Britain in Global Politics Volume 2

Security, Conflict and Cooperation in the Contemporary World

Edited by **Effie G. H. Pedaliu**, LSE-Ideas and **John W. Young**, University of Nottingham

The Palgrave Macmillan series Security, Conflict and Cooperation in the Contemporary World aims to make a significant contribution to academic and policy debates on cooperation, conflict and security since 1900. It evolved from the series Global Conflict and Security edited by Professor Saki Ruth Dockrill. The current series welcomes proposals that offer innovative historical perspectives, based on archival evidence and promoting an empirical understanding of economic and political cooperation, conflict and security, peace-making, diplomacy, humanitarian intervention, nation-building, intelligence, terrorism, the influence of ideology and religion on international relations, as well as the work of international organisations and non-governmental organisations.

Titles include:

Christopher Baxter, Michael L. Dockrill and Keith Hamilton (*editors*)
BRITAIN IN GLOBAL POLITICS VOLUME 1
From Gladstone to Churchill

John W. Young, Effie G. H. Pedaliu and Michael D. Kandiah (*editors*)
BRITAIN IN GLOBAL POLITICS VOLUME 2
From Churchill to Blair

Security, Conflict and Cooperation in the Contemporary World
Series Standing Order ISBN 978–1–137–27284–3 (hardback)

You can receive future titles in this series as they are published by placing a standing order. Please contact your bookseller or, in case of difficulty, write to us at the address below with your name and address, the title of the series and the ISBN quoted above.

Customer Services Department, Macmillan Distribution Ltd, Houndmills, Basingstoke, Hampshire RG21 6XS, England

Britain in Global Politics Volume 2

From Churchill to Blair

Edited by

John W. Young
Professor of International History, University of Nottingham

Effie G. H. Pedaliu
Fellow, LSE-Ideas

and

Michael D. Kandiah
Director, Witness Seminar Programme, Institute of Contemporary British History, King's College London

palgrave
macmillan

First published 2013 by
PALGRAVE MACMILLAN

Palgrave Macmillan in the UK is an imprint of Macmillan Publishers Limited, registered in England, company number 785998, of Houndmills, Basingstoke, Hampshire RG21 6XS.

Palgrave Macmillan in the US is a division of St Martin's Press LLC, 175 Fifth Avenue, New York, NY 10010.

Palgrave Macmillan is the global academic imprint of the above companies and has companies and representatives throughout the world.

Palgrave® and Macmillan® are registered trademarks in the United States, the United Kingdom, Europe and other countries.

ISBN: 978–0–230–36039–6

This book is printed on paper suitable for recycling and made from fully managed and sustained forest sources. Logging, pulping and manufacturing processes are expected to conform to the environmental regulations of the country of origin.

A catalogue record for this book is available from the British Library.

A catalog record for this book is available from the Library of Congress.

Saki Dockrill

Contents

Foreword: Remembering Saki Dockrill, by Professor Sir Lawrence Freedman ix

List of Key Publications by Saki Dockrill xii

Preface xvi

Acknowledgements xx

Notes on Contributors xxi

List of Abbreviations xxiv

1 Britain and the Origins of the Religious Cold War, 1944–47 1
Dianne Kirby

2 'Journey into a Desert': British Perceptions of Poland's Western Territories, 1945–48 22
Alastair Noble

3 British Propaganda and Countering Illegal Immigration into Palestine: The *President Warfield* or *Exodus 1947* 42
Kate Utting

4 Britain, the United States and the Issue of 'Limited War' with China, 1950–54 62
Kevin Ruane

5 'To Stay or to Walk': The British and the Defence of Domestic Jurisdiction at the United Nations, 1950–56 82
Edward Johnson

6 'A Cardinal Point of Our World Strategy': The Foreign Office and the Normalisation of Relations with Japan, 1952–63 100
Antony Best

7 Anglo-American Diplomacy and the Congo Crisis, 1960–63: The not so Special Relationship 119
John Kent

8 The US Embassy in London and Britain's Withdrawal from East of Suez, 1961–69 139
John W. Young

9 'We Were always Realistic': The Heath Government, the European Community and the Cold War in the Mediterranean, June 1970–February 1974 159
Effie G. H. Pedaliu

10 'At the Top Table': British Elites' Perceptions of the UK's International Position, 1950–91 179
Michael D. Kandiah and Gillian Staerck

11 The British Embassy in Washington and Anglo–American Relations during the Blair Governments, 1997–2007 198
Michael F. Hopkins

12 Beyond the Horizon 218
Peter Hennessy

Index 239

Foreword: Remembering Saki Dockrill

Professor Sir Lawrence Freedman

I do not think I am the only person to view the Department of War Studies at King's College, London, as a sort of extended family. Perhaps because of its singular subject matter, or its inclusive approach to interests and disciplines, it creates extraordinarily strong bonds and loyalties. For so many years at the heart of this family were the Dockrills, Mike and Saki. This was a remarkable partnership. Mike was recruited to the department as a lecturer while it was still in its infancy. Saki came as a graduate student in 1982, the year that I arrived. Both became professors in the department. Together they enriched not only the lives of numerous students, by being excellent teachers and excellent company, but also the lives of their colleagues, through their commitment to the department and what it stood for, and above all for their friendship and good humour. The loss of Saki, one half of this partnership, therefore was not just a matter of losing a valued colleague. It meant losing one of the family, somebody with whom you could share life's ups and downs, somebody with whom there was always lots to talk about.

Saki Namura was first brought to my attention by Mike as we strolled around Windsor Great Park, in what I guess was October 1985, in the days when the whole of the department, all staff and students, could be accommodated at Cumberland Lodge. Two Saki-related issues were discussed that day. I believed them – quite erroneously – to be closely linked. The first issue was 'was it a problem that Mike and Saki were forming an attachment?' The second was would I supervise her thesis? I presumed the second question was to ease the answer to the first. Saki was no longer a teenager and it was hard to object to the romance, but I could see why it might be a problem if there was supervision involved. So, I agreed to supervise. Except, Mike was not her supervisor. This I only discovered decades later.

Fortunately, supervising Saki was a delight. Looking back, I still find her achievement astonishing. Here she was, having had a good solid Japanese education and taught for five years at a private school, spending only one year in England, at the University of Sussex, doing an MA in international relations, before coming to King's. Yet she chose a topic – British attitudes to German rearmament – that required making sense of intense debates over European security at the height of the Cold War, depending on substantial archival research. She struggled with the English language only in pronunciation. From her written English you would never have guessed she was not a native speaker. And so, the chapters came – thoroughly researched, carefully analysed, clearly written, with that attention to detail that became the hallmark of all her work, and providing a new angle on a familiar topic that deservedly gained the approval of Cambridge University Press.

Every topic she researched, everything task she took on, she brought this extraordinary industry, care, commonsense. Whether on German rearmament, or President Eisenhower's national security policy, or Britain's withdrawal from East of Suez, her books became standard texts, simply because it was evident to any reader – and you can see this in the reviews – that this was a scholar who set herself exacting standards and would worry at an issue until she had satisfied herself that she had a solution.

All this required great ambition and drive. When her thesis was over and she had returned from a period at Yale University, before she waltzed through an interview to become a lecturer in the department, we managed to keep her on the books through sundry research projects. I confess that I often portrayed her as an Asian specialist. She was grateful for the work but I recall her carefully explaining to me, with one of her steelier looks, that if she had wanted to be an Asian specialist she would have stayed in Asia and that actually she had come to Europe because she wanted to study Europe. I should note, however, that we did eventually collaborate on a piece on Hiroshima. It was a measure of her growing self-confidence as a historian that she was starting to illuminate Asia's international history, as she had already done for Europe and North America in her final project on Japan and the Pacific War, just as it was a reflection of her growing confidence as a commentator on contemporary affairs that had led her to write her final book on responses to 9/11. Her sense of her identity and her place, not just in the College, but among international historians and her new country, was now secure. Not only did she take on British citizenship, but she also became a committed Anglican.

Not long before the dreadful diagnosis of leukaemia, my wife and I had dinner with Mike and Saki. It was a happy occasion, but my strongest recollection is of a point in the conversation where she insisted, 'I don't want to be "just a professor"'. It seemed to me that Saki was never 'just' anything, but her message was that she still had much to give and to prove – to herself if not to others. I have no doubts that, were it not for the illness, she would have found roles, not only in the College but elsewhere, in which her industry, competence, compassion and attention to detail would have allowed her to make even more of a mark. Instead, she had to turn her energy and her fortitude to fight the cancer.

I was about to say that I want mainly to remember the Saki of that dinner, before the disease, at the top of her game, charming and witty, curious about people and things, determined and optimistic as she looked forward to the future. But it is quite impossible to forget the Saki who so bravely fought the disease, resilient in her suffering, which was often considerable, analytical about her predicament, not for a moment abandoning her charm and wit, retaining her commonsense and exquisite sense of style, displaying to the end her concern for others and commitment to scholarship. We all miss her.

List of Key Publications by Saki Dockrill

Monographs

Britain's Policy for West German Rearmament, 1950–1955 (Cambridge University Press, 1991).

Eisenhower's New Look National Security Policy, 1953–1961 (Macmillan/St Martin's, 1996).

Britain's Retreat from East of Suez: The Choice between Europe and the World? (Palgrave Macmillan, 2002).

The End of the Cold War Era: the Transformation of the Global Security Order (Hodder Arnold/OUP, NY, 2005).

Edited volumes

From Pearl Harbor to Hiroshima: The Second World War in Asia and the Pacific, 1941–45 (Macmillan/St Martin's Press, 1994).

Controversy and Compromise: Alliance Politics between Britain, the Federal Republic of Germany and the United States (Philio, 1998).

Cold War Respite: The Geneva Summit of July 1955 (ed./author with G. Bischof) (Louisiana University Press, 2000).

L'Europe de l'Est et de l'Ouest dans la Guerre froide 1948–1953 (ed. with Georges-Henri Soutou, Robert Frank, and Antonio Varsori) (Presses de l'Universite de Paris Sorbonne, 2002).

Advances in Cold War History (ed. with G. Hughes) (Palgrave Macmillan, 2006).

Over Thirty Years: The United States and the Legacy of the Vietnam War (ed. with Jon Roper) (Palgrave Macmillan, November 2007).

The North Korean Nuclear Crisis (ed. with Rosenau and Bluth) (Palgrave Macmillan, forthcoming).

Articles

'The evolution of Britain's policy towards a European army 1950–54', *Journal of Strategic Studies*, (1989), 12/1.

'Hirohito, the Emperor's Army and Pearl Harbor', *Review of International Studies*, (1992), 18.

'Cooperation and suspicion: The United States' alliance diplomacy for the security of Western Europe, 1953–54', *Diplomacy & Statecraft*, (1994), 5/1.

'Retreat from the continent? Britain's motives for troop reductions in West Germany, 1955–1958', *Journal of Strategic Studies*, (1997), 20/3.

'Forging the Anglo-American global defence partnership: Harold Wilson, Lyndon Johnson and the Washington summit, December 1964', *Journal of Strategic Studies*, (2000), 23/4.

'Britain's power and influence: Dealing with three roles and the Wilson government's defence debate at Chequers in November 1964', *Diplomacy & Statecraft*, (2000), 11/1.

'Does a superpower need an Alliance?', *Internationale Politik*, (2002), 3/3.

'After September 11: Globalisation of security beyond the Transatlantic Alliance', *Journal of Transatlantic Studies*, (2003), 1/1.

'Dealing with Fear: Implementing the Bush Doctrine of Preemptive Attack', *Politics & Policy*, (2006), 34: 344–373.

Chapters in edited collections

'The Partition of Europe 1947–48: an Overview', in Antonio Varsori and Elena Calandri (eds), *The Failure of Peace in Europe, 1943–48* (Basingstoke and New York: Palgrave Macmillan, 2002).

'The Anglo-American Linkage between Vietnam and the Pound: 1964–68', in Christopher Goscha and Maurice Vaïsse (eds), *La Guerre du Viet-Nam et l'Europe (1963–1973)* (Paris: Bruylant, 2003).

'Hiroshima: A Strategy of Shock' (co-authored with L. Freedman), in Gordon Martel (ed.) *The Second World War: Reader* (Routledge, 2004).

'Eisenhower's Methodology for Intervention and Its Legacy in Contemporary World' politics, in Dennis Showalter (ed.), *Forging the Shield: Eisenhower and National Security for the 21st Century* (Imprint Publications, 2005).

'Dealing with Fear: Implementing the Bush Doctrine of Pre-emptive Attack', in John E. Owens and John W. Dumbrell (eds), *America's 'War on Terrorism': New Dimensions in U.S. Government and National Security* (Lanham, MD: Lexington Books, Rowman & Littlefield, 2008).

'Defense and Détente: Britain, the Soviet Union, and the 1968 Czech Crisis', in Gunter Bischof, Stefan Karner and Peter Ruggenthaler (eds), *The Prague Spring and the Warsaw Pact Invasion of Czechoslovakia in 1968* (Lanham, MD: Lexington Books, 2010).

Cold War History Series, Palgrave Macmillan
General Editor: Saki Dockrill

Günter Bischof, *Austria in the First Cold War, 1945–55: The Leverage of the Weak.*

Christoph Bluth, *The Two Germanies and Military Security in Europe.*

Dale Carter and Robin Clifton (eds), *War and Cold War in American Foreign Policy, 1942-62.*

Saki Dockrill, *Britain's Retreat from East of Suez: The Choice between Europe and the World, 1945–1968.*

Martin H. Folly, *Churchill, Whitehall and the Soviet Union, 1940–45.*

Michael F. Hopkins, Michael D. Kandiah and Gillian Staerck (eds), *Cold War Britain, 1945-1964: New Perspectives.*

John Gearson and Kori Schake (eds), *The Berlin Wall Crisis: Perspectives on Cold War Alliances.*

Ian Jackson, *The Economic Cold War: America, Britain and East–West Trade, 1948–63.*

Saul Kelly, *Cold War in the Desert: Britain, the United States and the Italian Colonies, 1945–52.*

Dianne Kirby (ed.), *Religion and the Cold War.*

Wilfred Loth, *Overcoming the Cold War: A History of Détente, 1950–1991.*

Erin Mahan, *Kennedy, De Gaulle and Western Europe.*

Steve Marsh, *Anglo-American Relations and Cold War Oil: Crisis in Iran.*

Donette Murray, *Kennedy, Macmillan and Nuclear Weapons.*

Effie G. H. Pedaliu, *Britain, Italy and the Origins of the Cold War.*

Andrew Roadnight, *United States Policy towards Indonesia in the Truman and Eisenhower Years.*

Kevin Ruane, *The Rise and Fall of the European Defence Community: Anglo-American Relations and the Crisis of European Defence, 1950–55.*

Helene Sjursen, *The United States, Western Europe and the Polish Crisis: International Relations in the Second Cold War.*

Antonio Varsori and Elena Calandri (eds), *The Failure of Peace in Europe, 1943–48.*

Global Conflict and Security since 1945 Series, Palgrave Macmillan Editors: Professor Saki R. Dockrill and Dr. William Rosenau, RAND

Vesselin Dimitrov, *Stalin's Cold War: Soviet Foreign Policy, Democracy and Communism in Bulgaria 1941–48.*

James Ellison, *The United States, Britain and the Translantic Crisis: Rising to the Gaullist Challenge, 1963–68.*

Peter Lowe, *Contending with Nationalism and Communism: British Policy towards South-East Asia, 1945–65.*

Jon Roper, *Over Thirty Years: The United States and the Legacy of the Vietnam War.*

T.O. Smith, *Britain and the Origins of the Vietnam War: UK Policy in Indo-China, 1943–50.*

Ken Young, *Weapons Systems and the Politics of Interdependence.*

Preface

During her fruitful career, Saki Dockrill worked on a wide range of historical subjects. For this collection of chapters by her colleagues and friends, we have focused on just one, that of British foreign policy after 1945. They cover a broad field, however, from relations with Japan and China, through European and African developments, to defence planning in Whitehall; they include also political, economic, defence, ideological and religious dimensions and, even, 'futurology'. The chapters in this collection aspire to offer fresh insights and new interpretations of the way in which a weakened Britain conducted its foreign policy and foreign relations in order to protect its interests and retain an influence in international affairs. The book aims at presenting its readership with comprehensive and wide-ranging perspectives on Britain and the World in the Cold War and post-Cold War eras.

Dianne Kirby discusses the religious dimension of the Cold War and how, in the context of the Cold War, religion became a place where Western cold warriors promoted the sense that the Cold War was about the defence of Western civilisation and Christianity and not, as it might otherwise appear, a struggle for power. She states that the British led the way in the religious cold war, cautiously and covertly, but also effectively.

Alastair Noble's contribution focuses on early post-war Poland. It describes the conditions British policy-makers faced in the aftermath of the conflict, involving the rebuilding and recasting of state and society by an externally backed new order. He outlines the British position on Poland as the Iron Curtain descended. He concludes that despite the inhospitable terrain of post-war Eastern Europe, British efforts were not in vain and secured the foundations of a lasting Polish settlement.

Kate Utting demonstrates that the current fascination with news management and 'spinning' by British governments in support of their policies is nothing new. She argues that the post-war Labour government had a sophisticated appreciation that success in pursuing policy aims depended on its ability in persuading its target audiences to support its policy over the future of the Palestine Mandate. She comes to the conclusion that no amount of propaganda could, post-Holocaust, challenge international perceptions of the illegitimacy of British rule in Palestine nor overcome the damage caused by the pursuit of misguided policy.

Kevin Ruane revisits a critical episode in Anglo–American relations, during the Korean War, when it looked for a time as though the British could side with the Soviet Union in opposing the American initiative in the UN to condemn China 'as an aggressor'. The recent opening of the Cabinet Secretary's Notebooks has revealed, in more detail, the way in which the Attlee government wrestled with the possibilities and implications of a break with the United States as well as the exact lines along which the Cabinet split in early 1951. He maintains that this was a clash of differing US and UK visions of what the United Nations stood for and that the legacy of the 'branding' of China would be seen in 1954 when the other great Asian Cold War 'hot' war, Indochina, reached its climax, and the British and Americans again found themselves badly at odds over the correct course of action.

Edward Johnson continues with the theme of the UN. He concentrates on the 1950s, the critical period during which the British government fought to keep the management of colonial questions from the prying eyes – as the British saw it – of the United Nations. His particular focus is on the British defence of the question of domestic jurisdiction through article 2(7) of the UN Charter and whether the British might withdraw from parts of the UN in protest at the UN seeking to discuss colonial questions.

Antony Best attempts in his chapter to throw light on the under-researched area of post-war Anglo–Japanese relations and also to explore the irony in which the need to contain Soviet expansion meant that Britain found itself on the same side with its former enemies from the Second World War. He examines the motives that led Britain to normalise this very difficult relationship with Japan. He contends that the impetus to normalisation was influenced by both Cold War and commercial considerations.

John Kent grapples with the theme of postcolonial crises and he deliberates on how 'special' the 'special relationship' was under such circumstances. His chapter covers Anglo–American disagreements on the Congo over the secession of Katanga during the period from the Kitona agreement at the end of 1961, to the differences at the Nassau conference.

John Young grapples with some of the issues raised in one of Saki Dockrill's most significant publications, her monograph *Britain's Retreat from East of Suez*. He focuses on the vital question of maintaining friendly relations with the United States. His chapter surveys the debate from the perspective of the US Ambassador in London, how his embassy interpreted British decision-making, how well it was informed and what it did to influence British leaders.

Effie Pedaliu examines the impact of the European Community on British foreign policy. She discusses the extent to which, during Edward Heath's premiership (18 June 1970 to 28 February 1974) Britain's preparations to join the European Community (EC) led to the 'Europeanisation' of its policies towards the Mediterranean. Her chapter also looks at how Britain handled its reduced ability to project military power in the Mediterranean and retain influence during the years of détente when the Mediterranean became a major field in East–West conflict and the sea became an area where many contended.

Michael Kandiah and Gillian Staerck analyse the *Weltanschauung* of the British ruling elites. They seek to illuminate the British policy-making elites' individual and collective narratives and perceptions by examining broad historical themes and significant events, such as Anglo–American relations, the UK's attitude to European integration, the Cold War, decolonisation and defence strategy. In order to get a more nuanced understanding, the chapter considers also how policy-makers approached specific issues, like British policy towards Rhodesia, Anglo–German relations, the Helsinki Accords, the Falklands War, the Defence Reviews from Sandys (1957) to Nott (1981), and the impact of the US Strategic Defense Initiative (SDI) on UK policy-making.

Mike Hopkins returns to the theme of the 'special relationship' and how it was invigorated during the Blair years after seeming to decline after the end of the Cold War. He suggests that as this was a relationship conceived originally in war, it has always appeared at its strongest when tested by conflict. He seeks to evaluate the nature and effectiveness of the Blair governments' (1997–2007) relations with two American presidents – Bill Clinton (1993–2001) and George W. Bush (2001–2009) and their secretaries of state Madeleine Albright, Colin Powell and Condoleezza Rice. In particular, it focuses on the contribution of the British Embassy to the development of policies. He concludes that Blair saw the Anglo–American relationship as vital to British interests.

The volume ends with a wide-ranging thinking chapter by Peter Hennessy which spans the whole timeline of the volume. He explores a succession of government-led attempts to reduce *uncertainty* by trying to anticipate events, good and bad, and to increase the chances of good happening and to reduce the prospects of the harmful. Today, what is called 'horizon-scanning' is a trans-Whitehall activity on a substantial scale. Hennessy argues that in its various guises, the horizon-scanner's craft has been central to the British state's preparations for the worst and that the pursuit of top-of-the-range horizon-scanning has been a kind of Holy Grail for Whitehall.

The editors and contributors hope that, in its intellectual rigour, use of archives and clarity of ideas, the book can stand as a fitting memorial to Professor Saki Ruth Dockrill.

Acknowledgements

There are many people without whom the book would not have come to fruition. The editors wish to thank all the contributors for joining them in this celebration of Professor Saki Ruth Dockrill's work. We are grateful to the following archives and libraries that provided the contributors with source materials: The National Archives at Kew, London; the US National Archives and Record Administration, College Park, Maryland; Birmingham University Library; Churchill College Archive Centre; the John F. Kennedy Library, Boston, Massachusetts; the Lyndon Johnson Library in Austin, Texas; and the Virginia Historical Society, Richmond. Special thanks are due to the editors of Volume I, Chris Baxter, Mike Dockrill and Keith Hamilton for their good advice and good humour. All of us, editors and contributors, would like to extend thanks to those who have acted as peer-reviewers for the chapters in this volume. Their comments have been invaluable. Above all, our thanks go to James Ellison (QMUL) and Jimmy Athanassiou for reading many of our drafts offering comments and helping us to crystallise and refine our arguments. Jen McCall and the staff at Palgrave Macmillan have proven to be an exceptional publishing team, from their initial interest in the project to its eventual publication. We are grateful to Alamy.com and the office of Tony Blair for permission to use the cover image of the former Prime Minister. In the course of preparing this volume, the three editors suffered family bereavements. They wish to extend their thanks for the support they have received from their families and, of course, their thanks to those they have lost: Dorothy Bethwaite Young, George N. Pedalios and Jessica Kandiah.

Notes on Contributors

Anthony Best is Senior Lecturer in History at the London School of Economics and a specialist in British policy towards the Far East in the twentieth century, with a particular focus on Anglo–Japanese relations. His most recent edited collections include *The International History of East Asia, 1900–1968: Trade, Ideology and the Quest for Order* (2010) and *Imperial Japan and the World, 1931–1941* (2011).

Lawrence Freedman has been Professor of War Studies at King's College London since 1982, and Vice-Principal since 2003. He was elected a Fellow of the British Academy in 1995 and awarded the CBE (Commander of the British Empire) in 1996. He was appointed Official Historian of the Falklands Campaign in 1997. He was awarded the KCMG (Knight Commander of St Michael and St George) in 2003. He was appointed in June 2009 to serve as a member of the official inquiry into Britain and the 2003 Iraq War. Professor Freedman has written extensively on nuclear strategy and the Cold War, as well as commentating regularly on contemporary security issues. His most recent book, *A Choice of Enemies: America Confronts the Middle East*, won the 2009 Lionel Gelber Prize and Duke of Westminster Medal for Military Literature.

Peter Hennessy is Attlee Professor of Contemporary British History at Queen Mary, University of London, a Fellow of the British Academy and in 2010, he entered the House of Lords as Baron Hennessy of Nympsfield. Before joining QMUL in 1992, he was a journalist for twenty years with *The Times*, *The Financial Times*, *The Economist* and with the BBC. His books include among others: *Never Again: Britain 1945–51* (1992), *The Prime Minister: The Office and Its Holders since 1945* (2000), *The Secret State: Whitehall and the Cold War* (2002), *Having It so Good: Britain in the Fifties* (2006).

Michael Hopkins is Associate Professor of History at the University of Liverpool and an expert in US foreign policy-making and Anglo–American relations. His most books include *Oliver Franks and the Truman Administration: Anglo–American Relations, 1948–1952* (2003), *The Washington Embassy: British Ambassadors to the United States, 1939–77* (co-edited with Saul Kelly and John W. Young, 2009), and *The Cold War* (2011).

Edward Johnson is Reader in Politics at Birmingham City University. He has written widely on British policy in the United Nations, over Suez, Cyprus, Spain and Greece, and on the role of the Secretary-General. He is the co-editor, with Keith Hamilton, of *Arms and Disarmament in Diplomacy* (2008). He is the Vice-Chairman of the British International History Group.

Michael D. Kandiah is Director of the Witness Seminar Programme, Institute of Contemporary British History, King's College London. Together with Gillian Staerck they have edited several academic volumes, including *Cold War Britain* (2003), *Asia: British Documents on Far East Asia* (1998); and *PROfiles, British Government Documents 1964* (1995). They are co-convenors of the International History Seminar.

John Kent is Reader in International Relations at the London School of Economics and has written on British imperial policy, the Middle East and sub-Saharan Africa. He was the editor of British Documents on the End of Empire, Series B, Volume 4, *Egypt and the Defence of the Middle East, 1945–1956, Parts 1–3* (1998). He has written books on Britain and the Origins of the Cold War, French and British colonialism in West Africa and an international history of the Cold War with John Young. His most recent monograph is *America, the UN and Decolonisation: Cold War Conflict in the Congo* (2010). He is presently working on 'The Mismanagement of British Decline: Foreign Policy and Defence Strategy 1945–68'.

Dianne Kirby is Reader in American Studies at the University of Ulster and an expert in the religious dimension of US and British foreign policy. As well as a number of articles and essays, her publications include *Church, State and Propaganda* (1999) and *Religion and the Cold War* (2003).

Alastair Noble currently works in communications in Whitehall. He was a Historian in the Foreign and Commonwealth Office from 2002 to 2009. As well as being the author of *Nazi Rule and the Soviet Offensive in Eastern Germany, 1944–1945* (2008), he has written numerous academic articles and contributions to edited volumes.

Effie G. H. Pedaliu is a Fellow at LSE-Ideas. She is the author of *Britain, Italy and the Origins of the Cold War* (2003). She has written widely on British and American Cold War policy, the Cold War Mediterranean, human rights, Vietnam and NATO. Her book *The Contemporary Mediterranean World* will be published in 2014. She is a member of the peer review college of the AHRC and co-convenor of the International History Seminar.

Kevin Ruane is Professor of Modern History at Canterbury Christ Church University. He has published extensively on Anglo–American relations, European security in the 1950s and the Vietnam War. His publications include *The Rise and Fall of the European Defence Community: Britain, the United States and the Crisis of European Defence 1950–55* (2000) and *The Vietnam Wars* (2000). He is currently working on a study of Graham Greene's Vietnam-based novel, *The Quiet American.*

Gillian Staerck was formerly a Research Fellow at the Centre for Contemporary British History. Together with Michael D. Kandiah, Gillian has edited several academic volumes, including *Cold War Britain* (2003), *Asia: British Documents on Far East Asia* (1998), and *PROfiles, British Government Documents 1964* (1995).

Kate Utting is Senior Lecturer at King's College London in the Defence Studies Department at the Joint Services Command and Staff College (JSCSC), the Defence Academy of the United Kingdom. Her publications include: 'Beyond Joint – Professional Military Education for the 21st Century: The United Kingdom's Post Defence Training Review Advanced Command and Staff Course', *Defence Studies,* 2009 and 'The Strategic Information Campaign: Lessons from the British Experience in Palestine, 1945–1948', *Contemporary Security Policy,* 2007; *British Techniques of Public Relations and Propaganda for Mobilizing East and Central Africa During World War II* (as Kate Morris, 2000). She is a co-convenor of the International History Seminar.

John W. Young has been Professor of International History at the University of Nottingham since 2000. He previously held chairs at the universities of Salford and Leicester. His publications include *Britain and European Unity, 1945–99* (2nd edn, 2000), *The Labour Governments 1964–70: International Policy* (2003) and, as co-editor, *Twentieth Century Diplomacy: A Case Study in British Practice, 1963–76* (2008). He is the Vice-Chairman of the British International History Group and a co-convenor of the International History Seminar. He was a member of the History panel for the RAE 2007 and in 2012 he was appointed to the History panel for the REF 2014.

List of Abbreviations

In the Text

BAOR	British Army of the Rhine
CAF	Central African Federation
CENTO	Central Treaty Organization
CFR	Church of England Council on Foreign Relations
CIA	(American) Central Intelligence Agency
CK	Compagnie du Katanga
CO	Colonial Office
CRO	Commonwealth Relations Office; Commonwealth Office (in 1966–8)
CSK	Comité Spécial du Katanga
DEA	Department of Economic Affairs
EEC	European Economic Community
EFTA	European Free Trade Association
EPC	European Political Cooperation
FCO	Foreign and Commonwealth Office
FO	Foreign Office
GATT	General Agreement on Tariffs and Trade
GCHQ	Government Communications Headquarters
HMG	His (Her) Majesty's Government
IRD	Information Research Department, FO
JCP	Japanese Communist Party
JIC	Joint Intelligence Committee
MFN	Most Favoured Nation
MI5	British counter-intelligence and counter-subversion service
MI6	British Secret Intelligence Service
MLF	Multilateral (Nuclear) Force
MOD	Ministry of Defence
MP	Member of Parliament
NATO	North Atlantic Treaty Organisation
OECD	Organisation for Economic Co-operation and Development
OPD	Overseas Policy and Defence Committee
PRC	People's Republic of China
RAF	Royal Air Force
SEATO	Southeast Asia Treaty Organization

UK	United Kingdom of Great Britain and Northern Ireland
UMHK	Union Minière du Haut Katanga
UN	United Nations
UNC	United Nations Command in Korea
US	United States
USSR	Union of Soviet Socialist Republics
WEU	Western European Union

In the Notes

CAB	Cabinet
CF	Country File
CMND	Command Papers
COS	Chiefs of Staff
CRO	Commonwealth Relations Office (Commonwealth Office 1966–8)
DDEL	Dwight D. Eisenhower Library
DEFE	Ministry of Defence
DOHP	Diplomatic Oral History Project
FCO	Foreign and Commonwealth Office
FO	Foreign Office
FRUS	Foreign Relations of the United States
HC Deb	House of Commons Debates (Hansard)
HSTL	Harry S. Truman Library
LBJL	Lyndon B. Johnson Library
LPL	Lambeth Palace Library
NAA	National Archives of Australia
NARA	National Archives and Record Administration (US)
NSF	National Security File
PM	Prime Minister
PREM	Prime Minister's Office
RG	(US National Archives) Record Group
TNA	The National Archives (UK)
WHCF	White House Central File
YML	York Minister Library

1
Britain and the Origins of the Religious Cold War, 1944–47

Dianne Kirby

The study of religion in the international arena has exponentially increased in the course of the past decade to the point of establishing its own subgenre, not least in the study of the Cold War. Saki Dockrill's role in the latter process was key. She accepted an edited book on *Religion and the Cold War* for her Palgrave Macmillan series long before scholarly recognition had been accorded to the subject. A decade later, a book of the same name noted that it was built on the foundation established by the original book.[1] This chapter is a token of gratitude for Saki's commitment to what was at the time a pioneering work.

Today, American scholars lead the way in emphasising the importance of religion to their nation's Cold War and in its assumption of world leadership.[2] Elizabeth Edwards Spalding argues that the origins, early decisions and policies of the Cold War cannot be satisfactorily explained without reference to religion. She suggests that neglect of the personal piety of the first Cold War president, Harry Truman, meant scholars missed 'the unique post-war liberal internationalism' he fashioned.[3] William Inboden, a former White House staffer who also worked in the State Department's International Religious Freedom Office, supports Spalding's argument. He attributes great importance to Truman's personal religious convictions and believes religion was a key causal factor leading to the Cold War. Conceding the importance of other causal factors – balance of power realities, security concerns and ideology – Inboden's thesis is that, taken apart or even together, they do not explain why the United States, so shortly after the Second World War, was prepared to step into 'yet another cataclysmic global conflict'. To understand that, consideration must be given to spiritual factors. Truman and subsequently Dwight D. Eisenhower instinctively recognised the Soviet regime's inherent evil: 'It would be hard to conceive a more stark division in the world than between those nations who believed in God and those nations who outlawed such belief.' Inboden argues that the prospect of a world dominated by the godless Soviets not only prompted America to assume the mantle of world leadership, but also meant other nations rallied to the cause:

> Differences over political structures and economic systems and even national interests, though important in their own right, paled in comparison with the prospect of a world ruled by evil, a world devoid of spiritual values, a world without God. If ever there was a cause to fight, this was it.[4]

A belief in American exceptionalism is implicit in the approaches of both Spalding and Inboden. However, by focusing exclusively on the US, both miss the wider dynamic of the religious dimension of the Cold War. This chapter explores the way in which the origins of the 'religious cold war' have roots in British policies, reflecting not so much an instinctual aversion to evil, such as Truman felt, but a more mundane vying for power in strategic locations between two European powers, which brought into play all the traditional instruments of state, religion included.

Religion and the Soviet state

Secular modernity supposedly relocated religion out of the public and into the private sphere to domesticate and de-politicise religious faith. The extent to which this remained an un-realised project was tellingly revealed during the Second World War, when Christianity was invoked by all the belligerents for political and military purposes.[5] The British played a key role, owing to links between the Church of England and the Russian Orthodox Church, in facilitating the rehabilitation of the image of the Soviet regime in the religious sphere.[6] Within British ruling circles, there was some reluctance to present too positive an image of the Soviet regime. The Foreign Office (FO) wanted the Soviet Union to appear an acceptable wartime ally for the sake of the anti-Axis alliance, but was concerned not to endorse or legitimise the communist state. Marxist atheism had been a crucial component in demonising the Bolsheviks and government officials were wary of wartime propaganda that might have unwelcome repercussions once hostilities ceased. The FO was deeply conscious of the extent to which, by its persecution of religion, the Soviet regime had inflicted more damage on itself than western propaganda could ever hope to do. The FO carefully monitored Soviet attitudes toward and treatment of religion, including the 1934 Congress, which accepted the policy of popular front governments and collaboration with Christians 'of revolutionary temper'. Subsequently the new 1936 Soviet Constitution theoretically allowed full civil rights of citizenship for priests and freedom for the conduct of religious cults.[7]

The Church of England Council on Foreign Relations (CFR), with which the FO enjoyed cordial relations, also discussed the significance of these changes.[8] It noted that Stalin had taken it upon himself to clarify their importance. Claiming that the Soviet Union was in a stage of socialism in which the class struggle was over and in which minds and habits were to be modelled by education, not by force or administrative measures, Stalin had repudiated previous calls for decisive and merciless struggles with religious prejudices. The necessity now was patiently to explain their harm. The report observed how, at peace conferences, Soviet spokes-people were keen to present a positive perspective on the Soviet attitude toward religion. Ignoring the huge numbers of religious people being oppressed in the course of the Great Purge, it denounced the 'most absurd and ridiculous rumours' about religious persecution, a 'poisonous weapon of lies for the purpose of preparing war against the only socialistic state in the world'. Rather, it was posited, communists esteemed those with religious belief and took care not to offend them. Acknowledging that the USSR was willing to 'soft-pedal' on world revolution and make a truce with religious bodies abroad, the CFR report recognised that Stalin was: 'more favourable to collaboration with capitalist states than to stirring up revolution in them'. The report's conclusion is of particular note. It observed that Stalin was presenting Soviet achievements as a model to be copied, not owing to compulsion but to appeal. In addition to the more obvious implications, it revealed Stalin's grasp that his religious policy was counterproductive at home and abroad.[9]

In 1903, although the Second Congress of the Russian Social Democratic Labour Party had demanded separation of church and state, and church and school, it had insisted on unrestricted freedom of conscience.[10] In October 1917, the Bolsheviks declared the new Soviet State to be non-religious, not anti-religious, whilst the Bolshevik decree of 1918 'on freedom of conscience and religious societies', theoretically safeguarded 'free practice of religious customs'.' Religious believers were not denied admission to the party because opposition to religion was subordinated to the class struggle. Nevertheless, Bukharin and Preobrazhensky's *ABC of Communism*, which popularised the party programme of 1919, still advocated attacking religious institutions and popular religious prejudices.[11] Still, it remained the case that some religious bodies, Christian and Muslim, managed to flourish under the new regime. Indeed, the Bolshevik separation of Church and State was welcomed by the Roman Curia as a blow to Russian Orthodoxy and revived Vatican aspirations to convert Russia to Roman Catholicism. Hence, the spectacle at the 1922 Genoa conference, where the Bolshevik Foreign Minister and the Pope's representative toasted one another in public. The Vatican was less celebratory about the progress of the various Protestant bodies.[12] Evangelical Christians, for example, increased their adherents from about 100,000 to over a million in the first decade of Soviet rule.[13]

Research into attitudes toward religion amongst the Bolshevik elites has revealed, not simply a distinct failure to understand Russian religion in all its manifestations, but, most significantly, the lack of an agreed religious policy. Fierce opponents of religion, moderate sympathisers toward it and even believers existed at all levels of the Communist Party. Political and economic considerations mattered more than ideological imperatives. There was no single office overseeing religious policy. Instead, there arose a series of overlapping initiatives and commissions, all subject to wide local and regional variations, as well as bureaucratic confusion.[14] Policies were inadequately resourced and vacillated between repression and concession. In addition to proving ineffective, they were often counter-productive.[15] The enthusiastic implementation of campaign-like initiatives often produced outcomes at variance with what was intended by central planners. The defective and contradictory anti-religious institutions such as the Central Standing Commission on Religious Questions and the League of the Militant Godless are indicative of the extent to which the Soviets lacked a coherent, intelligible plan to construct an atheist state.[16] That the eradication of religion was far from a government priority was discernible from the low value placed on the work of such institutions, their under-resourcing and lack of direction. Nonetheless, the maltreatment inflicted on the faithful under Stalin horrified the wider world and became a key component in the propaganda attacks on the Soviet experiment. When Hitler invaded the Soviet Union, a British survey, which covered 'the more intelligent members of all sections of the population',' demonstrated that of all those who felt there were obstacles to a proper understanding between Great Britain and the Soviet Union, 72% named Soviet treatment of religion as the chief difficulty.[17]

The Anglo-Soviet alliance confronted the British Ministry of Information, particularly the Religions Division, with a substantial problem: 'It must be realised ... that the whole spiritual presentation of our case is hampered by the Soviet record (especially by the officially favoured Anti-God movement).' Axis-controlled wireless stations daily made derisory play with the religious factor, mocking Britain's hypocrisy in claiming spiritual values.[18] With German propaganda proclaiming Germany to be the champion of Christianity against godless Soviet atheism, official British views conflicted as to whether or not London should actively promote religious freedom in the USSR, either through direct pressure on Moscow or covert encouragement of the Orthodox Church.[19] The FO opted for non-intervention. Reviewing the situation in June 1942, Herbert Waddams, an Anglican priest and Senior-Assistant Specialist of the Religions Division, stated that Soviet authorities had many reasons for a deep distrust of Christians outside Russia interfering in their country. Christian opinion had been hostile ever since the Revolution and Waddams saw this as the most important single factor in the present situation. He endorsed the FO's non-interventionism, observing:

> The paramount consideration is that confidence should be established in the minds of the Soviet authorities that Christians outside Russia have no counter-revolutionary intentions of any kind. ... The Soviet authorities must first be convinced that a spiritual alliance with worldwide Christianity is entirely to their advantage. When that conviction is established everything else will follow as a matter of course.[20]

Subsequent developments confirmed the potential gains of this policy. In 1943, a *Sobor* (council of bishops) was allowed to meet to elect an Orthodox Patriarch and an exchange of delegations took place between the Anglican and Russian Orthodox Churches.

Soviet religious policy was transformed in June 1941, to aid the cohesion of the Russian people and reduce the attraction of Nazi propaganda. No official agreement emerged between Church and State until September 1943, by which time Stalin was making policy with an eye to the post-war settlement in Europe. By then, religion had become a crucial consideration in defeating Hitler, maintaining the wartime Alliance, securing the territories newly incorporated into the Soviet sphere, and strategically spreading Soviet influence.[21] Stalin had emphatically impressed upon him the extent to which religious systems of belief were powerful determinants that he could neither ignore nor overcome, but which he might use to his advantage. Throughout the Soviet bloc, the nexus between religion and national identity, the congruence, at times, of church-state interests, not to mention the importance of religion in the rest of the world, meant it had to be considered by Soviet policy-makers.[22] Stalin implemented links and structures intended to secure compliant religious institutions responsive to top-down authoritarian policies, which effectively precluded any possibility of the gradual withering away of religion in the way predicted by Marx. By 1946, the Church appeared securely established with roles in both foreign and domestic policy. After years of isolation, the Church began re-establishing its influence outside Russia, making contact with the Patriarchs of other Orthodox churches, pursuing friendly relations with the Anglican Church, and helping annul the Treaty of Brest, as a consequence of which it absorbed a large number of parishes in Ukraine.[23]

Although his efforts were clumsy and completely repudiated by the Vatican, Stalin even attempted reconciliation with the Pope in the spring of 1944.[24] In the 1930s, the institutional Catholic Church had been crushed, but with the War's end bringing more than 50 million Catholics into the Soviet sphere of influence, it also brought overtures to the Vatican offering a deal: 'Potential enemies could be neutralised in return for concessions which would permit Catholics to exercise their faith without molestation'.[25] In Byelorussia and Ukraine, the revival of non-Orthodox religions caused concern to the Soviet government, especially the large number of Greek-Catholic (Uniate) churches, whose allegiance belonged to the Vatican. Reports on the Vatican and the Uniate Church in Ukraine were sent directly to Stalin. The chair of the Council for Russian Orthodox Affairs, Georgii Karpov, set out a strategy for weakening the control of the Catholic Church in the liberated areas and reducing the international influence of Pius XII. Karpov suggested that the Russian Orthodox Church call a World Council of Christian churches: 'In order to withstand the claims of the Vatican for pre-eminence in the world.' The plan was for invited church leaders to discuss a series of issues, including, 'the total groundlessness of the Catholic dogma that the Roman Pope is God's representative on Earth' and evidence of 'the Vatican as a patron of Hitler during the war'.[26] This audacious scheme bore an uncanny resemblance to, and was an inverted mirror of, the idea of a Christian front against communism, articulated by Cardinal Pacelli, subsequently to become Pope Pius XII, during a tour of the US in 1936.[27] Moreover, Karpov's intention that the Russian Orthodox Church should appear to act of its own volition, not at the behest of the state, reflected the same preference to maintain the appearance of ecclesiastical independence the British Ministry of Information's Religions Division had required from the churches working with it during the war.[28]

Religion and the British state

Church-state relations do not conform to a single formula or rule of politics. However, the nature of the church–state cooperation evidenced in Britain and the USSR suggested a common conviction that for most men there are two foci in life – God and country – two rival allegiances that could be reconciled for mutual benefit. Russian Orthodox hierarchs, moreover, believed it their duty to 'save' the state's communist rulers.[29] They were also naturally concerned about the long-term survival of the Orthodox faith and hoped for some re-assertion of their spiritual authority. The Russian Orthodox Church emerged from the war, cognisant that its basic well-being and that of the faithful required it to cooperate with the Soviet state. The prevailing view in the Anglican hierarchy of the nature of their relationship with the state was not the subjugation by one of the other, but a partnership equally beneficial to both.[30] Within this context, cooperation with the state was regarded as a prerequisite. A CFR memorandum stated:

> Our experience in this war has conclusively shown how political objectives are related to religious beliefs. For purposes of work the two may be separated, but they must go hand in hand and must not be allowed to be contradictory in any particular. The religious and the political must be two aspects of the same activity.[31]

Anglican activities in the ecclesiastical sphere had long complemented those of their political counterparts. The informal understandings and shared outlooks, the mutual empathy that characterised the church–state relations enjoyed by British government elites and the Anglican hierarchy, were regarded as of particular significance in winning American support. Along with FO concern about Soviet influence, there emerged worries that 'the process of inducing the United States to support a British resistance to Russian penetration in Europe', would be 'tricky'.[32] Churchmen, who already enjoyed a good track record of eliciting American empathy for British policy during the war, were enrolled to help reverse positive attitudes generated in the course of the wartime alliance toward the former Soviet ally. They were also required to help 'educate' publics on either side of the Atlantic about the threat potential that the Soviet Union now presented to world peace.[33]

Keenly aware of the extent to which churches could be conduits of influence, the FO worried about the developing relationship between the Soviet state and the Russian Church. Whereas many sincere Christians hoped the new position of the Russian Church in Soviet society might revive and strengthen the Orthodox faith throughout the Soviet bloc, the FO feared that what would really be strengthened would be the Soviet regime, particularly in areas of strategic interest to Britain. As early as 1943 warnings emanated from Cairo that the Soviet government intended to use the Russian Orthodox Church as a means of extending its influence in the Middle East.[34] Intelligence reports drew attention to the 'Slav peril', which it was thought church–state cooperation would exacerbate:

> a further reason why the disarmament *sine die* of Germany is foolish is that Hitler is uniting the Slav countries against him as Napoleon united Germany and Italy (to our present sorrow), and that pan-Slavism is the real menace of the future. The future in question may not be so very far distant, as Communism is *very* active underground in all the Balkan countries (not to mention France, Germany and Switzerland).[35]

The spectre of a resurgent Pan-Slavism also worried CFR's Secretary, J.A. Douglas, an expert on the Orthodox church. Prior to the wartime visit to Moscow by the Archbishop of York, Cyril Forster Garbett, in autumn 1943, Douglas penned a lengthy missive on British relations with the USSR:

> The most difficult of all problems is the growing *panslavism* of U.S.S.R. Panslavism has been in Russia since Russia began – c/o the Messianic vision that Russia is to remodel the world crusade fashion which lies behind 'Moscow the Third Rome'. There are very definite signs that Stalin is envisaged as realising the dream of Ivan the Terrible of his Tsardom – Peter the Great, Katherine, Nicolas 1st, etc. The new Soviet Socialist Russia has the Messianic vision to make the world what it should be. Unless I am mistaken, this type of panslavism is the dynamic in the idealist U.S.S.R. weltanschaung of today. It will appeal in a way to the Orthodox Russian who accepts Communism, and its allure will make *him* enthusiastic and will have an effect upon non-Communist Russian Orthodox. Its scope probably at present very

> definitely includes not only Orthodox Balkan religio-nationalists (Serbs, Bulgarians, Rumanians, Greeks) but the Latin Poles and Czechs and Croats etc: and it has its eye on Constantinople.

It appeared to Douglas, with his close ecclesiastical contacts throughout Eastern Europe, that the prospect of cooperative, perhaps even amicable, relations between the Soviet state and the Russian Orthodox Church were a cause of regional consternation:

> If the above *is* correct, at least it is what *even before the war* showed forth such as Abp (sic) Stefan of Sofia and Nicolai Velimirovic anticipated: and without precisioning this detail or the other the Poles and Serbs are convinced that the U.S.S.R. is going out for panslavism. For such a programme the influence of the Orthodox Church might be a very important factor.[36]

Wary that the Anglican delegation to Moscow would lend legitimacy to the new relations between church and state in the Soviet Union, the Roman Catholic newspaper the *Tablet* forcefully articulated its alarm at the prospect of a combination of Orthodoxy with communism in the wartime context of heightened patriotism and religious revival:

> We should do well to recognise that the radical changes which Russian Communist ideology has undergone, and its transformation into a fiery national patriotism, have narrowed the gulf separating the messianic spirit of Communism from the messianic spirit of the Orthodox Church. The tradition of 'Holy Russia' with an inspired mission toward mankind is ancient and ingrained. Under the stress of some intense emotion such as that of the present moment, the Orthodox conception of a messianic Russia might well merge with the Marxist conception of a messianic proletariat, effecting a fusion of ideas the consequences of which would be incalculable.[37]

Religious spheres of influence and Anglo-Soviet Cold War

In 1944–45, the Orthodox Church, under Stalin's influence, seemed ready to respect the British sphere of influence in Europe. During the course of the fraternal visits undertaken in the latter stages of the war by the Russian Patriarch, Alexei, he significantly omitted the Greek Orthodox Patriarch at Constantinople, regarded as a British protégé.[38] But, there was clear potential for a clash of religious spheres in south-eastern

Europe, which mirrored political competition between Moscow and London. In this context, also noteworthy was a visit to Greece by Archbishop Garbett. Stalin and Churchill had agreed in the 'percentages agreement' of October 1944, that Greece was to be in the British sphere of influence. FO correspondence makes it quite clear that Garbett's visit was part of an exercise to reinforce the political power of the British appointed Regent, Archbishop Damaskinos, following British military intervention in Greece.[39] Subsequently the FO gave serious consideration to the rejuvenation of the Greek Patriarchate at Constantinople, obviously as a counter to the Moscow Patriarchate, requesting official responses to the proposal.

The British Embassy in Moscow made explicit the political role it perceived the Russian Church to have assumed:

> While there is no doubt that the Orthodox religion in this country is still a living and independent force, which the Soviet Government failed to destroy, the present working arrangements certainly provide for the traditional subordination of the Russian Church in all matters of foreign policy to the interests of the State. The Soviet Government must be well aware of the important role which the Orthodox Church plays throughout South Eastern Europe and in the Levant, and although of course 'democratic forces', in the Soviet sense of the word, are those to which Moscow appeals in the first place, the Soviet Government are most unlikely to ignore the possibility of influencing opinion through religious channels likewise...The prestige abroad of the Russian Church as the biggest of all Orthodox churches is certainly being fostered in this and other ways, such as the successive visits of prelates from other Orthodox countries which have been going on ever since the Grand Assembly for Aleksei's enthronement in February.

The Embassy was, nonetheless, wary of proposals from the British Chancery at Athens outlining counter-activities, warning that 'on present showing Moscow would probably come out of it better than Athens' and advising:

> Closer contact between the Moscow Patriarchate and other Patriarchates is an inevitable development; and while we should certainly watch it carefully and remember that the Moscow Patriarchate is in effect an organ of the Soviet Government, it would we think be bad tactics for us to openly stand out against it....without ourselves

> encouraging a direct conflict between our own proteges in Athens and possibly Istanbul and the proteges of the Soviet Government.[40]

A warning was circulated to British embassies, in August 1945, about the Russian Church claiming a coincidence of interest between it and the Soviet state, defined as:

a) closer relations with the Slav nations;
b) the spread of Soviet influence in the Near and Middle East;
c) a design to put pressure on Turkey to restore the former prestige and dignity of the Oecumenical Patriarch of Constantinople (including the return of Santa Sophia);
d) the proposal to call as soon as possible an Oecumenical Council of all 'freedom loving Christians';
e) the reconciliation with the Moscow Patriarchate of the dissident Russian Orthodox communities in exile;
f) and exposure of the alleged relationship between the Catholic Church and Fascism.

Concern about 'the reconciliation with the Moscow Patriarchate of the dissident Russian Orthodox communities in exile' applied particularly to the United States. Britain already viewed American power as the safeguard against Soviet power. An amicable understanding between two anti-colonial, anti-imperialist powers could only prove, in the mind of the FO, detrimental to British interests. There was anxiety for the Empire in a post-war world disillusioned with and critically questioning the system that had delivered slump, fascism and war, in the context of a weakened Britain confronted by the appeal of a creed that appealed to the poor and dispossessed, particularly should it be reinforced by religious faith and friendship with the US. With Truman seemingly following the same accommodationist policies toward Moscow pursued by Roosevelt, the British FO observed with some trepidation the anticipated return of the Russian Orthodox Church in the US to the jurisdiction of the Moscow Patriarchate, worried it might provide a conduit there for Soviet influence.[41]

During the war, religion had proven crucial in consolidating the wartime alliance and it potentially offered the means of further reducing the gulf that remained between Stalin and his allies.[42] In 1942, George Kennan observed that the reported relaxation in Soviet hostility toward religion was in the best interests of the regime, in Soviet controlled territories and abroad. Kennan, very significantly from the man who was to become known as the father of containment, indicated that once the war was over, 'if the Kremlin could be induced to tolerate religion at home and to receive the proffered cooperation of western religious movements in the spirit of friendliness and confidence, I believe one of the greatest barriers to a sound future peace would have been removed'.[43] This was entirely possible. Kremlin policies toward religion were clearly flexible. Stalin's pragmatism meant account would be taken of the Soviet Union's relative weakness and the need to maintain wartime cooperation with its promise of American loans and reparations.[44] Although there were anti-Soviet Russian Orthodox Church leaders in the US who had opposed American wartime aid to the Soviet Union, congregations had gone ahead of their priests in the desire to recognise their affinity with the country that bore the brunt of the Nazi onslaught. According to Metropolitan Benjamin, Exarch of the Moscow Patriarchate in North America, similar transfers of parishes were taking place in South America.[45] British officials therefore kept an eye on the ecclesiastical negotiations, helped in part by the Episcopal Church in America, which was suspicious of the Moscow Patriarchate, taking a low view of its activities in Yugoslavia and the Balkans generally. It furnished the British Consulate in New York with confidential documents of a meeting between its Advisory Council on Foreign Relations and Metropolitan Benjamin, the Head of the Russian Orthodox Church in the US, warning that most Orthodox communities were destitute and any offer by the Russians to underwrite them would likely be accepted.[46] Further inside information came to the Consulate from the son of a former imperial Russian diplomat attached to an Orthodox theological seminary in New York.[47]

To British relief, as American policy toward the USSR hardened, prospects for reunion were accordingly diminished. The deteriorating relations between Washington and Moscow took its toll on the negotiations, as did attacks from the Roman Catholic Church in America. The Metropolitan Gregory, representative of the Moscow Patriarch, was called a 'professor of atheism at the Soviet Atheistic College' by Monsignor Fulton J. Sheen, Professor of Philosophy in the Roman Catholic University of Washington, who charged him with attempting 'to win over the Russian Orthodox Church in the United States for Stalin'.[48] In mid-November 1947, Gregory left America, observing that antagonistic influences had prevented negotiations from reaching a satisfactory conclusion. With evident satisfaction, the British Ambassador in Washington, Lord Halifax, reported to Bevin, 'The possibility of increased Soviet influence over the great majority of the Orthodox communicants in this country, who are alleged to number over one million, thus seems to have been eliminated for the present'.[49] The move was equally welcomed by the Roman Catholic Church in America.[50]

The FO regarded Roman Catholicism as 'one of the most powerful anti-Communist influences'. Careful not to be openly identified with the Vatican, which was 'rather in disgrace all over Europe for trimming during the war,' the FO still determined to support the Vatican's anti-Soviet stand by 'inconspicuous means'.[51] One suggestion emanating from the British Minister to the Holy See, Sir D'Arcy Osborne, was that the Church of England should support Papal anti-communism. In May 1946, Osborne emphasised how the Pope spoke 'as much of and on behalf of Christianity, as of the Catholic Church', a factor he wanted brought to the attention of the Anglican Church.[52] He subsequently wrote to J.V. Perowne, the FO representative on the CFR committee, that he 'should like to have a talk with someone on your Anglican Committee about rather a delicate question, the fact that it is left to the Pope to defend Christianity against marxian materialism and the Russian anti-religious campaign.…'.[53] Osborne was subsequently informed that the head of the Northern Department, Christopher Warner, would be glad to discuss his idea.[54] Following Osborne's meeting with Warner, Perowne arranged for him to meet the Bishop of Chichester, George Bell, Chairman of CFR.[55] Osborne subsequently received an enquiry from Warner about his meeting with Bell on anti-communism.[56] Although further correspondence on the matter has been retained by the FO, Bell's subsequent activities, until his aversion for nuclear weapons came to prevail, were those of an 'ecclesiastical cold warrior'.[57]

One topic discussed by Osborne, Warner and Bell could have been the possibility of the two major faiths behind the Iron Curtain, Roman Catholic and Orthodox, combining against communism. During a May 1946 visit by Richard Parsons, Bishop of Hereford, to the Serb Orthodox Church in Yugoslavia, ostensibly to renew ties of friendship, there occurred a 'very impressive demonstration which must have been extremely unwelcome to the Yugoslav Government.' It was, if not organised, at least welcomed by the Serb Orthodox hierarchy, which appeared to relish the prospect of political martyrdom: 'The Acting Patriarch was indeed confidently and cheerfully predicting that he and most of his clergy would be arrested, but probably not until the Bishop had departed.' During the visit, the British Ambassador, George Clutton, arranged a meeting on the 'neutral ground' of the Embassy between Parsons and the Apostolic Nuncio, Bishop Joseph Hurley. Hurley had previously been the Bishop of Florida and the principal American representative on the staff of the Cardinal Secretary of State. Although the meeting was not revealed to the Yugoslav authorities, Parsons pointedly told the Acting Serb Orthodox Patriarch, Metropolitan Joseph, that it was to take place. Clutton reported his response to the FO:

> He was extremely pleased at the idea, but begged Dr Parsons to warn Bishop Hurley that all his movements and every activity of the Nunciature were being watched by the secret police. He then said that when Bishop Sergei of Kirovgorod had visited Yugoslavia he had brought with him a message from the Patriarch of Moscow expressing his wish that the Serbian Church should associate itself with the Russian in denouncing the Catholic Church. The Metropolitan would, however, have nothing to do with such a proposal and informed Bishop Sergei that the Serbian Church, having lived side by side with the Catholic Church for centuries, knew what the Catholic Church stood for, whereas the Russian Church knew nothing whatsoever about the matter. More interesting still, the Metropolitan informed Dr Parsons that what the Yugoslav Government feared most was a rapprochement or coalition between the Orthodox and Catholic Churches. All their efforts were directed on keeping these two powerful influences in Yugoslav life apart. At present such a coalition was not practical politics, but he, the Metropolitan, had the matter well in mind, and when the time was ripe he would take the necessary action.[58]

Comments in a 'Top Secret' report written for the FO by Waddams, the CFR secretary, who had accompanied the Bishop, confirmed that Roman Catholic-Orthodox cooperation had been discussed: 'I was very much impressed by the positive and enlightened attitude of the Metropolitan on the subject of relations with the Roman Catholics. I am inclined to believe he will be ready to cooperate when such action becomes practical politics. At present it seems that in this field, as in others, his hands are to some extent tied by the opinion of his people'.[59] Equally significant, Clutton's despatch, also referred to:

> a confidential report from His Majesty's Consul at Sarajevo in which extremely circumstantial details were given of an underground movement in Bosnia and Hercegovina with connections in Zagreb and Belgrade for the formation of a coalition of representatives of the Catholic, Orthodox and Moslem Churches. The aim of the combination was to force a new general election in an attempt to obtain a different and non-communist regime.

Interestingly, early the following year when the FO requested the responses of its East European missions to the possibility of Archbishop Garbett visiting their respective domains, the response was decidedly restrained. The times were not considered propitious and fears were expressed that the visit would prove counter-productive. Bucharest advised of a clash of dates in Bulgaria with a Russian delegation and warned: 'It is clearly important that the visit should not clash, and that we should avoid any appearance of competing with the Russian Orthodox Church'.[60] From Sofia came two responses, an official reply, to be shown to the Anglican Church, and a private reply for Warner, which explained:

> I have borne in mind not only the fear expressed by the FO that a visit of a Church of England Hierarch to Bulgaria might be taken as approval of the present political regime, but also the desire of His Majesty's Government as expressed in [a despatch] of April 14, not to appear too prominently in the role of 'official opposition' to the local Government. I think that at a later stage a visit of the kind proposed might provide a most useful encouragement to the Opposition, but from this point of view I think that it is premature at present. I would rather wait till we have got rid of the major obstacle to Bulgaria's freedom i.e. the outward sign of Russian control in the shape of the presence of Russian armed forces.[61]

The official policy of cooperation with the USSR required that Britain not be seen to side openly with opposition to the communist regimes: 'the appearance of great power cooperation was publicly maintained, but the remorseless focus of British policy was directed toward securing an effective Western alliance to contain Soviet might in Germany, in Europe, and throughout the world.'.[62] However, as American policy toward Moscow hardened in 1947, reflected in the Truman Doctrine and Marshall Plan, British behaviour changed.

America and the religious Cold War

On 22 August 1947, Orme Sargent, the Permanent Under-Secretary of the FO, informed Garbett, 'we are all in favour of your visit to Yugoslavia and Hungary…'.[63] FO approbation was bestowed at the same time as an exchange of letters, between Truman and Pius XII. The exchange was facilitated by Myron C. Taylor, the President's personal representative to the Pope, which was widely interpreted to herald an anti-

Communist crusade, a spiritual corollary to the military and economic initiatives of the Truman Doctrine and the Marshall Plan and sharing the same objectives.[64] Like the Truman Doctrine, it was ideological and potentially universal. Like the Marshall Plan, it hoped to drive a wedge between the Soviet Union and the emerging bloc of satellite states in Eastern Europe. As Taylor reported to Truman following his audience with the Pope:

> In a lengthy discussion we reviewed prospective religious influence and canvassed various plans that have been proposed to you and by you for cooperating in some parallel or common action the power of various religious orders with the objective of conveying to those who are hopeless in many places both within the Russian orbit and outside of it such assurances that their misfortunes have not been forgotten in the stress of other controversies in states in closer proximity to the western powers and particularly to the United States.[65]

Truman's instruction to Taylor to consult with the Patriarchs of Istanbul and Athens, potential counters to the influence of the Russian Orthodox Church, worried Pius XII. He advised Taylor against such an approach at that time 'in so open and direct a manner but that some other method should be devised, perhaps through the Anglican group which would be of equivalent effect'.[66] That the Pope should be recommending the services of the Church of England was significant. Equally significant was that Taylor first approached Halifax, the former ambassador to the US, who subsequently had discussions with both Anglican archbishops. Afterwards, he told Taylor that Garbett was scheduled to visit the Balkans and would 'do his best in the direction you suggest'.[67] That direction can be gauged from the fact that, in both Czechoslovakia and Yugoslavia, Garbett had meetings with the leading representatives of the Roman Catholic Church. The Roman Catholic Bishop of Prague 'talked about cooperation over peace, especially about general action against what he described as "the common enemy"'.[68] In his meeting with the Yugoslav leader, Marshal Josip Tito, Garbett made representations on behalf of the Roman Catholic Church, warning of potentially adverse repercussions from Britain should they not be heeded.[69]

The Apostolic Nuncio was provided with a summary of what had transpired between Garbett and Tito. Hurley passed the information to the Vatican and Garbett was later informed that 'the Holy See was greatly interested in this conversation and wished you to know of their deep appreciation and gratitude for all you had said'.[70] It appeared that church and state in Britain were working together to signal their support for the US-Vatican alliance, which the President and Pope alike had openly flaunted. The day after publishing the highly symbolic letter exchange between the pair, the *New York Times* reported that Catholic organisations planned to print tens of thousands of copies to be distributed among the faithful, including in Eastern Europe.[71] Taylor's assistant, J. Graham Parsons, reported from Rome that: 'The Vatican Secretariat of State had circulated to all missions accredited to the Holy See a brochure in which the letters were printed in six different languages.' He suspected they were also circulating clandestinely where necessary 'in eastern languages as well'.[72]

As the traditional papal stance in international affairs was a studied neutralism, Parsons expressed surprise at the extent to which the Pope openly sided with the US. However, it became increasingly clear that, in the religious sphere, Truman was also determined to adopt an overt confrontational stance. The election of Archbishop Athenagoras of North and South America, an American citizen, as Patriarch of Constantinople, the primary position in the Orthodox world, was virtually flaunted by Truman, who had him flown in his personal presidential plane to Istanbul to assume his new position.[73] The President thus directly signalled to Moscow his good relations with, and support for, the heads of the two major religions in the Soviet sphere of influence, Roman Catholicism and Eastern Orthodoxy, each closely connected to the national identity, history and sentiment of key countries in the region.[74] For the Soviets, it threatened the dreaded combination of Roman Catholicism and Orthodoxy against Soviet communism, supported by the world's strongest economic and military power and its ideological foe, America.

Conclusion

As Anglo-Soviet tensions grew in 1945–47, the FO recognised and acted upon the potential importance of organised religion in combating the spread of communism.[75] The attitudes of Britain's foreign policy-making elites toward the Soviet regime derived from ingrained suspicion of and longstanding rivalry with Tsarist Russia, not just ideological opposition to Soviet communism. Their use of religion to counter Soviet influence and assert their own in areas of strategic interest was traditional diplomatic practice. However, the British soon moved further, endorsing and supporting America's anti-Soviet crusade with its messianic dynamic and rejection of the policy of cooperation Truman had inherited from Franklin D. Roosevelt. The US took over and transformed the religious cold war, for which Britain had been the forerunner. At the end of the war, Truman led a nation, anxious for peace, that without a discernible threat was divided about whether or not it should have a global role.[76] As the US moved from its traditional isolationism toward globalism and world leadership, Soviet intentions were over-simplified, particularly with regard to the Soviet treatment of and attitude toward religion. Following the example of his Democratic presidential predecessors, Woodrow Wilson and Franklin D. Roosevelt, Truman summoned up the 'righteous nation' narrative to engender national unity in support of an interventionist foreign policy. The notion of being divinely chosen that has informed the very concept of America from its colonial beginning, required not simply the idealisation of America, but the demonisation of the 'other'. Designating the USSR as godless, and hence evil, precluded validation or explanation, excluding negotiation and compromise as evidence of weakness. It allowed the Truman administration to shift America into permanent military, political and economic intervention on a world scale despite the tremendous cost. Truman's appropriation and use of religion transformed what in essence was great power rivalry into a politico-religious enterprise that was to have profound implications in domestic and international arenas.

The British origins of the religious cold war are yet another example of the way in which London 'helped shape the contours of the Cold War not just in terms of strategic geography, but also in its language and concepts.' Sean Greenwood's analogy with post-war technology – 'Britain was capable of remarkable invention, but others outpaced them in their application'[77] – is an apt description of how Britain's cautious and covert religious cold war was transformed by the US into the means through which America arrogated the spiritual and moral power associated with organised religion for its own strategic purposes. Equally important, the way America's presentation of the Cold War, as a cosmic struggle between good and evil, was supported by the church and the state of its transatlantic partner enhanced American conviction about its exceptionalism and world role, confirming its perception of itself and its justification for global intervention. The consequences of Church support should not be underestimated. The relationship of religious institutions with temporal power is longstanding, intricate and varied, sustained not only by their claims to command life's purpose and meaning but, perhaps above all, the ability to sanctify and legitimise secular power.

Notes

1. Dianne Kirby, (ed.), *Religion and the Cold War* (Basingstoke: Palgrave /Macmillan, 2003); Philip E. Muehlenbeck, (ed.), *Religion and the Cold War: A Global Perspective* (Nashville: Vanderbilt University Press, 2012), vii.
2. The most recent example is Andrew Preston, *Sword of the Spirit, Shield of Faith: Religion in American War and Diplomacy* (New York: Knopf, 2012).
3. Elizabeth Spalding, *The First Cold Warrior: Harry Truman, Containment, and the Remaking of Liberal Internationalism* (Lexington: University Press of Kentucky, 2006), p. 9.
4. William Inboden, *Religion and American Foreign Policy, 1945–1960* (New York: Cambridge University Press, 2008, pp. 4–5.
5. Conrad Cherry (ed.), *God's New Israel: Religious Interpretations of American Destiny,* (Chapel Hill: North Carolina University Press, 1998); William Van Den Bercken, 'Holy Russia and the Soviet Fatherland', *Religion in Communist Lands*, 15/3 (1987), pp. 264–277; S.M. Miner, *Stalin's Holy War: Religion, Nationalism, and Alliance Politics, 1941–1945* (Chapel Hill: University of North Carolina Press, 2003).
6. Dianne Kirby, 'Anglican-Orthodox Relations and the Religious Rehabilitation of the Soviet Regime during the Second World War', *Revue d'Histoire Ecclesiastique*, 96/1–2 (2001), pp. 101–123.
7. Ian McLaine, *Ministry of Morale: Home Front Morale and the Ministry of Information in World War II* (London: Allen and Unwin, 1979).
8. CFR performed for the church the same function as the FO did for the state. From its inception it ensured that its functions were, if not always complementary at least not opposed to the FO, helped by the fact that an FO representative sat, informally, on the CFR committee.
9. 'The New Soviet Constitution and Religion', 4 April 1938, p. 10; Lambeth Palace Library (LPL), Papers of the Church of England Council on Foreign Relations Papers (CFR), OC 191.
10. Ralph Carter Elwood, (ed.), *Resolutions and Decisions of the Communist Party of the Soviet Union, Volume I: The Russian Social Democratic Labour Party 1898-October 1917* (Toronto: University of Toronto Press, 1974), pp. 42–3.
11. N.I. Bukharin and E.O. Preobrazhensky, *The ABC of Communism,* (Harmondsworth: Penguin, 1969), pp. 299–301.
12. A. Manhattan, *Vatican Imperialism in the Twentieth Century* (Michigan: Zondervan Publishers, 1965).
13. P. Steeves, *Keeping the Faiths: Religion and Ideology in the Soviet* Union (New Jersey: Holmes and Meier, 1989), pp. 85–86.
14. Arto Luukkanen, *Party of Unbelief: the Religious Policy of the Bolshevik Party, 1917–1929* (Helsinki: Studia Historica, 1994).
15. In the official 1937 Soviet census, more than half the respondents declared themselves believers. Assuming that many preferred not to disclose such information, there must have been considerably more.
16. Daniel Peris, *Storming the Heavens: The Soviet League of the Militant Godless* (New York: Cornell University Press, 1998).
17. LPL, Temple Papers, Martin to Temple, undated, but probably May/June 1943.
18. The National Archives (TNA), Kew, INF1/790, 'The Question of Religion in Russia: Its Bearing on Allied Propaganda', 1 October 1941.

19. TNA/INF1/788, undated memorandum.
20. TNA/INF1/790, 'Notes on the Question of Religion in Russia and its Bearing on Allied Propaganda', 25 June 1942.
21. Miner, *Holy War*.
22. Dimitry Pospielovsky, 'The "Best Years" of Stalin's Church Policy (1942–1948) in the Light of Archival Documents', *Religion, State and Society*, 23/2 (1997), pp. 139–162.
23. LPL/CFR, 'The Russian Church and the Eastern Patriarchates', 12 April 1950.
24. Isaac Deutscher, *Stalin* (Harmondsworth: Penguin, 1972), pp. 506–7. On individual churches in the Soviet bloc, see Peter Kent, *The Lonely Cold War of Pope Pius XII* (Montreal: McGill-Queen's University Press, 2002).
25. Dianne Kirby, 'Truman's Holy Alliance: The President, the Pope and the Origins of the Cold War', *Borderlines: Studies in American Culture*, 4/1 (1997), pp. 1–17.
26. Anna Dickinson, 'Domestic and Foreign Policy Considerations and the Origins of Post-war Soviet Church–State Relations,' in Kirby, *Religion*, pp. 23–36.
27. Harry S. Truman Library (HSTL), Myron Taylor Papers, Taylor to Pius XII, 20 June 1951.
28. Kirby, 'The Church of England and "Religions Division" during the Second World War: Church–State Relations and the Anglo-Soviet Alliance', *electronic Journal of International History*, 1/1 (May 2000).
29. LPL/CFR, 'The Russian Church and the Eastern Patriarchates', 12 April 1950.
30. See Andrew Chandler, 'The Church of England and the Obliteration Bombing of Germany in the Second World War', *English Historical Review*, October 1993, pp. 920–946.
31. LPL/CFR, Waddams memorandum, 11 February 1944.
32. TNA/FO371/47881, 2 April 1945.
33. Dianne Kirby, 'The Archbishop of York and Anglo–American relations during the Second World War and early Cold War, 1942–55', *The Journal of Religious History*, 23/3 (October 1999).
34. TNA/FO371/36963/N6339, Shone to FO (FO), 19 October 1943.
35. TNA/INF1/785, FO to Ministry of Information, undated, 1943.
36. York Minster Library (YML), Garbett Papers, Douglas to Garbett, 23 August 1943.
37. *The Tablet*, 18 September 1943, p. 138.
38. LPL/CFR, 'The Russian Church and the Eastern Patriarchates', 12 April 1950.
39. Dianne Kirby, *Church, State and Propaganda* (Hull: Hull University Press 1999), pp. 127–137.
40. TNA/FO371/48349 Moscow to FO, 10 August 1945.
41. TNA/FO371/44632, FO to New York, 13 August 1945.
42. Kirby, 'Anglican-Orthodox Relations'.
43. Franklin Roosevelt Library, Myron Taylor Papers, PSF Diplomatic Box 52, Kennan to Taylor, 2 October 1942.
44. Pospielovsky, 'Stalin's Church Policy'.
45. TNA/FO371/44632, FO to New York, 13 August 1945.
46. Ibid., New York to Washington, 27 April 1945, and Washington to FO, 6 May 1945.
47. Ibid., New York to Washington, 6 May 1945.
48. *Religion and the People*, June 1947.
49. TNA/FO371/66409, Halifax to Bevin, 17 November 1947.
50. *The Lamp*, January 1948.

51. TNA/FO371/56885, Minute, 14 May 1946.
52. LPL/CFR, Perowne to Waddams, 27 May 1946.
53. TNA/FO371/66294, Osborne to Perowne, 6 June 1946.
54. TNA/FO371/66294, Perowne to Osborne, 18 June 1946.
55. TNA/FO371/66294, Perowne to Osborne, 22 June 1946.
56. TNA/FO371/66294, Warner to Osborne, 13 August 1946.
57. Dianne Kirby, 'Bishop George Bell and the Cold War', *Contemporary Church History,* 21/2 (2008), pp. 349–372.
58. TNA/FO371/59501, Clutton to Bevin, 5 June 1946.
59. TNA/FO371/59501, Waddams to FO, undated.
60. TNA/FO371/47174, Sarrel to Bevin, 1 May 1947.
61. TNA/FO371/66989, Sterndale-Bennet to Warner, 7 May 1947.
62. Anne Deighton, *The Impossible Peace: Britain, the Division of Germany, and the Origins of the Cold War,* (Oxford: Oxford University Press, 1990), p. 6–7.
63. TNA/FO371/66989, Sargent to Garbett, 22 August 1947.
64. *New York Times,* 28 August 1947.
65. HSTL, Truman papers, White House Central File (WHCF), Box 46, Taylor to Truman, 27 August 1947.
66. Ibid., Taylor to Truman, 25 September 1947.
67. Ibid., Halifax to Taylor, 24 October 1947.
68. YML, Garbett Papers, 'Travel Diary…, October–November 1947', p. 16.
69. Ibid., p. 34.
70. Ibid., Peake to Garbett, 5 April 1948.
71. *New York Times,* 30 August 1947.
72. HSTL, Parsons' Diary, 24 September 1947.
73. Demetrios Tsakonas, *A Man Sent by God: the Life of Patriarch Athenagoras of Constantinople* (Brookline: Holy Cross Press, 1977).
74. Dennis Dunn, (ed.), *Religion and Nationalism in Eastern Europe and the Soviet Union* (Boulder: Lynne Reinner, 1987).
75. See also Dianne Kirby, 'The Church of England in the Period of the Cold War, 1945–56', PhD, Hull University, 1991.
76. Walter Russell Mead, *Special Providence: American foreign policy and how it changed the world* (New York: Routledge, 2002).
77. Sean Greenwood, *Britain and the Cold War 1945–91* (Basingstoke: Macmillan, 2000), pp. 139, 194.

2

'Journey into a Desert': British Perceptions of Poland's Western Territories, 1945–48

Alastair Noble

Documents highlighting the experiences of British diplomats in early post-war Poland describe conditions in an environment dealing with the aftermath of conflict, involving the rebuilding and recasting of state and society by an externally backed new order.[1] This chapter highlights three main areas pertaining to the process. First, it illustrates Foreign Office (FO) reporting, frequently the product of experienced officials who had served in Poland before 1939. Secondly, it outlines the British position on Poland as the Iron Curtain descended. Finally, the chapter focuses on the situation in Stettin, the most insecure of Poland's post-war western territories.

Return to Warsaw

When British diplomatic representatives returned to Warsaw in 1945 they entered a wasteland.[2] The first to arrive was Robin Hankey, who flew in as *chargé d'affaires* on 14 July 1945.[3] Upon his arrival, he received a despatch from Sir John Anderson, the acting head of the government whilst the Prime Minister, Winston Churchill, and the Foreign Secretary, Anthony Eden, attended the Potsdam Conference. The despatch, approved by Eden before he left, provided instructions following Britain's recognition of the new Polish Government of National Unity earlier that month. London viewed the Soviet authorities and the Red Army as the real powers in Poland, noting from afar that, 'The Red Army seems to have been running riot, living on the country and despoiling it.' The Soviets controlled all communications. The new government was composed of re-appointees from the old, Communist-led Provisional Government with the addition of a handful of national figures, including Stanislaw Mikolajczyk, latterly Prime Minister of the Polish Government-in-Exile in London. The Communist President, Boreslaw Bierut, retained his post and it was 'clear, of course, that the Soviet Union will retain a predominant influence in Polish affairs'.[4]

Hankey was struck by the 'ruin, desolation and misery' he encountered and told Eden: 'Warsaw is unrecognisable. Many streets are still not cleared and work is proceeding slowly. The people all show signs of their sufferings and many look hungry and ill. Ministry of Health are concerned in containing the number of typhus and typhoid cases'.[5] He also provided a snapshot of the awkward working conditions at the undamaged and lively Hotel Polonia, the fourth floor of which housed the British Embassy:

> We have had a most difficult time here. There are only two telephones in the hotel, both downstairs in the Foyer. To get to the Ministry of Foreign Affairs over in Praga you had to ring 3 numbers, one after the other, and one of them was always engaged. Now they have moved over to Warsaw it is only slightly better. Therefore it has been practically impossible to make appointments unless somebody sent transport.[6]

The Polish leadership cadre had been devastated by the war. Political, academic and religious leaders were murdered by the Germans. In eastern Poland, during their occupation between September 1939 and June 1941, the Narodny Kommissariat Vnutrennikeh Del (NKVD) (Soviet People's Commissariat of Internal Affairs, Soviet secret police) organised four waves of deportations to the Soviet interior. Katyn became a byword for Soviet atrocities against the Polish intelligentsia, but this one mass grave was the final destination for a fraction of the Poles killed by NKVD executioners. The Polish Government-in-Exile, distant and openly derided by Stalin, following the severance of relations in April 1943, no longer enjoyed even London's recognition. Hankey described the new regime:

> The new Poland bears little resemblance to the old. The administration is riddled with corruption. Ministers and officials receive salaries about 1/10th of what they need to live on and all the rest has to be picked up in other ways...Most of those with a westernised mentality have been eliminated and one meets with a much more Russian type of outlook. They are, however, even more sensitive than the Poles before the war.[7]

The British ambassador, Victor Frederick William Cavendish-Bentinck, arrived on 20 August. Formerly an Assistant Under-Secretary in the FO, his diplomatic career included a spell as Third Secretary in Warsaw between 1919 and 1922. During the war he had been the young, but effective Chairman of the Joint Intelligence Committee (JIC).[8] He, too, reflected on the devastation of Warsaw, where the 'eerie and awesome' ruins seemed to epitomise the Polish character 'both romantic and grandiose'.[9] Bentinck was sympathetic towards the Poles, mindful of their 'achievements in clandestine as well as overt warfare against the Germans' and he regarded their intelligence officers as 'the best people by far'.[10] He was at the head of an embassy staffed by officers with experience of Poland and the region, some having experience of wartime intelligence work.[11] They were well informed and at least at the outset were able to travel widely in relative freedom.

Poland's western frontier

The Polish authorities claimed at the beginning of June 1945 that 85% of the German population had left the eastern German territories. Warsaw set about filling these lands with Poles. There was space for 7,500,000.[12] They hoped that one million Poles would be settled there by the end of July 1945. In a proclamation issued in early July, the four main political parties stressed: 'The ancient lands are returning to the Motherland. Today all efforts should be directed towards organizing the economic life of the lands retrieved from the Germans. Hands and brains are needed to wipe all German traces from the face of our country'.[13] However, the British and American governments maintained that no binding decisions had been taken at the Potsdam Conference on Poland's western frontier; this remained a matter for a future peace conference. But, even before Potsdam, the British press considered that President Truman and Churchill were faced with a *fait accompli*. The Diplomatic Correspondent of *The Times* wrote on 14 July 1945:

> Largely it will be a matter of asking Mr Truman and Mr Churchill to agree to what has already been done. The new frontiers have been proclaimed for many months past both by Moscow and by the Polish Provisional Government, and lately the Soviet Military Command has handed administration within the extended areas over to the Poles.[14]

Prior to Potsdam the Polish authorities did all that they could to ensure their *de facto* annexation of the western territories. They had emptied the 'frontier belt' of Germans through so-called 'wild expulsions', simply driving out the German population in a westerly direction at short notice. But, large swathes of these districts were soon deserted as no Poles had settled and the food situation remained 'calamitous'.[15] As the British occupation zone in Germany bulged to overflowing, Sir Alexander Cadogan, the Permanent Under-Secretary at the FO, outlined the difficulties of negotiating on the frontier with Stalin at Potsdam. On 21 July, he wrote:

> We've been having a row with Joe about the Polish Western frontier, and trying to stop him bagging from the area he wants to allot to the Poles all the produce that it used to contribute to the supply of Germany. We, in the west of Germany, have got millions of Germans to feed and support, and if a great part of their normal source of supply is snaffled by Joe, our difficulties will be considerably increased.[16]

Following the arrival in Potsdam of the new Prime Minister, Clement Attlee, and his pugnacious Foreign Secretary, Ernest Bevin, after Labour's General Election victory, there were tough discussions with the Polish delegation. However, the British came to the depressing realisation that the Poles and Soviets would only settle for a border along the line of the western Neisse.[17] Finally, on 31 July, Attlee and Bevin agreed to this. Ultimately worthless pledges were extracted from Bierut and his cronies for free elections, to be held no later than 'the early part of 1946', and for freedom of the press. Stalin stated that the Red Army would be largely withdrawn from the territories under Polish administration.[18] The FO's Research Department concluded that, 'The tide of history has been reversed and the Teuton's *Drang nach Osten* is replaced by a Slavonic *Drang nach Westen*'.[19] Attlee and Bevin comprehended the likely finality of the agreement on Poland's western frontiers. Attlee recalled in his memoirs: 'In our view the Russians were asking too much when they demanded the Oder-Neisse Line for Poland, thus expelling the Germans from lands which were almost wholly inhabited by them. We were obliged to accept the position pending a peace settlement, but it was obvious that, once settled in this sense, it would be difficult to change the boundary'.[20]

Bevin's telegram to Bentinck of 23 August 1945, highlighted the Potsdam discussions and 'the decision to entrust the administration of the territory west of the 1937 German-Polish frontier to the Polish Provisional Government'.[21] Bevin wanted free elections promptly and freedom of religion and the press. However, he thought that the Communists 'with Soviet support if not on Soviet instructions...are aiming at a regime much nearer to the Soviet model'. He hoped to widen the British net in Poland and instructed 'that the appropriate British Consulates should be established as soon as possible and that British officials should tour the western territories ... and indeed as much as possible of the country'.[22] Arrangements were initiated with the Americans, to coordinate consulates and provide maximum coverage.[23]

British officials travelled widely across Poland in the immediate post-war period although they were accompanied by Polish security personnel, ostensibly for their protection.[24] In mid-September 1945, Bentinck told London that economically Poland was 'basically in a bad way'. The Soviets controlled the key coal and textiles industries, otherwise 'the people of this country are largely engaged in taking in each other's washing'. Many were simply buying and selling goods at ever increasing prices. As Poles left central Poland for the former German lands in the west, Bentinck cautioned, 'I am certain they will not find this a land flowing with milk and honey'.[25] Hankey and Michael Winch, the embassy's First Secretary, visited Silesia from 21 September. They estimated that 1,400,000 Germans remained. All inhabitants were existing 'under conditions of considerable hardship in which the Germans come off worse and are encouraged to leave the country individually.' Indeed, 'the Germans, whilst not actually expelled, are being in fact faced with the alternative of leaving voluntarily or starving.' The transient nature of Polish settlement was also noted: 'The Poles are the more disinclined to put much work and effort into their holdings owing to the prevailing uncertainty as to the future of the territory. This uncertainty increases steadily as the western part of the province is approached.' Meanwhile, if relations with the Soviets were bad, the visitors discerned tension within the Polish communities between native Polish Upper Silesians and the more culturally backward and disorderly settlers. The settlers said the Silesian Poles were 'virtually German'.[26] The embassy's First Secretary (Commercial), G.L.G. Holliday, took a Co-operative parliamentary delegation, led by the Labour peer Lord Palmer, around Poland in October 1945.[27] These trips gave the British observers an opportunity to gauge the mood and to estimate Soviet troop numbers. In general, it was noted that the security police were even more hated and feared, most Poles hoped that the Red Army would leave soon and Poles still had warm feelings towards the United Kingdom, and Churchill in particular.[28]

Bentinck was not unduly sympathetic about the plight of the Germans but this cut little ice with the Polish Government. The US ambassador, Arthur Bliss Lane, a friend of Bentinck since they had both served in

Poland in 1919, wrote that the Warsaw press still insisted that the British and the Americans were more concerned about the return of the Germans to Germany than in the return of Polish displaced persons to Poland.[29] Lane added in early December 1945 that: 'The British have been seriously criticized here on the ground that they have been more mindful of the well-being of the Germans than of the Poles. The Polish press, encouraged by the Soviet Gov't, has emphasized British softness towards the Germans'.[30] Lane also cited Bentinck's lack of support for the German case:

> Bentinck says he fully agrees with me as to the unwisdom of making representations to Polish Govt re alleged inhumane treatment of Germans as it would merely serve to irritate Poles and would not alter conditions which Bentinck claims have been exaggerated by Germans transferred from Poland.[31]

The plight of the starving German refugees arriving in Berlin from the east was well covered across the British press and appeals to alleviate their suffering regularly arrived at the FO. When Bentinck received a telegram from London authorising him to act in tandem with the Americans over the 'alleged mistreatment of Germans', Lane reported his reaction: 'As Bentinck was authorized and not instructed to make representations he proposes like Nelson at bombardment of Copenhagen to hold his telescope to his blind eye'.[32] Others recognised German suffering, but pointed to the broader picture. When he returned to London in 1946 to head the FO's Northern Department, Hankey responded to appeals on behalf of the Germans by saying that the conditions in some Polish camps were indeed 'horrifying'. However, he stressed that he would have been 'much more deeply moved if I had not myself been to the extermination camps at Maidanek and Oswiecim [Auschwitz]'.[33] In contrast, Bentinck wrote, seemingly without irony, in September 1945 that 'The slaughter of Jews in this country has made the towns a good deal cleaner and has certainly decreased the number of middle-men'.[34]

The 'wild west'

To illustrate the British outlook on events in greater depth, a close focus will now be placed on their impressions of Stettin (renamed Szczecin by the Poles), on the Oder's west bank. The Polish Government in London had argued for the Gulf of Stettin in December 1942. Stalin first mentioned giving Stettin to Poland when he met Mikolajczyk in the Kremlin, on 3 August 1944. The British government expressed isolated support for this proposal three months later in an attempt to bolster Mikolajczyk.[35] As the war neared its conclusion, Stettin became an evermore shattered prize. Bombing had reduced much of it to ruins. A Scandinavian SS volunteer described the city in 1945:

> Stettin, on 22 January, was a sad sight. The inner city had been more or less blown away, or burned down, by British and American bombers. Piles of broken household goods, bricks and rubble framed the streets in front of the facades of blackened houses. Between them moved pale, dead-tired and after five years of clothes rationing, threadbare people who, with resolute defiance and fighting-spirit, still went about their daily occupations.[36]

Despite the last ditch propaganda rhetoric, the Nazi *Gauleiter*, Franz Schwede-Coburg, did not defend Stettin as a fortress, in marked contrast to the bloody and prolonged struggles for Königsberg and Breslau. Stettin fell to the Red Army on 26 April 1945. It was 40–45% destroyed. The Soviets soon displayed a particular interest in the port facilities, dismantling cranes and dockside machinery and shipping it back to Russia. The Polish takeover of the administration of Stettin, which they claimed along with all the German territory east of the Oder-Neisse Line, was ignored by the Soviet-controlled media in Germany.[37] In July 1945, Hankey reported that the Poles had taken over the administration of the main part of Stettin on the Oder's west bank. The naval dockyard, however, remained in Soviet hands.[38] The Polish coastline had increased from a mere 54 miles in 1939 to 310 miles, but the few Polish naval officers were sceptical about how much they would actually control. One told a visiting French military attaché that the coastline was said to stretch from Königsberg to Stettin, 'but without Königsberg and without Stettin'. It was even rumoured that Stettin was destined to be Czechoslovakia's outlet to the sea.[39]

At Potsdam it was agreed, 'pending the final determination of Poland's western frontier', to leave the territories east of the Oder-Neisse Line, extended west of the Oder to incorporate Stettin and Swinemünde, under Polish administration. FO observers concluded that it was unlikely that the decision would be reversed despite the inclusion of the provisos: 'the *fait accompli* for which the USSR and Polish Provisional Government have striven has been successful in securing acceptance by the Western Powers'.[40] Informed Germans brought details of conditions in Stettin in the summer of 1945 to the attention of the Allied control authorities in

Berlin. They said that typhoid was rife and people were receiving only the most meagre of bread rations. German money was not accepted. The only way to procure zlotys to buy a few potatoes was to sell remaining personal possessions. The looting and requisitioning of houses was commonplace and the Polish authorities turned a blind eye to feeding the remaining Germans whilst making every effort to encourage their 'voluntary evacuation'.[41]

Brigadier Richards, the British Military Attaché in Warsaw, journeyed to Stettin with First Secretary Winch, in October 1945, and noted that the Warsaw-Poznan road was 'in good condition, as far as Polish roads go'. But, 'There is an abrupt and striking change as soon as the 1939 frontier is crossed... The roads are worse in the immediate neighbourhood of Stettin, where heavy fighting took place and traffic was no doubt heaviest.' Rail travel was no better. The journey from Poznan to Stettin, not much more than 100 miles, took about 18 hours. Richards noted that the large-scale looting of cattle, horses and carts was continuing and Red Army garrisons were visible in the towns. He also reported, 'It was never long before some individual would come up with some frightful tale of oppression and wrong generally at the hands of the Russians'.[42] He described the area between the rivers Oder and Warthe and remarked that: 'The Russians have made a desert and we call it peace... What the Russian and Polish forces could not carry away they have burned or destroyed. One sees very little signs of cultivation... In less than a year the land seems to have gone back to nature'.[43] Richards witnessed the arrival of the first batches of Polish Displaced Persons at Stettin in October 1945. He remarked, 'They seemed in good heart and in high spirits at their return to Poland. I heard nothing worse than good natured chaff. Alas, they do not know what is in store for them'.[44]

Another British official visited the Oder's west bank north of Stettin and viewed the power plant and the Pölitz synthetic oil facility. He saw Red Army personnel systematically ransacking houses and loading their contents on to lorries. The Poles could not use Stettin's port but large Soviet ships did arrive empty and leave full. Moreover, Polish administrators who had attempted to assume control in the area in early October were robbed of valuables and clothing.[45] Little had been done to settle Poles into the area around Stettin, which remained full of Red Army troops 'at the best ill-disciplined, and at the worst marauding deserters'. As the British had foreseen at Yalta and Potsdam, 'the Poles have bitten off far more territory than they can chew for some time to come.' Again it was observed that the Germans were not expelled but were faced with the alternative of leaving voluntarily or starving.[46] Winch reckoned that 60,000 Germans remained in Stettin, half were children or the elderly. Voluntary migration of the Germans was encouraged by the Poles through the requisitioning of homes at short notice, the withdrawal of ration cards from those without work, and by unfair exchange rates. However, whilst the Poles tried to administer the city, the Soviets retained control of the port, the Oder and the only road bridge across the river.[47]

Charles Lambert in the *Daily Herald* talked of 'Poland's Western Desert', the '"Promised Land" of Desolation'. Here 'vast expanses of once rich agricultural area lie untilled, homes have been plundered and stripped. Livestock, horses and cattle have gone. Most of the farm machinery has gone, too. This is the empty land to be resettled by the Poles.' It was in stark contrast to the enticing posters, radio broadcasts and press reports in central Poland, which proclaimed, 'Make your fortune in the West' where there was 'Land and Work for All'. Some Poles who had tried to settle in the new lands had already returned home. Many Polish farmers had seen their livestock requisitioned by Soviet troops living off the land.[48] When Lambert visited Stettin in October 1945 it was 'a half-ruined city of 40,000 Poles and 60,000 Germans.' Shots rang out through the 'black ruins'. Soviet deserters and Polish gangsters were blamed for the crime and chaos. Lambert pitied the Polish administration. He viewed them as pioneers trying to do their best with limited resources.[49] Another report, in *The Times* in December 1945, mentioned that 'communications are haphazard' and 'security is precarious'. Poles dubbed the region the 'wild West'. The Soviets had stripped it of everything valuable: 'A tour of these lands reveals villages that have been destroyed, farms without cattle or horses, towns where the population has dwindled and factories without machinery'.[50]

Stettin played a major role as an exit point from Poland by sea or rail to the British zone of Germany, as arrangements for the repatriation of eastern Germans were formalised in February 1946.[51] A *Times* correspondent reported from Stettin, seemingly convinced of the orderly nature of the deportations in April 1946, with families being kept together and no suggestion of ill-treatment. Only the very elderly were said to be sad and, indeed, 'some looked healthy and many of the children had rosy cheeks'. Doctors and nurses were said to be on the ships and trains, tending to the sick and infirm. But the correspondent underlined that: 'Few hid their convictions that the deportations are "only temporary" and that they will come back some day though they always looked round to see who was within hearing when they said so'.[52] Observers reckoned in March 1946 that Stettin had around 80,000 inhabitants, comprising 50,000 Germans and 30,000 Poles. The port would be capable of handling transatlantic shipping and the Poles were expecting to use it to export coal to the Soviet Union and Scandinavia, to receive military personnel returning from the UK and Italy, and to handle United Nations relief supplies.[53] However, requisitioned goods were still being sent east. Reports in April 1946 suggested that large cases filled with dismantled German factory machinery were being loaded onto Soviet ships in the port.[54]

Joseph Walters, the British Vice-Consul in Stettin, stated in April 1946 that it was 'still considered unsafe to venture on foot into any part of the town after dark.' Shooting was heard throughout the night and 'a number of bodies are invariably found the following morning'. Despite the efforts of Red Army detachments and the Polish militia, violent bands lurked in the ruins. Walters reported: 'I myself on two occasions from my bedroom window, have witnessed a pitched battle lasting for several minutes between such bands and the militia in which the latter brought into action a heavy machine gun'.[55] Residential buildings that were undamaged or could be repaired were taken over by the Soviets. Empty dwellings on the outskirts and in sparsely populated areas remained empty because of the security situation. Relatively few Poles were attracted to Stettin. Most new arrivals tried to leave. It was hoped that the city would be re-populated with repatriated Poles from the west and by Poles from the former eastern districts. About 35,000 Germans were removed by train in March 1946. The British hoped that the more efficient sea route between Lubeck and Stettin would operate, repatriating 7,500 Poles and a similar number of Germans every week. Food prices in Stettin were high as it was dangerous to bring in produce, but shops remained open and 'having the money, one can buy as much as one wishes'.[56] Polish reports that the Soviets had handed over part of the port were not fully accurate, as this five kilometre stretch on the Oder's east bank included the Soviet Naval HQ and other wedges of territory closed to the Poles. Here, amongst the tangled mass of twisted girders, smashed machinery and bombed warehouses, the systematic stripping continued.[57]

A clean up of Stettin was launched before the liberation anniversary celebrations of April 1946. The authorities wanted to impress visiting correspondents and officials and the city was renamed Szczecin. The local press predicted that 'these celebrations will represent an important political argument in our struggle to retain this land, by the healthy propaganda of our obvious right to Western Pomorze'.[58] The Communists were also pleased that representatives from all states with diplomatic missions in Poland had come to the celebrations, as their attendance indicated the intention of their governments to support Poland's new western frontiers.[59] Some 30,000 visitors came, but the event was somewhat soured for the Communists by the youthful audience's heckling of Bierut and their chanting of the name of Mikolajczyk, who was looking on.[60] At the end of May, Walters still came to the conclusion that the feeling that Stettin would not remain Polish or that the port would be internationalised was so strong as to 'appear to be the cause of the apparent indifference to any long term policy for the development of the town'.[61] Polish settlers were also in a state of 'great consternation' at the arrival of 14,000 Jews, thought to be from Russia and with no grasp of the Polish language. Walters said that the Poles consoled themselves with the belief that the Jews would not stay in the city and that Stettin was simply a stop on their journey to the west.[62] By mid-June, the influx of Jews was unabated and Walters reported that they numbered around 21,000 in a later report he said that their numbers may have reached 25,000, more than 30% of the city's Polish population.[63] However, he noted that Jews still did not seem to envisage Stettin as a permanent home. As their numbers diminished during the summer, the population viewed them with 'indifference' and Walters advised that 'no major incidents of maltreatment or of victimisation have been reported'.[64]

Despite the intensive efforts of the Polish authorities to remove all Germans by 31 May 1946, around 15,000 were said to remain in mid-June.[65] By the end of June, the authorities claimed that the Polish population of Stettin had reached 99,000 and 23,000 eastern Poles arrived in May. In July, Walters reported that the Poles hoped that the entire port would be returned to them by the year's end but he was critical of their 'half-hearted' rebuilding, which suffered from the lack of labour, material and equipment.[66] Colonel Ronald Hazell, a wartime SOE officer now employed by the United Baltic Corporation, visited Stettin on 19 September 1946. He noted that the Soviets were still moving out German loot, but he thought that in the working of the port 'the Russians now seem to have changed their tactics and are assisting the Poles in every way.' Travelling through Pomerania, Hazell observed that 'Soviet troops 'are very thin on the ground' but Stettin was 'still strongly occupied and appears to contain at least one Divisional HQ'. However, remaining barriers in Stettin were manned by the Poles who checked civilian and military road transports.[67]

The Byrnes speech and the status of Stettin

Following the speech by the US Secretary of State, James Byrnes, at Stuttgart on 6 September 1946, the issue of Poland's western frontier, including Stettin, again came to prominence. Byrnes questioned the permanence of the Oder-Neisse Line and held out the prospect to the Germans that they might regain some of the territory lost at Potsdam. In discussions with Byrnes in Paris earlier in the month, Bevin recalled that at Potsdam and then in the House of Commons, he had stressed that the German-Polish frontier 'would be left for the peace conference'. Bevin added: 'Everybody in England knew that this question was not finally settled. We should certainly take a strong line, in view of the Poles' conduct, before we finally accepted a frontier on the Oder'.[68]

Bentinck, however, realised that the relentless Communist attacks on British policy were proving effective. In late May 1946, he had listed Warsaw's complaints, which he considered had some substance. One of them was Britain's reluctance to accept the Oder-Neisse Line as final. Britain's attitude was 'contrasted in the Polish press with the Soviet Government's unequivocal acceptance of the frontier'.[69] Bentinck witnessed the progress of Polish settlement. He had passed through the area around Schwerin and Landsberg in January 1946 where 'the scene was apocalyptic'. By September 1946, the situation had 'greatly improved' with nearly half of the land under cultivation and only a few habitable houses still empty. He concluded that the Poles were there to stay: 'Unless the Soviet Government are prepared to return to Germany some of the territory which was placed under Polish administration by the Potsdam decision last year, I think it will be very difficult to dislodge the Poles.' He argued that the transfer of the Western Territories to Poland could not be reversed and that Britain should recognise this.[70]

Bentinck again summed up the situation on 25 October 1946. He had visited all the former German lands under Polish administration and thought that 'very considerable foreign assistance' would be needed to rebuild and develop them. He added:

> Whilst I thought, when I left for this post last year and still think that it was unwise to hand over so much territory to the Poles, I do not believe it would be possible to reverse this decision, even if we were ready to sacrifice our position in this country by doing so.[71]

He noted that the Poles were most anxious about Stettin, but 'I do not believe it will be possible to turn them out'. To fully utilise the port, they had to retain Swinemünde at the entrance to the channel. Bentinck favoured a slight frontier 'tweak' to give the Poles more breathing space at Swinemünde. Stettin was the natural outlet for Lower Silesia and to return it to Germany would 'nullify our position here'. However, he hoped that safeguards could be introduced so that the Germans would not be excluded from using the Oder and Stettin's port facilities.[72]

Visiting journalists also noted the changes. *The Times* Warsaw correspondent wrote on 19 December 1946 that 'Szczecin and its hinterland are quickly becoming de-Germanized.... The port is gradually becoming Polish and is soon to be the main outlet for the export of Silesian coal and other products.' This visitor was 'struck by the rapidity which the Poles have colonized this considerable territory. Its stolid Teutonic character has disappeared, and it has become an extension of Poland essentially Slav in atmosphere.' The Poles claimed that over 3,000,000 people had settled in the west. This correspondent concluded that the initial stage of Polish colonisation was 'an outstanding feat of ingenuity and improvisation'.[73] Meanwhile, Walters reported from Stettin that Bevin's speech in the House of Commons on the western territories had met with 'bewilderment... at the policy adopted by HM Government towards Poland'. He stressed 'It cannot be understood, why having been forced to give up a portion of its territory in the east in exchange for promised territories in the west, Poland is now facing the prospect of having to give up part of these western territories.' On Stettin's streets, Walters detected that by December 1946 the growing strength of the militia had helped reduce violent crime but housebreakings continued to rise. He believed that if the Soviet and Polish patrols cooperated in the evenings much crime could be checked.[74] Meanwhile, shortcomings such as blazes in Stettin and forest fires in the adjacent countryside in the summer of 1947, which were caused by accidents, carelessness or youths playing with live ammunition were simply blamed by the Communist press on sabotage by the dwindling band of Germans.[75]

Communist stranglehold

At the end of 1946 Bentinck reported that fear stalked Poland. There was 'Fear of the Soviet Union, fear of the resurrection of a powerful and vengeful Germany, and above all fear of the Security Police'.[76] He predicted that Moscow's nominees would retain power after the election and would intensify their efforts to drag Poland into the Soviet orbit, but they were confronted with two major obstacles, 'the character of the Polish people and the influence of the Roman Catholic Church'.[77]

The Communists had held a referendum in June 1946 as a prelude to elections. The vote on the senate's abolition was fixed and the fraudulent conduct of the referendum was evident to British observers. After Bentinck had delivered a note to the Polish Government highlighting the 'grave irregularities', the campaign against him was cranked up. His old friend Count Grocholski was arrested on charges of illegal underground activity and wartime collaboration with the Germans.[78] Polish officials approached the FO seeking Bentinck's removal. Their supporters in Parliament and in the press criticised him as old school, out of step with the new government.

Despite Bentinck's great knowledge of Poland, the FO decided to move him on: he was earmarked as the next British ambassador to Brazil. In the meantime, the Polish election of 19 January 1947, conducted in an atmosphere of intimidation and terror with Mikolajczyk's Peasant Party officials being murdered, arrested and threatened across the country, gave the government bloc an overwhelming majority. Prior to Bentinck's departure, the blows still continued to fall. On 23 January, US ambassador Lane finally decided that he had seen enough. He submitted a resignation letter in which he concluded: 'For all practical purposes my mission to Poland is ended. I believe I could do more by educating American public opinion as a private individual than I can by remaining in Poland'.[79] The British Embassy's press reader Mrs Marynowska was arrested on 29 January 1947. Despite having no access to secret material she was sentenced to 12 years' imprisonment for passing secrets to Bentinck.[80] He made a 'sorrowful departure from Warsaw in February 1947' and his career ended in personal tragedy. Following a messy and very public divorce case, he was forced to leave the Diplomatic Service.[81]

Nevertheless, some British parliamentarians and officials were impressed with the reconstruction of the western territories. Lewis Silkin, the visiting Minister of Town and Country Planning, summarised the situation at the end of 1947: 'The devastation caused throughout Poland, including the new territories, is almost undescribable, and is probably worse than anywhere else in the world'.[82] Silkin reported the enthusiasm he had encountered: 'The people with whom we spoke regard themselves as pioneers and are full of the thrill and excitement of creating what amounts to a new civilisation. There are relatively few Germans left in the new territories and these are mostly key workers, in mines, or those engaged in indispensable tasks for the time being, but it is the desire of the Poles to expatriate every single German at the earliest possible moment'.[83]

Nonetheless, progress was slow. The British embassy believed that the population of the Western Territories was between 5 million and 5,250,000 in September 1947. Some 250,000 were Germans awaiting repatriation. Around 1,000,000 were German citizens who had obtained Polish citizenship or were claimed by the Poles. The total grain crop for 1946–47 was less than half the pre-war normal. Industrial production was only 25% of the pre-war level. Settlement was hindered by the lack of equipment and housing. Nevertheless, the new British ambassador, Sir Donald Gainer, concluded that 'Poles are still not anxious to settle in the western territories, but the determination to retain these territories is the one subject on which all Poles are united'.[84] A despatch from Warsaw in October 1948 reported that 'Poles of all classes and categories have done a remarkable job on the reconstruction of their country.' They were doing this 'in spite of a Government most of them detest, because their strongest instinct has always been for national survival against a hostile environment. It is certainly not... for any love of the new order'.[85] President Bierut, other ministers, Soviet military leaders and various Slav representatives had attended the handover ceremony transferring Szczecin from Soviet control to Polish administration, on 29 June 1947. Speakers stressed that the Oder had become 'the western frontier not only of Poland but of all the Slav nations'.[86] However, the FO dated the rebuilding of Stettin to the late 1950s when the Poles were finally given the security of tenure by the Soviets. In 1959, the *New York Times* reported that 'the roots are going down in the port on the Oder'.[87]

Conclusion

The return to Poland did not have a happy ending for Bentinck, Hankey and the other British diplomatic staff. Western governments had insufficient power on the ground to achieve their political goals for Poland. The Soviets and their stooges called the shots and the direction of travel soon became evident. After 1945, as the Communists followed a path of political consolidation towards a one-party system, ordinary Polish citizens tried to rebuild their lives and many settled their families in the western territories. Their efforts were not in vain and they secured the foundations of lasting Polish settlement. Bentinck, a friend of Poland but certainly no friend of the Polish Communists, correctly predicted that the Polish character and the influence of the Roman Catholic Church would always make Poland difficult terrain for Communism. For the Germans who escaped to what became the Federal Republic, nostalgia pangs and expellee associations kept memories of the *Heimat* warm. But, despite sometimes heated rhetoric and rumoured political intrigues, the Oder-Neisse Line has never been revised.

Notes

I would like to thank my former colleagues in the Foreign and Commonwealth Office Historians, Professor Patrick Salmon, Dr Keith Hamilton and Dr Stephen Twigge for their comments on an earlier draft of this chapter.

1. R. Butler and M.E. Pelly (eds), *Documents on British Policy Overseas* (hereinafter *DBPO*), *Series 1*, Volume I, *The Conference at Potsdam July-August 1945* (London: HMSO, 1984); M.E. Pelly, H.J. Yasamee and K.A. Hamilton (eds), *DBPO, Series 1*, Volume VI, *Eastern Europe 1945–1946* (London: HMSO, 1991).
2. Warsaw had been reduced to rubble by a combination of *Luftwaffe* bombing and fighting in September 1939, the eradication of the Jewish ghetto (April-May 1943), the heavy street fighting of the Warsaw Rising (1 August–3 October 1944) and systematic German demolitions following the Rising's brutal suppression. On the political background see especially A.J. Prazmowska, *Civil War in Poland, 1942–1948* (Basingstoke: Palgrave Macmillan, 2004).
3. Robert Maurice Alers Hankey, 2nd Baron Hankey (1905–1996), had served in Warsaw between November 1936 and September 1939. He was promoted to First Secretary in August 1939.
4. *DBPO, Series 1*, Volume I, document 160.
5. Ibid., document 161.
6. *DBPO, Series 1*, Volume VI, document 4. The Hotel Polonia was a former railway hotel which had served as a wartime German headquarters. The US Embassy was also housed in it and ambassador Lane described the dining room as 'spy-infested and garish': Arthur Bliss Lane, *I Saw Freedom Betrayed* (London: Regency Publications, 1949), p. 111.
7. Ibid.
8. Cavendish-Bentinck, later 9th Duke of Portland (1897–1990), was known as Bill Bentinck. Colleagues recalled his demeanour as Chairman of the JIC and noted that he may have been the youngest member of that body 'but he did not stand in awe of admirals, generals or air marshals'. He was uniquely well informed about intrigues within the offices of the War Cabinet and adopting a tactic he would later use in Warsaw he would not disclose his sources but instead would grip the attention of his audience by remarking 'My dog Angus tells me...': Noel Annan, *Changing Enemies: The Defeat and Regeneration of Germany* (London: HarperCollins, 1995), pp. 60–61.
9. *DBPO, Series I*, Volume VI, Calendar to document 4.
10. Stephen Dorril, *MI6: Fifty Years of Special Operations* (London: Fourth Estate, 2000), p. 255.
11. Ibid., pp. 254–256. Patrick Howarth, *Intelligence Chief Extraordinary: the life of the Ninth Duke of Portland* (London: Bodley Head, 1986), 213–215. As a comparison with the United Nations Relief and Rehabilitation Administration relief workers' knowledge of Poland, see Jessica Reinisch, '"We Shall Build Anew a

Powerful Nation": UNRRA, Internationalism and National Reconstruction in Poland', *Journal of Contemporary History*, 43/3, (2008), pp. 451–476, particularly, pp. 462–64.
12. Foreign Office, *Weekly Political Intelligence Summaries, Volume 11, January–June 1945* (London: Kraus International Publications, 1983), No. 296, 6 June 1945.
13. *The Times*, 14 July 1945.
14. Ibid.
15. The National Archives (TNA), Kew, FO1049/86, report by Winch following visit to Stettin (Szczecin) and West Prussia, 25 October 1945.
16. David Dilks (ed.), *The Diaries of Sir Alexander Cadogan* (London: Cassell, 1971), p. 768.
17. Ibid., p. 775.
18. Ibid., p. 777 and see p. 778.
19. Foreign Office, *Weekly Political Intelligence Summaries, Volume 12, July–December 1945* (London: Kraus International Publications, 1983), No. 305, 8 August 1945.
20. Clement R. Attlee, *As It Happened* (London: William Heinemann, 1954), p. 149.
21. The homogeneous Catholic Poland that Bentinck and Hankey had returned to was radically different to the ethnically and religiously diverse pre-war country. Eastern Poland was annexed by the Soviets in September 1939 after the Molotov-Ribbentrop Pact. When the Red Army returned in 1944 it was clear from Soviet pronouncements that the best the Poles could hope for was the Curzon Line. Eastern Poland, frightfully scarred by the NKVD's murders and deportations of 1939–41, by the liquidation of its large and visible Jewish communities by the Nazis and by the bloody internecine guerrilla warfare with Ukrainian nationalists would not be administered by Warsaw. Poland was moved physically westwards. Its eastern provinces were 'ceded' to the Lithuanian, Belorussian and Ukrainian Soviet Socialist Republics. Possible compensation in the form of Germany's eastern provinces seemed likely but the extent of the claim appeared to be dependent on the deliberations of a planned peace conference.
22. *DBPO, Series I*, Volume VI, document 8.
23. Before 1939 there was British representation in the cities of eastern Germany with Vice-Consulates in Stettin, Breslau and Königsberg (closed in 1934) and a Consulate-General in the Free City of Danzig. On the Polish side of the pre-war frontier, there were Vice-Consulates in Gdynia, Katowice and Poznan. Representation was thinner in post-war People's Poland, comprising a Consulate-General in Gdansk, a Consulate in Katowice and a Vice-Consulate in Szczecin. In the last, Joseph Walters (1911–1969), was at the helm. Walters was appointed Vice-Consul on 24 March 1946 and became Consul at Poznan in June 1949.
24. For the first post-war year, Poland was not as yet a police state but as the Communists asserted their authority through the Security Police, British officials found operating conditions more difficult. Some were physically attacked: see TNA/FO371/56414.
25. Bentinck remarked that until the Red Army arrived, Polish peasants 'were enjoying a period of unprecedented prosperity' as the Germans directed agriculture efficiently and paid for produce: TNA/FO371/47651/N12791/96/55, Bentinck to Warner, 19 September 1945. See also FO371/47651, N15519/96/55,

copy of article in *Daily Herald*, 8 November 1945, for examples of the Soviets taking Polish coal and textiles at minimal prices.

26. TNA/FO371/47651/N 14038/96/55. The British visitors concluded that in Silesia: 'The Russian army swarms everywhere and its discipline seems to have suffered severely. There are numerous parties of marauders and deserters who recognise no military authority. Everyone tells stories of rape and plunder by Russian troops even in Breslau and Liegnitz. These incidents are making orderly settlement virtually impossible. Public feeling amongst Poles is reaching a point at which notice will have to be taken of the situation by the Polish Government.'
27. Howarth, *Intelligence Chief*, p. 215. Holliday had been Vice-Consul at Katowice in 1936–1938. He concluded that 'many conversations showed that the general fear and dislike of Russian soldiery on the part of the Polish population has not diminished'. He mentioned 'the large acreage now under the plough between Warsaw and Krakow and between the 1939 frontier and Lodz' but he observed that 'the situation is very different to the west of the old frontier, where for mile after mile the fields are covered with scrubby grass and weeds.' An official in Breslau told Holliday that there were 50,000 Poles in the city and 200,000 Germans. The latter had to wear a distinguishing white armband and their numbers were falling daily in the face of 'Voluntary Evacuation' trains, which headed out of the city: *DBPO, Series I*, Volume VI, document 54.
28. In the summer of 1946, the JIC estimated that 405,000 Soviet troops were in Poland. Hankey said that even when he had been in Warsaw there were no more than 300,000, adding 'our embassy in Warsaw travel widely and are extremely well informed': TNA/FO371/56414/N12216/21/55, Hankey minute, 28 September 1946. Bentinck was 'much impressed by the small number of Soviet forces' following visits across Poland in the summer of 1946. However, Soviet personnel were embedded in the Polish Army and administration, particularly in the Security Police: see TNA/FO371/56414/N12216/21/55, Warsaw to FO, 24 September 1946. Soviet troop numbers had been dramatically reduced during the winter of 1945–46. Bentinck reported in March 1946 that the upsurge of underground activity throughout the country, involving as many as 80,000 activists in late 1945, would provoke harsh Soviet counter-measures and the return of Red Army units: see Dorril, *MI6*, p. 257.
29. See Lane to Acting Secretary of State, 21 and 22 September 1945, in *Foreign Relations of the United States* (hereinafter, *FRUS*), *1945*, Vol. II, *General: Political and Economic* Matters (Washington: US Government Printing Office, 1967), pp. 1278–1280.
30. Lane to Secretary of State, 4 December 1945, *FRUS 1945*, Volume II, pp. 1318–1319.
31. Ibid., p. 1322, Byrnes to Lane, 10 December 1945.
32. Ibid., p. 1323, Warsaw to Washington, 12 December 1945.
33. TNA/FO371/66217/N8482/1118/55, Hankey to Vyvyan, 11 July 1947.
34. TNA/FO371/47651/N12791/96/55, Bentinck to Warner, 19 September 1945.
35. Stanislaw Mikolajczyk, *The Pattern of Soviet Domination* (London: Sampson Low, Marston & Co., 1948), pp. 81, 114–116.
36. Thorolf Hillblad, *Twilight of the Gods* (Solihull: Helion, 2004), p. 21.

37. Foreign Office, *Weekly Political Intelligence Summaries, Volume 12*, No. 303, 25 July 1945.
38. *DBPO, Series I,* Volume 1, Document 320.
39. TNA/FO371/47651/N12988/21/55, report of Captain Mazoyer, French military attaché in Moscow, following a visit to Gdansk and Gdynia, mid-June 1945.
40. Foreign Office, *Weekly Political Intelligence Summaries*, Volume 12, No. 305, 8 August 1945.
41. TNA/FO1049/227, *Conditions in Germany*, 1 September 1945.
42. TNA/FO371/47651/N 14925/96/55, Richards journey to Stettin and Return, October 1945.
43. Ibid.
44. TNA/FO371/47723/N 14872/433/55, Richards memorandum, 21 October 1945.
45. TNA/FO371/47723/N 14872/433/55, Richards memorandum, 23 October 1945.
46. TNA/FO1049/86, Bentinck's covering letter to Winch's report, 27 October 1945.
47. TNA/FO1049/86, report by Winch, 25 October 1945.
48. TNA/FO371/47651/N 15519/96/55, excerpt from *Daily Herald*, 7 November 1945.
49. Ibid.
50. *The Times*, 14 December 1945.
51. Ibid., 19 February 1946.
52. Ibid., 24 April 1946
53. Ibid., 25 March 1946.
54. *The Times*, 25 April 1946.
55. TNA/FO688/45, Stettin General Report, No 1, 4 April 1946.
56. Ibid.
57. Ibid.
58. TNA/FO688/45, Stettin General Report, No 2, 22 April 1946.
59. Lane, *Freedom Betrayed*, pp. 165–66.
60. TNA/FO688/45, Stettin General Report, No 2, 22 April 1946; Mikolajczyk, *Soviet Domination*, 173.
61. TNA, FO688/45, Stettin General Report, No 3, 26 May 1946.
62. Ibid.
63. Ibid., Stettin General Report, No 4, 12 June 1946; Stettin General Report, No 5, 21 July 1946.
64. Ibid., Stettin General Report, No 5, 21 July 1946.
65. Ibid., Stettin General Report, No 4, 12 June 1946.
66. Ibid., Stettin General Report No 5, 21 July 1946.
67. TNA/FO371/56414/N12988/21/55, letter Cleugh to Chancery, British Embassy, Warsaw, 23 September 1946.
68. TNA/FO371/55853/C11287/3520/18, Paris to FO, 2 September 1946.
69. Howarth, *Intelligence Chief*, pp. 214–215.
70. TNA/FO371/55853/C11287/3520/18, Bentinck to Warner, 13 September 1946.
71. TNA/FO371/55853/C13234/3520/18, Bentinck to Warner, 25 October 1946.
72. Ibid.

73. *The Times*, 19 December 1946.
74. TNA/FO688/45, Stettin Monthly Report, 10 December 1946. In the Commons, on 22 October 1946, Bevin said Britain could hardly agree to the permanent establishment of the boundary, unless it was satisfied that assurances given by the Polish Government at Potsdam were being carried out and that the Poles could repopulate the area after the Germans had been driven out: see TNA/FO371/55853/C14375/3520/18, minute of 12 November 1946.
75. TNA/FO371/66217/N 10823/1118/55 and N14024/1118/55.
76. Howarth, *Intelligence Chief*, p. 212.
77. Ibid.
78. Ibid., p. 220; Lane, *Freedom Betrayed*, pp. 181–182.
79. Howarth, *Intelligence Chief*, p. 221; Lane, *Freedom Betrayed*, pp. 183–92.
80. *Keesing's Contemporary Archives, 1946–1948*, p. 9096. Bentinck and Lane were named as the beneficiaries of secret information in the major high treason and espionage trial of December 1947.
81. Ibid., pp. 221–223; Percy Cradock, *Know Your Enemy: How the Joint Intelligence Committee Saw the World* (London: John Murray, 2002), p. 24. See also *The Times*, 28 March 1947, 7 November 1947 and 6 July 1948.
82. TNA/CAB129/22/343, 31 December 1947.
83. Ibid.
84. TNA/FO417/45, Poland: Annual Report for 1947, 25 February 1948.
85. TNA/FO417/45, Allen to Bevin, 15 October 1948.
86. *Keesing's Contemporary Archives, 1946–1948*, p. 8697.
87. TNA/FO370/2808, *The Status of Stettin*, memorandum by the FO's Historical Adviser, 1965, quoting *New York Times*, 6 April 1959 and 26 April 1959.

3
British Propaganda and Countering Illegal Immigration into Palestine: The *President Warfield* or *Exodus 1947*

Kate Utting

The seemingly intractable problem of Palestine that exercised the British government between 1945 and 1948, has been considered from the diplomatic viewpoint and as a case study in British counterinsurgency.[1] British propaganda, the calculated intent on the part of government to persuade target audiences to behave or think in a certain way, in pursuit of policy aims, is the focus of this chapter.[2] This is a study of the complexities of propaganda, through the management of information conducted by the British government during the controversial negotiations on the future of the Palestine mandate. It demonstrates that the current fascination with government news management in support of their policy is nothing new. The post-war Labour government appreciated that success in Palestine depended on persuading target audiences to support its policy. This chapter is a case study of failed propaganda, which highlights the themes and challenges faced by the government, over the summer of 1947, in dealing with the illegal immigration ship known to the British government as the *President Warfield* and to the Zionists as *Exodus 1947*.[3]

Between 1945 and 1948, the British government tried to implement a long-term policy over Palestine, which would preserve British political, economic and strategic interests in the Middle East while influencing the day-to-day decisions over the future of the Mandate. They favoured an agreed solution to create an independent Palestine, some form of unitary state, which would guarantee British military facilities and maintain the Arab goodwill on which Britain's general position in the Middle East was predicated. But, there was no clear plan in the sense of a positive proposal that would deliver the strategy that would fulfil British strategic requirements. Instead, there were broad policy assumptions – that any settlement leading to independence had to be agreed, and not just agreed between Britain, the Arabs and Jews living in Palestine, but also supported by the United States and countries in the Middle East. With hindsight, this was perhaps both unrealistic and ambitious, but given the assumptions and wider policy interests at the time it was an unsurprising aim. For this policy to succeed, the two leading departments, the Foreign Office (FO) and the Colonial Office (CO), had to integrate it with a comprehensive propaganda effort, which would control information received at home and abroad. In this period Palestine was 'almost daily reading for the world'.[4] In general, Britain adopted a traditional approach to propaganda: a news and facts-based effort, letting facts speak for themselves. Domestic opinion in Britain had to be convinced not to oppose the government's efforts to reach a solution, but the main targets of British propaganda were audiences abroad. British policy had to reconcile the differing objectives and opinion of four constituencies: Arab, Jewish, American and, as part of the need to gain cooperation against illegal immigration, the wider international opinion of the Mediterranean powers in particular.

Kenneth Morgan argued that the 'disaster and tragedy' of the Labour government's policy towards Palestine can largely be explained by Foreign Secretary Ernest Bevin's mishandling of public relations, 'defects of style and presentation rather than of substance'.[5] Fritz Liebreich has also argued that British policy became 'mired in insensitive blunders and public relation disasters'.[6] These criticisms overstate the potential and role of propaganda in furthering policy objectives. The British may have lost the propaganda war, but this was not for a lack of consideration of the publicity dimension of policy. It was Britain's inability to reconcile competing interests, especially pledges to the Arabs and Jews, with her own national interests that produced failure in Palestine. As Ivone Kirkpatrick, a senior FO official, recognised, 'Propaganda is never effective unless it is linked with policy'.[7] While the government searched for a political settlement, on the ground in Palestine Britain faced an insurgency. If an insurgency is a political legitimacy crisis of some kind,[8] the counterinsurgents' propaganda campaign may only be effective if their legitimacy can be successfully demonstrated. While British propaganda emphasised the use of insurgent terrorist and illegal immigration methods as 'illegitimate', Zionist propaganda turned British attempts to stop Jewish immigration into Palestine to their advantage. The Zionists were conscious of the importance of propaganda, well aware of their relative asymmetric weakness in relation to other forms of British power and military force'.[9]

Central to the insurgency problem in Palestine in 1945–48 was illegal immigration.[10] The Arabs and Jews saw immigration as 'a stepping-stone for a Jewish State'[11] and the Arabs consistently refused to compromise on this issue. While the armed struggle was a 'hard sell' for the Zionists,[12] illegal immigration pursued clandestinely by the *Aliyah Beth Haganah* organisation of the Jewish Agency, played much better in propaganda terms. Whether you were a religious Jew or a Revisionist Zionist, whether you supported the creation of a Zionist state or saving Holocaust survivors, Palestinian Jews could agree on supporting illegal immigration in a way they could not over the use of terrorist tactics. A CO assessment was that 'The Jewish community in Palestine, from its official leaders down to the individual Jew in the street or settlements, is resolutely committed to a policy of assisting illegal immigration'.[13] The Jewish Agency's propaganda line was that countering immigration into Palestine was illegal and contrary to the Mandate. The British made consistent mistakes in its handling of the issue, with Zionist propaganda scoring repeated successes in their portrayal of Palestine as the only haven for the remnant of European Jewry and, more extremely, in their portrayal of the British as the instruments of Hitler's end game. In three years, the British went from the liberators of Bergen–Belsen to the natural successor of Adolf Hitler. Britain's perceived illegitimacy over immigration became a critical vulnerability in her attempts to achieve a settlement of the Palestine problem.

Political settlement and illegal immigration

The difficulty for Clement Attlee's government when it took power in July 1945, was that the wartime Labour party had endorsed a pro-Zionist policy: independence for Palestine would be rapidly followed by a transfer of populations in which the Arabs would be encouraged to move out as the Jews moved in. The party was not however, 'emotionally pro-Jew, but only rationally "anti-anti-Semitic"'.[14] The new government did not understand that many Jews did not see their future in Europe and the Zionist desire to get to Palestine was seen as 'essentially irrational'.[15] Palestine had hit the post-war political agenda in June 1945 with the publication of the Earl G. Harrison report commissioned by President Truman on the conditions of Displaced Persons (DPs)[16] in European camps, with special reference to the position of Jews. Throughout the summer, Truman lobbied the British government to allow the immediate admission of the estimated 100,000 Jews in DP camps.[17] This associated two problems in public perception, which the British government wished to separate, and which dogged them in their dealings of the future of the Mandate: the problems facing European Jewry and the political future of Palestine. There was a new urgency about the future of Palestine, as some decision would have to be taken by the Labour government in anticipation of the expiry of the immigration quota of the 1939 White Paper, expected in November 1945. The *Haganah* had set out an ambitious plan for illegal immigration and in a speech David Ben Gurion said: '...we have to fight for a large and free *Eretz Israel* and its must be remembered that we are the last hope of the Jews in Europe'.[18] This idea of Palestine as the 'last hope' became a consistent theme of Zionist propaganda.

The British response was seen in the context of wider Middle East interests. To maintain vital Arab friendship, Arab states were asked to accept immigration at a rate of 1500 a month beyond that set in the 1939 White Paper, until a long-term solution was devised. It was this decision to continue the White Paper and restrict Jewish immigration to 1500 a month that set them on a path to dispute. By the end of 1945, the British correctly identified that illegal immigration would increase and the first reaction was to attempt to stop the immigrant ships from sailing in the first place. Attempts to deal with the challenge of the Jewish insurgency were made against the background of the search for a political settlement. Between August 1945 and October 1946, the British sought to take advantage of Truman's interest in the fate of the 100,000 Jews by pursuing an Anglo–American Committee of Inquiry (AAC) to investigate the problems of DPs in Europe. Following the failure of this initiative, between October 1946 and February 1947 the British tried to achieve a negotiated settlement between Arabs and Jews at the London Conference. When this Conference failed, the British referred Palestine to the United Nations (UN) without any recommendations and the Special Committee on Palestine (UNSCOP) was established in May 1947.[19] In Palestine, reference to the UN did not lead to a calming of the security situation. The gamble that the two sides, and the Zionist terrorist organisations in particular, would moderate the intensity of their activities while the issue was considered at the altar of international public opinion, did not pay off.

From the spring of 1947, illegal immigration became *the* major security issue facing British authorities in Palestine. A central problem was that no amount of propaganda could, after the Holocaust, act as a corrective for international perceptions of the illegal immigration issue. Britain found itself increasingly morally isolated on this issue. Between 1940 and 1947, the Royal Navy intercepted 47 illegal immigration ships and interned over 65,000 Jews in camps in Cyprus. So great was the challenge posed by the problem of illegal immigration, that two of the three Palestine desk officers in the FO Middle Eastern Department devoted their time to it.[20] In April 1947, the government's Defence Committee established both an Official Committee and a Ministerial Committee to deal with the subject. This involved the government in a variety of co-ordinated initiatives involving the FO, the CO, the Ministry of Transport, the military, navy and British intelligence to try and break the illegal immigration traffic from Europe. Even the Washington Embassy had an illegal immigration committee.[21]

Stopping immigration at source

The first stage of the strategy against illegal immigration was a military blockade of Palestine by the Royal Navy (RN) Palestine Patrol[22] and an attempt to stop illegal immigration traffic at source through diplomacy and propaganda. British effectiveness in countering illegal immigration depended, to a large degree, on the cooperation they received from other states and they were reluctant to engage in propaganda that would expose the complicity of states and organisations in this traffic.[23] The government thought that the 'exodus' was fuelled by Zionist propaganda. The intelligence service MI5 reported that Zionist propaganda amongst DPs would increase and that 'any Jew asking for resettlement in Europe is to be publicly denounced as a traitor to his nation'.[24] The problem of a potential mass movement of Jews from Europe was compounded by the Arabs believing that the British government could stop this if they really wanted to: 'they suspect that she is not prepared to antagonise the Jews by doing so…they remember the action which was taken against them in the Arab rebellion and they judge failure to mete out equal measures as a sign of weakness'.[25]

The government tried to control the movement of Jews in Europe, and in particular, the land frontiers of Italy and Greece in order 'to check the exodus from other European countries'.[26] Diplomatic pressure was applied and publicity about the 'facts' of illegal immigration was given to Italy, Greece, Romania, the Netherlands, Czechoslovakia, Austria, Turkey, Poland, France and the USSR.[27] But securing inter-state cooperation proved difficult. Even after the Polish Kielce pogrom in July 1946, British attempts to achieve denouncements of anti-Semitism by the

Catholic Church proved elusive.[28] Similarly, the FO doubted that appeals to the Soviets would work and suspected them of 'actively assisting this traffic'. The British position would 'be stronger if we can at least tell the Arab governments and others concerned that we have asked the Russians to assist in the suppression of this illegal traffic'.[29]

The British accumulated evidence of illegal immigration collusion between the UN Relief and Rehabilitation Agency and the Jewish Agency[30], but found it difficult to publish this information because of sensitivities involved in criticising allies.[31] The biggest challenge was to secure the cooperation of the American government. While the AAC deliberated, London took a cautious line against exposing American complicity in illegal immigration traffic. Advertisements appeared in the American press by Zionist organisations, like the American League for a Free Palestine (ALFP) to raise funds to support illegal immigration. An ALFP advertisement ran: 'give us the money…we will get them there! It costs 250 dollars to move one concentration camp victim from Europe to Palestine'.[32] From mid-1946, the British made representations to the American government about this type of newspaper advertisement. In early 1947, Lord Inverchapel, British Ambassador to Washington, asked Secretary of State James Byrnes to take decisive action against the press advertisements but, while sympathetic, he said that his government 'had no legal means of preventing the newspapers from publishing advertisements'.[33] The FO wanted to publish the facts about illegal immigration in the US, but the Embassy doubted this would be effective as, although American opinion was not pro-Zionist, it was 'apathetic' about British difficulties and the Arab case. Furthermore, there was 'the ordinary human interest in the successful "under-dog"'.[34]

The Cyprus decision and *refoulement*

As a result, it proved impossible to stop illegal immigration at source and the British faced a crisis of overwhelming immigrant numbers. The second stage of British policy against illegal immigration was the August 1946 decision to send intercepted immigrants to Cyprus. The Chief of the Imperial General Staff, Lord Montgomery argued that 'Illegal immigration must be stopped or war in Palestine with Arabs as well as Jews was inevitable'. He did not want immigrants to land in Palestine but to be 'sent elsewhere'. Arab reactions, it was argued, would be 'favourable' and the 'possibility of a war on two fronts in Palestine averted'.[35] The decisions over illegal immigration were taken in the context of the most significant terrorist act against the British in Palestine: the bombing of the military–administrative headquarters in the King David Hotel, on 31 July 1946. Alan Cunningham, the High Commissioner, pleaded with London that, while military action against the perpetrators proceeded, action needed to be taken 'to avoid Arabs taking the law into their own hands'. The bombing had altered his view on illegal immigration and he felt 'no more Jewish immigrants should be allowed into Palestine until a final solution' was found. He argued for the 'withdrawal of quota and diversion of a legal immigrant ships preferably to points of departure'.[36]

The Cabinet agreed on the diversion to Cyprus on 7 August. It was noted that these measures would only be necessary for the next few weeks, as an Anglo–American agreement over future immigration of the 100,000 into Palestine would 'automatically reduce the likelihood of substantial illegal immigration'.[37] In announcing the decision, the government would not be 'apologetic' and they stated 'no country in the world' had been 'a better or more consistent friend of the Jewish people than Britain'.[38] A *Daily Herald* editorial supported this 'inevitable' transhipment decision 'which must surely be endorsed by fair-minded men of every race and religion'.[39] In the US, however, the policy increased 'anti-British feeling'.[40] Instead of deterring immigration, the Cyprus decision 'only encouraged organisers of illegal immigration'.[41] What was supposed to be a temporary solution dragged on, as the government searched for agreement at the London Conference. British options had reduced and, with an ever increasing flow of illegal immigration anticipated, London looked for other places to send illegal immigrants, including Kenya, Greek or Italian islands, Libya, Aden and Somaliland.[42]

By September 1946, the RN was concerned with the increasing challenge of dealing with the traffic. The Jews used 'faster ships' and had become 'more violent'; they were now in a 'fanatical state' of mind and might sabotage its ships in harbour, with a resultant loss of life and negative 'propaganda'.[43] In December, the RN suggested it might intercept ships under the right to 'self-defence' but the Lord Chancellor, Lord Jowitt, doubted whether it was justified under international law.[44] He argued that the right of visit and search was a 'belligerent right', not to be exercised in time of peace. Self-preservation could only be claimed if it could be demonstrated that a particular immigrant ship was 'loaded with arms and ammunition'; action could be justified before an international court on the grounds that 'importation of the arms and ammunition would lead to civil war' but he thought this 'unwise' and did not 'like this as a precedent'.[45] The Cabinet decided against the Admiralty's request.[46]

The London Conference failed to produce a political agreement and the British duly referred Palestine to the UN. In February 1947, the High Commissioner argued that the government should 'face facts': from the 'purely humanitarian angle everyone must be anxious to see the question of displaced persons cleared up'.[47] The choice was either to increase the immigration quota or undertake 'other action short of war with the Jews'. The Cabinet rejected the idea of increasing the immigration quota, as it would lead to 'active resistance from the Arabs'.[48] Instead, on the diplomatic level, London tried to obtain a UN General Assembly Resolution on illegal immigration in May, by asking the UN Secretary-General, Trygve Lie to 'appeal to all Member States to take the strictest precautions, in so far as they are concerned, to prevent the transit through their territory and the departure from their ports of Jews attempting to enter Palestine illegally'.[49] British Missions in Europe, US and the Middle East were instructed to 'give all possible publicity' to the illegal traffic using factual material supplied from London to 'demonstrate that the traffic...was a 'racket', 'organised and financed by Zionists in the US'.[50]

The Ministerial Committee on Illegal Immigration even considered supplementing the 'white' factual propaganda of press articles and radio talks, with 'black' propaganda, but it was argued that, 'The Jews are being impelled to emigrate by a strong feeling of uncertainty about their future in Europe and a fanatical nationalism. It is not clear that we have the material for effective counter propaganda to these inducements'.[51] In the summer of 1947, MI5 estimated that over 35,000 potential illegal immigrants were strategically located for embarkation to Palestine together with 37 ships.[52] With policy options narrowing and the illegal immigration traffic predicted to continue unabated, the government considered the possibility of introducing a new method of *refoulement,* in effect 'an admission of the failure of the Cyprus deterrent'. *Refoulement* was first recommended by the High Commissioner in response to the King David bombing. It meant that 'a ship that brought an immigrant without legal right of entry to this country was required to take him back again'.[53] In the context of countering illegal immigration, *refoulement* would mean the forceful return of Jews to the country of embarkation. However, there were clear dangers in this policy and, from the outset, it was anticipated that there would be a tremendous outcry of Jewish and American opinion.[54]

The President Warfield

In May 1947, Bevin decided that the government should 'not shirk from taking drastic action' and the *Warfield* became the 'test case' of the new policy of *refoulement*, designed to deter subsequent attempts at illegal immigration.[55] It also became a Zionist 'propaganda coup of the first order'.[56] In March, the *Warfield,* with accommodation for approximately 4500 passengers, sailed from the US under the Honduran flag, manned by a crew of *Haganah* and *Palmach* members and American volunteers.[57] She arrived in La Spezia, Italy on 24 April, picking up stores and fuel illicitly. She also attempted to load immigrants, but was unable to do so owing to the Italian authorities. On 12 June, she left La Spezia with a certificate valid for coastal traffic only and eventually arrived in Sète, where she embarked illegal immigrants. The French authorities refused the *Warfield* permission to sail on the grounds that her navigation certificate issued was invalid but, on 11 July, she cut her cables and sailed for Palestine, shadowed by HMS *Mermaid*.[58]

As the *Warfield* approached Palestine, the ship broadcast a message via the illegal broadcasting unit, *Kol Israel* (The Voice of Israel).[59] The broadcast stated that 4500 Jews 'were returning home after 2000 years in exile'. It condemned the British for 'actively assisting in the extermination of six million Jews', labelling them as 'dammed slave merchants' who 'traded with Jewish blood during the war and you are continuing to do so now. You are paying with red Jewish blood for black oil.' They included a particular appeal to the members of UNSCOP requesting that they collect 'first-hand evidence' of the 'suffering of our people' and 'British brutality'.[60] At 2 a.m. on 18 July, the destroyers HMS *Childers* and HMS *Chieftain* moved in, rammed the *Warfield* from both sides and boarded it while the crew transmitted radio commentaries to Palestine, 'to gain maximum publicity and sympathy'.[61] On 19 July, the ship docked at Haifa. Two members of UNSCOP, the Swedish chairman of the committee, Justice Emil Sandstrom, and Vladimir Simic, the Yugoslav delegate, witnessed the operation. According to American journalist Ruth Gruber, Sandstrom was shocked by what he saw and declared, 'Britain must no longer have the mandate over Palestine'.[62] The CO's man on the spot, Donald MacGillivray, reported that Sandstrom 'fully sympathised with the deplorable and sad plight of "the pawns in the game", but was sickened by the use made of them by the Zionist propaganda machine' and he realised 'that the resistance and the propaganda surrounding its fatal consequences had probably been staged primarily for the Committee's benefit'.[63] The Arabs welcomed 'this step as a sign of firmness' and 'compared it favourably with the 'alleged weakness and leniency towards the terrorist movement'.[64]

There was intense public speculation about the destination of the *Warfield* Jews and whether they would be sent to Cyprus, or an alternative destination. Publicity for *refoulement* to France would concentrate on the 'inhumanity of the Jewish organisers in their gross overcrowding' of the ship.[65] The success of *refoulement* depended on the cooperation the British government received from France. Paris suggested that 'full facts' about the *Warfield* should be publicised, but it was 'essential' that reference to French undertakings should be avoided, as this would 'only make more difficult task of securing French agreement to return the President Warfield's passengers to France'. The preoccupation with persuading the French suggests that no one looked beyond securing their agreement to take in the *Warfield* Jews. Once agreement had been reached, it was publicised that the destination of the *Warfield* immigrants was France. HMG did not want to be drawn into the legal aspects of *refoulement* but whatever the legal justification, the decision was not perceived as legitimate, it seems, by anyone other than London and the legal advisers in the FO.[66]

While the *refoulement* of the *Warfield* Jews was welcomed in Arab capitals, it did not play well with European or American public opinion despite the publicity preparations. Duff Cooper, the Ambassador to France, expressed his annoyance with 'the lack of assistance we had received from the Press Section of the Quai D'Orsay.[67] The French population sympathised with the Jewish immigrants from a humanitarian view and as national atonement for the treatment of the Jews during the Vichy period, but also as an opportunity to take revenge on the British for their intervention in Syria, in 1945.[68] The Paris press, from Right to extreme Left, criticised British action. *Humanite* referred to the three British ships *Runnymede Park, Empire Rival and Ocean Vigour* as 'a floating Auschwitz'.[69] Further controversy arose when allegations were made that the RN's boarding of the *Warfield* occurred outside territorial waters. In a 'virulent' editorial in the American newspaper, *PM*, this was characterised as an act of 'piracy'. The FO confirmed 'the initial stages of this operation did in fact take place outside territorial waters' but instructed the Washington Embassy not to 'admit this'.[70]

The three British transports took the *Warfield* Jews to Port de Bouc, where they were invited to disembark. A small fishing vessel called 'through loudspeakers for the immigrants to remain where they were' and, by 5 August, only 96 volunteers had disembarked.[71] The situation deteriorated and it became clear that the immigrants would not disembark without the use of force. In view of the refusal, alternative destinations were discussed both within the British government and publicly in the media; the *Daily Herald* published the story that Hamburg would be the port of destination, should the French option fail. At this stage, the FO opposed the transfer of the immigrants to the British zone of Germany, but the CO regarded a return to Cyprus as 'virtually out of the question' and could not 'accept the defeat implicit in return to Cyprus'. The authorities in Palestine favoured the UK over Cyprus as Cyprus would be a 'bitter blow for British prestige' and would encourage all dissidents.[72] At a Cabinet meeting on 31 July, Bevin warned that the *Warfield* Jews might have to be sent back to Germany. The Cabinet merely took note – there were no objections to this proposal.[73] But, the High Commissioner reiterated his objections to Germany as a destination for the *Warfield* Jews, as 'excitement and anger would once more be aroused', which would be unfortunate given the 'new-found determination of the general body of Jews to step up their domestic struggle against terrorism'.[74]

The *Warfield* Jews continued to refuse to disembark. A meeting of the Illegal Immigration (Official) Committee on 5 August recommended that the immigrants should be landed in Hamburg and sent back to France by train.[75] The CO noted the High Commissioner's objections to Germany, but explained that this decision had been made on 'practical grounds of accommodation available and the capability of the transports to make the requisite voyage'.[76] Public justification for this decision included the argument that Germany was the only place, outside Cyprus, that could accommodate these numbers and that the Jewish Agency had the influence to persuade the immigrants to disembark in France but had chosen not to. The 'facts' of the British case were outlined: it was not the British government's fault; France was partly to blame and the illegal immigrants were not prisoners. The French government offered to re-admit all the Jews to France; 'none of them are obliged to proceed to Germany'; it was their own choice if they declined the French offer. In answer to the question, 'why Germany?' the reply was to be given that there was 'no place in British colonial empire which could be made ready in short time to take such a number of illegal immigrants'.[77] Once the Jews refused their last chance to disembark at the Port de Bouc in France on 21 August, the British government took the fateful decision to send them to Germany, their original point of departure – and the ultimately logical end point to the policy of *refoulement* for a government that had run out of alternatives. On 22 August, the three transport ships sailed for Hamburg.

While force had not been used at Port de Bouc to disembark the *Warfield* Jews because of international opinion, the same consideration did not apply to the decision to send them to Germany. Washington warned about the possible negative impact on Anglo–American relations of this decision:

> the forcible return of these people to the country which was so recently the scene of the worst anti-Semitic atrocities would almost certainly cause a wave of American indignation, spreading considerably beyond the normal circle of Zionist agitators.[78]

The *Palestine Post* referred to the German decision as the 'crime of Hamburg'.[79] More widely it was viewed as 'a crime against humanity' and 'a political error of the first magnitude'.[80] On 23 August the Jewish Agency Executive issued a statement criticising it as the 'latest action in the squalid War against the Jews' and gave details of British errors. The statement argued that there was 'no established truth in assertion that Jews refused to land from ship under Zionist threat and propaganda'; on the contrary they had resisted 'mental and physical torture' deliberately inflicted by the British. The British were the illegal ones, their fight against Jewish immigration disregarded 'every law of humanity, every obligation under mandate and main principles of charter of United Nations'. The CO considered an 'official rejoinder' to this statement, but felt it would 'aggravate an already highly charged and emotional situation'.[81]

The British embassy in Paris was so frustrated with the negative publicity about the *Warfield* that they suggested extreme measures to undermine the Zionist case, by using intelligence to counter claims that many of them have been '"fighters for freedom" in the war' and to publicise the countries of origin of passengers; how many had fought Germans; how many had been in concentration camps and how many were known terrorists.[82] But the *Warfield* was a British propaganda failure and even in the British press, reaction was incredulous. A leader in *The Times* described it as 'An Act of Folly'. The government had 'badly underestimated the courage and fanaticism of the Jews themselves' and 'the remarkable capacity of Zionist propagandists to misrepresent British policy'. Most of all 'it underestimated the sympathy with which people everywhere feel for the Jewish survivors of Nazi persecution ... to send these Jews back to Germany of all places, will horrify millions'.[83]

On 8 September 1947, the *Warfield* Jews finally arrived in Hamburg and were met by 1000 fully armed British troops, backed by 1500

German police. Zionist propaganda exploited the *Warfield* incident 'to devastating effect...as decisive proof of British depravity, callousness and moral bankruptcy'.[84] The repercussions of this incident produced condemnation from those not usually critical of British policy in Palestine. The reasons for this were the evil connotation of Germany where the Jews were concerned and the feeling that, whatever the legal rights and practicalities of the matter and the desire to seize the initiative may have been, it was a mistake to take this step at a moment when the UN was about to consider the whole question. Any retreat, like sending the *Warfield* Jews to Cyprus would undoubtedly have been exploited by anti-British propagandists. Nevertheless, there had been a clear failure to think through *refoulement* and HMG had not considered the possible refusal of the *Warfield* Jews to disembark in France. At the beginning of September, it was decided there would be no more *refoulement* to Germany because of the burden on the British administration there.[85] How far incidents like the *President Warfield* influenced the findings of UNSCOP is also unclear.[86] As far as the British propaganda campaign in support of its policy on Palestine was concerned it was clear that no amount of propaganda could overturn the perceived illegitimacy of this British policy.

Aftermath

From the end of 1947, the British organisation to counter illegal immigration wound down. The fear of arms smuggling into Palestine became the new preoccupation, as it could directly affect the security situation and British plans for withdrawal. In public, however, for wider interests of maintaining Arab goodwill, the policy of countering illegal immigration was maintained. In October 1947, the Illegal Immigration Committee was subsumed into the Palestine Committee and withdrawal became the priority. After the UN General Assembly vote in favour of the partition of Palestine between Arabs and Jews on 29 November, Britain still faced the challenge of maintaining law and order. Given British interests in the Middle East, London did not wish to be seen as responsible for implementing the partition solution, which would antagonise Arab states on whose cooperation Britain's political and strategic system in the Middle East depended. Instead, publicity efforts concentrated on preserving Anglo–Arab friendships. In spite of the attempts to present the withdrawal in the best possible light, the reality was that British policy had failed. Palestine descended into disorder and civil war.

During this period, it was anticipated that illegal immigration would continue at an even higher rate. The Illegal Immigration Committee recommended that Britain should pursue *refoulement* to Italy and, subject to the resolution of certain legal and practical difficulties, to Bulgaria and Romania. They believed the problem with the *Warfield* had been the failure to use force to disembark immigrants at the Port de Bouc and that, in future, no such operation could be undertaken, 'until we are sure of the full cooperation of the government concerned including the use of force at the port disembarkation by our own troops on board ship'.[87] Sofia however reported there was no chance of *refoulement* to a Black sea port in cooperation with the Bulgarian government.[88] Without states with whom to cooperate, *refoulement* was effectively dead. Meanwhile, Britain also attempted to highlight the 'Cold War' dimension of Palestine, linking Jewish illegal immigration and Soviet policy.[89] But, it was recognised, albeit belatedly, that the desire to emigrate to Palestine was also the result of renewed post-war persecution of the Jews in Eastern and Central Europe. Because of this, caution was recommended on publicising the link between the USSR and the illegal immigration traffic and the FO decided they needed to be 'very careful and very certain of our facts'. As long as the link was made to 'communists' rather than specifically to the USSR, the FO decided (on the advice of MI5) that, if the 'facts' were 'skilfully presented', no one could avoid the conclusion that, 'if a person is a non-Jew, and also a member of the Communist Party he is surely a communist agent'.[90]

It was one of the great ironies of Britain's attempts to obtain international action on the illegal immigration front that it achieved its greatest success *after* the decision to withdraw from Palestine. With the establishment of the International Refugee Organisation (IRO), in October 1947, Britain aimed to achieve 'the early liquidation of the refugee problem, which is the source of so many other political and economic difficulties which are embarrassing to us.' The government took steps to encourage more countries to join IRO and give financial support for schemes of resettlement, which would 'deprive the Zionists' of their 'raw material'.[91] On 17 November, the General Assembly passed a resolution inviting member states 'not to accord aid and protection to individuals or organisations which are engaged in the promoting or operating of illegal immigration or any activities designed to promote illegal immigration'.[92] For Britain, this came too late to have an appreciable effect on the situation on the ground in Palestine or to lead to an alteration of their decision to withdraw.

In December, the Defence Committee was concerned about the possibility of arms smuggling into Palestine and the challenge of emptying the Cyprus camps by May 1948, when the Mandate ended. MI5 reported that the *Haganah* was to 'suspend illegal immigration to Palestine in favour of shipping arms to the defence of the new state by the same clandestine methods'.[93] An increase in the immigration quota was considered, but 'it would be necessary to take the Jewish Agency fully into our confidence' and the plan was unlikely to 'remain secret'. Instead, the present number of certificates allocated to illegal immigrants from Europe would 'remain unchanged', but 'without any formal announcement'; an increase of a few hundreds in the number of Jews admitted to Palestine each month should be made 'in order to enable the camps in Cyprus and Germany to be cleared more rapidly'; and 'special groups of Jewish children' would be admitted outside the quota.[94]

In Palestine, as the partition decision began to sink in, British assessments of Arab opinion predicted a bloody solution to the problem: 'it has been said openly and by the most moderate elements that any efforts to implement partition would be violently opposed'.[95] In spite of the partition plan calling for the immediate relaxation of immigration controls, the Cabinet chose not to increase the immigration quota.[96] A general amnesty for illegal immigrants was considered to have 'unacceptable political repercussions'.[97] Instead, it was agreed that every effort would be made and every opportunity would be taken in the General Assembly to make it clear publicly what British policy was and the need for the international community to face up to its responsibilities.[98] While it was clear that the administration in Palestine would be unable to hold back the illegal immigration traffic beyond February, the publicity line was firm; 'on the general question of a legal immigration we should maintain our previous attitude that HMG were determined to control the traffic so long as they remained responsible for the government of Palestine'.[99] Secret reassurances were made to the Palestine Commission about some relaxation of the immigration quota on humanitarian grounds but, as seen above, this was not to be publicised. The FO News Department were informed about the scheme and told, 'that it is in our best interest to say nothing'.[100] It proved impossible to empty the Cyprus camps before the end of the Mandate and by 15 May approximately 24,000 immigrants remained there, the hope being that they would be out by 1 August, the date set for the final British military withdrawal.[101]

Conclusion

As far as the specific propaganda challenges faced by the British government in Palestine are concerned, the record demonstrates that London was conscious of the constituents of a successful propaganda campaign and attempted to conduct one, albeit with mixed results. Key target audiences were identified and in the circumstances appropriate propaganda themes, stressing British legitimacy and fairness, were adopted. However, the British did understand the insurgents' propaganda aims but failed to see how they would exploit British vulnerabilities. The problem was one of policy, not propaganda. Britain's competing strategic priorities were never reconciled and one 'key' target audience never emerged; instead several audiences competed. Moreover, the tempo of events and the unrelenting nature of the illegal immigration challenge proved greater than Britain's ability to deal with them in a way that ensured London's version predominated in perceptions of what occurred. Thus the British propaganda effort, like its policy, was often on the defensive, reacting to events rather than proactively controlling them.

The example of the *President Warfield*, a monumental policy failure and public relations gaffe, illustrates the frustrations felt by the British government in the thankless task of administering Palestine. At no point did they achieve the policy or propaganda initiative. Instead, in the attempt to counter illegal immigration, there was a series of incremental and short-sighted decisions, as options narrowed from the blockade by the Palestine Patrol, through the decision to deport illegal immigrants to Cyprus and finally to *refoulement*. The potential negative implications of these decisions were neither fully appreciated nor foreseen. Once the decisions had been taken to make an example of the *Warfield*, the die had been cast and any retreat would equally have been exploited by anti-British propagandists. By the summer of 1947, Britain could not please anybody fully and her policy aims were irreconcilable; they could not accommodate Jewish, Arab and British interests in reaching a solution. Immigration was at the heart of the Palestine insurgency and the government demonstrated that they had misunderstood the *Zeitgeist* – misunderstood the transformative impact of the Holocaust, misunderstood the aims of political Zionism and misunderstood what played to the Arab streets. The *Warfield* became symbolic of the loss of British moral authority. The story of the survivors of the concentration camps won in the battle for international public opinion and trumped legality in countering immigration into Palestine. This case study demonstrates the limits of propaganda in pursuing policy goals. Even 'good' propaganda could not, and indeed cannot, remedy the damage done by a 'bad' or misguided policy. Propaganda should not be seen in isolation, or as a substitute for policy. If the policy is misconceived, lacks credibility or is illegitimate, then a proactive propaganda campaign alone cannot deliver success.

Notes

The analysis, opinions and conclusions expressed or implied in this chapter are those of the author and do not necessarily represent the views of the Joint Services Command and Staff College, the UK Ministry of Defence or any other government agency.

1. For example, W.R. Louis, *The British Empire and the Middle East, 1945–51* (Oxford: Oxford University Press, 1984); Michael Cohen, *Palestine and the Great Powers, 1945–48* (Princeton: Princeton University Press, 1982); Martin Jones, *Failure in Palestine* (London: Mansell, 1986); William Roger Louis and R. Stookey (eds) *The End of the Palestine Mandate* (London: IB Taurus, 1986); David Charters, *The British Army and Jewish Insurgency in Palestine, 1945–47*, (Basingstoke: Macmillan, 1989); David French, *The British Way in Counter-Insurgency, 1945–1967* (Oxford: Oxford University Press, 2011); John Newsinger, *British Counterinsurgency: from Palestine to Northern Ireland* (Basingstoke: Palgrave, 2002); Bruce Hoffman, *The Failure of British Military Strategy within Palestine 1939–1947* (Jerusalem: Bar-Ilan University Press, 1983).
2. Propaganda is used here in a non-pejorative sense as shorthand for information/perception management. This chapter builds on my work (published under the name C.J. Morris) 'The Labour government's policy and publicity over Palestine 1945–7' in Anthony Gorst, Lewis Johnman and Scott Lucas (eds) *Contemporary British History 1931–61: Politics and the Limits of Policy* (London: Pinter, 1991) and Kate Utting 'The Strategic Information Campaign: lessons from the British experience in Palestine, 1945–1948', *Contemporary Security Policy*, 28/1 (2007).
3. For details of the voyage see: Aviva Halamish, *The Exodus Affair: Holocaust survivors and the Struggle for Palestine*, (London: Vallentine Mitchell, 1998); Ruth Gruber, *Exodus 1947: the ship that launched a nation* (New York: Union Square Press, 2007); David C. Holly, *Exodus 1947* (Maryland: Naval Institute Press, 1995). The British government always referred to the ship as the *President Warfield* and, since the focus of this chapter is the British perspective, the name *Warfield* is used.
4. The National Archives (TNA), CO537/4206, Stubbs, Public Information Office Report for January–December 1946.
5. Kenneth O. Morgan, *Labour People, Leaders and Lieutenants: Hardie to Kinnock* (Oxford: Oxford University Press, 1989), p. 158.
6. Fritz Liebreich, *Britain's Naval and Political Reaction to the Illegal immigration of Jews to Palestine, 1945–1948* (London: Routledge, 2005), pp. 6–7.
7. TNA/FO371/56885/N6092, Kirkpatrick memorandum, 15 May 1946.

8. Bard E. O'Neill, *Insurgency and Terrorism: inside modern revolutionary warfare* (New York: Brassey's, 1990), p. 13.
9. Giora Goodman, 'Palestine's Best: The Jewish Agency's Press Relations, 1946–1947', *Israel Studies*, 16/3, (2011).
10. On the challenge of illegal immigration and Britain's response, see: Ze'ev Venia Hadari, *Second Exodus: The Full Story of Jewish Illegal Immigration to Palestine, 1945–1948* (London: Valentine Mitchell, 1991); Liebreich, *Political Reaction*; Ninian Stewart, *The Royal Navy and the Palestine Patrol*, (London: Frank Cass, 2002); Arieh J. Kochavi, 'The Struggle against Jewish Immigration to Palestine', *Middle Eastern Studies*, 34/3, July 1998.
11. Joseph Heller, 'The Anglo-American Commission of Inquiry on Palestine, 1945–46: the Zionists Reaction Reconsidered', in Elie Kedourie and Sylvia Haim (eds), *Zionism and Arabism in Palestine and Israel* (London: Frank Cass, 1982), p. 156. In 1933–36, over 130,000 Jews arrived in Palestine and the Jewish population there increased about 80%. By July 1945, 10,938 immigration certificates of the 75,000 allotted by the White Paper remained: Kochavi, 'Struggle', p. 146.
12. For the relative significance of militancy and illegal immigration in Zionist counterinsurgency against British rule, see Joseph Heller, *The Stern Gang: ideology, politics and terror, 1940–1949* (London: Frank Cass, 1995); Saul Zadka, *Blood in Zion: how the Jewish Guerrillas drove the British out of Palestine* (London: Brassey's, 1995) and Norman Rose, *"A Senseless, Squalid War" Voices from Palestine 1945–1948* (London: Bodley Head, 2009).
13. TNA/CO537/1794, Mathieson minute, 1 April 1946.
14. Richard Crossman, *Palestine Mission: a personal record* (London: Hamish Hamilton, 1947), p. 27.
15. Liebreich, *Political Reaction*, p. 27.
16. Refugees were homeless people who remained within the borders of their native countries; DPs had been forcibly evicted from their homes during the war; 'infiltrees' were homeless people who voluntarily moved to Allied zones after VE Day. Jews constituted 20% of all DPs. See, Amikam Nachmani, *Great Power Discord in Palestine: the Anglo-American Committee of Inquiry into the problems of European Jewry and Palestine, 1945–1946* (London: Frank Cass, 1987), p. 8.
17. British estimates agreed with the 100,000 figure: TNA/CO537/1705, Dobkin report, 30 May 1946.
18. TNA/CO537/1742, Kellar to Martin, 7 December 1945.
19. Morris, 'Labour's government's policy', pp. 173–186 and Utting, 'Strategic Information Campaign', pp. 52–55.
20. TNA/FO371/61806/E3863, IIP(47)2, 7 May 1947.
21. TNA, CO537/2368, Robertson to Smith, June 1947.
22. Stewart, *Royal Navy*, chapter 5.
23. TNA/CO537/1800, Illegal immigration summary, No. 8, 25 October 1946.
24. TNA/CO537/1742, Kellar to Smith, 30 January 1946.
25. TNA/CO537/1739, Gutch to Smith, 20 March 1946.
26. TNA/CO537/1793, Mathieson to Secretary of State, 15 February 1946.
27. TNA/CO537/1798, Beith note, 23 August 1946; TNA/CO537/1797, FO to Prague, 7 August 1946.

28. TNA/CO537/1798, FO to Warsaw, 20 August and reply, 21 August; Russell to Baxter, 21 August; Vatican to FO, 22 August; FO to Warsaw, 27 August; Warsaw to FO, 29 August and Warsaw to FO, 31 August 1946.
29. TNA/CO537/1795, FO to Moscow, 9 June 1946; TNA/CO537/1799, Moscow to FO, 5 September 1946.
30. Liebreich, *Political Reaction*, 94; TNA/CO537/1798, FO to Geneva, 14 August 1946; TNA/CO537/2398, MI5 Illegal Immigration Review, No. 1, 15 May–15 June 1947; TNA/CO537/2398, Higham minute, 26 June 1947.
31. TNA/CAB128/5, CM(46)3, 8 January 1946.
32. TNA/CO537/1734, Washington to FO, 22 April 1946.
33. TNA/FO371/61799/E207, Washington to FO, 4 January 1947.
34. TNA/CO537/1799, Maclean to Baxter, 16 September 1946.
35. TNA/CO537/1795, Note for Hall on COS meeting, 29 July 1946.
36. TNA/CO537/1726, Palestine to CO, 25 July 1946.
37. TNA/CAB128/6, CM(46)75, 30 July 1946.
38. Ibid., CM(46)77, 7 August 1946; TNA/FO371/52628/31, FO to Paris, 11 August 1946.
39. TNA/CAB128/6, CM(46)78, 14 August 1946.
40. *Daily Herald*, 14 August 1946.
41. Stewart, *Royal Navy*, p. 134.
42. TNA/CO537/1808, Mitchell to Creech Jones, 21 November 1946; CO537/2385, IIP(47)12, 9 May 1947.
43. TNA/CO537/1799, Dodds to Beith, 18 October 1946, containing C-in-C Mediterranean to Admiralty, 23 September 1946.
44. TNA/CAB128/6, CM(46)104, 10 December 1946.
45. TNA/CO537/2389, CP(46)465, 18 December 1946.
46. TNA/CAB128/6, CM(46)107, 19 December 1946.
47. TNA/CO537/2333, Palestine to CO, 348, 17 February 1947.
48. TNA/FO371/61803, DO(47)7, 12 March 1947; TNA/CO537/2334, CO to Palestine, 21 March 1947.
49. TNA/CO537/2337, Beeley Report on UN Assembly, April–May 1947, 7 June 1947.
50. TNA/FO371/61841/E4108, FO to Missions, 23 May 1947.
51. TNA/FO371/61811/E5001, Luke to Bevin, 7 June 1947 and minutes of Ministerial Committee on Illegal Immigration, 10 June 1947.
52. TNA/CO537/2398, MI5 illegal immigration review, No. 2, 16 June–15 July 1947.
53. Kochavi, 'Struggle', p. 164.
54. TNA/FO371/52544/E7182/4/31, Wikeley minute, 27 July 1946.
55. TNA/FO371/61807/E4149, IIP(47)15, 15 May 1947.
56. Jones, *Failure*, p. 272.
57. Rose, *Voices*, p. 156.
58. TNA, CO537/2400, Martin minute, 11 July 1947.
59. Holly, *Exodus*, p. 157.
60. TNA/CO537/2400, CID Report, 22 July 1947.
61. Rose, *Voices*, pp. 158–9
62. Gruber, *Exodus*, p. 92.
63. TNA/FO371/61876/E6848, MacGillivray to Martin, 21 July 1947.

64. TNA/CO537/2280, District Commissioner's Office, Haifa, report – 16th-31st July 1947.
65. TNA/FO371/61816/E6648, 19 July 1947.
66. TNA/CO537/2400, FO to Paris, 18 and 21 July; TNA/FO371/61846/E6687, FO to New York, 28 July 1947.
67. TNA/FO371/61819/E6831, Paris to FO, 28 July 1947.
68. Halamish, *Exodus*, pp. 40–1 and p. 55; Hadari, *Exodus*, chapter 14.
69. TNA/FO371/61819/E6867, Paris to FO, 30 July 1947.
70. TNA/CO537/2400, FO to Washington, 21 and 24 July 1947.
71. Stewart, *Royal Navy*, pp. 131–2.
72. TNA/CO537/2400, minutes by Higham and Martin, and Palestine to CO, 30 July 1947.
73. TNA/CAB128/10, CM(47)66, 31 July 1947.
74. TNA/CO537/2401, Palestine to CO, 8 August 1947.
75. TNA/CO537/2400, Martin minute, 6 August 1947.
76. TNA/CO537/2401, CO to Palestine, 9 August 1947.
77. Ibid., FO to Berlin, 19 August, and CO to Palestine, 20 August 1947.
78. TNA/FO371/61822/E7490, Washington to FO, 14 August 1947.
79. TNA/CO537/2401, Palestine to CO, 21 August 1947.
80. TNA/FO371/61822/E7744, Palestine to CO, 22 August 1947.
81. TNA/CO537/2401, Palestine to CO, 1614, 24 August 1947.
82. TNA/FO371/61826/E8439, Paris to FO, 27 August 1947.
83. *The Times*, 22 August 1947.
84. Rose, *Voices*, p. 161.
85. TNA/CO537/2404, Sargent to Lloyd, 2 September 1947.
86. Halamish, *Exodus*, chapter 12.
87. TNA/CO537/2368, CO to Palestine, 26 September 1947.
88. TNA/CO537/2404, Sofia to FO, 3 October 1947.
89. TNA/CO537/2404, Beith minute, 18 September 1947.
90. TNA/FO371/68516/E1817, minute by Fellowes, 16 February, Warner and Beith, 18 February 1948.
91. TNA/FO371/61956/E9456, Wilkinson memorandum, 8 October 1947.
92. TNA/FO371/61832/E10760, Cable to Higham, 25 November 1947.
93. TNA/CO537/2383, Scherr to Evershed, 15 December 1947.
94. TNA/CO537/2369, Higham undated minute and DO(47)26, 11 December 1947.
95. TNA/CO537/2280, District Commissioner's Office, Haifa, fortnightly report – 16th–30th November 1947.
96. TNA/FO371/61833, Beith minute, 17 December 1947.
97. TNA/CO537/2273, CO to Palestine, 24 December 1947.
98. TNA/FO371/68613/E929, CO to Palestine, 27 January 1948.
99. TNA/FO371/68661/E2616, Higham to Beith, 20 February 1948.
100. TNA/FO371/68532/E1715, Beith minute, 13 February 1948.
101. TNA/CO537/3945, DO(48)7, 31 March, and Cyprus to CO, 7 May 1948.

4

Britain, the United States and the Issue of 'Limited War' with China, 1950–54

Kevin Ruane

It is a well-established staple of the literature that the Korean War exposed the 'special relationship' to one of its earliest and sternest Cold War tests. British and American support for the United Nations (UN) in condemning the North Korean attack on South Korea in June 1950, together with their subsequent military contributions – vast in the case of the US, still significant on the UK side – to the United Nations Command (UNC), helped foster an outward impression of unity. Behind the scenes, however, the Labour government of Clement Attlee and the Democratic administration of Harry S. Truman were often divided. Historians have given due consideration to a number of Korean issues insofar as they impacted on Anglo–American relations. These include: British reluctance to bow to American pressure to match moral disapproval of North Korea's actions with a military commitment to the UNC; the decision to cross the 38th parallel into North Korea, in October 1950, followed by China's entry into the war; the possible use of nuclear weapons and the Truman-Attlee talks of December 1950; and British concerns about the bellicosity of UN commander, General Douglas MacArthur.[1] Compared with these matters, the Truman administration's efforts in 1951 to secure a UN resolution denouncing the People's Republic of China (PRC) as an aggressor for its Korean intervention has received less attention.[2] Yet this issue brought into sharp relief many British misgivings about the conflict.

US strategists questioned the wisdom of confining hostilities to the Korean peninsula once China was a belligerent, and the Attlee government worried that Washington would use the resolution to justify punishing China through the imposition of a naval blockade and widespread bombing. Sometimes referred to as the 'MacArthur strategy', because of the UN commander's espousal of targeting China, the Truman administration preferred the term 'limited war'.[3] In London, Pierson Dixon, Deputy Under-Secretary at the Foreign Office (FO), spoke for many when he likened a Sino-American war to a 'useless struggle between the whale and the elephant.' It might easily 'start a chain of events which would bring the Soviet Union into the war, perhaps initially in the Far East but almost certainly in Europe in a longer or shorter time'.[4] As we know, no wider war ensued. Instead, in July 1953, an armistice was signed. By then, the leading actors in the Anglo–American drama had changed: Churchill and the Conservatives were back in power in Britain and the Republican Eisenhower was in the White House. But the danger of war with China still managed to bedevil relations. Should the communists break the peace, the Eisenhower administration favoured not limited but all-out war against China, including the use of nuclear weapons. In spring 1954, the issue of punitive action suddenly shifted locale to Indochina, where France faced defeat in its eight-year war against the communist-led Viet-Minh. Washington sought an international coalition to intervene militarily to salvage the French position, but London wanted nothing to do with the so-called 'united action' plan. As this article concludes, the British approach to Indochina was shaped to a significant degree by the experience of Korea, with US-led intervention in Vietnam viewed by London as a possible prelude to war with China.

The January 1951 crisis

On 30 November 1950, President Truman caused an international stir when he revealed that his administration was giving active consideration to the use of nuclear weapons in Korea.[5] The previous month, UN forces had crossed the 38th parallel into North Korea with the aim of establishing an independent, unified and democratic country. Massive PRC intervention in defence of the North destroyed this hope and, by the time Truman made his statement, UN troops, the overwhelming majority of them American, were in headlong retreat and the US government was reportedly thinking of abandoning Korea to prepare for a war with and in China.[6] In early December, Attlee flew to Washington, seeking an assurance that nuclear weapons would not be employed without advance consultation with London. He also restated his government's opposition to any widening of the war to China and reiterated his desire to see both a peaceful resolution in Korea and a wider Far Eastern settlement with the PRC. Truman accepted the principle of consultation insofar as it was practicable in an emergency, but in other respects the discussions were unsatisfactory from a British standpoint.[7] 'We appear not to have convinced the Americans of the need to make a serious effort to reach a political settlement with the Chinese and not to have shaken them in their intention to undertake some form of "limited war" against China', Dixon told the Foreign Secretary, Ernest Bevin. 'If matters are left like this, it seems inevitable that the United States at least will be drawn into war-like operations against China. Two results seem certain to flow from this: (a) the Far Eastern theatre will inevitably take priority over the European theatre, however much the Americans say that they put Europe first; (b) the temptation to Russia to act in Europe will be greatly increased'.[8] According to the British Chiefs of Staff, their American counterparts, believing general war with the USSR was inevitable, maintained 'the sooner we got it over the better'. The US Joint Chiefs appeared willing to contemplate action against China that risked escalation into World War III with a fatalism that the UK chiefs refused to share.[9]

British concerns peaked in the period immediately following the Truman-Attlee talks. By mid-December, UN forces had stemmed the Chinese onslaught and there was a lull in the fighting before, on 1 January 1951, the PRC renewed the attack, sweeping across the 38th parallel in great force. Against this sombre backdrop, the US served notice that it intended to table a UN resolution condemning China as an aggressor and demanding unspecified 'collective measures' by way of punishment.[10] The British accepted the fact of Chinese aggression, but were reluctant to support the US proposal, because it would antagonise the PRC and so damage ceasefire prospects. There was also concern that the Truman administration, amid domestic criticism for the alleged failings of its Far Eastern policy, would use the resolution to legitimize a limited war with China.[11] As the Chiefs of Staff pointed out, 'there is in fact no such thing as "limited war"' and '[we] find it almost impossible to believe that open general war against China in the Far East could fail to spread, sooner rather than later, to war on a world wide scale, with Russia fully engaged'.[12]

Having decided the American initiative was dangerous, London considered how to convey this unwelcome message to Washington. 'Our best course', William Strang, the FO Permanent Under-Secretary, decided, 'is to state our views plainly and firmly and patiently both in private, and in public when necessary, but always with the intention of working for agreement rather than for a breach'.[13] Bevin agreed. If the resolution were passed 'the existing danger of a wider conflict would become much more grave', but through 'wise diplomacy' the Americans could be brought to see sense.[14] Buoyed by the backing of Commonwealth leaders, Attlee wrote to Truman on 8 January detailing British doubts and advising against any plan to 'substitute for a policy of localising the conflict in Korea a policy aimed at limited action against China'.[15] The President's response was brusque: 'if the truth be that aggression has occurred let us not shrink from stating that truth because of the fact that the power which launches it is formidable. If we take that attitude the great common problems which you and we have are insoluble'.[16] Dean Acheson, the Secretary of State, told Bevin that any failure to condemn China 'would create a wave of isolationism in this country which would jeopardize all that we are trying to do with and for the Atlantic Pact countries'.[17] Coming at the moment when the Senate was debating whether to send large numbers of American troops to garrison Western Europe, the warning hit home. 'We must *not* lose U.S. support in Europe', Bevin avowed, a view echoed by the Cabinet and the Chiefs of Staff.[18]

On 17 January, with Chinese armies still advancing and Beijing having rejected another UN ceasefire proposal, the Americans circulated a draft resolution, denouncing the PRC and proposing 'additional measures'.[19] In London, a perturbed Bevin told the Cabinet that the imposition of sanctions would wreck ceasefire prospects and 'seriously increase the risk of general war in the Far East.' He therefore proposed to press the Americans to settle for straight condemnation.[20] This decoupling mission got nowhere; by the time Bevin next addressed the Cabinet, on 22 January, the original resolution had been formally tabled in the UN's Political Committee. For all Washington's assurances that economic measures were the limit of its ambition, the Foreign Secretary feared military action was lurking in the background. Against this, he also worried that an open US–UK split would boost 'isolationists' in Congress, jeopardise the 'all-important' US defence commitment to Europe, and render the North Atlantic Treaty Organisation (NATO) stillborn.[21] That same evening, Bevin was taken to hospital suffering from pneumonia. From his sick-bed, he relayed to the Cabinet his conviction that 'in the last resort we should have to vote for the United States Resolution'.[22]

As it happened, the man who took over the FO was no natural last-resorter. Kenneth Younger, the Minister of State, had previously tried but failed to persuade his colleagues to vote against a resolution which, if passed, would mean 'that we are, in effect, at war with China'. Now, with Bevin removed from the centre of policymaking, he again challenged what he called 'the dangerous stupidity' of US policy.[23] It may be, as Robert Beisner has argued, that Acheson was determined to confine the war to Korea and restrain Cold War hot-heads in Washington. Younger, however, suspected the Americans were 'rather spoiling for a chance to hit back on China by any means at their disposal, reckless of the consequences to others', and it was this perception that informed his approach to Korea.[24] Senior FO officials, as well as Ambassador Oliver Franks in Washington, shared this worry, though, like Bevin, they were prone to giving the Truman administration the benefit of the doubt. Not so Younger, who stepped up his campaign for 'independence of USA in foreign policy'.[25]

On 25 January 1951, the Cabinet gathered for what Hugh Gaitskell, the Chancellor of the Exchequer, described as a 'short and emotional' meeting.[26] The case for supporting the Americans in the UN was posited in terms of avoiding 'lasting damage' to US–UK relations and the importance of keeping in step with the 'older Commonwealth' (Australia, New Zealand and South Africa, though not Canada, had agreed to back the US). The counter-arguments included: the Chiefs of Staff's appreciation of the 'serious effects of any extension of the conflict with China' on Commonwealth interests in the Far East; the risk of estranging the 'new' Commonwealth, especially India, which opposed the resolution; public opposition in Britain to a war with China 'which might easily broaden out into a Third World War'; and concern that passage of the resolution would shut the door to a peaceful settlement. Cabinet Secretary Norman Brook's handwritten notes confirm that Younger played a bullish role. To vote with America 'when everyone knows we oppose their policy would see our international standing and influence destroyed forever', he declared. 'If ever we are to stand against the US, this is the time.' Younger was supported, *inter alia,* by Jim Griffiths (Colonial Secretary), Herbert Morrison (Lord President of the Council), Aneurin Bevan (Health Minister), John Strachey (War Office), and Hugh Dalton (formerly Chancellor). After abstention was rejected as 'a weak course for a great Power to take on a major issue', ministers opted by majority verdict to vote against the US resolution in the General Assembly.[27] The decision, Younger acknowledged, 'was against the balance of FO opinion, and against what everyone thought Ernie [Bevin] would have done'.[28]

Had the vote been held the following day, Anglo-American relations would surely have been brought to a point of rupture. As it was, the debate was delayed. Meanwhile, on 26 January, the Cabinet reversed its decision. How is this turnaround to be explained? Top

FO officials had been badly rattled by the original decision and made their unhappiness clear to Younger, but this in itself was not decisive. Nor was the ailing Bevin's *in absentia* contribution that 'I can't let a pal down when I'm in a fight with him'.[29] Of far greater significance was the manoeuvring of Gaitskell, the arch last-resorter in the Cabinet, who decried the 'anti-Americanism' of the Younger clique and warned Attlee that, unless the Cabinet's decision was annulled, he would have to consider resignation. This threat was bound to make an impression on a Prime Minister defending a slender parliamentary majority. Then, overnight, came news of an Israeli initiative at the UN, designed to weaken the link in the resolution between condemnation and sanctions. Action on additional measures, the Israelis suggested, should be contingent on a further exhaustive effort by the UN's Peace Observation Commission to bring about a ceasefire. These developments quickly fused, the Israeli intervention enabling Gaitskell to insist that the Cabinet revisit its decision. The Chancellor harboured few illusions about US policy, noting that while the Americans 'talk of a limited war…we all feel that there is probably no such thing, and the worst of it is that the Chinese would probably retaliate, if blockade is organised against them or if the Americans bomb them, by occupying Hong Kong and moving south through Indochina.' Even so, if the Truman administration refused to shift its position, he saw no option other than to vote with the Americans, even if this meant having to 'go with them in China'.[30]

When the Cabinet reassembled, a majority of ministers agreed that if the Americans accepted the Israeli proposal – itself quite possibly a hidden-hand US initiative – this would make possible an affirmative UK vote and 'contribute immeasurably to the maintenance of good relations with the United States'. However, the decisive factor in bringing the government to reverse course was the forceful performance of the Prime Minister. Attlee was now convinced, or had been convinced by Gaitskell, of the rectitude of voting for the resolution. When Griffiths warned of a split between the new and old Commonwealth, Attlee rounded on him. 'Be realistic', he snapped, Britain '[c]an't throw over *all* our friends for fear of Asian attitude'. It was too much to expect the Americans to drop all mention of sanctions and he urged caution; otherwise Britain could end up 'losing all by pressing for too much'. The Cabinet ended with an agreement to vote for the resolution if amended; otherwise abstention would be necessary.[31] 'The PM was now quite firm and very good', Gaitskell wrote approvingly afterwards.[32] As for Younger, he had been uncharacteristically quiet, but his diary offers an explanation. Even as the Cabinet voted to oppose the Americans, he had decided that 'abstention is good enough', although it had still been 'wise to *threaten* to vote against, since it scared the Americans who are frantically trying to devise compromises' via the Israelis 'in order to get our vote'.[33] In the end, then, Younger was also a last-resorter, but he could console himself with the knowledge that the government's obstructionism so delayed the resolution's progress that, by the time it was put to the vote, the Korean battlefield situation had improved and the momentum in Washington for action against China had correspondingly slowed.[34]

The crisis eases

On 29 January, the Cabinet learned that the US government had agreed not to act before the UN had exhausted all ceasefire options. If the Americans were sincere, Attlee judged, then the government would have 'substantially achieved our two principal objectives', namely to prevent the issue of sanctions undermining ceasefire prospects and, by extension, to keep alive the possibility of a negotiated settlement.[35] After receiving assurances from Washington, on 1 February the UK voted for the aggressor resolution in the General Assembly, where it passed 44–7, with 9 abstentions.[36] This represented a victory for the 'America right or wrong' faction in the Cabinet, but it had taken the Israeli 'card of re-entry' (as Strang put it) and Gaitskell's resignation threat to bring it about. The tactical victory, insofar as the Americans *did* compromise, belonged to Younger.[37]

The resolution was denounced by Beijing, but British fears of a Chinese sideswipe at Hong Kong or Indochina went unrealised.[38] Meanwhile, in Korea, the front line began to stabilise. By March the Attlee government was talking of new chances for peace. MacArthur, however, retained dreams of advancing north again, taking the war directly to the PRC. When he made these views public – deliberately sabotaging his own government's nascent efforts to broker a truce – the British were outraged. 'Our principal difficulty is General MacArthur', protested Herbert Morrison, who had succeeded the dying Bevin as Foreign Secretary. 'He seems to want a war with China. We do not...Here we seem to have a case of a commander publicly suggesting that his policy is not the stated policy of his government, not subject to the control of his own government, and whom his government is, nevertheless, unwilling and unable to discipline'.[39] Morrison was wrong. On 11 April, Truman fired MacArthur.

Acheson moved swiftly to 'cash in' on British euphoria at the general's demise, pressing the Labour government to accept the principle of retaliation against China should UN forces come under air-attack from aircraft launched from Manchuria.[40] On 3 May, the Cabinet, abandoning its firm opposition to a geographical widening of the conflict, endorsed the US proposal. Ministers were undoubtedly swayed by the fact that General Matthew Ridgway, a soldier they respected, was now in charge of the UNC. They also felt obligated to the Truman administration, following the Senate's recent vote to send troops to Europe. The Cabinet further recognised that denying the Americans freedom to retaliate would be inconsistent with UK support for the aggressor resolution.[41] Even so, what Franks called 'MacArthuritis' lingered; FO officials, the Chiefs of Staff, Britain's UN delegation, and Franks' embassy all voiced concern lest the US find some excuse for war with the PRC.[42] The Cabinet therefore determined to make 'absolutely clear' to Washington 'that we must be consulted before a decision was taken to authorise retaliatory bombing [to any Chinese action], even though the bombing was to be carried out solely by United States forces'. If a large-scale Chinese assault was launched, UK support would probably be automatic, but if it was of lesser intensity, ministers reserved the right to decide for themselves whether counter-action was merited. Knowing that placating the Americans would be anathema to many in the Parliamentary Labour Party, Attlee kept the decision secret.[43]

The failure of the Chinese spring offensive marked their last effort to fashion an outright military victory and, in July 1951, ceasefire talks opened. Yet, this did not lessen US interest in limited war. When the talks stalled in August, Washington proposed a range of punishments if the PRC resumed heavy fighting, including bombing China and a naval blockade. In London, the Chiefs of Staff and the Cabinet's Defence Committee objected that such measures would not only be ineffective in degrading China's war-making capacity but would run 'a very grave risk of global war'.[44] Then there was the vexed issue of consultation. The Truman administration 'feel that the decision as to what measures may be necessary to ensure the safety of United Nations forces (the bulk of which are in any case American) must, in the last analysis, be theirs alone', the Washington embassy reported. 'We say that we must play our part in the decision because we should be involved in its consequences'. But while the Americans claimed to understand British anxieties, they were 'hardly likely to bind themselves not to act without our concurrence in circumstances involving the safety of large numbers of American troops', even if (as the UK Chiefs of Staff believed) 'a possible consequence were an extension of the Korean campaign to global war'.[45] With little prospect of altering the US attitude the British were left to trust in Ridgway's 'discretion and wisdom', and by Autumn the dispute had been put into 'cold storage'.[46]

Churchill and Eden take office

Following the Conservative election victory in October 1951, Younger predicted that 'one of the shocks coming to [the] Tories now they are in power is to find that the predominance of US is not just due to the weakness of Labour Ministers, but is one of the facts of life'.[47] Korea was a case in point. 'No one here knows what is going on', Churchill was soon complaining. 'We must try to penetrate the American mind and purpose'.[48] The new Foreign Secretary, Anthony Eden, likewise felt that '[o]ne of the greatest dangers in Korea is of the Americans taking the bit between their teeth and going ahead, without consulting any of their allies, on steps which may have consequences affecting us all'.[49] Beyond this shared interest in consultation, Eden and Churchill rarely saw eye-to-eye on the Far East. The Prime Minister took the Korean War seriously because British lives were at stake, but in most other respects the affairs of Asia, especially following Indian independence, lagged behind Western Europe and the Middle East in his global priorities. He was invariably unhappy when disagreements over China upset the wider harmony of Anglo–American relations. At best, China was a bargaining counter: if Britain were to 'meet the Americans over China, which really does not matter to us', then 'they in turn might meet us about Egypt or Persia, which matter a lot'.[50] In contrast, Eden invested the Far East with high importance, not least because he worried that US adventurism could spark a regional, or even a global, conflict and he soon pursued a dual containment strategy predicated on hemming in China while holding the US back from extreme action.[51]

Towards the end of 1951, the Truman administration proposed that any Korean armistice should be accompanied by an Anglo–American warning to the communists of dire consequences if they broke the peace.[52] 'This was the first time since the Korean war began that the Americans had seen fit to consult us on any matter of major policy,' Churchill pointed out. However, his inclination to fall in with US wishes was resisted by the FO and Chiefs of Staff, who questioned both the necessity of a warning and the American preference for punishing communist infractions with bombing and blockade.[53] Following Anglo–American discussions, it was agreed that the warning should be issued by the UN, specifying that, in the event of a 'major' breach of the armistice, it would 'in all probability' be impossible to confine hostilities to Korea. The Americans had wanted a stronger form of words – to wit, a communist breach '*will* result in hostilities outside Korea' – but Eden rejected this as 'too positive and menacing' and successfully argued for more ambiguous phrasing.[54] Still, restraining Washington might be difficult. If the Chinese upset a settlement, Acheson warned Eden, 'we should have to go after them ... if they jump on us, they will be for it ... no holds will be barred'.[55]

In January 1952, Churchill and Eden visited Washington, where Eden spent much of his time fretting in case his chief sold the pass on the Far East in the hope of winning American backing for the British position in the Middle East. Churchill shared the US military's estimate of the consequences of limited war, opining that 'Russia would start World War III when she wanted to' – she 'certainly would not do so merely to honour her pledge to China' – and he was therefore 'not unduly worried about bombing targets in Manchuria'.[56] When the Americans restated their interest in bombing and blockade should the Korean talks collapse, Churchill said that in the Far East the 'role of leader squarely belonged to the United States' and pledged his government to 'do its utmost to meet US views and requests in relation to that area.' These remarks left not just Eden but others in the UK party 'a good deal concerned by the PM's readiness to give away our case'.[57] Churchill affirmed his faith in American leadership when he addressed Congress on 17 January, adding that 'if the truce we seek is reached only to be broken our response will be prompt, resolute and effective'.[58] Back in Britain, these words were interpreted by Labour as proof the Conservatives had signed-up to 'the MacArthur policy of carrying the war to China'.[59] Irked, Churchill revealed in Parliament that the Attlee administration had first compromised the principle of confining the war to Korea. All he had done was second Labour's decision on retaliation if UN forces came under air assault from Chinese aircraft. The hapless Attlee sat 'hunched up like an elf just out of its chrysalis ... turning slowly white' as his secret was laid bare.[60]

While Churchill used China to score parliamentary points, others in the government faced up to the potentially incendiary consequences of US policy. In the FO, Strang described China as the 'black spot' in Anglo-American relations and warned that 'as usual the Americans are trying to entangle us ... [O]bjective: war with China', while the Chiefs of Staff continued to rue the complacency of their US counterparts in believing that the USSR would steer clear of any Sino-American war.[61]

In Korea, meantime, the ceasefire negotiations had fallen foul of a dispute over the repatriation of prisoners-of-war and London worried the Chinese might try to break the political deadlock by launching a new offensive. In the event, it was the Americans who struck first. On 23 June, US air and naval aircraft bombed power plants on the Yalu river in the largest combined air attack of the war. The targets were not on Chinese soil, but a disturbed FO felt that the attack came perilously close to an unprovoked extension of the war. Even though London had not been informed in advance, Churchill's first instinct was to avoid an open display of Anglo–American disunity. Eden, however, was livid. Barely a month had passed since Acheson assured him that Washington would do nothing to provoke war with China. It was with great reluctance that he bowed to Churchill's wish to mute his public criticism, but when he next met the Secretary of State it was to demand 'no more surprises'.[62]

Eisenhower and Korea

To British policy-makers, the June 1952 bombing was symptomatic of a general aversion to consultation on the part of the Democrats.[63] The victory of a Republican, Dwight D. Eisenhower, in the November presidential election, was therefore welcomed as an opportunity for a fresh start. At the same time, the need for close US–UK cooperation seemed greater than ever, in light of alarming Republican campaign rhetoric about winning the Cold War.[64] When it came to Korea, the FO doubted that the new administration would tolerate a continuation of the stalemate, though officials were gratified that Eisenhower 'sedulously avoided discussion of the MacArthur policy in respect of Communist China' during the election.[65] Once in power, the Republicans indulged in a good deal of sabre-rattling, including warnings to Beijing that nuclear weapons would be used if the Korean deadlock continued. The problem for the British was that, if the communists refused to yield, the war would drag on and the US government might succumb to the temptations of a nuclearised MacArthur strategy. Whether in those circumstances the Republicans would be inclined to consult fully with London was uncertain. 'In dealing with our allies', the new Secretary of State, John Foster Dulles, observed, the US 'must strike a balance between allied unity and American freedom of action ... To be committed to "consultation" on every step is to be exposed to veto by those consulted, with consequent handicaps on freedom of action'.[66]

The communists did yield and, on 27 July 1953, a Korean armistice was signed. This was welcomed by the British insofar as it cleared the way for their long-standing goal of a general Far East settlement with China, involving the seating of the communists in the United Nations and transferring Taiwan to PRC authority. However, the Americans flatly refused to give China satisfaction on either count and announced that if the proposed Korean political conference, which was to prepare a peace treaty, failed to make progress, they would abandon the diplomatic track. What they would do then was unclear, but Selwyn Lloyd, the FO Minister of State, visiting the US in August, detected 'an emotional feeling about Communist China and to a lesser extent about Russia which borders on hysteria'. The Korean armistice 'has made people more jumpy even than the hostilities'.[67] By Autumn, with the political conference stagnant, the British themselves were jumpy. Should the peace fail, the Chiefs of Staff expected the US to 'go all out for a clear cut victory...driving the Chinese out of Korea and...reunifying the country by force of arms'. However, because these plans would require 'unrestricted use of unconventional weapons' against China and thus 'heighten the risk of general war' with the USSR, they preferred to confine retaliation within Korea.[68] The Cabinet accepted this military appreciation, but with Britain a party to the UN warning issued following the armistice and in the agreed wording of 1951, its capacity for resisting American pressure to target China was limited.[69]

Matters came to a head in December 1953, when American, British and French leaders gathered at Bermuda. Eisenhower privately confirmed to Churchill that the US would use nuclear weapons, both in Korea and against China, if the armistice crumbled. The Prime Minister not only failed to raise any objection, but told Eisenhower their conversation 'put him in a position to say to Parliament that he had been consulted in advance and had agreed'.[70] When Eden learned what had happened he was shocked, declaring the implications of US plans 'too horrible for the human mind to contemplate'. But, given Churchill's record of propitiating the Americans on the Far East, his conclusion that 'W[inston] failed to notice [the] significance' of the President's words was charitable. More likely, the Prime Minister hoped to trade UK backing on Korea for American support for his pet project, a summit with the post-Stalin leadership in Moscow. 'We have always recognised that it would probably be impossible to avoid bombing Chinese aerodromes beyond the Yalu,' Eden reminded him. 'But we have never given, or been asked to give, approval to widespread bombing of China proper nor, of course, to the use of the atom bomb, or to a blockade.' There was no such thing as limited war. If the USSR backed China, Britain would be in 'immediate danger' of nuclear attack.[71] Eden did his job well. When Churchill next met the President, he withdrew his blank cheque approval, citing in explanation the ease with which London could be destroyed in a war with the Soviet Union.[72] Afterwards, Eisenhower vented his frustration in his diary. The British looked upon 'the use of the atom bomb as the initiation of a completely new era in war' and 'cling to the hope (to us fatuous) that if we avoid the first use of the atom bomb in any war, that the Soviets might likewise abstain.' US thinking 'has come a long way past this kind of conjecture and hope' to arrive at 'the conclusion that the atom bomb has to be treated just as another weapon in the arsenal'.[73]

At Bermuda, the British were given an outline of the Eisenhower administration's 'New Look' national security strategy, approved by the President a few weeks earlier. Its aims cohered to the Democrats' strategy insofar as they sought to contain the communist bloc by maintaining strong defensive positions but, in terms of means, the Republicans emphasised reliance on cost-efficient nuclear weapons rather than expensive conventional arms. However, if the US nuclear arsenal failed to deter the communist bloc, Washington stood ready to engage in massive (nuclear) retaliation against the source of aggression, be it China or the USSR.[74] On the eve of his departure for Bermuda, Eisenhower listened to a presentation by Admiral Arthur W. Radford, Chair of the Joint Chiefs of Staff, on plans for nuclear targeting of the PRC's military–industrial infrastructure if the communists reignited the Korean war. To the President these plans represented 'all-out war against Communist China' and he insisted on advance 'approval and understanding' from America's key allies. It follows that the evident lack of British support at Bermuda was not only a personal disappointment to Eisenhower, but strengthened the hand of those in his administration who bridled at conceding a veto over US strategy to inconstant partners.[75]

Intended to alarm, and hence contain, the USSR, the New Look convinced the British that 'the very nature of the retaliatory power at the Americans' disposal is such that any decision to retaliate becomes one of cataclysmic potentialities'.[76] This danger was much in Eden's thoughts as he prepared a paper on Korea for the Defence Committee in early 1954. Although the UK was still committed to join in a military response to a violation of the armistice, the fact that the Americans were now bent on delivering a shattering nuclear blow to China prompted a reconsideration of basic policy. As Eden put it, the use of nuclear weapons 'against an enemy in the Far East might be so serious for the United Kingdom that we cannot agree to such action in advance and must insist upon being consulted at the time before it is taken.' This open-ended reference to 'an enemy' implicitly acknowledged that Korea was not the only Asian Cold War hot spot where the Americans might confront communism with the ultimate weapon. Indeed, by the time that the Defence Committee approved Eden's paper in April 1954, Indochina had emerged as the likeliest test-case for massive retaliation.[77]

The Indochina crisis

The Indochina crisis erupted just as news of a powerful US hydrogen bomb test in the Pacific spawned anxieties that thermo-nuclear developments were out of control. On 9 March an agitated Churchill wrote to Eisenhower of his fear that 'several million people would certainly be obliterated by four or five of the latest H-Bombs' and how the United Kingdom's 'smallness and density of population emphasizes this danger to us'.[78] Four days later, in north-west Vietnam, the Viet-Minh attacked the French base at Dien Bien Phu in what quickly developed into the decisive battle of the Indochina war. At the end of the month, with the French in trouble, the Eisenhower administration issued a call for 'united action'.[79] Accepting that the New Look's nuclear components were of limited value in the circumstances prevailing in Vietnam, the Americans fell back on a conventional response, the creation of a coalition to intervene to buttress the French position and ensure that the loss of one battle did not lead to a general collapse. In order to obtain war powers from a Congress still bitter at the scale of US losses in Korea, the administration needed allies to share the burden, hence the concept of united action. However, this in turn gifted to those allies the very power of veto that so perturbed the likes of Dulles and Radford. In Britain's case, it was a power swiftly exercised. On 31 March, the FO and Chiefs of Staff, in a combined position paper, insisted that '[a]ny direct intervention by the armed forces of any external nation ... would probably result in Chinese intervention, with the danger that this might ultimately lead to global war. Our influence should therefore be used against these more dangerous forms of deeper United States involvement.' With an international conference, due to open in Geneva in late April, devoted to Korea and Indochina (and to which the USSR, PRC and Viet-Minh were invited), the Churchill government had little hesitation in rejecting a military solution in favour of a diplomatic one.[80]

The extent to which the UK approach to Indochina was a reaction to the more minatory features of US policy towards Korea is seldom acknowledged, but the linkage is clear.[81] London, worried that Vietnam would provide the Americans with a post-Korean pretext for war with the PRC, came to view Radford (whom Eden thought was 'spoiling for a fight with China') as the MacArthur of Vietnam.[82] On 24 April, Eden told the Cabinet that the admiral believed 'the time was ripe... to take direct military action to check the ambitions of Communist China', a view which underestimated both the 'grave risk that the Soviet Union would feel obliged to intervene' and the danger that US plans might 'be the first step towards a third world war'. There was '[n]o talk yet of using atomic bombs', he said, but Dulles had recently 'made it clear that US would feel free to use atomic weapons in retaliation – not necessarily in [the] place they had been attacked.' In other words, if united action prompted Chinese intervention in Vietnam, the PRC itself might be hit. For this reason, both the Cabinet and the Chiefs of Staff fully backed the Foreign Secretary in his quest for a negotiated settlement.[83]

The Americans made one last attempt to win round the British, on 26 April, when Radford turned up in London and met privately with Churchill. For Eden, now in Geneva for the start of the conference, the prospect of this encounter filled him with 'the terrors' lest the Prime Minister give way to the Americans.[84] For once, he need not have worried. Radford pressed hard, telling Churchill that this was 'the critical moment at which to make a stand against China', and that the USSR, being 'frightened of war', would not act to save the PRC, but he got nowhere. The British people 'would not be easily influenced by what happened in the distant jungles of S.E. Asia,' Churchill retorted, 'but they did know that there was a powerful American base in East Anglia and that war with China, who would invoke the Sino-Russian Pact, might mean an assault by Hydrogen bombs on these islands.' Neither he, nor his government, could 'commit ourselves at this moment, when all these matters were about to be discussed at Geneva, to a policy which might lead by slow stages to a catastrophe.' When the record of the meeting reached Eden he wrote just one word on the bottom of his copy: 'Good'.[85]

At the conference itself, Eden took the view that the best insurance against US intervention, hence a wider war, was to make the peace process work. In contrast, Dulles appeared to be playing for a diplomatic collapse: on 3 May, he left Geneva, handing leadership of the US delegation to his deputy, Walter Bedell Smith, who later admitted to a bungled wrecking tactic. Eden saw Dulles off at the airport. 'The trouble with you, Foster', he told him, 'is that you want World War Three'.[86] Even with the more amenable Smith to work with, Eden remained anxious. On 22 May, he calculated that it was 'still even money we may reach an armistice' and confessed to being 'more than ever convinced of dangers of 3rd world war if we don't'.[87] Returning to London two days later, he assured Cabinet colleagues that he would continue to strive for a compromise at Geneva because he was 'gravely concerned about the dangers of the alternative courses of action which the United States Government were likely to favour if a settlement were not now secured by negotiation'.[88] In the end, Eden's greatest contribution to peace in Indochina was to prevent the collapse of the conference following Dulles' departure and to ensure that France, China and the Viet-Minh, once they decided to negotiate seriously (as they did from mid-June), had a ready-made forum in which to operate. On 21 July 1954, the Geneva settlement brought the Indochina war to a close.

Conclusion

For more than four years, from 1950 onwards, the British foreign policymaking elite largely accepted the premises of last-resortism when dealing with the US in Korea and in the Far East generally. Until, that is, the 1954 Indochina crisis saw the Conservative government not only refuse to back US policy but, at Geneva, actively to thwart it. Leading the charge in this regard was Eden. In contrast to Younger, a stand-in Foreign Secretary prone to spasms of self-doubt, Eden was at the height of his powers as a diplomatist and a dominating Cabinet presence. Fearful the Americans would use Indochina as a springboard for the 'limited war' with China they were denied during the Korean conflict, and certain that if that war became unlimited the USA would unloose its nuclear arsenal, he felt there was no option other than to reject 'united action' and, with it, the principle of last-resortism. Yet, Indochina proved to be a false dawn. Two years later, the Suez crisis brutally exposed the limits of British independence of the United States in foreign affairs and led, in January 1957, to the end of Eden's short premiership. Thereafter, last-resortism, nestling between the extremes of obsequious obedience of Washington's will and damaging opposition to US policy, resumed its place as the compromise of choice for British policy-makers. 'If we cannot effectively change American ... policy, then we must, it seems to me, resign ourselves to a role of counsellor and moderator', Pierson Dixon wrote in 1951. 'But we should accept the disagreeable conclusion, in the end, that we must allow the U.S. to take the lead and follow, or at least not break with them. It is difficult for us, after several centuries of leading others, to resign ourselves to the position of allowing another and greater Power to lead us'. More difficult for Eden, it would seem, than for most.[89]

Notes

1. See Sean Greenwood, '"A War We Don't Want": another look at the British Labour Government's commitment in Korea, 1950–51', *Contemporary British History*, 17/4 (2003), pp. 1–24; Laura Belmonte, 'Anglo-American Relations and the dismissal of MacArthur', *Diplomatic History,* 19/4 (1995), pp. 641–67; Peter Lowe, 'An Ally and a Recalcitrant General: Great Britain, Douglas MacArthur and the Korean War, 1950–51', *English Historical Review,* 105/416 (1990), pp. 624–53; Michael Dockrill, 'The FO, Anglo-American Relations and the Korean War, June 1950–June 1951', *International Affairs*, 62/3 (1986), pp. 459–76; Rosemary Foot, 'Anglo-American Relations in the Korean Crisis: the British Effort to Avert an Expanded War, December 1950–January 1951', *Diplomatic History,* 10/1 (1986), pp. 43–57.
2. For a recent exception see Robert Barnes, 'Branding an aggressor: the Commonwealth, the United Nations and Chinese intervention in the Korean War', *Journal of Strategic Studies*, 33/2 (2010), pp. 231–253.
3. *Life,* MacArthur and Asia', 25 September 1950.
4. The National Archives (TNA), Kew, TNA/FO371/92067/2G, Dixon minute, 6 January 1951.
5. *Public Papers of the Presidents of the United States, 1950,* press conference, 30 November 1950, at http://trumanlibrary.org/publicpapers/viewpapers.php?pid=985
6. William Stueck, *Rethinking the Korean War* (Princeton: Princeton University Press, 2004), p. 125.
7. TNA/TNA/FO371/83019/13G, Washington to FO, 7 December 1950.
8. Ibid., Dixon to Bevin, 8 December 1950.
9. TNA/DEFE4/38, COS(50) 206th, 14 December 1950.
10. TNA/FO371/92767/80G, US memorandum, 4 January 1951.
11. TNA/FO371/92767/58G, Younger to Bevin, 2 January 1951; TNA/FO371/92756/23G, COS(51) 7th, 8 January 1951; TNA/CAB128/19 CM(51) 5th, 22 January 1951; *Documents on British Policy Overseas, Korea 1950–1951* (London: HMSO, 1991), (hereinafter *DBPO Korea*), 291, FO to Ankara, 12 January 1951.
12. TNA/CAB21/3269, COS to Washington, 29 December 1950.
13. TNA/FO371/92067/2G, Strang minute, 3 January 1951.
14. TNA/CAB128/19, CM(51)1st, 2 January 1951; PREM8/1439, Bevin to Attlee, 12 January 1951.
15. TNA/FO371/92766/47G, FO to Washington, 8 January 1951; Barnes, 'Branding', pp. 240, 245.
16. *Foreign Relations of the United States 1951*, Vol. VII (Washington: US Government Printing Office, 1983), (hereinafter *FRUS*), pp. 39–40.
17. TNA/FO371/92766/47G, Acheson to Bevin, 8 January 1951.
18. TNA/CAB195/8, CM(51)4th, 18 January 1951; PREM8/1439, Bevin to Attlee, 12 January 1951; TNA/FO371/92607/9G, COS(51)16th, 22 January 1951.
19. *DBPO Korea,* 308, New York to FO, 17 January 1951; TNA/FO371/92771/237G, Strang minute, 25 January 1951.
20. TNA/CAB128/19, CAB195/8, CM(50)4th, 18 January 1951.
21. *Ibid,* 4th and 5th, 18 and 22 January 1951; TNA/FO371/92768/101G and 104, FO telegrams to Washington and New York, 18 January 1951.

22. *DBPO Korea*, p. 321.
23. Geoffrey Warner, (ed.), *In the Midst of Events: the FO diaries and papers of Kenneth Younger, February 1950–October 1951* (London: Routledge, 2005), hereinafter *KYDP*, pp. 45–7, pp. 52–9.
24. Robert L. Beisner, *Dean Acheson* (Oxford: Oxford University Press, 2006), pp. 411, 423; *DBPO Korea*, pp. 322–6.
25. *KYPD*, pp. 53–57; TNA/FO371/92771/238, Strang to Younger, 25 January 1951.
26. Philip M. Williams, (ed.), *The Diary of Hugh Gaitskell 1945–1956* (London: Jonathan Cape, 1983), p. 230.
27. TNA/CAB128/19, CAB195/8, CM(51) 8th, 25 January 1951.
28. *KYDP*, p. 60.
29. TNA/CAB195/8, CM(51) 9th, 26 January 1951; TNA/FO371/92771/238, Strang to Younger, 25 January 1951; *DBPO Korea*, p. 334.
30. Williams, *Gaitskell*, pp. 225–32; Ben Pimlott, (ed.), *The Political Diary of Hugh Dalton, 1918–40, 1945–60* (London: Jonathan Cape, 1986), pp. 501–04.
31. TNA/CAB128/19, CAB195/8, CM(51) 9th, 26 January 1951.
32. Williams, *Gaitskell*, p. 232.
33. *KYDP*, p. 60.
34. William Stueck, *The Korean War: an international history* (Princeton; Princeton University Press, 1995), pp. 126, 129.
35. TNA/CAB128/19, CM(51) 10th, 29 January 1951; TNA/FO371/92771/215, 220, New York and Washington telegrams, 27 January 1951.
36. *DBPO Korea*, pp. 342 and 346.
37. *KYDP*, pp. 59 and 61.
38. Stueck, *History*, p. 157.
39. TNA/CAB129/44, CP(51)65, Younger memorandum, 1 March 1951; TNA/FO371/92809/44G, COS report, 21 March 1951; *DBPO Korea*, 387; TNA/FO371/92757/137G, FO telegram, 9 April 1951; *The Times*, 16 and 24 March, 7 April 1951.
40. *FRUS 1951*, Vol. VII, pp. 352–3; TNA/FO371/92063/16G, Acheson to Morrison, 1 May 1951.
41. TNA/CAB128/19, CAB195/8, CM(51) 33rd, 3 May 1951, and 35th, 10 May 1951.
42. *FRUS 1951*, Vol. VII, p. 296; TNA/FO371/92816/53, Jebb to Morrison, 14 April 1951; CAB21/3549, COS(51) 73rd, 30 April 1951.
43. TNA/CAB128/19, CM(51) 35th, 10 May 1951; *FRUS 1951*, Vol. VII, pp. 427–31.
44. TNA/CAB131/10–11, DO(51)102, COS memorandum, 7 September 1951, and DO(51) 22nd meeting, 10 September 1951; TNA/FO371/92810/77G, Makins to Attlee, 25 September 1951.
45. TNA/FO371/92758/70G, Tomlinson to Scott, 29 September, and reply, 10 October 1951.
46. TNA/FO371/92811/89G, COS(51) 171st, 30 November 1951.
47. *KYPD*, p. 96.
48. TNA/PREM11/112, Churchill to Eden, 16 November 1951.
49. TNA/FO371/92760/86G, Eden to Churchill, 19 December 1951.
50. Lord Moran, *Churchill: the Struggle for Survival 1940–65* (London: Constable, 1966), p. 355.
51. Kevin Ruane, 'Containing America: aspects of British Foreign Policy and the Cold War in South-East Asia, 1951–54', *Diplomacy & Statecraft*, 7/1 (1996), pp. 141–174.

52. TNA/FO371/92757/49G, FO telegram 1732, 22 November 1951; TNA/FO371 /92759/80G, FO telegram 1388, 5 December 1951.
53. TNA/FO371/92759/74G, 77G, Shattock minute, 23 November, and Dixon minute, 28 November 1951; PREM11/112, McLean to Alexander, 29 November 1951, and COS(S)(51) 3rd, 30 November 1951.
54. TNA/FO371/92759/75G and 76G, Rome to FO, 653 and 654, 29 November 1951; TNA/FO371/92759, Eden telegram 1432, 14 December 1951; TNA/CAB128 /23/CC(51) 16th and 19th, 11 and 20 December 1951.
55. TNA/FO371/92759/75G, Rome telegram 654, 29 November 1951; PREM11 /112, FO telegram 5, 2 January 1952.
56. TNA/PREM11/112, COS(S)(51) 3rd, 30 November 1951.
57. Harry S. Truman Library, Independence, Acheson Papers, Memoranda of Conversations series, Box 70, US–UK talks, 8 January 1952; TNA/CAB21/3057, US–UK talks, 8 January 1952; Evelyn Shuckburgh, *Descent to Suez: Diaries 1951–1956* (London: Weidenfeld and Nicolson, 1986), 32, January 1952.
58. *The Times*, 18 January 1952.
59. Richard Crossman, 'Churchill Comes to Washington', *New Statesman*, 19 January 1952.
60. Churchill Archives Centre, Cambridge, CHUR 2/517, Eden to Churchill, 6 January 1952; Nigel Nicholson, (ed.), *Harold Nicolson: Diaries and Letters 1945–62* (London, 1968), p. 222.
61. TNA/FO371/101259/22G, Strang minute, 21 January 1952; TNA/FO371 /101261/38G, COS(52) 38th, 11 March 1952; CAB131/12, D(52)13, COS memorandum, 25 April 1952.
62. TNA/CAB128/25, CAB195/10, CC(52) 62nd and 63rd, 24 and 26 June 1952; TNA/FO371/99577/343–344, Anglo–American talks, 26–27 June 1952; TNA /FO371/101058/78, Eden–Acheson meeting, 26 May 1952; Dean Acheson, *Present at the Creation* (New York: Norton, 1969), pp. 656–7.
63. TNA/FO371/125009/4, PUSD paper, 6 November 1952.
64. John W. Young, *Churchill's Last Campaign: Britain and the Cold War, 1951–1955* (Oxford: Oxford University Press, 1996), pp. 106–08.
65. TNA/FO462/6, FORD paper, 24 November 1952.
66. University of Birmingham Library, Avon Papers, AP20/1/27, Eden diary, 9 November 1952; TNA/FO371/103513/31, Dulles statement, 15 February 1953; Edward C. Keefer, 'President Dwight D. Eisenhower and the End of the Korean War', *Diplomatic History*, 10/3 (1986), p. 268.
67. Hansard, *House of Commons Debates*, 5th Series (*HC Deb*), Vol.518, col.895, 27 July 1953; TNA/FO371/103518/23G, Lloyd to Salisbury, 23 August 1953.
68. TNA/DEFE4/66, COS(53) 132nd meeting, 24 November, and JP(53)135(Final), 19 November 1953.
69. *The Times*, 8 August 1953.
70. Dwight D. Eisenhower Library (DDEL), Abilene, AWF International Series, Box 3, Eisenhower notes, 4 December 1953; Matthew Jones, 'US Nuclear Planning and "Massive Retaliation" in East Asia, 1953–1955', *Journal of Cold War Studies*, 10/4 (2008), p. 46.
71. Avon Papers, AP20/16/90, 91, Eden to Churchill, 4 and 7 December 1953; AP20/1/29, Eden note, undated; Shuckburgh, *Descent*, p. 114.
72. Jones, 'Nuclear Planning', p. 47.
73. DDEL, AWF International Series, Box 3, Eisenhower diary, 5 December 1953.

74. Saki Dockrill, *Eisenhower's New Look National Security Policy, 1953–61* (Basingstoke: Macmillan, 1996), pp. 19–71.
75. Jones, 'US Nuclear Planning', pp. 43–6; DDEL AWF International Series, Box 3, Eisenhower diary, 4–8 December 1953.
76. TNA/FO371/109135/1, Wenner minute, 18 January, and Maitland to Ross, 2 February 1954.
77. TNA/CAB131/14 D(54)8, Eden memorandum, 1 February, and D(54)5th, 14 April 1954.
78. *The Times,* 25 March 1954; PREM11/1074, Churchill to Eisenhower, 9 March 1954.
79. *The Times,* 30 March 1954.
80. TNA/FO371/112049/103G, FO-COS memorandum, 31 March 1954; TNA /DEFE4/69, COS(54) 36th, 31 March 1954.
81. For an exception, Matthew Jones, 'Great Britain, the United States, and Consultation over the Use of the Atomic Bomb', *Historical Journal,* 54/3 (2011), pp. 799, 827–8.
82. Shuckburgh, *Descent,* 171–72; TNA/FO371/112056/314G, Paris to FO, 24 April 1954.
83. TNA/CAB129/68, CAB195/12, C(54)155, 27 April 1954.
84. TNA/FO371/112060/454G, Colville to Makins, 28 April 1954.
85. TNA/FO371/112057/360G, Churchill–Radford dinner, 26 April 1954, and undated Eden minute.
86. Clarissa Eden, *A Memoir* (London: Weidenfeld and Nicolson, 2007), p. 160.
87. Avon Papers, AP20/45/49, Eden to Clarissa, 22 May 1954.
88. TNA/CAB128/27, CAB195/12, CC(54) 35th, 24 May 1954.
89. TNA/FO371/92067/8G, Dixon minute, 28 January 1951.

5

'To Stay or to Walk': The British and the Defence of Domestic Jurisdiction at the United Nations, 1950–56

Edward Johnson

When the United Nations (UN) first convened in January 1946, the Labour government of Clement Attlee had already said that it intended to put the new organisation at the heart of foreign policy.[1] However, by late 1946, Britain accepted that the UN was not likely to be the forum for international peace it had first hoped. The onset of Cold War tensions seeped into the Security Council from day one of its proceedings, seen most clearly in the Soviet Union's use of the veto. British disappointment in, and frustration with, the UN was not however confined to the proceedings of the Security Council. They also discovered, to their irritation, that the UN General Assembly, its Fourth Committee and the delegations to it, had a tendency to seek to confer a UN supervisory role in all colonial territories and thus pervert the Charter. This was noted as early as the second part of the First Session of the General Assembly in 1946 by the Colonial Secretary, Arthur Creech Jones.[2] This continued to be a source of annoyance to the British who looked for American support, often without success, to prevent discussion of colonial issues spreading across the UN. By 1950, Britain's permanent representative at the UN, Sir Alexander Cadogan, had indicated that relations with the US in the UN, while generally very good, were, over colonial issues, often a source of disagreement, with the Americans supporting the British line infrequently.[3] This was to continue throughout the following decade, one in which the British were to find themselves running against a tide of opinion in the UN over colonial issues and which presented them with some major diplomatic predicaments.

The issue of UN jurisdiction

Britain's difficulty specifically derived from the UN exercising its rights in the Trust territories and the colonies, or non-self-governing territories. The UN Charter had established an *active* role for the organisation in relation to those in the first category: Trust territories were administered under a mandate by a UN member. In these, the UN's purpose was 'to promote the political, economic, social and educational advancement'[4] of the inhabitants towards the development of political independence. In the cases of Togoland, Tanganyika and British Cameroon, the British were the administering power and had a duty to cooperate with the UN's Trusteeship Council. The other UN role was, from the position of the Charter, more *passive*. It applied to those colonial territories, the imperial possessions of Britain, France, Belgium, the Netherlands and Portugal. Article 73 exhorted those powers to assist the peoples of their dependent territories 'in the progressive development of their free political institutions, according to the particular circumstances of each territory.' The article also required the colonial powers to transmit information on technical, social and educational matters to the Secretary General. But this excluded political information. In the Trusteeship Council, there was a right to hear petitions and reports from individuals and groups within the Trust territory and organise fact finding visits: no such provision applied to the colonies.

The problem, which Creech Jones had noticed by 1946, was the tendency of the General Assembly's Fourth Committee, which received reports from the Trusteeship Council, to include in its Trusteeship discussions, consideration of colonial territories. Thus there was a blurring of the boundaries between what was legitimate UN business and what, to the colonial powers, was of no concern to the UN: the management of the imperial possessions. By 1960 the General Assembly, with a markedly larger number of newly-independent African states as members, was able to pass *The Declaration on the Granting of Independence to Colonial Countries and Peoples*, as resolution 1514(XV) of 15th December. After this date, the UN took a shift towards greater formal involvement in the political future of the colonies and their relationships with their colonial powers and as such it amounted to, in effect, a hidden amendment to the Charter. Yet, prior to this, the European colonial powers were fighting a rearguard action to prevent UN discussion while fully accepting that it would be involved in the development of the Trust territories. In general, the case against UN involvement was political, but the British also used a legal argument: that the management of the colonies was an internal matter and that article 2(7) of the UN Charter, covering domestic jurisdiction, precluded UN involvement or interference.

In the original drafts for the UN Charter, which had been tabled at the Dumbarton Oaks Conference in 1944, the idea of domestic jurisdiction was not covered: it formed neither part of the American nor British proposals.[5] However, it was not unusual for international treaties to exclude any reference to internal matters of signatory parties and the League of Nations Covenant had, in article 15(8), issued a self-denying ordinance in respect of disputes between parties where the origins lay 'solely within the domestic jurisdiction' of one of them. The question of protecting domestic jurisdiction seems to have been raised very generally at Dumbarton Oaks by Ben Cohen, a member of the US delegation to the Joint Steering Committee of British, American and Soviet representatives.[6] It was later refined by Cadogan, the British representative, when he proposed that the Security Council should, in its procedures for settling disputes through peaceful means, exclude any matters which were solely within the domestic jurisdiction of states. This was accepted by the Americans and, later, by the Russians.[7] Cadogan, with an eye on the post-war management of the Empire, wished to keep the UN at arm's length from British commitments but at the time, Gladwyn Jebb, a future head of the British delegation to the UN, thought it understandable that the UN would wish to become involved in domestic matters that might disturb international peace.[8] The question seemed to have been settled at the San Francisco Conference in 1945. Here, the four sponsoring states transferred the question from the section on pacific settlement to the chapter on principles, indicating that protection of domestic jurisdiction was to run through the whole of the UN and, further, that the only exception to the principle of non intervention in domestic matters was to be, as article 2(7) in its final form indicated, those involving enforcement measures under Chapter VII.[9] Thus the UN would be limited in its interventionist role. Yet, in spite of this, those such as the Australians, New Zealanders and South Africans were fearful that the UN might, at some future date, seek to ride roughshod over domestic matters, fears that were to be well founded.

The defence of article 2(7) remained the basis of the British case against the UN discussion of colonial issues in either the General Assembly or the Fourth Committee from 1946. However, within ten years the Foreign Office had changed its position in respect of one colony appearing as an item for discussion on the agenda of the General Assembly: Cyprus. By then, it assumed that Britain would lose any vote to exclude Cyprus from discussion, and it would be better to abstain while making the case that it reserved the right to oppose UN intervention in colonial matters. The change in the British approach was significant: it was borne of a recognition that political forces were moving against the colonial powers and the defence of article 2(7) was becoming ever more difficult. However in making that defence before 1956, the British were to be pulled in different directions by the Americans, who were generally keen to take a more flexible stand on article 2(7). This position was not shared by Britain's colonial NATO allies, France, Belgium and Portugal. The defence also called up tensions within the Commonwealth between those 'old' members: New Zealand, Australia and South Africa who took a less sympathetic and even hostile attitude to the UN, and India, Pakistan and Ceylon who were in the vanguard of leading the attack on the colonial powers. Even within Whitehall, there was some discord between the Foreign Office (FO), which tried to temper its frustration with the UN, and the more inflexible Colonial Office (CO), for whom the UN and particularly its Fourth Committee could do little right.

Foreign Office and Colonial Office approaches

By 1950, the British had indications of the intervening intentions of some UN members in the Fourth Committee. Then, a joint Indian and Pakistan draft resolution sought to streamline its work, but without differentiating its responsibilities in respect of Trusteeship issues and colonial territories. The British, while fully in support of efficiency, opposed the initiative even from these two Commonwealth members. London feared the gradual adoption of accountability for colonies by the Fourth Committee and eventually the General Assembly. In particular, the CO saw the resolution as giving the Indian government a licence to meddle: India was 'the most dangerous of the anti-colonial members' of the UN. Not only was it a fellow Commonwealth member, but its criticisms of colonialism were always given in a courteous and reasonable manner unlike those of strident anti-colonialists, such as Cuba or the Philippines. The Indians posed, therefore, an insidious threat and the British wanted the role of the Fourth Committee to be reduced thereby removing, 'opportunities for spectacular attacks on the Colonial powers'.[10] British concerns were sharpened the following year, when an Iraqi draft resolution in the Fourth Committee called directly for the affairs of colonial territories to be discussed. This was part of an Arab approach to widen the Committee's responsibility, previously signalled by its intent to discuss Morocco, an initiative which led to a French walk out. In light of Iraq's *démarche,* Winston Churchill, recently restored as Prime Minister, had given approval, without having time to refer to the Cabinet, for the British delegation to withdraw from the Committee if the resolution were adopted.[11] This threat of a walk out, with which the Colonial Office concurred, was not exercised, since the resolution was withdrawn before put to a vote, but the spectre of further intervention by the UN was clearly hovering.

In this context, the CO, seeking a clearer line on formal British policy particularly with regard to the Fourth Committee and the question of possible withdrawal, prepared a brief in March 1952. The subsequent discussion with the FO indicated the divisions over the prospect of a withdrawal from the proceedings of the UN. The CO view was that the head of the British delegation to the UN, or the Minister of State in attendance, should be given the authority to walk out from proceedings and be given notice of that authority *beforehand,* not merely when the question of discussion of colonial issues arose.[12] This signified the entrustment of powers from London to the British delegation in New York and was received without much enthusiasm by officials in the UN department of the FO, who saw it as far too rigid.[13] Selwyn Lloyd, the Minister of State, considered any *carte blanche* walkout tended to make the 'walkers-out' look ridiculous, although he did recognise that there might come a time when 'we shall have to refuse to have anything more to do with the work of the 4th Committee'.[14] In those circumstances, Lloyd did not feel prior authority should be given *publicly*. If the head of the delegation was devolved that power it would make sense only for him or her to know it, not the rest of the delegation – and certainly not others, those 'anti-colonial extremists' who might then deliberately force Britain into a difficult diplomatic position of having to withdraw. It was, in short for Lloyd, 'extremely dangerous' to build one's policy in the Fourth Committee on the basis of a walkout. Echoing these sentiments, the head of the UN department, Paul Mason, doubted that Anthony Eden, the Foreign Secretary, would 'bind himself to so rigid a procedure' as the CO proposed, rather expecting that a decision be taken on the merits of each case.[15] With this however, the CO was neither impressed nor satisfied[16] and, in the face of a departmental divide, Eden put the matter to Cabinet for clarification.

On 31st July 1952, the Cabinet discussed the Foreign Office memorandum, *Handling of Colonial Questions at the United Nations: the Question of Withdrawal in Certain Circumstances.*[17] The issue was not a straightforward one, as the paper acknowledged. The threat of withdrawal or its actuality, as a defence of domestic jurisdiction, might make some

UN members more reticent in their anti-colonialist approach and such a line would have the support of the fellow colonial powers and NATO members: France, Belgium and Portugal. However, withdrawal might prove an empty gesture, given that those of the French and South Africans in 1951 appeared to have been ineffective. It would not only put the British in the same light as them, but also of the other 'walker', the Soviet Union.[18] It might also undermine the idea of the UN as a forum in which differences were aired, precisely what the Foreign Office had always seen of value in the UN. Yet, the memorandum recognised there were some UN ambitions that would have to be resisted. Its 'right' to discuss colonial questions and establish any form of accountability for the management of colonies, receiving petitions from them, granting oral hearings or sending missions could not be conceded. Although the 'manoeuvre of withdrawal' was 'distasteful', the Foreign Office recommended the need to consider it as a last resort. Under Eden's guidance the Cabinet authorised the head of the British delegation to the UN to be given *prior* authority to *threaten* to withdraw from discussions in UN forums where Britain's colonial position was in danger of being discussed, but requiring political clearance from London before *actual* withdrawal took place, except in extreme circumstances.[19] Thus any application of these 'rights' of UN intervention should trigger the withdrawal or its threat as agreed by the Cabinet. However, what was envisaged was a limited withdrawal, related only to that particular case: it did not appear to cover a general withdrawal by Britain from all discussions of colonial affairs in the UN.

The approach of friends and allies

If the CO had no firm ally in the FO, it could perhaps have taken solace from the attitudes of France and Belgium. The French had experience of walking out in 1951, over Egyptian criticism of its administration of Morocco, an action which Selwyn Lloyd, thought 'most foolish'.[20] The Belgians were even more sensitive to the UN's creeping interference in colonial matters and in the light of this, both states took the line that by 1952, the time had come 'to call a halt to the encroachments of the United Nations…over the administration of colonial territories'[21] and sought a common approach to present with the British. This posed some problems for the British however. It became clear, in tripartite discussions, that the Belgians were more hostile to the UN than the CO and any attempts by the Europeans to present a united front at the UN would lead to potential embarrassment for the British who were keen to portray themselves as less rigid than their colonial partners. They therefore declined to include them in any discussions they had with the Americans about the approach to take in the UN.[22]

The relationship with the Americans over colonial issues at the UN was never easy for the British, as both Cadogan and Jebb noted in their annual reports. As allies, they stood fairly solidly in the Security Council against the obstructive and Cold War tactics of the Soviet Union, yet the relationship did not go so deep in the General Assembly, nor its Fourth Committee. For the Americans, the question of domestic jurisdiction was one which generated potentially conflicting views of the role of the UN. They, as much as any, wished to be protected from any outside intrusion in their domestic affairs. They had some experience of this, as it was an American initiative at Versailles in 1919 which, through Article 15(8) of the League of Nations Covenant, had raised the protection of domestic jurisdiction. This was to preclude any US Senate objection to the possible interference of the League into American internal affairs.[23] On the other hand, the US was a driving force behind the new UN and wished, perhaps more than any of the four sponsoring governments, to bring about a different form of international politics and behaviour in the post-war world, with the UN given more licence than its predecessor.

By 1949, the differences in the General Assembly were already becoming evident as Cadogan noted, with the British and American delegations only voting in the same way in two out of seventeen resolutions on colonial matters.[24] On the question of the Iraqi draft resolution in 1951, Washington had been conscious of the pressure to stand with the British and the French. But the Americans were also driven by their dislike of colonialism, as something to be eradicated from the new post-war world, and by domestic US public and Press opinion, which tended to side with the anti-colonialists.[25] They were aware that the British, and the French, considered their support in the Fourth Committee lukewarm and were in the event content to see the Iraqi resolution withdrawn, rather than to 'have to stand in support of the right of the Fourth Committee to discuss the political aspects of the economic, social and educational problems presented to it'.[26] The British were less than enamoured of this equivocation, placing the responsibility at the door of the diplomats in the American delegation to the UN, many of whom exhibited a strong liberal, anti-colonial make up. In particular, the US representative on the Fourth Committee, Channing Tobias, a black American, was seen by some in the Foreign Office and even in the US State Department, for all his abilities, as a mistaken appointment given that colonialism and the position of indigenous peoples formed much of the Committee's work.[27]

Others saw the authors of the difficulties, not in the US delegation bending the instructions from the State Department, but in the wider US government whose diplomatic stance was duplicitous. In this view, the Americans:

> instead of facing up to a difference of opinion with us, often palm us off with alibis within their own ranks e.g. they blame the 'negro vote' or Mrs. Roosevelt etc. etc. I don't think this is playing the game although it has the appearance of taking us into their confidence. I think we should insist on treating whichever American we are dealing with as a responsible American spokesman and rub their noses in the difficulties.[28]

The Americans were unwilling to participate in formalised meetings with the British prior to the annual General Assembly for fear of being thought part of a colonial bloc in the UN.[29] This American sensitivity towards colonialism was, as Jebb noted, augmented by their 'profound uncritical belief in free discussion', their certainty of the unstoppable force of nationalism and the concessions they were prepared to make to Asians and Arabs in return for support in the Cold War.[30] Added to this, the State Department lawyers took the view that mere discussion in the UN did not constitute intervention, and therefore did not breach domestic jurisdiction, a point which the Foreign Office legal advisor, Gerald Fitzmaurice was able to demolish in a later memorandum on the defence of article 2(7).[31]

A further complicating factor in the assessment of tactics to adopt in the UN was the role of Commonwealth states, in particular South Africa. In November 1951, the South Africa delegation had walked out of the Trusteeship Council over the dispute that South West Africa was not a mandated territory and therefore not subject to oversight from the Council, which had invited tribal chiefs to the UN to give evidence to it. South Africa used the defence of article 2(7) for this and for any attempts by the UN to discuss its *apartheid* policies. In September 1952, after the Cabinet had agreed the policy over a walkout, information was received that the Indian delegation was to press for South Africa's racial policies to be included on the General Assembly's agenda, which might force another South African walkout.[32] What was to be the British line in the UN, caught as they might be between two Commonwealth members? The Commonwealth Relations Office (CRO) sought guidance from the Cabinet through its paper *Relations with the Union of South Africa in the context of the United Nations*[33], in which it noted the significance of three factors. The first was that Britain had to maintain its own rights as a colonial power in the UN: it could not allow the UN a 'right' to intervene in any colonial administration, nor should it be given any encouragement to do so. At the same time, the British had to maintain their reputation as champions of liberal western civilisation; any move which appeared to endorse South Africa's position could create difficulties with Afro-Asian opinion and offend Indian and Pakistani feelings. Countering this was the strategic importance of the Simonstown naval base, and South Africa's value as both a source of key raw materials and an important market for British exports. In the event of a public British stand against the South Africans in the UN, the British High Commission territories of Basutoland, Swaziland and Bechuanaland could all have been on fragile ground economically, effectively held hostage by an irritated South Africa.

The CRO paper advised the British delegation to the UN that it might indicate its intention to vote against the inclusion of racial policies on the agenda of the UN and use its discretion to vote against, or abstain on, any resolutions subsequently proposed in debate. The Cabinet approved the CRO paper, including the recommendation to vote against inscription of the racial policy question if necessary, while recognising the delicate position the UN was placed in by South Africa.[34] The question created further complications because the British faced the problem that, having been prepared to support South Africa in defence of its domestic jurisdiction, they could be seen as hypocritical if they did not stand firm in other cases: one such being Tunisia in 1952. There, the French were prepared to acquiesce in it appearing on the agenda of the General Assembly. The CRO feared Britain might be thought of as playing fast and loose with article 2(7), if they overlooked domestic jurisdiction when one of their allies, France, felt able to deal with criticism in the UN, yet cynically invoked it in defence of a friend, South Africa, 'who has not get (sic) the moral courage to face open criticism'.[35] In the light of this, the CRO wanted more consistency to be applied, otherwise the British would find themselves in deep water. However, the FO felt it was difficult for the British to portray themselves as more dogmatic than the French over their own colony: they could not be more Royalist than the King![36] These very real stresses on the British were aggravated, later in 1952, when Belgium, a NATO partner and fellow colonial power, began to criticise the Indian government for its treatment of the Andaman and Nicobar islanders. This was itself a domestic matter, but one deliberately chosen by the Belgian government as a counter to the Indians. The British Ambassador in Brussels, not wishing Britain to be seen as close to Belgium, was prepared to press them to desist most forcefully.[37]

Seeking a firmer stance

In 1953, the CO wished once more to push for straight withdrawal, without any prior threat, from all discussions in the UN relating to colonial territories, but did not expect ministerial approval for this widening of the 1952 Cabinet decision.[38] Not only did the brief which was prepared to guide the British delegation in New York, not go further than the 1952 Cabinet decision on withdrawal but, to the disappointment of the CO, it also was unclear about what was meant by withdrawal. Was it limited to the discussion which had triggered it, or was a withdrawal to be more general and applied to all areas of the UN forums where colonial matters might be raised?[39] In the event, the British were forced to go rather further than the brief suggested, as a result of the Indian delegation raising the question of the Central African Federation (CAF) in the Fourth Committee, in October 1953. Although the Indian government had agreed with the British against this course of action, one of its delegation, Mrs Menon, broke cover and pressed for political information on the CAF, a breach, as the British saw it, of article 2(7).[40] In the proceedings of the Committee, Lord Hudson, for the CO, not only delivered a diplomatic dressing down to Menon, but warned the Committee that any discussion of the political affairs of the CAF would bring into question Britain's willingness to cooperate with it. This was a significant step beyond the Cabinet position of 1952 and one which could be interpreted as a forewarning of complete withdrawal from the Committee.[41] Hudson's Minister of State, Henry Hopkinson, suggested that the Cabinet decision of 1952 had in mind the need for Britain to cease cooperation with the UN on all colonial matters in the face of an approach like Menon's. Eden rejected this, noting that Hopkinson was 'not always a wise guide in these matters'.[42]

However, there is evidence that Eden and the FO were ready to toughen their stance. In order to head off any further embarrassment, the CO urged that Selwyn Lloyd, who was in New York, be authorised to withdraw the delegation from the Fourth Committee *without further reference* to London, as discussions on the CAF might arise without notice. This, too, marked an extension of the 1952 Cabinet decision but, in what seems a reversal of his more conciliatory line of 1952, Lloyd supported this and Eden agreed.[43] In the event of such a withdrawal, the CO and Lloyd wanted to go further and be allowed to warn the Fourth Committee that a point would have been reached, 'a parting of the waves', where Britain would have to review its position of participating in the work of the Fourth Committee – a restatement of Hudson's threat.[44] It was a warning which, in the event, did not have to be made but, significantly, it was one of which the Foreign Office was now ready to approve.[45] Eden's willingness to sanction withdrawal without further reference to London indicates the seriousness with which the British viewed the continuing UN pressure on it.

The question of how to manage a possible withdrawal also had to be considered. The reluctance of some in the Foreign Office not to abandon the Fourth Committee completely, was shown when Lloyd, again in a somewhat contrary fashion, suggested that the delegation might withdraw from the Committee while leaving the most junior official in the front seat, under orders to remain silent! Britain was coming under pressure from Canada and Norway not to leave yet. After much discussion, Eden overruled Lloyd who was ordered to ensure that, if the British did withdraw from the Committee, it would be a complete one: the anti-colonial powers wanted a presence in order to attack the British and an empty chair would deny them this luxury. An occupied seat would, moreover, appear to make withdrawal an idle threat and weaken the British case. If the British were to go, they had to go completely.[46] Happily for the delegation, it was spared the potential embarrassment of this action. Menon, although asked by the chair of the Fourth Committee to make no comment on colonial policies, did proceed to do so, but only to make a rather 'woolly' survey of developments in Britain's west African colonies, without calling for specific information from the British government.[47]

A change of policy

The position of firmness was reinforced, in 1954, when the Cyprus question appeared as an issue of domestic jurisdiction for the first time in the UN. The Greek government, seeking to draw international attention to Cyprus, with which it had ambitions of forming a union, attempted to raise it for discussion on the agenda of the General Assembly.[48] For the British, Cyprus was not merely a colonial question. Its significance was amplified by its strategic position as part of Britain's defence commitment to NATO. It was assumed to lie at a vital strategic point between Europe, Africa and the Middle East, playing an important role in the defence of Western oil interests and part of a set of military bases helping to contain the Soviet Union. Moreover, as the Suez Canal zone was to be evacuated in 1956, its significance was expected to grow.[49] Discussion of the Cyprus case in the UN would allow the Soviet Union licence to cause mischief. The British, therefore, thought it preferable that any consideration of a political settlement of Cyprus be shielded from public scrutiny.[50]

The British Cabinet decided to oppose inscription in the UN, confident that France and Belgium would provide political support in defence of article 2(7), but unsure of the American attitude.[51] The US appetite for open diplomacy in the UN, and past experience of American sensitivity towards colonial questions, left the British doubtful about Washington's position. Their fears were not ungrounded. In discussions in June 1954, Eden was convinced that the Secretary of State, John Foster Dulles, was either unaware of the sensitivity of Cyprus to the British or poorly briefed. Having sent an *aide-memoire* to Washington in January seeking American assurances over Cyprus, the British had to wait until July for a reply and when it arrived it failed to offer any promise of political support.[52] That same month, the CO Assistant Under-Secretary, Harry Bourdillon, sought State Department support, indicating that Cyprus would be the 'touchstone' of the ninth General Assembly for the British. He gave notice that they would withdraw from discussions if Cyprus was inscribed on the UN agenda and even raised the possibility of a re-appraisal of Britain's policy of cooperation with the UN in colonial matters.[53] In fact, Bourdillon was rather free in his interpretation of what the Cabinet had already agreed. Having been forewarned of Greek intentions, it had decided that in the event of inscription of the Cyprus case, the head of the British delegation be permitted to threaten to withdraw from discussions in the UN. But, this threat was only to be implemented after prior reference to London. This was a restatement of the 1952 Cabinet decision and an indication that the 1953 licence given to the head of the delegation had not been extended.[54] Yet again, however, the threats were not required. Although Cyprus was inscribed on the agenda against British protests, the Churchill government was able to get the issue talked out, by calling on the support of the New Zealand delegation to table a procedural resolution 'not to discuss' the Cyprus case any further. The Americans abstained on the inscription of Cyprus rather than vote with Britain, an act which severely disappointed Churchill to the extent that he sent President Eisenhower a personal telegram indicating his 'deep distress' at America's failure to support its ally in the UN.[55]

The fact that the British did not withdraw from the General Assembly, in spite of the inscription of the Cyprus item, indicated the anomalies of the instructions sent to the British delegation in New York. There was uncertainty over the 1952 Cabinet decision: did it hold for all sessions, or had it been limited in time? Consequently, the Cabinet Steering Committee on International Organisations prepared a master brief for 1955 to clarify the position. This reflected real differences between the Foreign and Colonial Offices over withdrawal but lent towards the compromise position of the former.[56] For the FO, the 1952 Cabinet decision had only applied to that session, even though Eden had agreed to its extension in 1953. It opposed the *general* policy towards UN discussion of its colonial territories being based on the *specifics* of the 1953 instructions to the Minister of State in regard to the CAF question. Consequently, as far as the Foreign Office was concerned, a limited withdrawal could be authorised *in extremis* without reference to London, but any major withdrawal or its threat, even *in extremis*, required approval from London.[57] The CO believed the FO had compromised on withdrawal and considered its interpretation of the 1952 Cabinet decision wrong: where the FO felt it was limited in time and scope, the CO considered it long standing and that it covered a major withdrawal.[58]

Given these divisions, the British were fortunate that the Cyprus case was not inscribed in 1955 and that the differences could remain dormant. The Eisenhower administration was reluctant to inflame divisions in the UN forums between two NATO states and the question of Cyprus was thus shelved. Yet, Dulles was opposed only to the timing of the Cyprus question being discussed, not the principle, noting it was 'contrary to our general policy to oppose inscription'.[59] In contrast, the French did what the British had yet to do and walked out of the General Assembly after Algeria had been inscribed on the agenda. But for the British representative at the UN, Pierson Dixon, 'it had not been a bad year for colonial questions'. Then again, he realised any victory might be short lived: the American position might not hold and the arrival of new members in the Assembly would surely complicate the discussion of colonial matters in the years to come.[60]

In spite of the American refusal to support discussion of Cyprus in 1955, the Foreign Office came to the conclusion that the US stance could not be taken for granted. The likelihood was that Britain would at some point in the future lose a vote on Cyprus and be unable to talk out the matter procedurally: there had after all been an indication of the way the wind was blowing in 1954. The Cyprus case was already becoming internationalised with the influence of Greece on one side and Turkey on the other and, from April 1955, the British were fighting a counter-insurgency operation against the pro-Greek EOKA movement. The FO thus took the startling decision in 1956, that it would no longer oppose inscription of the Cyprus item on the basis that it contravened article 2(7), but rather go on the offensive and seek to discredit the Greek case in the forums of the UN. To do this, in a clear reversal of the defence of article 2(7), the British were prepared to table their own resolution on Cyprus. Far from seeking to deny the UN the chance to discuss colonial issues, the FO were now actively participating in those discussions. However, the FO wanted it known that this approach did not prejudice Britain's general case over domestic jurisdiction and the defence of article 2(7).[61] This not only produced misgivings from Commonwealth states, but also from the CO and the CRO.

The South African government was concerned that article 2(7) was becoming something of a dead letter and even warned, with one eye on its *apartheid* policy, that it might reconsider its future in the UN if 2(7) were not defended.[62] The Australian and New Zealand delegations to the UN also had grave reservations about the British decision seeing it as the thin end of a wedge.[63] These Commonwealth states, having been steadfast in support of Britain's defence of domestic jurisdiction, were now being told it did not matter. They had support from the CRO, which wanted more consideration of their position especially as the British decision had not gone to Cabinet.[64] In the CO, there was further disquiet over the decision which, 'might encourage other attacks' on the principle of defending domestic jurisdiction and in these circumstances it would be necessary to 'stop the rot from spreading'.[65] However, as the Foreign Office noted, there were more Commonwealth states (Canada, Ceylon, India and Pakistan) who supported the British change of heart than opposed it.[66] The difficulty for the British was made more acute as it was Australia and New Zealand which provided diplomatic support in the UN over Suez in the same year. The discussion of the Cyprus question for that UN session was resolved by a resolution from, of all quarters, India, expressing the desire for peace in Cyprus through negotiations including all parties.[67]

The British were by now coming to the conclusion that, where there was sufficient political momentum in the UN to discuss colonial questions, it was, especially with the attitude of the United States, becoming far more difficult to threaten to withdraw from the proceedings as the French and South Africans had done in previous years. Subsequent briefs in defence of article 2(7) for the British delegation contained some important common features. Inscription was to be opposed (even though it had not been in the case of Cyprus) and a threat of limited withdrawal could be made *in extremis* without prior reference to London, but no threat of a major withdrawal could be made without such reference.[68] Yet the change of approach, not to oppose inscription over Cyprus in 1956, had removed much of the force of the British case for the defence of domestic jurisdiction. Their position over an actual, or merely a threat of, withdrawal from UN forums would have been even more delicate after the Suez crisis of 1956. Having vetoed two resolutions in the Security Council and placed themselves, for many UN members, in the same moral space as France and Israel, with their actions in Egypt, and the Soviet Union, with its invasion of Hungary, the British could not afford any further erosion of their standing and reputation in the UN. The need to regain some honourable position in the UN constrained Britain from forcing a showdown over colonial questions generally, and the defence of domestic jurisdiction in particular. In response the British found to their relief that in the years following Suez and the inscription of Cyprus, their position over colonial questions was less exposed than those of France, Portugal, Belgium and South Africa, all of whom provided easier targets for the anti-colonialists than did London.[69]

Conclusion

Thus, the British never did walk out from the UN over the defence of domestic jurisdiction. It seems somewhat extraordinary, having discussed in quite fine detail what might trigger a threat or even an actual withdrawal, that when opposition to the inscription of the Cyprus question appeared to be a lost cause, the British chose not to walk but rather to stay. The threat of withdrawal, or its actuality, would have been a diplomatic gesture from which the British might have gained some gratuitous, if momentary, satisfaction. But the substantive questions would still have remained and the British, as with the French and South Africans, would have had to return to the UN forums at some point. It was perhaps this that led Selwyn Lloyd to consider remaining with some physical presence when the threat came closest to being activated following Menon's apparent commitment to raise the CAF issue in the Fourth Committee in 1953. That Eden was prepared to consider walking out at that time reveals the extremes to which even the FO felt it was being pushed at the UN. Within Whitehall, for most of the time, there was generally a more conciliatory line that cooperation with the UN over colonial affairs was preferable to confrontation, whereas the CO was less willing to afford the UN any licence to infringe domestic jurisdiction. Meanwhile, the

CRO had the responsibility of balancing the opponents of article 2(7) – Canada, India, Pakistan and Ceylon – against its defenders – Australia, New Zealand and South Africa. The British government had also to take into account the approach of the French and the Belgians, fellow colonial powers and NATO allies, whose positions on article 2(7) were even more extreme than the CO. It was however, as so often with British policy in the UN in the 1950s, Washington's approach that was a key factor in influencing London. The British could never successfully rely on the Americans standing with them over the defence of domestic jurisdiction. This, plus the changing membership of the UN from 1955, with the increase in Afro-Asian states following colonial independence, revealed the way the political and diplomatic wind was blowing. In the face of such a change, the defence of article 2(7) through a threat of, or actual, walkout proved increasingly difficult to sustain.

Notes

1. The National Archives (TNA), Kew, FO371/50891/U8810, Attlee speech to the UN Association, Albert Hall, 10 October 1945.
2. TNA/CAB129/16, CP(47)5, 16 January 1947, *Report on Trusteeship and Supply of Information on Non-Self-Governing Territories.*
3. TNA/FO371/88392/UP107/1, *The United Nations: Annual Review of United Kingdom Delegation for 1949,* 15 April 1950.
4. UN Charter, Article 76b.
5. For the American proposals see Department of State, *Postwar Foreign Policy Preparation, 1939–1945* (Washington: US Government Printing Office, 1949), pp. 595–606. For the British ones, *Future World Organisation,* can be found at TNA/CAB66/52, WP(44) 370, 3 July 1944.
6. *Foreign Relations of the United States* (hereinafter *FRUS*), *1944,* Vol. I, *General,* (Washington: US Government Printing Office, 1966), p. 791.
7. *FRUS 1944,* vol. 1, p. 808 and pp. 838–839.
8. TNA/FO371/50809/ U4014, Jebb minute on Sir William Malkin's paper regarding domestic jurisdiction, 17 November 1944.
9. See the minutes of the 70th meeting, US delegation to the San Francisco Conference: *FRUS, 1945,* Vol. I, *General: the United Nations* (Washington: US Government Printing Office, 1967), pp. 1275–76.
10. See the 1951 Colonial Office brief prepared for the British delegation to the UN: TNA/CAB134/412, IOC(51)157, 26 October 1951.
11. TNA/PREM11/302, Strang to Eden, 26 November 1951.
12. TNA/FO371/101363/UP243/39, Colonial Office memorandum, *Note on tendencies in, and United Kingdom policy towards, the Fourth Committee,* February 1952.
13. TNA/FO371/101363/UP243/39, comments by Cecil Parrott, the Head of the UN Department and Paul Mason, its Superintending Under-Secretary, 3–4 March 1952.

14. TNA/FO371/101363/UP243/49, Selwyn Lloyd minute, 16 April 1952.
15. TNA/FO371/101363/UP243/39, Mason minute, 4 March 1952.
16. TNA/FO371/101363/UP243/48, Dunnett memorandum, 14 March 1952.
17. TNA/CAB129/53, C(52) 232, 8 July 1952.
18. The Soviet Union had walked out of the Security Council in January 1950 as a protest against the continuing inclusion of the Nationalist Chinese government and the exclusion of the newly formed Communist regime.
19. TNA/CAB128/25, CC(52) 75th, 31 July 1952.
20. TNA/FO371/101363/UP243/49, Selwyn Lloyd minute, 16 April 1952.
21. TNA/FO371/101394/UP2428/2, Hope to Jellicoe, 19 May 1952.
22. TNA/FO371/101394/UP2428/4, Parrott minute on Anglo–French–Belgian talks on Colonial Questions in the UN, 6 June 1952.
23. David Hunter Miller, *The Drafting of the Covenant*, vol. I (New York: Putnams, 1928), p. 276.
24. TNA/FO371/88392/UP107/1, *The United Nations: Annual Review of United Kingdom Delegation for 1949,* 15 April 1950, p. 6.
25. See the US Delegation to the UN's Working Paper on the competence of the 4th Committee, 23 November 1951, in *FRUS, 1951*, Vol. II, *The United Nations, the Western Hemisphere* (Washington: US Government Printing Office, 1979), pp. 663–665.
26. See the minutes of the US delegation to the UN, 26 November 1951, *FRUS, 1951*, Vol. II, pp. 671–672.
27. TNA/FO371/101363/UP243/32, Parrott to Hope, 4 February 1952.
28. TNA/FO371/101363/UP243/32, Dunnett's minute, 9 February 1952.
29. See informal meeting of British and American Officials in Washington, 25 September 1952: *FRUS 1952–1954*, vol. III, *United Nations Affairs* (Washington: US Government Printing Office, 1979), pp. 1258–1263.
30. TNA/FO371/107023/UP109/1, Jebb despatch, 11 June 1953.
31. TNA/CAB134/952, IOC (53) 175, 17 September 1953.
32. TNA/FO371/101331/UP2017/15, Delhi to CRO, 11 September 1952.
33. TNA/CAB129/55, C(52) 306, 24 September 1952.
34. TNA/CAB128/25, CC(52) 81st, 26 September 1952.
35. TNA/FO371/101331, UP2017/25, Cleary to Williams, 17 September 1952.
36. TNA/FO371/101384. UP2411/48, Record of the FO, CO and CRO meetings, 16 September 1952.
37. TNA/FO371/107064/UP243/1, Jellicoe to FO, 29 December 1952.
38. TNA/CO936/354, Hanrott minute, 7 May 1956, summarising the 1952 and 1953 approaches.
39. TNA/CAB134/952, IOC(53)148, 11 September 1953.
40. TNA/FO371/107111/UP2435/9, Mathieson minute, 23 October 1953.
41. TNA/FO371/107112/UP2435/38, Hudson speech, 26 October 1953.
42. TNA/FO371/107112/UP2435/20, Eden's marginal comments to Cope minute, 11 November 1953.
43. TNA/FO371/107111/UP2435/15, Cope's minute and Eden's agreement, 3 November 1953.
44. TNA/FO371/107111/UP2435/17, Lloyd to Eden, 7 November 1953.
45. TNA/FO371/107111/UP2435/16, FO to New York, 13 November 1953.
46. Ibid., Lloyd to Eden, 7 November, Jackson minute, 9 November, and Eden to Lloyd 13 November 1953.

47. TNA, FO371/107112/UP2435/36, Jebb to FO, 7 December 1953.
48. Eden's rejection of discussion of the Cyprus issue at a meeting with the Greek Prime Minister Papagos in September 1953, is discussed in E. Averoff-Tossizza, *Lost Opportunities: the Cyprus Question, 1950–1963* (New Rochelle: Caratzas, 1986), pp. 25–26.
49. TNA/COS(54)303, DEFE 5/54, 3 September 1954.
50. TNA, CO926/180, Intel. 140, *Cyprus*, 25 June 1954.
51. TNA/CAB128/27, CC(54) 53, 27 July 1954.
52. See TNA/FO371/112855/WG1081/398, *The United States Government and the Cyprus issue and tactics in the United Nations*, 18 August, 1954, which commented on FO371/112851/WG1081/274, US *aide-memoire* on Cyprus, 12 July 1954. This briefing paper went to Sir Ivone Kirkpatrick, Permanent Under-Secretary at the FO, and Selwyn Lloyd, the Minister of State. The American reply was not immediate and with reason. Dulles was so incensed by the British attitude over Guatemala that he let it be known that anyone seeking clearance for the American reply to the British would be 'thrown out of the room'. See FO371/112848/ WG1081/185, Salt to Young, 9 July 1954.
53. TNA/CO936/317, record of talks, 31 July 1954.
54. TNA/CAB128/27, CC(54) 53rd, 26 July 1954.
55. TNA/FO371/112863/WG1081/607, Churchill to Eisenhower, 18 September 1954.
56. TNA/CAB134/966, IOC(55) 114, 1 October 1955.
57. TNA/FO371/145265/UN1513/3, Colonial Office brief, *Intervention by the Fourth Committee in the affairs of British colonial territories*, July 1959.
58. TNA/CO936/354, Hanrott minute, 31 October 1955.
59. TNA/FO371/117658/RG1081/1041, Washington to FO, 17 September; and FO371/117659/RG1081/1072, Nutting to FO, 20 September 1955.
60. TNA/FO371/123744/UN22512/1, Dixon's Annual Review for 1955, 28 February 1956.
61. TNA/FO371/123959/RG10812/103, Dixon to FO, 23 October 1956, summarising his views to the 'old' Commonwealth delegations at the UN.
62. TNA/FO371/123959/RG10812/104, Record of the meeting of Commonwealth delegations to the UN, 16 October 1956; and FO371/123959/RG10812/133, on South African views.
63. TNA/FO371/123959/RG10812/103, Dixon to FO, 23 October 1956.
64. TNA/FO371/123963/229, Home to Lloyd, 27 October 1956.
65. TNA/FO371/145265/UN1513/3, Colonial Office brief, *Intervention by the Fourth Committee in the affairs of British colonial territories*, July 1959.
66. TNA/FO371/123960/RG10812/138, Pink minute, 29 October, 1956.
67. *United Nations General Assembly, Official Records*, 11th Session, 1st Committee, 856th meeting., 22 February 1957.
68. TNA/FO371/145265/UN1513/3, Colonial Office brief, *Intervention by the Fourth Committee in the affairs of British colonial territories*, July 1959.
69. TNA/FO371/145242/UN1011/1, Annual Review of 1958; and TNA/FO371 /153497/UN1011/1, Annual Review of 1959.

6

'A Cardinal Point of Our World Strategy': The Foreign Office and the Normalisation of Relations with Japan, 1952–63

Antony Best

One of the great ironies of the Cold War was that the new strategic paradigm created by the need to contain Soviet expansion meant that many members of the 'free world', including Britain, now found themselves ranged alongside their former enemies from the Second World War in the shape of West Germany, Italy and Japan. Indeed, the denial of all three of these countries to the Soviet bloc was one of the most important strategic goals in the post-war world. As Saki Dockrill demonstrated in her first book, this new reality meant that Britain had soon to contemplate and approve the rearmament of its recent German foe.[1] Moreover, in order to seal the security of Western Europe, it was necessary for Britain to encourage the development of a military alliance in the form of NATO that would see Italy join as a founder member in 1949, with West German entry coming in 1955.[2] These were undoubtedly tough decisions to take, for memories of the recent war naturally led many amongst the British elite and public to view these new allies with distaste and suspicion, but the exigencies of national security meant that sentiment could not be allowed to trump pragmatism.[3]

The relatively close relations that Britain was able to construct with West Germany and Italy within a few years of the end of the Second World War does raise the question of whether a similar policy of friendship and benevolence was extended to Japan. However, as Japan was on the other side of the globe in a region where British power was in any case in rapid decline, the issue of how Anglo–Japanese relations were revived in the post-war period and what place the Cold

War played in them has received little scholarly attention. Most of the work that has been produced on Anglo–Japanese ties in the years after 1945 has focused on only three areas: first, British policy towards the American-dominated occupation of Japan; second, the economic relationship in Southeast Asia in the 1950s; and third, bilateral diplomacy towards Third World issues in the 1960s.[4] As such, the central question of how Britain tried to normalise relations with Japan and what obstacles emerged to thwart that goal has tended to be neglected.[5] Yet, if it is contended that the Cold War was the dominant paradigm for British foreign policy, this particular relationship is surely worthy of study, for Anglo–Japanese relations carried with them a great deal of difficult cargo from the 1930s and 1940s. This chapter seeks to rectify this gap in our knowledge by looking at the evolution of Foreign Office policy between April 1952, when Japan regained its sovereignty, and March 1963, when Lord Home became the first British foreign secretary to visit Tokyo.

The Communist threat

When Japan once again became an independent nation in April 1952 its future was uncertain. On the surface, it appeared to be solidly within the Western camp. Its conservative government was led by a prime minister, Yoshida Shigeru, who clearly had close ties with the business community and little sympathy for socialism. In terms of its foreign relations, its diplomatic partners were almost exclusively from the 'free world', for at the San Francisco peace conference in September 1951 the Soviet Union and its allies had refused to sign the Anglo–American-designed treaty on the grounds that it was not open to amendment. Moreover, the Americans had insisted in late 1951 that Japan enter into trade relations with the Republic of China on Taiwan, thus aborting any Japanese effort to establish commercial ties with the People's Republic of China (PRC). Meanwhile, in the realm of national security, Japan was tied to the United States by the September 1951 security treaty, which provided the Americans with bases on Japanese soil and the freedom to use their forces to maintain regional security and even, at Tokyo's request, to quell domestic unrest.

Appearances, however, can be deceptive, for closer study of Japan reveals that it was in an unstable and potentially dangerous position. One important problem was that its economy was still in a fragile state and that it was struggling to restore the trade relations that had underpinned its past prosperity. In this respect, the American refusal to allow Japan to renew its traditional commercial ties with China was a significant drag on its recovery. Concerning its domestic politics, Yoshida's government was not in a particularly strong position, for the conservatives within the country were divided into a number of competing political parties and, even within his own Liberal Party, he faced opposition from the faction centred upon the recently de-purged Hatoyama Ichiro. Fortunately, the socialists were also divided, but there was no guarantee that the latter's disunity would be permanent and if they did unite and form a government they might well take Japan in a neutralist direction.[6]

This potential for economic and political instability in Japan was naturally a matter of serious concern for the Foreign Office, for even though Britain had not entered into any direct commitment to the former's defence, as it had with Germany and Italy, it was by no means indifferent to its fate. The Japan, after all, was a Great Power in terms of its economic and military potential. Moreover, even though British power was in decline in East Asia itself, it maintained significant interests in Southeast Asia and was still sensitive to the security concerns of Australia and New Zealand who were key components of the British Commonwealth. Japan may therefore not have been as important as Germany and Italy, but its future still mattered. Put simply, it was clear that Japan had to be kept within the free world and that Britain needed to consider what it could do to contribute towards this goal. As the British ambassador to Japan, Sir Esler Dening, put it in 1953, 'It must surely be a cardinal point of our world strategy to keep Japan on our side and to keep in step with the United States in this aim'.[7]

Before looking at the construction of British policy, it is necessary to investigate the precise nature of the Foreign Office's concerns about Japan's stability. The surprising aspect to this is the degree to which it was concerned about the position of the Japanese Communist Party (JCP). The idea that the left provided a profound threat to the stability of Japan is not one that resonates much in Cold War historiography, but the reality is that in the early years of Japan's renewed independence the JCP was seen as a real danger by British officials. For the Foreign Office, this became a grave concern in the summer of 1952 following the JCP-inspired violence at that year's May Day celebrations in Tokyo, which led Dening to warn that the JCP were willing to take advantage of any and every opportunity to expand their support.[8] Moreover, the ambassador's concern was underlined by the profound disquiet that Malcolm Macdonald, the Commissioner-General for

Southeast Asia, brought back from his July 1952 visit to the country, which led him to warn:

> The great peril in Japan is Communism. I do not suggest that the local Communists are likely to increase their strength greatly in the immediate future; but in my opinion there is real danger of their coming into power sooner or later during the next ten years.[9]

Such was the level of Foreign Office trepidation that in 1952–53 it sent an official from the Information Research Department (IRD) to investigate the local situation and at its own instigation entered into liaison with the American State Department and the latter's embassy in Tokyo about the scale of the threat.[10] Even this, however, which included insight into the CIA's view of the matter, did not bring much reassurance. To the Foreign Office, the American belief that the Japanese were now irrevocably committed to democratic government appeared unduly optimistic.[11] Its own assessment, as represented by a memorandum on 'Communism in Japan' from late 1952, was bleak:

> Communism in Japan is a serious threat both now and in the long run. Psychologically the Japanese might not be averse to an authoritarian regime of the Communist kind. There are many factors in the economic situation which lend themselves to Communist exploitation.[12]

In particular, British officials feared that the JCP might make serious inroads into the labour movement by infiltrating the leading umbrella organisation, Sōhyō, which might, in turn, have the unfortunate effect of marginalising and demoralising the democratic left.[13] Nor was Yoshida's fervent anti-socialism much of a comfort, for it was feared that his propensity for bringing in extreme anti-union legislation would only alienate workers and drive them into the hands of the left.[14] Moreover, adding a further level of concern was the fear of the effect that any shift to the left in Japan might have on countries in the region. In this respect, Dening observed in February 1953 that 'a Japanese accession to the communist camp' might have a very unfortunate influence 'upon large sections of people all over Asia'.[15]

Further aggravating the situation was the possibility, particularly after the announcement of the Mao-Khrushchev manifesto of October 1954, that the Soviet Union and the PRC might offer blandishments to Japan in the process of trying to open diplomatic relations. In the case of Beijing, it clearly held a powerful trade card, while Moscow could offer its own peace treaty, including a settlement of the territorial dispute over the Kurile Islands, and the withdrawal of its potential veto over Japanese entry into the United Nations. The danger in this was that some Japanese might well be tempted by such bait to flirt with neutralism and that the JCP might moderate its propaganda in an effort to stimulate such a change in Japan's foreign policy direction.[16] Linked to this was also a profound concern about the state of Japanese politics at the governmental level. The undulating political fortunes of the Yoshida administration, which was forced in 1952–53 to go to the polls twice within six months, did not inspire confidence. Moreover, there was concern about the exposés of corruption and cronyism which undermined public respect for the parliamentary system. Such was the level of despair that in August 1953 Dening wrote from Tokyo that:

> Eight years after the end of a most disastrous war and a mere fifteen months after the regaining of independence, the Japanese ship of state seems to be well under way on a course of incompetence in administration, political disunity and scant regard for the usually accepted parliamentary forms of government.[17]

From this he concluded that it would be possible for some strong but disruptive figure to emerge and exploit the chaos. The only room for optimism was that it was not clear that any such person existed.

The limits of foreign policy

The situation in Japan was therefore one that was seen as fraught with danger, but the question for the Foreign Office was: what could Britain do to assist in the task of maintaining Japan within the Western camp? In the security sphere, it was clear that as a key ally of the United States and the leader of the Commonwealth, Britain's opinion on issues such as Japanese rearmament mattered and it could therefore help the cause by adopting an understanding attitude. In this area, the Prime minister, Winston Churchill, took the lead, observing in March 1953 that he was, in principle, in favour of Japanese rearmament which 'might well be the only effective manner of balancing the growing power of Communist China in the decade'.[18] Meanwhile, in regard to domestic politics, the IRD and the embassy in Tokyo sought to enlighten Japanese opinion about the threat posed by communism. It was also hoped that a visit by a Labour Party delegation in August 1954 would bring the left in Japan to a greater understanding of social democracy and the proper role of opposition parties within parliamentary politics.[19]

However, the most obvious area in which Britain could assist was in the field of trade policy. Japan, like Britain, was a country that relied heavily on exports for its economic health and many of its best markets lay within the British Empire and the wider sterling bloc. The British government could therefore aid Japan most fruitfully by providing the latter's cotton textile and other consumer goods with easy entry into its colonial markets, thus contributing to a renewal of Japanese prosperity that would blunt the appeal of both the JCP and the Sino–Soviet bloc. To a degree this was also to Britain's advantage, for Japanese goods, particularly cheap textiles, were capable of making an important contribution to the restoration of stability in Southeast Asia, while Japan itself was a valuable market for a variety of raw materials, including Australian wool, Malayan rubber and Indian manganese. Moreover, as Noriko Yokoi has pointed out, the revival of this trade was seen as a vital element in the re-establishment of sterling as a global currency.[20] The problem, however, in this area was that the level of Japanese trade had to be carefully balanced. Britain could not allow Japan unrestricted access to its colonial markets without harming its own interests, for Japanese exports directly competed with British goods. This was particularly the case concerning cotton textiles as the colonies remained one of the few major markets for the mills of Lancashire. Nor was this simply a matter of the cotton industry's contribution towards Britain's balance of payments, for Lancashire was a key electoral battleground and the party in power could not afford to provoke its wrath. Moreover, the government had to remember that in regard to Japan, the legacy of the past weighed very heavily indeed because of the appalling treatment that the Japanese authorities had meted out to the Allied prisoners-of-war in Southeast Asia, and the hard times and unemployment that had been created as a result of Japanese economic competition in the 1930s. Nor did it help that the Japanese government was extremely slow to live up to its obligation under the peace treaty to provide compensation to former prisoners-of-war.

As a result of these counter-veiling factors the Foreign Office, despite its use of Cold War rhetoric, faced considerable opposition to its efforts to push for a liberalisation of British trade policy. The scale of the problem was made clear in early 1954, when a bad-tempered debate took place in the House of Commons over the government's decision to sign a new Sterling Payments Agreement with Japan, that allowed the latter to sell more goods to Southeast Asia in order to balance its trade with the Sterling Bloc. The Foreign Office's response to this criticism was to argue, in an April 1954 memorandum for the Cabinet, that a liberal attitude towards Japan was essential as the alternative was that the Japanese might be forced into collaboration with the PRC and thus imperil British interests. It was necessary for all policy decisions concerning Japan to take this consideration and for the government to try to change public feeling about the Japanese 'so as to bring it into closer accord with the overriding requirements of our national policy and interests'.[21]

The Cabinet duly accepted the memorandum as government policy, but its goals were easier to state than to achieve. This was particularly evident over the issue that arose in the second half of 1954 of whether Japan should be allowed to sign up to the General Agreement on Tariffs and Trade (GATT) and whether, if it did join, Britain should, under article 35 of the treaty, exercise its right not to extend Most Favoured Nation (MFN) status to Japan. As far as the Foreign Office was concerned there was no question but that Britain should accept Japanese entry and place its trade with the country on MFN lines, even though this would lead to even greater trade competition. In his memorandum for the Cabinet on this issue in December 1954, the Foreign Secretary, Sir Anthony Eden, warned of the dangers that might arise if Japan's bid were rejected. Noting that Yoshida had just fallen from power and been replaced by the 'anti-American' Hatoyama, who had been supported in his coup by the anti-Western socialist parties, he observed that, 'a period of unstable Government could lead to the breakdown of Parliamentary Government and to the establishment of a new dictatorship in Japan of the extreme left or possibly of the extreme right'.[22] In support of this view, a panic-stricken telegram from Dening was attached to the memorandum in which the ambassador emphasised the danger of alienating the Japanese through a public demonstration of British distrust at a time when the Soviets and the Chinese were engaged in 'offering more and more inducements to Japan to change her policy'.[23]

As the Minister of Defence, Harold Macmillan, observed in his diary in January 1955 the GATT issue presented the Cabinet with a fundamental dilemma, 'On the one hand we risk turning Japan towards China & the Communists. On the other, we risk losing Lancashire & the election'.[24] The centrality of the Cold War to our understanding of the post-1945 period might lead one to imagine that the international repercussions of invoking article 35 would necessarily trump the domestic, but this turned out not to be the case, for the Foreign Office's pleading proved in the end to be of no avail. As the Secretary of State for Commonwealth

Affairs, Lord Swinton, noted, the fact of the matter was that 'electoral expediency' dictated the need for the government to stand firm in defence of its own domestic interests.[25] Perhaps, if Japan's position within the Cold War had been more directly linked to British security interests then this decision might have been different. In the circumstances, however, it is clear that it would not have been an easy task for the government to sell this concession to a former enemy, especially as it might have entailed significant economic consequences.

The slow thaw begins

This domestic opposition to any outright concessions to Japan meant that between 1955 and 1957 Anglo-Japanese relations fell into a malaise, and the situation was not helped by the fact that Japan began to find its own reasons to criticise Britain.[26] This was most evident in the Japanese opposition to British nuclear tests in the Pacific which flared up in early 1957, but also emerged in regard to the Suez crisis of the previous year. The distance that existed between these two key pillars of the free world was evident in the realm of official visits. In 1955, both Dening and a number of MPs sympathetic to Japan stressed to Whitehall the need for more senior British figures to visit the country, but found the ministers at the Foreign Office reluctant to add Tokyo to the itinerary of their visits to Asia. Finally, in September 1956, it was arranged for the Chancellor of the Duchy of Lancaster, Lord Selkirk, to visit Japan, but this trip did not prove a success, for the Japanese foreign ministry made it clear that it felt distinctly underwhelmed by the presence of this relatively minor political figure.[27] Meanwhile, when Lieutenant-General Hayashi, the chair of the Japanese joint staff came to Britain in April 1957, it is telling that the Foreign Office was keen to emphasise to Tokyo that high-ranking military visitors need not wear uniform and that it would better if the general did not lay a wreath.[28]

It was only in areas away from the troubled direct relationship that the Foreign Office was able to pursue its favoured policy of trying to incorporate Japan more into the Western camp. In particular, it attempted to display Britain's goodwill by soothing Japan's re-entry into international society. It thus assisted in 1954 with Japanese membership of the Economic Commission for Asia and the Far East and the Colombo Plan, two institutions that were designed to funnel Western aid into South and Southeast Asia. Furthermore, in 1955–56 it supported Japan's entry into the United Nations (UN). In this policy, it acted in step with the Menzies government in Australia, which in August 1954 had followed the British lead by approving its own External Affairs Department memorandum arguing that Japan could not be allowed to drift into China's orbit.[29]

Not surprisingly, the Foreign Office were frustrated by the *de facto* public veto over any move towards closer relations and its concern was only reinforced after the re-opening of diplomatic relations between Japan and the Soviet Union, in October 1956, and Japan's entry into the UN two months later. Moreover, even though the Japanese domestic situation appeared more stable after 1955, when the conservative parties in Japan had merged together to form the Liberal Democratic Party, there was still uncertainty about the prospects for democracy. This was particularly the case after the autocratic Liberal Democratic politician and former war crimes suspect, Kishi Nobusuke, emerged as prime minister in early 1957. While the United States saw Kishi as a strong pro-Western leader, the Foreign Office had misgivings about his desire to pursue a more independent line in foreign policy, his potential to cause division domestically, and even his commitment to democracy.[30] In addition, it feared that the Americans still did not understand or trust those on the left who had merged in 1955 to form the Japanese Socialist Party and that this risked alienating the latter and pushing it towards, at the very least, a neutralist outlook.[31]

In the summer of 1957 the *chargé d'affaires* in Tokyo, William Harpham, wrestled with the problem of Japan's future course in a draft memorandum for the Foreign Secretary and again raised the prospect of the country potentially flirting with neutralism. He duly concluded that it might be a useful goodwill gesture if the Japanese foreign minister, Fujiyama Aiichiro, could be invited to London for talks after the opening of the forthcoming UN General Assembly session in September.[32] The Japan desk in London felt that this was a splendid idea and quickly persuaded the Foreign Secretary, Selwyn Lloyd, to issue an invitation. Indeed, Lloyd was so enthused as to issue an order that Fujiyama was 'to be treated "royally"'.[33] The subsequent visit appeared to go well, despite some hostile media coverage in Britain, and Fujiyama commented to the British ambassador on his return to Tokyo that the politicians and officials in Whitehall seemed more practical about world affairs than their American counterparts.[34]

While Fujiyama's coming to London proved a useful means of breaking the ice that had built up over the past two years, it was only a start. As such, Lloyd was only being truthful and sensibly cautious in May 1958 when he informed the new Japanese ambassador in London, Ōno Katsumi, that, while recently there had been an improvement in Anglo-Japanese relations, '...British public opinion needed nursing along step-by-step and we must not over-do things'.[35] Lloyd also took much the same line with Sir Godfrey Nicholson, the leading parliamentary advocate of closer Anglo–Japanese relations. He told him, in November of the same year that, while the British government 'fully understood the importance of Japan and wished for better relations', it was important that 'we did not run the risk of a snub to the Japanese from the British public who still felt strongly about the war'.[36]

Behind the scenes, however, the Foreign Office was emboldened to take a more active line towards building ties with Japan. In part, this came out of its conviction that it was simply in the British national interest to do so. However, it was also linked to pressure from the Eisenhower administration, for recent Anglo–American talks about East Asia in Washington had revealed the former's concern about Japan and its desire for Britain to assist in the task of keeping the Japanese tied to the free world.[37] The most noticeable change in Foreign Office policy was that, in 1958, it began to exchange low-grade intelligence reports about the external and internal politics of the PRC with the Japanese foreign ministry.[38] Although the closure of some records about the military links between the two countries makes it difficult to know how much cooperation had previously taken place, this does appear to be a significant shift for, as recently as 1954, concern had been raised about the ability of the Japanese government to keep foreign intelligence reports secret.[39] In addition, the Foreign Office also began to be more amenable to sharing its views on current issues, such as the formation of the United Arab Republic.[40]

A further stimulus to this process was that the Japanese government itself appeared genuinely to desire closer relations in an effort to reduce its reliance on the United States, especially after the second Taiwan Straits crisis of 1958.[41] Moreover, although the much-trumpeted Kishi Plan for development aid for Southeast Asia had proved abortive, the British did gain the impression in 1958–59 that Japan was at last showing a desire to play a responsible role in world affairs. This was particularly the case in regard to collaboration with Britain in the provision of development aid to the newly independent states of the Third World and its willingness to explain Western policy to the Afro–Asian bloc at the United Nations.[42] Accordingly, when Kishi more or less invited himself to Britain for a formal visit in July 1959, he was accorded a warm welcome, despite the distrust that had been displayed towards him only two years before. Moreover, the Foreign Office was, in turn, encouraged by the fact that this visit seemed to inspire considerably less hostile comments in the media than had taken place during the earlier visits by Yoshida and

Fujiwara.[43] The lack of overt opposition to Kishi's presence in Britain also tied into another significant factor that began to make a difference to Anglo–Japanese relations in the late 1950s, which was that the excessive concentration on Japan as an economic enemy had begun to decline as the focus of British trade shifted away from its former colonial markets to Western Europe. It was therefore now possible for the British government to start to give serious consideration to signing a new commercial treaty with Japan and reversing its stance over GATT rights without engendering a hostile wave of opinion at home.[44]

Towards normality

Encouraged by this warmer atmosphere, the Foreign Office sought in early 1960 to create momentum in Anglo–Japanese relations by pressing Macmillan to commit himself to a reciprocal visit to Japan. This proved a fruitless task, however, for the Prime Minister, faced with the need to get Britain into the European Economic Community and with Cold War tensions rising over Berlin, saw Japan as low on his list of priorities.[45] The Foreign Office refused though to give up without a fight and its contention that Japan should not be ignored was underscored by the violence that erupted in Tokyo in May and June 1960 when the Kishi government used dubious parliamentary tactics to force through ratification of the new US–Japan Security Treaty. For those concerned with policy towards Japan, the riots and protests confirmed them in their belief that the left could not be ignored and that more needed to be done to cement the country into the Western bloc.[46] Nor were the British officials the only ones who thought in this way, for the Italian government also made clear its concern about Japan's future course.[47]

The Foreign Office's drive for better relations also received a stimulus in the autumn of 1960 when two British politicians visited Japan. In October, the Conservative MP Julian Ridsdale, who had been an army language officer in Japan in the late 1930s, wrote to the Lord Privy Seal, Edward Heath, noting that Anglo–Japanese relations were still in the doldrums and that this would disadvantage Britain in Japan's burgeoning market for specialised industrial goods.[48] The other visitor was Lord Lansdowne, the Minister of State at the Foreign Office, who went to Tokyo to represent Britain at a Colombo Plan conference. He, too, felt that the Japanese desire for better relations was not being reciprocated and feared that Britain would lose out commercially.[49] Thus, when he returned to London, he proved amenable to pressure from his civil servants to write to the new Foreign Secretary, Lord Home, about the need to get Macmillan to go to Tokyo as an expression of Britain's goodwill. Against the background of the recent demonstrations in Japan, Lansdowne's letter in December 1960 duly warned of the possibility of neutralist feeling growing, and observed that:

> Japan is an undoubted asset to the Free World: but her importance for us lies not only in what she can do on our side but perhaps more so in what she could do if she were on the other. A Japan in the neutralist bloc would disrupt the Free World strategic position in the Far East; in the Communist bloc she would make the whole of the Western position in Asia virtually untenable.[50]

Subsequently Home forwarded this letter to Macmillan with his own seal of approval and the result was that the prime minister indicated that he might be able to visit Japan and Malaya in the autumn of 1961.[51]

The following year did, indeed, see a further warming of relations. In the political field, Ridsdale arranged for the establishment of an all-party Anglo–Japanese Parliamentary Group. Meanwhile, in the world of commerce, the director-general of the Federation of British Industries, Sir Norman Kipping, visited Japan and was able to gather evidence that challenged the common belief that its economy relied solely on low labour costs and cheating for its competitiveness. He was thus able to persuade the Federation to moderate its position on Japanese competition, which, in turn, removed one of the remaining obstacles to the conclusion of a commercial treaty.[52] Moreover, the royal link between the two countries, which had, aside from Crown Prince Akihito's controversial visit in 1953 for the Coronation, lain dormant since 1937, was revived with the visit of Princess Alexandra to Japan. What it did not involve, unfortunately, was a British prime ministerial visit. In June 1961, Macmillan decided that the situation in Berlin was too serious to allow him to be absent from Britain for any length of time, noting to Home that:

> I really do not think that it would be right for me to be absent from this country on what is after all a journey of comparatively secondary importance during what is likely to be a time of great difficulty here.[53]

This was then to be followed in 1962 by his cancelling another visit, due to the need to hold a Commonwealth conference about Britain's bid to join the EEC.[54]

Despite the low priority that Macmillan applied to Japan, the Foreign Office still persisted with its policy of seeing what could be done to improve relations with Japan and to seal its alignment with the West. It is worth noting that, although some progress had been made in this area, it was still felt that much more needed to be done. For example, in May 1961, Sir Edward Peck, the Assistant Under-Secretary responsible for overseeing East and Southeast Asian affairs, observed that, 'I would…estimate Japan's rehabilitation towards becoming a respectable member of international society has reached about the point that the Federal Republic of Germany reached some years before her admission to NATO – say 1951/52'.[55] Not surprisingly, the area of greatest importance was the conclusion of a new commercial treaty, but this was largely in the hands of the Board of Trade. Where the Foreign Office could help was in continuing to foster the intelligence exchange that had been established in 1958 and in endeavouring to see where the two countries might cooperate in regard to the Third World. Here, as Kweku Ampiah has noted, a potentially fruitful horizon opened in the form of possible collaboration in the provision of development aid to the newly independent states of sub-Saharan Africa.[56]

Further impetus to the improvement of relations was provided, in 1962, by the desire of the Japanese Prime Minister, Ikeda Hayato, to visit Britain. As a leader whose primary focus was increasing Japan's prosperity, he was keen to improve his country's commercial links with Western Europe and engage in talks about trade liberalisation and possible Japanese membership of the Organization for Economic Cooperation and Development (OECD). With the two governments quickly settling on arranging the visit for November, Ikeda's impending arrival then provided a useful stimulus for the rapid completion of the negotiations for a new Anglo–Japanese Commercial Treaty, which was duly signed during his stay. In addition, during his time in London, Ikeda held a series of talks with Macmillan and Home which ranged widely over the current international agenda rather than just focusing on economic issues. In regard to the Cold War, Ikeda indicated that he was particularly interested in developing a bilateral exchange of information between Britain and Japan about the Sino–Soviet split.[57] From this proposal there subsequently developed the seed of an idea that was to achieve fruition in Tokyo in the following spring when Home finally became the first British Foreign Secretary to visit Japan – namely that the two countries should establish a half-yearly consultative forum at the ministerial level.[58] The Foreign Office saw this as a useful development, for it was seen as an excellent way not only of building trust, but also of overcoming the problem that the two countries had relative few common forums. Aside from the UN, Japan was not a member of NATO, SEATO or the Commonwealth.[59]

The first consultative forum duly met in Britain in September 1963, with the talks beginning at Home's ancestral home at The Hirsel, in the lowlands of Scotland, where the Foreign Secretary and Foreign Minister Ōhira Masayoshi also indulged in some grouse shooting. Amongst the subjects under discussion were East–West relations and the Soviet desire for a test-ban treaty, the international stance of the PRC, and the situation in Southeast Asia with particular attention to the establishment of Malaysia. Home's view was that the talks proved useful and he reported to the embassy in Tokyo that:

> I have the impression that the Japanese ... value this opportunity to exchange views outside the framework of normal diplomatic contacts as a concrete demonstration that they are full and important members of the free world "club".[60]

Thus, by 1963, it appears that Britain and Japan had finally shaken off the distrust and bitterness left over from the Pacific War and had begun a new era of closer cooperation. Economic relations were now rescued from the unsatisfactory doldrums in which they had sat while Britain denied Japan MFN status even though the latter was a member of GATT. In the political and security field a series of annual bilateral consultations at the ministerial level had been established which built up trust and mutual respect and showed that, although Japan was not a direct ally in the Cold War, it was still considered to be a significant strategic partner. Moreover, at the symbolic level Britain had now restored one of the links that Japan most prized – the royal relationship. Indeed, a series of reciprocal visits now began that would eventually include the monarchs themselves. While tensions would, of course, surface again in the future, to all intents and purposes relations were now normal.

Conclusion

Although Britain and Japan were theoretically on the same side in the Cold War, it should be evident from the above that the relationship between the two countries remained frosty for at least a decade after Japan regained its sovereignty in April 1952. This was not because the Foreign Office failed to realise the significance of Japan's place within the Cold War system. It was, in fact, all too aware of the need to keep Japan out of the clutches of the PRC and to prevent it associating itself with the neutralist bloc. The problem was twofold. Quite clearly the major obstacle was that the shadow of the Pacific War and the image of the unstoppable juggernaut of Japanese trade competition that had been formed in the 1930s dominated immediate post-war public and cultural perceptions of Japan. The result of this dichotomy between past hostility and present-day pragmatism was the development in the 1950s of a limited revival of political, cultural and commercial ties and the evolution of a relationship that superficially looked normal, but which, in reality, was carried out in a spirit of cold, distant formality. In addition, it was difficult for the Foreign Office to pursue its agenda because, unlike in the case of West Germany and Italy, the security of Japan did not have profound implications for the defence of Britain itself, because it was so distant. Moreover, if anything, it was seen as an American rather than a British responsibility. Nor, it should be added, was the threat to its pro-Western stance so grave as to create a sense of thunderstruck concern amongst the British public. There was no crisis to point to, but only an unsettling sense of malaise. This was enough to mobilise those policy-makers and parliamentarians most concerned with Japan but it was hardly likely to inspire acts of self-sacrifice in anyone else. It was therefore difficult to communicate the message that Britain must make concessions to its former enemy, for the only thing that could be seen at the popular level were the disadvantages rather than the benefits. It is also, of course, important that the only area in which Britain could substantially assist Japan was in the commercial field, for concessions here meant creating more unemployment in industrial Britain with the obvious impact that this would have on electoral politics.

The thaw with Japan thus had to wait until the hostility engendered by the Pacific War had dissipated to a degree and the Japanese had become less obvious trade rivals. Only then was the Foreign Office able to increase the momentum in Anglo–Japanese normalisation, but it is important to note that even in the late 1950s and early 1960s it was still wary of going too fast for fear that it might outrun the public's tolerance. The instinct to improve relations was still at this point heavily influenced by Cold War considerations. The fear that Japan might be lured towards China was not a nightmare that died easily and the Security Treaty crisis of 1960 certainly did not steady British nerves. It is, however, worth noting, as relations began to become closer in the early 1960s that commercial motives were increasingly coming to the fore in London. As the Japanese economy began its sensational rise there was a new awareness that Japan should not be seen solely as a competitor but also as a potential marketplace for British goods. Thus, there were reasons outside of Cold War motives for the sealing of normalisation in 1962–63.

The case of Britain's normalisation of relations with Japan in the post-war era is therefore important in a number of ways. It shows the degree to which, even at a time of heightened strategic tension when two states have a common enemy, their interaction is influenced by their own shared past and that it is difficult to overcome a bitter history. In addition, it reveals the role that domestic political considerations, and in particular, electoral politics, have on the shaping of foreign policy and the need to understand that, while, civil servants can impress with their eloquence and command of detail, it is in the end politicians who decide. These are not new points, but any chance to reiterate them needs to be taken, in order to uphold the standards of international history in which Saki Dockrill so firmly believed.

Notes

1. Saki Dockrill, *Britain's Policy for West German Rearmament, 1950–1955* (Cambridge: Cambridge University Press, 1991). See also Spencer Mawby, *Containing Germany: Britain and the Arming of the Federal Republic* (Basingstoke: Macmillan, 1999).
2. See Effie Pedaliu, *Britain, Italy and the Origins of the Cold War* (Basingstoke: Palgrave/Macmillan, 2003).
3. Sabine Lee, *Victory in Europe: Britain and Germany since 1945* (Harlow: Longman, 2001); and John Ramsden, *Don't Mention the War: The British and the Germans since 1890* (London: Little, Brown, 2006).
4. For the occupation period, see Roger Buckley, *Occupation Diplomacy: Britain, the United States and Japan, 1945–52* (Cambridge: Cambridge University Press, 1982) and Peter Lowe, *Containing the Cold War in East Asia: British Policies towards Japan, China and Korea, 1948–53* (Manchester: Manchester University Press, 1997). For the economic relationship, see Junko Tomaru, *The Postwar Rapprochement of Malaya and Japan, 1945–61: the Roles of Britain and Japan in Southeast Asia* (Basingstoke: Macmillan, 2000), and Noriko Yokoi, *Japan's Postwar Economic Recovery and Anglo–Japanese Relations 1948–1962* (London: Routledge-Curzon, 2003). For aspects of relations in the 1960s, see: Kweku Ampiah, 'Anglo-Japanese Collaboration about Africa in Early 1960s: the Search for "Complementarity" in the Middle of Decolonisation', *Journal of Imperial and Commonwealth Studies*, 39/2, (2011), pp. 269–95; James Llewelyn, 'Diplomatic Divergence: the Japanese and British Responses to Indonesia's Confrontation of Malaysia 1963–1966', *Asia-Europe Journal*, 4 (2006), pp. 583–605; and idem., 'Steadfast Yet Reluctant Allies: Japan and the United Kingdom in the Vietnam War', *Diplomacy and Statecraft*, 22/4, (2011), pp. 608–33. The following edited collections also contain valuable essays: Ian Nish and Kibata Yoichi, *The History of Anglo–Japanese Relations, 1600–2000: the Political–Diplomatic Dimension*, Vol. II, (Basingstoke: Palgrave/Macmillan, 2001); Iokibe Makoto, Caroline Rose, Tomaru Junko, and John Weste (eds), *Japanese Diplomacy in the 1950s: from Isolation to Integration* (London: Routledge, 2008), and Shigeru Akita & Nicholas J. White (eds), *The International Order of Asia in the 1930s and 1950s* (London: Routledge, 2009).

5. Three exceptions are: Peter Lowe, 'Uneasy Readjustment, 1945–58', and Tanaka Takahiko, 'Anglo–Japanese Relations in the 1950s: cooperation, friction and the search for state identity', in Nish and Kibata (eds), pp. 174–200 and pp. 201–34 respectively; and Yoichi Kibata, 'Peacemaking and After: Anglo–Japanese Relations and Japan's Re-Entry into International Society', in Hugo Dobson and Kosuge Nobuko (eds), *Japan and Britain at War and Peace* (London: Routledge, 2009), pp. 97–111. But even these are limited to analysis of the 1950s alone.
6. For Japanese politics in this period, see Tetsuya Kataoka, *The Price of a Constitution: The Origin of Japan's Postwar Politics* (New York: Crane Russak, 1991), pp. 101–23.
7. The National Archives (TNA), Kew, PREM11/3569, Dening to Eden, 7 March 1953.
8. TNA/FO371/99393/22, Dening to Eden, 13 May 1952.
9. TNA/FO371/99506/25G, MacDonald to Eden, 26 July 1952.
10. For the IRD mission, see TNA/FO371/105366/1, Dening to Eden, 16 January 1953. For liaison with the US, see FO371/99393/32, Watson to Pilcher, 28 July 1952; and FO371/105366/7G, Watson to Pilcher, 14 May 1953.
11. TNA/FO371/105366/7G, Pilcher minute, 30 May 1953.
12. TNA/FO371/99393/40, 'Communism in Japan', undated FO memorandum.
13. TNA/FO371/105366/17, Dening to Salisbury, 18 August 1953; and FO371/115227/8G, Higgins minute, 24 March 1955.
14. TNA/FO371/110403/49 Cortazzi minute, 15 September 1954.
15. TNA/FO1110/570, Dening to Eden, 17 February 1953.
16. TNA/FO371/110411/6, Dening to Eden, 14 October 1954; and FO371 /115227/8G, Higgins minute, 24 March 1955.
17. TNA/FO371/105365/74, Dening to Salisbury, 12 August 1953.
18. TNA/PREM11/407, Churchill note, 21 April 1953.
19. TNA/FO1110/6, Dening to Eden, 17 February 1953; FO1110/669/9, Redman to Bolland, 31 August 1954; and FO371/110499/10, Brain to Eden, 8 September 1954.
20. Yokoi, *Japan's Postwar Economic Recovery*, passim.
21. TNA/CAB129/66 C(54)92 *Japan's Postwar Economic Recovery*, Eden memorandum 8 March 1954.
22. TNA/PREM11/1039, C(54)391 'Japan and the General Agreement on Tariffs and Trade', Eden memorandum, 14 December 1954. See also Yokoi, *Anglo-Japanese Relations*, pp. 110–13.
23. TNA/PREM11/1039, Dening to Eden, 8 December 1954.
24. Diary entry 24 January 1955, in Peter Catterall (ed.), *The Macmillan Diaries: the Cabinet Years, 1950–57* (London: Pan, 2004), p. 384.
25. TNA/CAB21/3268, Swinton note, 26 January 1955.
26. TNA/PREM11/2163, Dening to Lloyd, 22 March 1957. See also Tanaka, 'Anglo-Japanese Relations in the 1950s', pp. 212–18.
27. TNA/FO371/121048/46, Dening to Morland, 12 October 1956.
28. TNA/FO371/127564/5, Mayall to Selby, and /12, Lloyd to Dening, 29 March 1957.
29. National Archives of Australia (NAA), Canberra, A1838 3103/10/1, Part 1, Prime Minister's Committee Decision no. 53 PM, 17 August 1954. For

Japanese entry into the Colombo Plan, see Daniel Oakman, *Facing Asia: A History of the Colombo Plan* (Canberra: Pandanus Books, 2004), pp. 98–111.
30. TNA/FO371/127529/11, Coulson to Lloyd, 8 July 1957, and /14, Morland to Coulson, 29 July 1957.
31. TNA/FO371/133651/14, de la Mere to Trench, 27 May 1958.
32. TNA/FO371/127529/16, Harpham to Lloyd, undated [August 1957]. Harpham hesitated about sending this despatch to the Foreign Secretary and thus decided to forward it privately to the Japan desk first, see /16, Harpham to Morland, 6 August 1957.
33. TNA/FO371/127531/38 Langridge to McNab, 17 September 1957.
34. TNA/FO371/127532/59 Lascelles to Morland, 22 October 1957. For Fujiyama's visit, see also Tanaka, 'Anglo–Japanese Relations in the 1950s', pp. 218–21.
35. TNA/FO371/133597/18, Lloyd minute, 12 May 1958. For a good review of Anglo–Japanese relations after 1958, see Christopher Braddick, 'Distant Friends: Britain and Japan since 1958 – the Age of Globalization', in Nish and Kibata (eds), *Anglo–Japanese Relations*, pp. 263–312.
36. TNA/FO371/133598/51, Lloyd minute, 17 November 1958.
37. TNA/FO371/133599/1, Morland to Lascelles, 7 January 1959. See also FO371/141236/3G, Home to Ottawa, Canberra, and Wellington, 15 April 1959. It appears that the files on Scott's conversations in Washington are retained.
38. TNA/FO371/141515/1 Chancery Tokyo to Far Eastern Department, 24 December 1958. Attached to this letter were Japanese reports on the visit that the North Korean leader, Kim Il-Sung, had recently made to the PRC and the recent CCP conference in Wuhan. The file that covers the start of the intelligence exchange, FO371/133634, is retained.
39. TNA/FO371/110444/49, Marten to Pulverman, 30 June 1954.
40. TNA/FO371/133584/1, Dalton minute, 7 February 1958.
41. See Braddick, op.cit, p. 266.
42. TNA/FO371/141437/53 'Visit of the Japanese Prime Minister', FO Briefing Paper, undated [July 1959?]
43. TNA/FO371/141439/94, Lloyd to Morland, 28 July 1959.
44. TNA/CAB21/5576, *Japan's Postwar Economic Recovery*, ad-hoc meeting, 26 January 1960. For the lessening of the economic tensions, see Yokoi, *Anglo-Japanese Relations*, pp. 129–39.
45. TNA/FO371/150579/3, Macmillan to Lloyd, 5 January 1960.
46. TNA/FO371/150565/24, Morland to Lloyd, 24 June, and Trench minute, 4 July 1960.
47. TNA/FO371/150569/3, Trench minute, 27 July 1960.
48. TNA/FO371/150580/29, Ridsdale to Heath, 5 October 1960.
49. TNA/FO371/150581/37, Lansdowne to Lloyd, undated draft letter [December 1960].
50. TNA/FO371/150581/40, Lansdowne to Home, 9 December 1960.
51. TNA/FO371/150581/40, Home to Macmillan, 12 December 1960.
52. Yokoi, *Japan's Postwar Economic Recovery*, pp. 149–50.
53. TNA/FO371/158493/59, Macmillan to Home, 15 June 1961.
54. TNA/FO371/164971/19, Samuel minute, 2 April 1962.
55. TNA/FO371/158492/38, Peck minute, 16 May 1961.

56. See Ampiah, 'Anglo–Japanese Collaboration', pp. 269–95.
57. TNA/FO371/164976/21, records of Macmillan–Ikeda meetings, 12 and 14 November 1962.
58. TNA/FO371/170759/28, record of Home–Ohira meeting, 3 April 1963.
59. NAA/3103/11/51, Part 3, Vines to Griffiths, 3 June 1963.
60. TNA/FO371/170757/55, Home to Morland, 13 September 1963.

7

Anglo–American Diplomacy and the Congo Crisis, 1960–63: The not so Special Relationship

John Kent

The Congo Crisis marked the beginning of a short period in which Africa assumed special international importance both in the Cold War and in the process of decolonisation. It would be too simplistic to say that, for Washington, the Cold War was the main issue at stake in the Congo, whereas for the British the real question was the nature of decolonisation. Especially if it is assumed, arguably incorrectly, that the Cold War, as it came increasingly to involve newly independent states in the less developed world, was essentially about security, nuclear weapons and the containment of the Soviet threat. The reality was that, for John F. Kennedy's administration, the Cold War was about the values, or ideology, of capitalist democracy, which were necessary to strengthen the Western bloc against the forces of totalitarian communism that could, or so it was perceived, take root in Africa. It was about preventing radical left-wing ideas, under the guise of 'nationalism', from gaining acceptance in newly independent states and disrupting the transfer of power to pro-Western or non-aligned leaders. However, for Europeans, achieving stability through ensuring that 'moderate' Africans assumed power was not mainly about containing the Soviets, or even communism (which never had significant appeal in Black Africa); it was about preserving British, French or Belgian interests. In the Congo, elections providing for the transfer of power to Patrice Lumumba were never seen by Belgium, the former colonial power, as compatible with their particular economic interests. For Washington, international elements of the Cold War, making US actions seem acceptable in the eyes of the world, also meant using the United Nations (UN) as a screen for American goals. However, long before the suspicious death of UN

Secretary-General Dag Hammarskjöld, in a September 1961 air crash, serious problems occurred with the Belgians, which created international difficulties for the Kennedy administration. Even the removal of the leftist Patrice Lumumba from power, achieved as this was by the Belgian *sûreté* murdering him, while solving some important problems, added others.[1]

By January 1961, as Kennedy settled into office, US Cold War African priorities were clashing with the neo-colonial aims of some in Brussels, Katanga and London. For some Europeans, the process of 'neo-colonial decolonisation' had to be linked to the Cold War, but in ways that would prevent US and UN aims being achieved at the expense of British and Belgian economic interests. The conflict between the British and Americans deepened in 1962, impacting on the Nassau conference between Kennedy and British premier Harold Macmillan, although existing accounts tend to play down the issue.[2] Conflict over the Congo eventually even trumped the demands of the Anglo–American 'special relationship', as far as Africa and its prime, if brief, Cold War importance were concerned. The Belgians, also NATO partners, despite, or because of, being the former colonial power, eventually emerged from the Congo crisis in better Cold War odour with Washington than did the British.

For Washington, the challenge was to reconcile the NATO alliance, involving European powers, with establishing the allegiance of newly-emerging African states. But for the Belgians especially, the Congo's problems meant the Cold War's main role was initially to justify their actions after they failed to prevent Lumumba forming a government.[3] The Cold War atmosphere was produced less by Soviet actions and Lumumba's supposed communist links than by what others invented. The result of the misperceptions has been to justify a general model of decolonisation and high political decisions in an international context. Economic realities in the Congo and the benefits of the intermixing of Belgian state and private capital, especially British, have been ignored. Furthermore, the importance of the operating profits of the *Union Minière du Haut Katanga* (UMHK), the main company developing the mineral resources of the Congo, have been neglected. In fact, the decolonisation process in the Congo was not comparable to British or French Africa, and was an exception in the struggle between US Cold War needs and European post- or neo-colonial requirements. The territory's real significance lies in the roles played by European neo-colonial elements not normally considered significant in explaining the end of colonial rule.

Independence and secession

By March 1960, three months before Congolese independence, there was an awareness in Washington that Belgian settlers in southern Katanga were seeking a union with Britain's white-dominated Central African Federation (which embraced present-day Zambia, Malawi and Zimbabwe) and that Belgian companies wanted to see a Katangan secession.[4] This would enable economic control of mineral-rich southern Katanga to be kept out of any left-wing African hands. It came even before Lumumba's election as premier threatened to affect the taxation and foreign exchange position of the leading copper and cobalt producer, the UMHK. In other words, there were already those eager to prevent the European economic benefits of colonialism passing to Africans inheriting political power. The first indication something serious was afoot came when, according to the British Foreign Office (FO), Belgian troops arrived in Elisabethville, the capital of the Katanga region, on 10 July.[5] That was one day before the pro-western Moishe Tshombe declared Katanga an independent state, specifically because of the 'neo-communist government in Leopoldville', the Congolese capital. The justification for the troop deployment provided by Brussels was the threat to European lives that followed from the mutiny of the *force publique* (the Belgian-officered Congolese army) on the night of 5–6 July. The Belgian action was the first attempt to establish a neo-colonial state to protect the financial interests of Belgium and Britain.

The FO was initially not too troubled by the prospects of Lumumba as prime minister. Ian Scott, the former Leopoldville consul-general and first ambassador to the newly independent state, was clearly unsympathetic to King Baudouin's independence day speech on 30 June, which celebrated the end of colonialism by praising King Leopold's nineteenth-century 'achievements' in the Congo. Despite the horror and resentment Leopold provoked at the time, Baudouin provided a list of the alleged benefits Belgium had brought the Congo.[6] The situation became of greater concern for both London and Washington in the wake of the Security Council resolutions of 14 and 22 July, which called for the deployment of UN troops to assist the Congo government in maintaining order and, more importantly, secure the withdrawal of Belgian troops. These resolutions were followed by another on 9 August calling for Belgium to withdraw its troops 'immediately' from Katanga, where they provided support for Tshombe's secessionist regime. The Belgians were defying the UN by not even beginning to withdraw their troops. Hence, the US was confronted with the epitome of their decolonisation dilemma, torn between support for their European allies and the Cold War need to create viable states free from colonial control. Yet, there was little they could do except try to persuade Belgium of the broader African Cold War interests which far exceeded, in US eyes, whatever economic benefits the Katanga secession might provide European enterprises with.

Having rejected calls from Lumumba for military assistance the day after Katangan secession was declared, Dwight D. Eisenhower's administration was determined aid should only go through the UN.[7] The British, especially the Colonial Office (CO), were increasingly hostile to UN interference, but Washington believed its own influence over the UN would serve to protect the West's Cold War interests. By using the UN, any association with the colonial powers would be internationalised and accusations about 'American imperialism' reduced. The problem was that radical elements in the emerging African states were supportive of Lumumba and the UN Resolutions; yet a NATO member was defying the Security Council for apparently neo-colonial reasons. When UN troops began arriving in the Congo on 15 July, Belgian troops, now deemed to be committing aggression against an independent state, still gave no indication of withdrawal. Lumumba and President Joseph Kasavubu therefore turned to the Soviets, threatening to ask them to intervene 'if the Western camp does not stop its aggressive action.' This was followed, on 17 July, by an ultimatum that, if the Belgians had not complied with the UN resolutions within the next 48 hours, the threat would be carried out.[8] But it never was. The Cold War came to the rescue of the Europeans. The Belgians had already tried to invoke it when the Belgian foreign minister, Pierre Wigny, told London that the army mutiny was an organised communist plot against whites.[9] Scott however rejected the claim, noting that Brussels was 'not willing to accept a transition to the sort of relationship that the British now enjoy with former dependent territories'.[10]

In London, outside the FO and CO, others were concerned by the prospect of left-wing Africans achieving political power. The consequences of Lumumba's election for British economic interests in the Congo led some right-wing Conservatives to favour preserving the Tshombe regime. The Tanganyika Concessions Chairman, Captain Charles Waterhouse, a member of the UMHK board, along with a fellow board member and former government minister, Lord Selborne, approached FO officials on 13 July. Their concern about the Congo situation centred on the interests of shareholders in Tanganyika Concessions and its holdings in the UMHK. Waterhouse's Brussels contact was telling him that directors of the *Société Générale Belgique*, including most of the UMHK directors, had passed a unanimous resolution in favour of an independent Katanga as indispensable for the security of their interests. Waterhouse lobbied the FO to pressure the Belgian government to act in accordance with *Société Générale's* wishes.[11] No Western country could openly recognise or support a secession based on neo-colonial advantages gained at the expense of a newly independent state.[12] However, two days later Wigny summoned the British, French and American ambassadors to tell them he hoped they would all give encouragement, short of recognition, to Tshombe's regime.[13] The FO decision, in effect to do nothing, meant tacit acceptance of the advantages Katangan secession was providing for European capital.

The overthrow of Lumumba

Once the claims of a Soviet or communist threat could be substantiated, however tenuously, by contacts between Lumumba, Kasavubu and Khrushchev this provided a convenient cloak to hide the latent divisions between the US and its European allies over the Katangan secession. The American position, outlined for the National Security Council by the Assistant Secretary for the Bureau of African Affairs, Joseph Satterthwaite, was to refuse to recognise Katanga, 'while not closing the door completely in view of the possibility that Katanga is all that can be salvaged for the West'.[14] The FO policy objectives, defined after the meeting with Waterhouse, were a settlement between the legal, democratically elected government in Leopoldville and Tshombe's secessionist regime 'that preserves Western interests'. To give this practical effect, the FO insisted that no UN troops (which could end secession) should be allowed into Katanga 'as long as law and order prevails'.[15] These underlying Anglo–American differences were to become more evident as the crisis developed and the Kennedy administration ushered in a new approach to the African continent.

Meanwhile, in July 1960, once the 'Soviet intervention' in the Congo occurred, it was used to justify Western policy and preserve neo-colonialism in Katanga. Wigny lost no time in adding new colours to the Cold War picture that the Belgians were painting in the Congo. He told the US, British and French ambassadors on 16 July that 'Lumumba's activities of the past few days...have now made it clear that the Congo's problems must be looked at in the context of the East–West struggle. This means that the essential thing is to get rid of Lumumba. From now on he can only be a source of trouble and an instrument for a Soviet take over in the Congo'.[16] Wigny was helped by a common belief, whether derived from flawed Cold War perceptions, neo-colonial aims or a desire for 'moderation' in decolonisation processes, that something had to be done about Lumumba. Despite the Soviet reluctance to provide any form of military support and Moscow's provision only of food aid and transport aircraft, albeit on a bilateral rather than UN basis, the Cold War die was cast. It's, and Lumumba's, fate were sealed by the actions of Secretary-General Hammarskjöld, who was unwavering in his attachment to the West, justified by 'keeping the Cold War out of Africa'. This effectively meant keeping the Soviets out and the West in, hopefully in a better guise than Belgian colonialism. Hence, the American dilemma over support for the UN while Belgian troops remained in defiance of the legitimate Congo government and UN resolutions. The dilemma could be overcome if Lumumba and his opposition to European backed secession and the Belgian military presence were removed. Western unity in the face of a communist threat to the Congo could then look more credible than divisions over the neo-colonial Katangan regime.

Hammarskjöld changed his mind about sending UN troops into Katanga when Tshombe warned, in August, that he would treat this as a declaration of war. Lumumba's removal in the face of Belgian intransigence then became even more necessary.[17] He, as was his right, might demand that UN forces left the Congo. Their departure would deliver a blow to the UN and to the West's prestige, and the Americans would then be unable to act through the UN in the Congo. If the Belgian breach of UN resolutions continuing to be castigated by Lumumba and exploited by the Soviets in neo-colonial terms, then the Cold War situation would become more disadvantageous for the West. But, the elimination of Lumumba would avoid such a disastrous scenario. The first stage of this process was Lumumba's dismissal by his president and erstwhile rival, Kasavubu, on 5 September. Whatever the constitutional rights and wrongs of the presidential dismissal of Lumumba, and the latter's refusal to accept it, the fact was that the subsequent stalemate provided an opportunity for the ambitious Colonel Joseph Mobutu. With control of much of the Congo's army and 'unauthorised' support from Larry Devlin, the CIA station chief, Mobutu launched his first coup in mid-September, arrested Lumumba and dispensed with parliament. Congo was then governed by a college of commissioners.[18] At the crucial moment in the coup, troops in Stanleyville who were loyal to Lumumba were prevented from flying to Leopoldville by UN troops, occupying the city's airport.[19] Yet, this decisive involvement occurred when a UN resolution prohibited such actions, while calling for UN troops to enter Katanga 'for the full implementation of the present resolution'.[20]

Kennedy takes office

With Lumumba's murder becoming public knowledge in mid-February, the Cold War threat of bringing the Soviets into Africa, which he allegedly embodied, had to be transferred to his leading supporter, the lethargic and ineffective Antoine Gizenga. By then, Kennedy was in the White House, bringing a new US approach, not just to Africa and the Congo, but to the less developed world in general. At the heart of this lay more than anti-communism and a desire to reduce the threat presented by thermonuclear weapons. It reflected a belief that the existing problems the world faced could be tackled and overcome. Kennedy embodied aspirations for a future in which the beneficial operations of capitalism, assisted by the state, would bring a new and ultimately successful dynamic to the struggle between free enterprise and communism. This was an optimistic vision, in which Cold War success against communism would build a better world, notably for the less developed states that were throwing off the burdens of colonialism. The development process in Africa would not be built on the colonial foundations of European capitalism, but on freer and more open competition, represented by American values. Ensuring that democratic capitalism, influenced by these US values, would be welcomed by the newly-emerging nations of Africa, was seen as a crucial Cold War task by the new administration. Whatever the importance of Latin America under Kennedy, it was Africa where the expected benefits of capitalist development and economic progress were particularly significant, and which now provided the clearest Cold War challenge. An important American aim was to ensure that the newly independent states were not disrupted by left-wing forces *or* prevented from attaining their independence by the relics of colonialism. Both would risk the instability that would provide opportunities for the baleful tenets of communism. The fact that instability was generally produced by the failures of capitalism was never noticed in the march to the new frontier. The politics of development were at the heart of Anglo–American differences during the Kennedy administration. Nothing could have provided a bigger contrast between the Macmillan and Kennedy administrations than the way in which European enterprise was expected to adapt to the end of colonial rule in the Congo.

On entering the White House the Kennedy administration immediately embarked on a 'New Policy' in the Congo. Its ultimate aim was to counter Gizenga's semi-independent regime in Stanleyville, by creating a 'moderate', parliamentary Leopoldville government favourable to the West. The UN was even keener to restore democracy in the Congo, which was eventually accomplished in August 1961, assisted by considerable CIA bribes. The establishment of the government of the former trades unionist, Cyrille Adoula, free from left wing or radical nationalist influence, allowed attention to refocus on ending Katangan secession, still vital for a unified Congo state. By now, the UN resolutions demanding the withdrawal of Belgian troops had been superseded by the need to remove the mercenaries who were a vital part of Tshombe's armed forces, or *gendarmerie*, in Katanga. No sooner had a new UN representative arrived in Elisabethville than UN troops, now in that city, tried to remove the mercenaries.[21] However, using troops to enforce UN resolutions against Tshombe and strengthen the new regime in Leopoldville was not welcomed by the British, with their 'do nothing' policy that had allowed the secession to continue.[22]

The first signs of what the British Cabinet were told were UN local representatives taking steps beyond removing Tshombe's 'military advisers' (that is, the mercenaries) came in late August 1961. These steps, if they included removing civilian advisers, could be represented as interference in internal affairs and the Foreign Secretary, Lord Home, proposed to inform Hammarskjöld, who was killed shortly afterwards, that stability in Katanga depended on maintaining the Tshombe administration – not a view that would be welcomed in Washington. The Cabinet saw dangers of disorder spreading and communism threatening the Congo, but nothing appeared to be noted about the threat to UMHK and British financial interests.[23] As tension between Adoula and Tshombe mounted, the distinction between the British position, of preserving the Tshombe regime, ostensibly to keep out communism, and the US view, that maintaining Adoula was vital to prevent the appeal of communism, was becoming clearer. In November 1961, Kennedy, George Ball, the Under-Secretary of State, Mennen Williams, the Assistant Secretary for African Affairs, and Adlai Stevenson, US Ambassador to the UN, discussed how to get agreement between Tshombe and Adoula with David Ormsby Gore, the British Ambassador in Washington. Ormsby Gore felt there was no point in approaching Tshombe about a meeting with Adoula, until the former could be assured that the latter would not take military action against him.[24]

The contrast between the Kennedy administration, with its focus on a new future for Central Africa as a key element of its Cold War strategy, and the Macmillan government's Conservative party members, frequenting social clubs with links to white settlers and their Central African enterprises, could not have been starker. These Conservatives had often 'entertained' America's Ambassador to London, David Bruce, at their London clubs, visits to which were an essential part of his ambassadorial role. The views he encountered at these wealthy men's institutions were duly reported to the State Department.[25] In Washington, as the Americans were informed by Ormsby Gore that 'Tshombe ran a much better show' than the other Congo 'governments' that had appeared since independence, Bruce was informed by London's conservative elite that the UN was either bent on destroying the Congo's sole source of wealth or turning the territory over to Soviet domination. Either way the real losers would be the remaining whites, and the lucky ones in such an event 'might be those thought culinary acceptable and there would be cold missionary on many a sideboard'.[26] Thus, as the second round of Congo fighting approached, elements in the ruling Conservative party displayed their concern about the future of the illegitimate Katangan regime, despite London openly adopting a shared Anglo–American commitment to the re-integration into the Congo of Katanga. Sections of the Conservative party and government were also vehemently opposed to giving the UN more responsibilities, while the US, with its contrasting experiences of colonialism, had radically different expectations of the UN role in the Congo. The Kennedy administration was loathe to see the UN leaving the Congo with its 'tail between its legs', which was what the British government, left to itself, would have wanted.[27]

The Kitona agreement

Open Anglo–American disagreement was avoided, for the time being, despite UN Security Council Resolution 169, of 24 November 1961, which authorised the new Secretary-General, U Thant, to 'take vigorous action including the use of force, if necessary, for the immediate apprehension ... of all foreign military and para-military personnel not under UN command and mercenaries'.[28] Meanwhile, the degree of unity achieved by Adoula was fast disappearing with Gizenga choosing to leave the government and again base himself in Stanleyville. The second round of fighting in the Congo on 5 December was at Tshombe's instigation, as he hoped to seize the moment before UN forces had the opportunity to make the military preparations required to implement Resolution 169. In Washington, Kennedy was kept reminded of the goals of using UN military strength to promote reconciliation between Adoula and Tshombe.

For Dean Rusk, the Secretary of State, the UN should not be prevented from implementing its mandate as this 'would destroy for good the image of the US as a supporter of the UN's collective effort'.[29] The same conclusions had been reached by the US Ambassador, Edmund Gullion, in Leopoldville and by the National Intelligence Board.[30] Rusk, however, was in Paris for a NATO Council in mid-December, and was subjected to very different views by the British, French and Belgians.[31]

As Home and Macmillan prepared for a Commons debate on the Congo, they formally proposed a ceasefire to U Thant, which the Secretary-General decided to put to the UN Congo Advisory Committee. Ball, acting Secretary of State in Rusk's absence, discussed the ceasefire proposal with Kennedy but was eager to avoid ceasefires in the middle of implementing UN resolutions. Capitulation by the UN could bring the fall of Adoula and the re-emergence of Gizenga, with possible Soviet involvement.[32] Kennedy was prepared to accept a ceasefire, but on condition that Tshombe agreed to meet Adoula to discuss the re-integration of Katanga. This idea was put to the Cabinet in London.[33] It served to paper over the Anglo–American disagreements and produced the Kitona agreement, between Adoula and Tshombe, in December 1961, on the principle of Katangan re-integration. But the Anglo–American differences remained over the UN's role and the requirements of European capital which in the Cold War could not be easily reconciled with emerging African states. The practical details of implementing Kitona proved difficult however. Constitutional provisions for greater provincial autonomy, the incorporation of Tshombe's armed forces into the Congo army had to be arranged, and the sharing of tax revenues and foreign exchange decided. Robert Gardiner, the leading UN civilian representative who took up his post in February, produced the idea of joint technical commissions to deal with such problems. As the French pointed out, such a process was unnecessary as nothing but money was involved and it was 'well known that the *Société Générale* was in the control of the Belgian government'.[34] Therefore if the UMHK, rather than cooperating with Tshombe could be made to apply pressure on him, the secession would end. Not only would the UMHK suffer losses in the short term if it did but Paul-Henri Spaak was not initially inclined to pressure them to do so.

Economic questions of Katangan integration into the Congo involved the same neo-colonial issues as the secession of 1960. The implications for the UMHK and Tanganyika Concessions were significant, linked to the ties between the colonial state and private enterprise in Congo's colonial history. The plain fact was that the Belgian government refused to hand over its part-ownership of significant economic assets to the new state, as would normally have been expected with independence. The *Comité Spécial du Katanga* (CSK) established by King Leopold, received 40% of the royalties on mineral mining on behalf of the Belgian Congo government, with 40% going to Tanganyika Concessions and currently worth, according to the FO, about £15 million per annum. This was not the only British income going back to the days of King Leopold, as Tanganyika Concessions also had shareholdings in the *Compagnie du Katanga* (CK), which owned one third of the CSK's share portfolio, which were described by the Foreign Office as substantial but indeterminate.[35] There were also Tanganyika Concessions' shares in the UMHK itself – 50% until the Great Depression and by independence 14.5% with additional voting rights. The final 'neo-colonial' element was the fact that the Belgian Government appointed four of the six directors of the CSK and had merged parastatals (government owned but autonomously administered public corporations), such as the Congo River Board and the national bank with shares and bonds issued by profit-making private companies into what was known as the Congo Portfolio, managed by boards in Brussels. Its holdings were worth 37.5 billion Belgian francs (earning one billion francs per annum in 1959) and were not immediately transferred on independence.[36] The situation was made more difficult by Tshombe cancelling the pre-independence agreement between the CK and the Belgian colonial government to dissolve the CSK. One third of the *Comité's* holdings were meant to go to the *Compagnie* and two thirds to the government but, after secession, Tshombe appropriated these for his Katangan state.

Concerns about Tshombe continuing to play for time in implementing the Kitona agreement grew, as he and Adoula began talks on the Kitona implementation process in March 1962. The already dire financial situation of the Congo was worsening and the money necessary to keep the UN operation going beyond the end of the year appeared in doubt.[37] U Thant was therefore keen to resolve the crisis before then, which only increased the likelihood of further armed conflict. The new British ambassador, Derek Riches was clear that serious pressure on Tshombe would result in him destroying major UMHK installations, as he had threatened to do, and thus the status quo should be accepted *faute de mieux*.[38] However, on 29 March the State Department's Bureau of Intelligence and Research produced an assessment of the consequences of maintaining the status quo. This would likely end in chaos and lead to pressure to reduce the UN's role as the chosen US agent. Adoula would then be dependent on external aid, which could well be provided by the

Soviets.[39] One proposal to put pressure on Tshombe was a tax collection plan, with the installation of customs officials in Elizabethville to ensure that revenue went to the legitimate government.[40] That scenario was precisely what the British feared because of the likelihood of Tshombe taking retaliatory action, which would place the value of their own investments in jeopardy. Ambassador Gullion was convinced Tshombe was relying on the UN running out of money, so something clearly had to be done when the latest Adoula-Tshombe meeting broke up on 16 April with a commitment simply to resume talks in May.[41] The Americans wanted to co-ordinate policies with Britain and Belgium, despite their differing views. Washington hoped the Belgians could provide much needed expertise in the Congo through French-speaking technicians. As a result, the US proposed a tripartite meeting to discuss the best way to proceed. The crux of the secession problem was whether forceful measures could be agreed upon that would get Tshombe to take irreversible steps to re-integrate Katanga into the Congo.[42]

The Anglo–American rift

The May tripartite meeting, held in London, was chaired by Lord Dundee, a FO Minister of State, whom Ormsby Gore described to the Americans as 'a fool'.[43] The meeting was so important to Kennedy that he sent a personal letter to Ambassador Bruce emphasising that time was running out. While the Americans wanted a peaceful re-integration, if Tshombe remained obdurate 'we must be prepared to pursue actions which could involve the UN in the use of force.' He had to be disabused of the notion that this would never happen and Bruce should make sure that those with financial interests got the message that the failure to re-integrate Katanga into the Congo would be a commercial disaster.[44] A few days earlier, Sir Brian Urquhart had explained to the Americans why the Congo was seen as so important in London. Urquhart was a former FO official, who had worked with Gladwyn Jebb on the establishment of the UN. When Hammarskjöld became Secretary-General in 1953, he appointed Urquhart as one of his advisers. He later replaced Conor Cruise O'Brien as the UN representative in Elizabethville. Urquhart explained to US officials that the reason for the Anglo–American differences were not due simply to the relationship between the Foreign Secretary and the Chairman of Tanganyika Concessions. The lack of British enthusiasm for Katangan re-integration was the result of the influence within the government of the Conservative Party's chief financial backers who 'almost to a man were the principals in Tanganyika Concessions'.[45] In 1962, in contrast to the present day, the nature or extent of donations to the Conservative Party and its election campaigns did not have to be revealed.

The two-day tripartite meeting (which the French were extremely irate at not being invited to, or even informed about) began on 15th May, with the chair emphasising Home's concerns about the 'disaster' that might result if punitive measures were taken against Tshombe. Therefore, progress in achieving re-integration should depend on inducements offered to Tshombe and Adoula. It was patently obvious by now that the British were keen to prevent any pressures being applied to Tshombe that might subsequently risk force being used. They maintained, difficult though it was to do, that Adoula's intransigence over refusing to accept changes to the *loi fondamental,* which would provide Katanga with greater local autonomy, was the real problem. Wayne Fredericks, the American Deputy Assistant Secretary of State for African Affairs, pointed out that, as part of the key US goal of agreeing on how best to apply pressure on Tshombe and overcome his delaying tactics, the disaster resulting from the failure to re-integrate would be equal to the destruction of Katanga. In other words, it could prove a disaster on a greater scale than that which might affect dividends due to Tanganyika Concessions shareholders or the assets of UMHK installations. The interesting Cold War difference with the Lumumba situation and the role of Tshombe was that, whatever their respective legitimacies or legalities, the former's removal/elimination because of his left-wing, nationalist views could enable different Western concerns to be fused into an anti-Soviet crusade. With Tshombe and Katanga, supported by the Belgians, this could not apply. Thus, the British argued that force would produce chaos, as the collapse of the Tshombe government would lead to the UN taking over Katanga; while the Americans argued that ruling out force would lead to chaos, by bringing about the collapse of the Adoula government and opening the door to a communist takeover of the Congo.[46]

Another issue, directly connected to this fundamental disagreement about the priorities of the interests of European capital, was the idea of putting pressure on UMHK and Tanganyika Concessions. But on this, Bruce, as on securing support for pressure on Tshombe that might involve force, had to confess to 'almost complete failure'. Overnight, between the conference sessions, the Belgians drafted a paper which reflected some elements of tripartite agreement. This was discussed on 16 May, but there was no way of bridging the gap between the British and the Americans. In a private meeting between Bruce, Dundee and the Belgian representative, Robert Rothschild, Dundee said he had been instructed by Home to oppose any measures that might lead to involve hostilities. If a resolution were tabled in the Security Council that threatened a renewal of fighting, then the UK would veto it and would probably withdraw its financial contribution from the UN operations in the Congo.[47] These points were repeated by Dundee at the conference, where he also initially opposed restrictions on the Katangan *gendarmerie* as this would indicate 'a lack of trust in Tshombe'.[48] With no further progress being made, Bruce concluded at the end of the conference that the State Department would be unable to accept the points of agreement.[49] Ruling out the use of force, given President Kennedy's views, was a particularly crucial point. However, with Ormsby Gore repeating the British view on the use of force to Rusk, there could be no agreed way forward.[50] In reporting to Washington, Bruce added that he was 'impressed by mobility and helpfulness within limits of Belgian position compared to that of Britain'.[51] Letters exchanged between Macmillan and Kennedy on 25 May and 1 June could not paper over the cracks.

The result was that, although actions by the Belgian government in 1960 had seriously damaged their relations with the US over the Congo, these were now improving. After May, the Americans co-operated more closely with the government of Paul-Henri Spaak, due in no small part to the British government's determination to put the interests of Tanganyika Concessions before the cultivation of good relations with Washington over the Congo. Precisely the opposite view was always taken by Spaak, on his return to power in the spring of 1961. The British government asked the Kennedy administration not to reveal the extent of the disagreement between Washington and London. Meanwhile, the Adoula-Tshombe talks stalled and were finally abandoned in late June. With the reactionaries in the UMHK 'hiding behind the skirts of British directors from Tanganyika Concessions', the Americans were left in no doubt that Tanganyika Concessions was significantly more hard line than UMHK.[52] In this situation, the clear Anglo–American disagreement could no longer be fudged. In the short term, this had no real significance other than in emphasising the joint approach of the Americans and Belgians, who merged Gardiner's UN plan into a programme involving the risk of force, so as to escalate the pressure on Tshombe. The British were informed of this in July. Washington was still eager, as far as possible, before risking force or applying economic sanctions on Tshombe, to reach a common Western position. On four occasions in July the British Cabinet discussed, or were given information on, the Congo, but Britain remained at odds with the US interpretation of events. Ormsby Gore continued to express his views to American officials and Bruce informed the State Department that, although he did not doubt the British desire to see the re-integration of Katanga, London only wanted to achieve that if the 'stability of mining operations, and revenues dependent on them [could be] preserved'.[53]

On 27 June, the American–Belgian proposals were put to the UN and, although U Thant wanted more time for Gardiner's commissions to work, the State Department draft eventually became the UN plan for the re-integration of Katanga, in a process known as 'national reconciliation'. The British were presented with the latest proposals at a meeting in August, together with French and Belgian embassy officials, in Washington and were invited to provide comments on the drafting process.[54] This led to the August 1962 agreement on the UN Reconciliation Plan, but London was excluded from plans to guarantee progress on its implementation should Tshombe fail to go beyond verbal acceptance of the national reconciliation process. In a real way, the British, left on the sidelines as mere recipients of information, were nearing their 1950s nightmare of 'being classed with the French' in the Congo crisis.[55] This may also have served to advance changes to the fundamental Anglo–American relationship from one of cooperating on how best to approach problems and achieve common goals from shared perspectives, to one that was often limited to providing information. The CIA had defined the consequences of allowing Tshombe to maintain the secession as producing the 'failure of American policy in the Congo' with 'obvious ramifications throughout Africa'. That would produce 'a sharp decrease in American prestige and influence in the UN [and] in underdeveloped countries in general'. The communist bloc would be provided with a psychological weapon to mount an anti-American campaign, particularly in Africa and Asia, the vital Cold War areas. 'In short, 2 years effort, millions of dollars of economic aid and immeasurable prestige would be lost and victory turned to defeat'.[56] When so much was at stake for the Americans, the extent of the disagreement with Britain may well have had a long-term corrosive effect on special Anglo–American relations, over and above the decline of British power in the world.

The British were assisted in reducing the short-term impact of the Congo disagreement with the Americans by the ending of secession in January 1963, after Tshombe fled in the face of UN forces. It proved that British fears, about their investments in the copper mining industry being at risk unless there was agreement on reconciliation by persuasion, were unfounded. The end of the secession avoided any dire international consequences and the fears of Adlai Stevenson, who had expressed himself 'deeply disturbed by the British refusal to participate in effective measures of economic pressure on Tshombe', which could result in the failure of the Western attempts to deal with the Congo crisis.[57] At the end of the day, the secession was not ended by coordinated pressure on Tshombe or by a plan carefully thought out and executed by the US, the Belgians or the UN. The explanatory value of rational choice theory was devoid of significance, as what finally instigated the end of Tshombe's regime was the catalyst that alcohol and two particular drunks provided. Their actions and the subsequent reactions were played out as American, European and UN officials helplessly struggled even to get information about what was going on.[58]

Conclusion

Under Kennedy, the value of the UN and the success of US Cold War strategy in the less developed world were believed, in Washington, to depend on the ending of Katangan secession. Ironically, the Cold War threat, in all its basic misconceptions about the expansion of Soviet power in Africa, had first been unleashed by the Belgians in order to rouse the US to preserve the unrestricted profits of European capitalists in the former colony. As it turned out, the Kennedy administration had sufficient awareness of the real Cold War requirement of winning over Africans to the benefits of Western capitalism US style. Hence, preserving the unconstrained profits of European capital did not figure amongst its priorities. The Cold War irony came full circle when, in 1962, the protectors of European capital were faced with the administration's arguments about the potential costs of failing to get Tshombe to end secession, which for Washington would result in the fall of Adoula and open the door to communism. As a result, the British government, which had become the leading protector of European capitalism in the Congo, even resorted to arguing that the communist threat to Africa was being exaggerated by the Americans.[59]

The Cold War has often been evoked in different circumstances to justify a supposed Soviet threat under the ill-defined, but all-pervasive blanket of security. In the Congo, when Africa and the process of ending colonial rule were briefly of prime international importance, the Cold War was used to conceal those aspects of decolonisation, including neo-colonial ones, that did not easily fit into the dominant 'end of Empire' framework. 'Moderate indigenous nationalists demanding, and their responsible rulers granting, the 'right' form of independence in difficult and problematic circumstances were not the whole story of decolonisation in Africa. Nor was the complex array of specific pressures and responses emanating from international influences sufficient to flesh out such a framework in the Congo. The needs of European capital to survive the sudden end of Belgian colonial rule without damage have to be factored into a Cold War ideological – not security – framework of decolonisation. There was no long-term aim to prolong colonialism, but a short-term requirement to mitigate European companies' economic losses. In London, that was important enough politically to supersede the primacy of standing alongside the Americans, and arguably constituted another important milestone in the Anglo–American special relationship. The British took another step along the road from the dominant and special position of genuine consultation on policy, to one dominated by receiving information and being 'classed with the French'.

Notes

1. Ludo de Witte *The Assassination of Lumumba* (London: Verso, 2003).
2. Nigel Ashton's account in *Kennedy Macmillan and the Cold War* (Basingstoke: Palgrave, 2002) has over forty pages on interdependence and the British nuclear deterrent, and eighteen on the Congo.
3. National Archives and Records Administration (NARA), College Park, Maryland, RG59/CDF755A:00, 1960–63, Box 1831, Cumming Memorandum, 17 June 1960. See also Catherine Hoskyns, *The Congo since Independence* (Oxford: Oxford University Press, 1965), pp. 74–7, and John Kent, *America, the UN and Decolonisation: Cold War Conflict in the Congo* (London: Routledge, 2010), pp. 14–15.
4. NARA/RG59/CDF755A:00, 1960–63, Box 1831, Elizabethville to State, 7 March 1960, Brussels to State, 11 March 1960, and Salisbury to State, 14 March 1960.
5. The National Archives, (TNA), Kew, FO371/146642, Nicholls (Ambassador to Brussels) report on developments in the Congo 10 July 1960.
6. TNA/FO371/146639, Leopoldville to Foreign Office (FO), 1 July 1960.
7. *Foreign Relations of the United States* (FRUS), *1958–60, Vol. XIV, Africa* (Washington: US Government Printing Office, 1988), memorandum of conversation, Herter-Eisenhower, and Assistant Staff Secretary to Goodpaster, both 12 July 1960.
8. NARA/RG59/CDF770G:00, 1960–63, Box 1954, Leopoldville to State, 15 and 18 July 1960.
9. TNA/FO371/146639, Nicholls to Hoyer-Millar, 7 July 1960.
10. TNA/FO371/146646, Leopoldville to FO, 22 July 1960; FO 371/146639 Leopoldville to FO, 14 July 1960, and Leopoldville to FO, 20 July 1960.
11. TNA/FO371/146634, Boothby minute, 13 July 1960.
12. The advantages gained by the new state of Katanga were in the form of the customs duties and taxes paid to Elizabethville rather than Leopoldville. For

Tshombe personally (although having considerable wealth from his father's position as chief of the Lunda people), to offset considerable expenditures on mercenaries and weapons, never mind bribes, by 1962 he had accounts in Belgium, France, Switzerland, Italy and the US. For the UMHK the main advantage was in the percentage of their foreign exchange earnings they were able to receive in hard currency from the Bank of Katanga (45% of foreign exchange earnings as compared to 20% from the Leopoldville government) to use for purchases and payments of dividends to European shareholders, although such payments were suspended in 1962.

13. TNA/FO371/146442, Nicholls diary-letter to Hoyer-Millar, 19 August 1960.
14. NARA/RG59/CDF755A:00, State Department memorandum, 'Analytical Chronology of the Congo Crisis' up to January 1961, undated.
15. TNA/FO371/146442, Nicholls diary-letter to Hoyer-Millar, 17 July 1960.
16. NARA/RG59/CDF755A:00, State Department memorandum, 'Analytical Chronology of the Congo Crisis', up to January 1961, undated.
17. FRUS, 1958–60, XIV, Memorandum of conversation, Herter-Scheyven, 5 August 1960.
18. Larry Devlin, *Chief of Station, Congo* (New York: Public Affairs, 2008).
19. NARA/RG59/CDF755A:00, State Department memorandum, 'Analytical Chronology of the Congo Crisis' up to January 1961, undated.
20. UN Security Council Resolution 146, 9 August 1960, at: http://daccess-dds-ny.un.org/doc/RESOLUTION/GEN/NR0/157/35/IMG/NR015735.pdf?OpenElement.
21. For the UN military actions in August–September 1961, see Kent, *America, the UN and Decolonisation*, pp. 60–68.
22. See Conor Cruise O'Brien, *To Katanga and Back: a UN case history* (London: Hutchinson, 1962) for an account of his time in Elisabethville; and Kent, ibid., pp. 56–7, for how he misrepresented the US position.
23. TNA/CAB128/35, CC (61) 49th, 5 September 1961.
24. NARA/RG59/CDF770G:00, 1960–63, Box 1966, memorandum of conversation, 7 November 1961.
25. Kent, *America, the UN and Decolonisation*, p. 77.
26. JFKL/NSF, Country Series, Congo, Box 29A, London to State, 7 December 1961.
27. NARA/RG59/CDF770G:00, 1960–63, Box 1966, memorandum of conversation, 7 November 1961.
28. Resolution at:<http://daccess-dds-ny.un.org/doc/RESOLUTION/GEN/NR0/171/68/IMG/NR017168.pdf?>.
29. JFKL/NSF, Country Series Congo, Box 27A, Memorandum for the President from Dean Rusk, 'Courses for the US in View of Fighting in Katanga', 7 December 1961.
30. NARA/RG59/CDF770G:00, 1960–63 Box 1967 Leopoldville to State, 11 December 1961; *FRUS 1961–63, Vol XX*, Special National Intelligence Estimate (NIE), 'Possible Developments in Katanga', 7 December 1961.
31. *FRUS, 1961–63, Vol XX*, State to Rusk, 11 December 1961.
32. JFKL, George Ball papers, Box 2, record of telephone conversation, Ball–JFK, 11 December 1961.
33. TNA/CAB128/35, CC(61)74th, 14 December 1961.

34. NARA/RG59/CDF770G:00, 1960–6,3 Box 1973 Paris to State 11 July 1962 JFKL/NSF, Country Series, Congo, Box 31, Brussels to State, 12 July 1962.
35. TNA/FO 371/161516, Nicholls to Stevens, 6 March 1962.
36. 100 francs was about 3 dollars.
37. JFKL/NSF, Country Series, Congo, Box 28A, CIA Memorandum, 12 February 1962.
38. JFKL/NSF, Country Series, Congo, Box 30, Leopoldville to State, 9 April 1962.
39. JFKL/NSF, Country Series, Congo, Box 28, Memorandum by Hilsman, 29 March 1962.
40. JFKL/NSF, Country Series, Congo, Box 28, Briefing paper for Anglo–American–Belgian talks on the Congo, undated.
41. NARA/RG59/CDF770G:00, 1960–63, Box 1971, Leopoldville to State, 19 April 1962.
42. JFKL/NSF, Country Series, Congo, Box 30, State to Brussels, 27 April 1962, and State to London, 11 May 1962.
43. JFKL, Ball papers, record of telephone conversation, Ball–McGhee, 27 May 1962.
44. JFKL/NSF, Country Series, Congo, Box 28, Draft letter Kennedy to 'David', 13 May, which formed telegram 6054 to London, 14 May 1962.
45. JFKL/NSF, Country Series, Congo, Box 30, Telegram 3657, USUN to State, 4 May 1962; Kent *America, the UN and Decolonisation*, p. 90. The political importance of the issue for high policy can be gauged by the fact that in 1961, when the crisis in Central Africa hit British territories in the wake of the Monckton report, the Congo was brought to the attention of the British Cabinet on fifteen occasions, as compared to the four times that the Central African Federation featured. In the following year, 1962, Central African Federation issues were raised in Cabinet twenty times, compared to twenty-seven times for the Congo.
46. JFKL/NSF, Country Series, Congo, Box 28, Ormsby Gore to Rusk, 10 January 1962, and Record of Tripartite talks morning session, first day, in London to State, 15 May 1962.
47. Ibid., London to State, 16 May 1962.
48. Ibid.
49. Ibid., The key documents on the London conference are all included in *FRUS, 1961–63, Vol XX*. As Bruce predicted, the paper the conference produced was unacceptable to the State Department because of the measures proposed in the transition period to independence and the inadequate measures of pressure on Tshombe: *FRUS, 1961–63, Vol XX*, State to Leopoldville, 19 May 1962.
50. JFKL/NSF, Country Series, Congo, Box 28, Ormsby Gore to Rusk, 18 May 1962.
51. Ibid., London to State, 16 May 1962.
52. JFKL/NSF, Country Series, Congo, Box 30A, Leopoldville to State, 22 June, State to London, 21 June, and Leopoldville to State, 25 June 1962.
53. NARA/RG59CDF770G:00, 1960–63, Box 1978, Memorandum of conversation between Rusk, Ormsby Gore and others, 12 July 1962; JFKL/NSF, Country Series, Congo, Box 31, London to State, 13 July 1962.

54. JFKL/NSF, Country Series, Congo, Box 31, State to London, 7 August 1962.
55. TNA/FO 371/102834, War Office memorandum, 'Middle East Garrison', 25 June 1953.
56. JFKL, Brubeck papers, Box 382A, CIA Information Report, 'Prospects for the Congo in the event of a Failure of the UN Reconciliation Plan Situation Appraisal', 5 October 1962.
57. JFKL/NSF, Country Series, Congo, Box 31, USUN to State, 8 August 1962.
58. For details on the drunks and the impact of alcohol on the end of secession see Kent, *America, the UN and Decolonisation*, pp. 137–144.
59. TNA/CAB128/36, CC(62) 73, 6 December 1962.

8
The US Embassy in London and Britain's Withdrawal from East of Suez, 1961–69

John W. Young

One of Saki Dockrill's most significant publications was her monograph, *Britain's Retreat from East of Suez*.[1] In this, the first archival study of the subject, she set Britain's reassessment of its defence priorities in a broad context, looking not only at withdrawal from Southeast Asia and the Persian Gulf, but also at relations with the North Atlantic Treaty Organisation (NATO) over such questions as nuclear-sharing and the size of the British Army of the Rhine (BAOR). She showed that, in reducing spending, the British initially sought cuts in NATO; yet, by 1968, the Wilson government was set on a European future, eager to abandon the world role and enter the European Economic Community (EEC). Saki also looked at the debate over particular weapons systems, such as aircraft carriers and the US-manufactured F-111 aircraft, both vital to a world role. Some previous writers emphasised that the January 1968 decision to quit military bases East of Suez by the end of 1971, was *the* vital turning point in the process of retreat.[2] Others argued it merely marked an acceleration of earlier decisions, especially those announced in July 1967.[3] But, Saki looked further back, seeing harbingers of retreat under the Conservative governments of 1959–63.[4] Throughout the discussions, a vital question was the need to maintain friendly relations with London's main ally, the United States, which, concerned about its own defence burden, could hardly welcome Britain's retreat. This essay looks at the East of Suez debate from the vantage point of the US Ambassador in London, looking at how his embassy interpreted the various stages of British decision-making, how well it was informed about the debate and what it did to influence British leaders.[5]

The Bruce embassy

David Bruce was in London for eight years from March 1961. He had already served as ambassador to France (1949–53) and West Germany (1957–60), and had close links to Great Britain. He was an intelligence officer in London during the Second World War and his wife, Evangeline, was the granddaughter of a Conservative MP. His time in London had already attracted some academic discussion, its appeal boosted by his fascinating diary.[6] He was highly respected on both sides of the Atlantic for his professionalism and, while he was never personally close to Presidents John F. Kennedy (1961–63) or Lyndon B. Johnson (1963–68), was known to 'have the ear of the White House…'.[7] A telling example of his access to Downing Street is the fact that he met Macmillan in January 1963, immediately after French President Charles de Gaulle vetoed the first EEC application.[8] Bruce presided over one of the largest US diplomatic establishments. Particularly significant in dealing with the Labour government was the Deputy Chief of Mission after 1964, Philip Kaiser who, since his time at Oxford University in the 1930s, had come to know several future Cabinet ministers.[9]

Nelson Lankford has argued that it was Lyndon Johnson's lukewarm attitude to foreign policy that allowed Bruce to 'come into his own as Ambassador to Britain' in a way that had been impossible under Kennedy, who was a close friend of the British Ambassador to Washington, David Ormsby Gore, and got on well with Macmillan.[10] When Labour took office in October 1964, the new premier, Harold Wilson, had high hopes of establishing close relations with the White House, but Johnson never showed any sign of reciprocating.[11] Despite the supposed pre-eminence of Britain's Washington embassy in the relationship, there was plenty of transatlantic business for Bruce to conduct in the 1960s. In particular, three persistent concerns loomed large in the Ambassador's mind and had long-term significance for Anglo–American relations. The first was Britain's economic decline relative to its major competitors, like America, Germany and Japan. Throughout Bruce's time in London, the British economy was dogged by balance of payments problems and low growth. This economic weakness forced the government into expenditure cuts, which, in part at least, led to the second major challenge, Britain's withdrawal from its world role. The third problem was America's growing involvement in the Vietnam War, which stretched US resources and made it difficult for Washington to think of filling the power voids left by its ally's retreat.

Holding the position, 1961–66

In economic terms, Britain had never properly recovered from the financial strains of the Second World War and, by the late 1950s, with its global system of defence bases and expensive welfare state, was living beyond its means. Under Macmillan there was a situation of 'stop-go economics', whereby attempts to boost domestic demand led to increased imports, which in turn damaged the balance of payments position and forced a return to deflation. In such a situation, it was inevitable Britain should try to make savings in its overseas commitments. The 1957 Defence White Paper aimed almost to halve military manpower within five years. However, this proved difficult to achieve, not least because Britain clung to its great power ambitions. In October 1961, the Macmillan government laid down Britain's strategic roles as being: to contribute to nuclear deterrence; to defend Western Europe from the threat posed by the Soviet bloc; and to maintain the presence East of Suez. The last was intended to help preserve world order, defend the Commonwealth and guarantee stable conditions for trade, which was vital to national wealth. Any hopes of cutting expenditure in Southeast Asia were reduced, in 1963, when forces were committed to protect Malaysia–Singapore, thanks to the threat posed by neighbouring Indonesia, in the so-called 'confrontation', a period of tension marked by cross-border raids and diplomatic abuse. To adhere to a ceiling on defence spending of 7 per cent of Gross National Product, it seemed easier to cut manpower in Europe, where the size of the BAOR fell from 77,000 in the mid-1950s to 51,000 in 1962. Despite doubts from the Treasury, the Conservatives also maintained ambitious equipment programmes including, in 1963–64, decisions to build a new aircraft carrier and develop an advanced tactical, strike and reconnaissance aircraft, TSR-2. In June 1963, Lord Home, the Foreign Secretary (soon to succeed Macmillan as premier), wrote, '*We have rejected the idea that we should "choose between Europe and a world role"*. We have worldwide interests and must therefore have available a worldwide presence to protect them'.[12]

Given the Conservatives' determination to maintain the world role, Bruce could be content with British defence policy in this period. Neither does he seem to have recognised any contradiction between the fulfilment of a world role and his own desires for a stable British economy and membership of the EC. He also approved British opposition to Indonesia.[13] Such concern as existed on the US side, concerned London's commitment to NATO. When, in the light of tension with the Soviet Union over Berlin in 1961, Kennedy urged NATO members to increase their defence efforts, Bruce realised this would sit uneasily alongside Britain's need for retrenchment.[14] In February 1962, when the US government learnt the content of Britain's upcoming Defence White Paper, it provoked what Bruce termed 'deep disappointment' and led Kennedy to complain in a personal message to Macmillan.[15] But Bruce commented that, 'As long as they continue to finance their independent nuclear deterrent, and keep the present ceiling on their total military expenditures, there is little chance, in my opinion, of BAOR being adequately manned and equipped'.[16] Fortunately for Macmillan, as tension over Berlin eased, so did US concern about the BAOR and whereas, in early 1962, Washington would have welcomed Britain's abandonment of the nuclear deterrent, by the end of the year Kennedy had offered the Prime Minister Polaris missiles with which to deliver it.

By October 1964, when Harold Wilson narrowly won power, there was a serious balance of payments deficit of £400 million. Yet, Labour ruled out devaluation of the Pound and wanted Washington to support the currency. The Americans were willing, partly because a devaluation of the Pound could lead to speculation against the Dollar. Washington helped put together a $3 billion support package for Sterling following Labour's first budget. While hoping that Britain would maintain its key role in Western defence, Americans wanted to see Labour reduce its domestic spending plans, but it was always clear that there might be some cutbacks East of Suez. A weekend ministerial meeting in November 1964 agreed, under Treasury pressure, to a ceiling of £2 billion on defence spending (at 1964 prices) by the financial year 1969–70. A comprehensive review of defence spending was launched and some aircraft projects were scrapped, with cheaper alternatives to be bought 'off the shelf' from America. TSR-2, for example, was replaced by the F-111. Another meeting, in June 1965, discussed the possible reduction of bases East of Suez, but the British still intended to maintain a presence there, perhaps withdrawing from Singapore to a base in Australia. The White Paper of February 1966 was very much a compromise on East of Suez. It planned major reductions in the Mediterranean and Middle East, and lower spending in the Far East once the 'confrontation' with Indonesia ended. East of Suez, Britain would not 'undertake major operations of war except in co-operation with allies.' The aircraft carrier planned by the Conservatives was cancelled, but the F-111 was still seen as a means to exercise power in the region. In 1969–70 Southeast Asia would still absorb over a third of the defence budget and no date was set to leave Singapore.[17]

Faced by this cautious approach to defence cuts, the Americans showed only limited concern about British plans. During Labour's early months, Bruce's greatest concern in the defence field was still Europe. He hoped Wilson would not rule out participation in the so-called 'Multilateral Force', which involved a system of nuclear-sharing among NATO allies and was designed to prevent West Germany seeking nuclear weapons. This issue dominated the first Wilson–Johnson summit in December 1964. Then again, the Americans also took the opportunity at the meetings to express their support for Britain's world role; it was clear that they were anxious to see this maintained.[18] The Prime Minister had warned the Ambassador in the wake of the November 1964 Chequers meeting that Labour could not maintain current expenditure on the world role, but he also described himself as an 'East of Suez man'[19] and Bruce's diaries during the defence review only intermittently suggest worries about Britain's commitment to the region. This picture confirms Saki Dockrill's finding that, from Washington's perspective, 'details about the current Defence Review coming from London were vague and fragmented'.[20]

In February 1965 the Ambassador, fearing another 'run' on the Pound, expressed doubts as to whether Britain's payments problems could be surmounted 'without a large cutback in prestige expenditures abroad' and he was aware that some in London favoured a wholesale withdrawal from East of Suez.[21] One of these was the deputy Prime Minister, George Brown, who told Philip Kaiser that, while he understood the US wanted Britain to remain East of Suez, it should be possible to dispense with some commitments there.[22] At one point, in September, British civil servants even told a US team that 'the jig is up as far as the UK being able indefinitely to maintain its base' at Singapore was concerned. However, Bruce wondered if this was 'not part of a play to induce the US and others to take over part of their east of Suez burden'.[23] In October 1965, the Shadow defence secretary, Enoch Powell, told the Conservative Party conference that the East of Suez position must be reconsidered, leading Bruce to note that 'this will alarm people at home'.[24] He was certainly correct in this judgement. The Under-Secretary of State, George Ball, had argued a few months earlier that it was in US interests to prop up the Pound, because otherwise Britain might save money by withdrawing from East of Suez, leaving Washington to pick up the commitments on a permanent basis. And in June, the Defense Secretary, Robert McNamara, told the British Chancellor of the Exchequer, James Callaghan, that US support for Britain in its financial difficulties 'was conditional on their-being no change in Britain's world-wide political commitments'.[25] In mid-September, Bruce accompanied Ball to meetings with Wilson, where the Under-Secretary 'pointed out in detail the disastrous consequences if the word should be spread that Western power might be withdrawn or diminished' and warned 'neither the US nor Australia had any intention of letting the British off the hook' in Southeast Asia'.[26]

In November 1965, Wilson's Secretary of Defence, Denis Healey, told McNamara, that Britain hoped that in future the US, Australia and New Zealand would play a greater role in defending Western interests in the Indian Ocean. This reflected British plans for sharing burdens with its allies around the world.[27] Nonetheless, it hardly suggested a wholesale withdrawal from East of Suez and the way the British portrayed the review was calculated to ease American fears. Thus, McNamara felt the F-111 purchase was 'the best evidence that [the British] intend to maintain their commitments east of Suez'.[28] The provisional findings of the defence review were a major item for a Wilson–Johnson summit, in December, ahead of which Bundy told the President, 'We need a British role at Singapore for as far ahead as we can see...'.[29] Wilson set out the decisions in a brisk manner and hinted at an eventual withdrawal from Singapore, after the 'confrontation' with Indonesia ended, but he said Britain intended to remain a force East of Suez after that. The complicated nature of his position is brought out in the American record:

> Not talking withdrawal – and only when confrontation ends; we know you cannot take our place; but for the long-run, and if confrontation ends, we can't keep up our present arrangements indefinitely; in the end we are thinking of a scheme involving withdrawal to northwest Australia.[30]

This two-sided approach does much to explain Saki Dockrill's judgement that, at the end of the talks, 'it was arguable how far the Americans had really appreciated the magnitude of Britain's plans to reduce its world commitments in relation to its financial capacity'.[31]

Bruce attended both the summit meeting and more detailed talks, with a British delegation led by Healey and Foreign Secretary Michael Stewart, in Washington in January 1966. Here, again, the British were keen to calm any fears of a premature withdrawal. On the one hand, they believed a withdrawal from Singapore was inevitable in the long-term (thanks to anti-colonialist pressures) and would buy only a limited number of F-111 aircraft. On the other hand, they planned to remain in the Persian Gulf, were investigating a base in northern Australia and wanted to develop 'quadripartite' co-operation with the US, Australia and New Zealand. Bruce felt they 'allayed American fears that they would no longer, in view of diminished economic and financial resources, play a global political and military role.' Despite substantial cuts, the British, 'with improved cost effectiveness should still command an important military establishment'.[32] All this confirmed American expectations, prior to the talks, that British proposals would 'involve comparatively minor and, from our viewpoint, generally manageable adjustments in their overseas military posture, at least for the next two or three years'.[33] Yet, it seems Bruce and his colleagues were deceived. There was already an element of dishonesty in the British position in that, once the 'confrontation' ended, and if it proved impossible to secure an Australian base, the only real option was a complete withdrawal from Southeast Asia.[34] The Ambassador's position in London does not seem to have given him any greater insight into the direction of Labour's defence cuts than that of Washington.

Sounding the retreat, 1966–67

A month after the White Paper, Wilson secured a clear majority in another general election, but only four months after that the future of Britain's defence posture was thrown into doubt by renewed pressure on Sterling. At the same time, political changes in Indonesia paved the way for an end to 'confrontation', which in turn allowed the British to contemplate an early withdrawal from Malaysia–Singapore. An initial round of further defence cuts was announced, as part of an emergency deflationary package, on 20 July 1966, and another defence review followed, with Brown, now Foreign Secretary, seeing Britain's future as lying in EC membership, the corollary of which was an end to East of Suez. A ministerial meeting in December agreed to discuss a full withdrawal from Southeast Asia and an interim White Paper, in February 1967, was followed within weeks by approval of a 'peripheral strategy', whereby forces would quit mainland Southeast Asia in 1975–76. Brown explained this concept to US, Australian and New Zealand representatives at a meeting of the South East Asia Treaty Organisation (SEATO), in Washington on 18–20 April. It was a pivotal moment in the history of British foreign policy. Predictably, his statement drew a negative US response, with McNamara and Secretary of State Dean Rusk unable to understand why an announcement had to be made so far in advance of the actual withdrawal. Such a step could only complicate the Western position in the region, at a time when the Vietnam War was at its height. Brown replied, not only that the Labour government must make budgetary savings and must announce these soon in order to placate its critics, but also that 'white faces' were increasingly unwelcome in Asia, and British defence chiefs needed to plan for a new future. The most the British would do to placate their allies was to preserve a 'capability' to intervene in the area after the mid-1970s. The White Paper of July confirmed these decisions. Privately, the British also decided to withdraw from the Persian Gulf, but they did not publicise this decision for fear of instability in the region, where British forces supported a number of Arab sheikhdoms.[35]

How successful were Bruce and the Embassy in discovering British intentions during this phase? As the July 1966 crisis struck, Bruce warned Washington about the British economy in dramatic terms:

> The country seems at the mercy of economic drift and unsuccessful improvisation... We must also contemplate the likelihood that they would require a further curtailment of Britain's ability to continue even at present planned levels the military commitments East of Suez and probably in Germany. I do not conclude that Britain is going down the drain, but every sluice gate is beginning to open.[36]

But economic experts in Washington, and even some of his own staff, felt such warnings too pessimistic.[37] When the Ambassador visited Washington shortly afterwards, to prepare for another summit, McNamara again urged that the British 'must maintain, even if in diminished strength, their semi-global military posture, especially East of Suez and in Germany', a view endorsed by the Secretary of State, Dean Rusk.[38] The US government briefly considered underwriting Britain's financial obligations in return for pursuing the kind of foreign policy Washington wanted to see – including a bid to enter the EC and the abandonment of the nuclear deterrent. Bruce, however, was among those opposed to such a dramatic offer.[39] As it transpired, Wilson, who was anxious to appear bullish in the face of the latest economic crisis, told Johnson 'that the UK will continue to carry its share of the load East of Suez'.[40]

The British continued to give out messages designed to reassure the Americans, such as Wilson's undertaking to Johnson, in November, that the position in Southeast Asia would be held, at least for the time being.[41] However, it is noteworthy that, even in Washington, some officials believed the burdens on Britain were becoming too great to sustain. As early as July 1965, Francis Bator, of the National Security Staff had warned it was too much to expect the UK to maintain the value of Sterling, cut domestic spending, remain East of Suez *and* keep a sizeable army in Germany.[42] In September 1965, Dean Acheson, a former Secretary of State, talked of Britain as a 'wizened island'.[43] And in October 1966, John Leddy of the State Department's Bureau of European Affairs hoped Washington would ignore a request, recently made by Wilson, to 'enlighten Brown on the importance of Britain's world role…'. Leddy argued, 'The Foreign Secretary is on our side…and I hope we will not discourage him by overstressing the East of Suez argument. They will do what they will East of Suez and I see no further mileage [in] belabouring the world responsibility there at the cost of Britain's responsibilities in Europe'.[44] Like Bator, Acheson and Leddy, Bruce, too, was concerned about Britain's economic strains and keen to see it join the EEC, but he never seems to have drawn the conclusion, in the clear way Leddy did, that it was therefore better to ease off the pressure on London to play a world role.

The British largely succeeded in hiding their plans for a rapid retreat from East of Suez from the Americans and other allies, until the very brink of Brown's announcement to SEATO in April. The uncertainty of the embassy about future British policy can be seen in a 1 March report from Kaiser, following 'the most massive, back-bench disaffection on any major issue since the Government has been in power', when its own MPs bitterly attacked the ambiguities in the Labour government's defence policy. Kaiser believed these ambiguities were deliberate:

> The present 'straddling' policy on East of Suez, while it displeases Little Englanders and Europe-Firsters, still holds heavy hints of retrenchment and ultimate withdrawal. To put this policy in clearer focus would alienate not just 'imperialists', but those who genuinely feel (and it is noteworthy that Wilson and Healey are both in this camp) that Britain does have a contribution to make in the area and that in any event this presence gives Britain a degree of influence on US policy which it would otherwise not have.

The London Embassy feared 'the effect of the debate will be to toughen British policy along lines least congenial to us', but also felt that the 'first test' was likely to be a contest over further cuts in the BAOR and that 'on balance, we would expect continuation of the essentially "straddling" defence policy…'.[45]

Washington knew, ahead of the SEATO meeting, that Brown's main purpose was to discuss East of Suez. The Americans prepared some arguments against further British cutbacks there, including one that there had been 'considerable progress made in recovering from the balance of payments crisis.' But one memorandum warned, 'we should recognize that at some point in the mid-70's we could well lose the British East Asian military presence altogether'.[46] By mid-April, then, the US understood that a dramatic British move was *possible*. However, the rumours only turned into reality a few days before the SEATO meeting, when a British journalist, Henry Brandon, leaked the story in the *Sunday Times* of 16 April.[47] This was highly embarrassing for the US embassy because, on 14 April, warned of the Brandon story, it reported only 'circumstantial evidence' in support of the journalist's claim, before arguing that 'on balance' the story was unlikely; if plans for a withdrawal did exist, the British 'have been at considerable pains to keep them from us.' Only on 18 April – the day the SEATO conference opened – did the embassy concede that the British Cabinet was indeed planning to leave East of Suez by the mid-1970s.[48] The US response was predictable. Bruce, who hoped the British would 'desist from making any such announcement as is contemplated', was asked to deliver a firmly-worded memorandum from Rusk to Brown. While sympathetic to Britain's economic difficulties, this expressed deep concern about 'making significant reductions in force unless and until there is a real change in the Vietnam situation.' If Britain persisted, it would encourage opponents of the Vietnam war to argue that there were no vital Western interests in Southeast Asia; it could lead some Senators to push for US military reductions in Europe; and it would be treated as 'a victory' by Communist states like China.[49] Other allied governments expressed similar concerns. The shock of Britain's move led Johnson to ask Wilson, when they met at the funeral of former German Chancellor Konrad Adenauer, whether the British government was 'going crazy' in planning to quit Southeast Asia.[50]

Over the following weeks, Bruce found that the British were no longer prepared to compromise much on cost-cutting, even for the sake of their American allies. He encouraged a visiting US official, William Benton, to raise the issue with Wilson in late April, pressing the case that any reductions should be made 'without fanfare or publicity', in view of the possible adverse effects 'in relation to Vietnam.' But Wilson commented that it was partly because of Vietnam that Britain did not advocate an even earlier withdrawal.[51] Even two Labour critics of Wilson, Woodrow Wyatt and Christopher Mayhew, told the Ambassador that the Prime Minister would push the reductions through and, despite Bruce's argument to the contrary, predicted Johnson would accept the position.[52] In early May, Brown asked to see Bruce privately. He again set out the British case for the cuts, but also revealed the offer to retain the 'capability' to re-intervene East of Suez after the mid-1970s. The Ambassador did not hide his strong feelings. He told Brown that an announcement of retreat, 'eight years in advance of it being carried into effect', was 'more likely to cause bitter controversy between the US and UK Governments than any other issue between us during the last few years.' Bruce tried to persuade the British to delay any final decision until Wilson and Johnson met, and in order to secure this he stated the situation in the starkest terms:

> ... the appearance of our being deserted (for that is how the project would be analyzed) in the midst of our Vietnamese involvement, by a Government assumed to be our most loyal ally, headed by a Prime Minister who had repeatedly declared himself an 'East of Suez Man', would seem to me unwise, provocative and absolutely unacceptable to us ... .[53]

The Ambassador was present when McNamara, on a visit to London a few days later, took up similar themes with Healey.[54] There was another written appeal on 12 May from Rusk to Brown about the withdrawal, which Bruce delivered personally.[55] During this time, as Saki Dockrill noted, US policy was co-ordinated with other allies to increase the pressure on the British.[56] Yet, over the following weeks, American feelings subsided. Ahead of the next Johnson–Wilson summit, Bruce reported that, 'Important as the Far East and Middle East are, for the British they are less compelling than domestic economics and politics ...' and explained:

> An announcement in July of substantial savings in [the East of Suez] area, looking ahead to what may be a stormy Labor Party Conference in September, is probably the juiciest bone he [Wilson] can throw his critics. It commends itself in both budgetary and foreign exchange savings ... and it appeals to the growing number who, for doctrinal or emotional reasons, want to reduce Britain's world role. Furthermore, it is thought by some to strengthen the Common Market bid.[57]

It was part of an ambassador's role, of course, to provide objective political reports on the state to which he was accredited and, in this telegram, Bruce showed he could understand Wilson's position, even if it ran counter to US interests. More surprising, perhaps, at the Johnson–Wilson encounter on 2 June, there were no fireworks over East of Suez. This may partly have been because, by coincidence, the meeting occurred as war broke out between Israel and the Arabs, a crisis that forced Britain and the US together.[58]

It was not that Washington had accepted the idea of British withdrawal, but there was no sign Wilson would back down. In late June, the US embassy believed that 'under almost any circumstances the British are going to be out of Singapore–Malaysia by mid-1970's.' Bruce felt London might yet be dissuaded from an immediate announcement of this, but he also believed such a 'planning assumption' would leak and be 'tantamount to a decision to get out.' Around this time, the Ambassador seems to have gained a fuller grasp of thinking within Whitehall. It was not only economic problems, popular opinion and a desire to focus on Europe that pointed away from the world role. Defence planners needed a long 'lead-time' to plan force levels and equipment procurement. In other words, even the British military chiefs wanted to settle the future of the world role in clear terms, abandoning any costly attempt to 'straddle' multiple roles. It is also noteworthy that Bruce was confused about Washington's purpose by now: did they really want to keep a British presence East of Suez after the mid-1970s, or did they simply want to forestall an early announcement of a rapid retreat?[59] There was another bout of protests about British intentions from America and other allies in mid-July, but London again rejected such pleas.[60]

Accelerating withdrawal, 1967–68

The drastic decisions of July 1967 did not end Labour's attempts to re-define Britain's defence posture. In November, there was another Sterling crisis, so severe that the government had to devalue the Pound, accompanied by more expenditure cuts and the replacement of Callaghan at the Treasury by Roy Jenkins. Like Brown, Jenkins was a critic of the East of Suez role and a keen advocate of focusing on EC membership. Before the year ended, he put forward a plan to retire from Southeast Asia by 1971 and from the Persian Gulf even earlier. Despite support from the Prime Minister, the Chancellor found tough opposition from some other ministers over the details. Healey was keen, for example, to retain the F-111 order. A series of divisive cabinet meetings in January, accompanied by pressure from the US and other allies, led to a compromise decision, announced on 16 January, to withdraw from both Southeast Asia and the Persian Gulf by December 1971.[61]

In this last, short phase of the debate, it is possible to trace Bruce's views and the work of his staff in some detail. In the wake of the unpleasant surprises of the previous April, the embassy was well aware of the possibility of dramatic British action. But they were also helped by disaffected individuals in the British government, who were willing to share their dismay over events. Even senior ministers, including Brown and Healey, were happy to reveal details of Cabinet discussions with US officials. It was not that the Foreign and Defence Secretaries were opposed to withdrawal in principle. Both, of course, had been deeply involved in planning the July 1967 cuts. But now, they opposed Jenkin's drive for a more rapid retreat, accompanied by the end of the F-111 purchase and, with it, any capacity for re-intervention. Bruce first seems to have become aware of differences inside the Cabinet on 6 January, after sending over a message from Rusk to Brown, which began, 'I am deeply disturbed by information which has just reached me that HMG may be considering accelerating its withdrawal from the Persian Gulf.' Bruce talked to Brown about this over the telephone and gathered the latter had 'been trying, to some extent vainly, to ... persuade his colleagues not to freeze their attitudes on defence matters until he has discussed these questions with the Secretary ... '. Bruce telegrammed Rusk to tell him that Brown seemed 'sympathetic to our views, but has encountered strong opposition in the Cabinet.' However, when Bruce saw Wilson, the latter was quick to downplay any problem and said he would discuss the issue with Johnson when they met for their next summit in February – which hardly suggests that he wanted to be open with his key ally about the scale of the new cuts.[62]

Confirmation of the bitter Cabinet debates came in a 'private chat' between Healey and the Embassy's Political–Military Counsellor, Ron Spiers, three days later, where the discussion, 'which lasted an hour, was frank and far ranging.' Healey claimed the position was better than it had been a month before, when he feared 'lunatic' Cabinet decisions, but a 'big majority' were in favour of a rapid withdrawal from Malaysia–Singapore and the Persian Gulf. He and Brown felt it made sense to leave the Gulf, but they were holding out for a longer timescale on leaving Southeast Asia. The Defence Secretary hoped to save much of the F-111 order, but complained that Wilson had 'led the pack' against this. In drawing this 'rather extraordinary conversation' to Rusk's attention, Bruce thought it 'impossible to predict what compromises may finally be reached' and felt it unlikely whether anything Rusk might say to Brown would 'necessarily alter what seems probable British action.' Significantly, Bruce also opposed any idea of threatening the British: it was merely 'essential ... we remain on record as still believing they should continue to honor their present obligations'.[63] However defeatist the Ambassador's judgement, it proved a realistic one. Over the following days, the contemplated withdrawals remained 'a stormy subject' but Jenkins largely got what he wanted.[64]

On 11 January, visiting Washington to explain the likely reductions, Brown had a 'bloody unpleasant' meeting with Rusk, who asked 'Why don't you act like Britain?' But this was preaching to the converted. Brown privately told the Americans that 'these were the saddest days of his life' and even encouraged Johnson to plead with Wilson for a rethink. Yet there was little hope this would achieve anything.[65] Bruce delivered the message, read over summaries of the Rusk–Brown talks and concluded, 'It looks as if the jig is up for any real British military activity after 1970 in the Far East, and probably in the Middle East. The Cabinet…seem to have decided Great Britain cannot have both guns and butter'.[66] On the 14th, the Embassy also heard 'through the grapevine' that the Cabinet had approved all the expected cuts, including cancellation of the F-111 purchase. At this point, Bruce's personal feelings spilled over in his diary: 'I feel these decisions in the military field represent a gross deficiency in good judgment. Once their forces leave an area, reentry will be more or less impossible'.[67] He was even more outspoken in a letter to Washington, saying the likely British cuts were 'calamitous, destructive, selfish, myopic, and threatening to world orderliness…. They constitute, perhaps, the most deplorable resolve, except for Munich, that any British Government has taken during the last 150 years.' He also used the cuts to defend his past reports:

> This Embassy has, I realize, for a long time been viewed in some Departmental quarters at home as over pessimistic in its assessment of the probable course of British foreign policies, especially as concerns defense commitments. The truth is, we have been witnessing the gradual, now accelerated, decline of a formerly great power…

Yet, he also concluded that, 'Reproaches from one nation to another, are seldom constructive'.[68]

There was another message from Johnson to Wilson on the 15th, declaring, 'if you decide to forego the acquisition of the F-111, everyone here will regard this as a total disengagement from any commitments whatsoever to the security of areas outside Europe.' The message had a threatening tone, with its hint of reductions in US military purchases from Britain.[69] But, in Bruce's words, 'the President lost both his pleas'. On the morning of Wilson's announcement of the new cuts, a 'tired and dispirited' Healey gave more, detailed information to Spiers, including the names of those ministers who had resisted the F-111 cancellation and precise voting figures from Cabinet meetings. Healey also confirmed US suspicions that there was a trade-off between domestic and international reductions: the F-111 cancellation was a 'sacrificial goat' designed to placate those who had hoped to raise the school leaving age. It was partly because of this meeting that Bruce commented on the 'wonderfully efficient' way his staff gathered information:

> They have built up a sort of intelligence system, and it is quite remarkable how forthcoming, on the basis of personal trust and friendship, some of their British counterparts have been in keeping them advised of what is going on behind the scenes.[70]

But it is doubtful whether this co-operation would have been so full had Brown and Healey not been so alienated by their own government's policy. The British had been much less forthcoming over their thinking on defence in 1965 and 1967. The Embassy's intelligence-gathering may have been much improved compared to those earlier occasions, but the lesson learnt was a simple one – that information on a government's inner machinations is most easily obtained when its members are happy to provide it.

Curiously, in reflecting on the January 1968 crisis, the Ambassador reserved his most withering comments for Healey, whose 'record in supporting defense measures now renounced was consistent.' To underline the point, Bruce listed several statements made by the Defence Secretary in recent years about the need to remain East of Suez and to purchase the F-111. Yet, Healey did not resign when these commitments evaporated. 'If he did, he would sink, at least temporarily, into political oblivion, which would not be to his liking'.[71] The Ambassador understood there would be little cost at election-time to Wilson from defence cuts: 'abdication of a world role has depressed the citizens, but has not seemed to have stirred up great popular resentment. In Britain, as far as elections are concerned, foreign policy is of minor interest ... '.[72] The real importance of the recent defence debates lay with political personalities. Summing up the situation for Rusk in late January, Bruce argued that they had strengthened Jenkins' position as a possible future Prime Minister. The ambassador also noted the 'unusual' alliance between Jenkins and Wilson, even though they had never been 'on especially good terms', and the fact that the F-111 had provided 'the greatest battle' because its cancellation signalled 'the abandonment by Britain of any global role or influence'.[73] As to Wilson's February summit with Johnson, Bruce predicted that 'the President will not reproach Wilson when the latter comes to Washington, but the Prime Minister will find himself regarded as a man with whom Lyndon Johnson would not care to go to a water hole'.[74] This proved too pessimistic. As so often, Johnson adapted himself to the continuing retreat of his ally with extraordinary restraint. Indeed this, the last Wilson–Johnson summit proved one of the warmest.[75]

Conclusion

Historians recognise a decline in the significance of the 'special relationship' in the 1960s, partly because the withdrawal from East of Suez, alongside the devaluation of Sterling, made Britain less valuable as an ally for Washington.[76] Yet, the friendly relations between the US Embassy and British governments throughout Bruce's ambassadorship lend weight to Alan Dobson's point that, whatever the decline in the *importance* of the relationship, bilateral links still retained a good *quality*.[77] Certainly, the Ambassador himself had easy access to British ministers, right up to the Prime Minister, when he needed to discuss issues. Nonetheless, looking at the East of Suez question, it is clear that an open and cordial atmosphere is no guarantee that an Embassy will be well-informed on a close ally's plans. For a long time in 1965–67, while it recognised a rapid retreat from Britain's world role were possible, the Embassy did not realise how seriously Labour ministers were contemplating such a step. The April 1967 announcement came as something of a shock to the Ambassador and his staff, not helped by the fact that a journalist had 'scooped' the story first. After that, they were more alert to the possibilities of a precipitate retreat but, as seen above, the Embassy's successful intelligence on British thinking in January 1968 was decisively helped by the readiness of Brown and Healey to reveal the inner workings of the Cabinet. However large and well-connected the Embassy was, it could not break down the secret workings of Whitehall unless helped from within. The record of the Embassy in predicting British policy was, therefore, mixed.

It is legitimate to ask, in light of this, how vital the Embassy was to the smooth functioning of transatlantic relations. It would be wrong of course to judge its value on one issue. Bruce's officials were involved in a plethora of subjects, from trade promotion to the provision of consular services, which arguably made the Embassy irreplaceable as an institution. However, political–security relations on such delicate issues as defence spending, the Western alliance and NATO, were also handled at a higher level, in talks between foreign and defence ministers and, at the highest level of all, at summits. Did a resident ambassador still have a meaningful role in exchanges on these topics? In answer to this question, it is surely significant that Bruce was often present at the most important meetings. He briefed the President before summits, acted as host to McNamara and Rusk when they visited London and delivered messages to Wilson, Brown and others. Ambassadors might not be as central to diplomatic contacts as they had been a century earlier, but they continued to oil the machine and, when a crisis blew up, were on the spot to handle the challenge. Bruce was also important it seems, for providing Washington with an objective understanding of why the British took the decisions they did, even if he disagreed with it. Then again, viewed in retrospect, it has to be asked whether he could not have been clearer in his own mind about the contradiction between recognising the dire state of the British economy and yet expecting the country to maintain its global position. In 1965–66, US-based officials like Bator and Leddy were aware that Britain could not bear all the burdens that Washington expected it to sustain. Acceptance of such an argument might have given greater clarity to US policy, had Bruce joined the chorus, and it might have made Washington more aware, at an earlier date, of the likelihood – and even the wisdom – of Britain's retreat from East of Suez.

Notes

I am grateful to the British Academy and the University of Nottingham for funding research into David Bruce's diaries and at archives in the United States.

1. Basingstoke: Macmillan, 2002. A more recent analysis on Southeast Asia is P.L. Pham, *Ending East of Suez: the British decision to withdraw from Malaysia and Singapore* (Oxford: Oxford University Press, 2010).
2. Jeffrey Pickering, *Britain's Withdrawal from East of Suez* (Basingstoke: Macmillan, 1998) and 'Politics and "Black Tuesday": shifting power in the Cabinet and the decision to withdraw from "East of Suez"', *Twentieth Century British History*, 13/2 (2002).
3. David Greenwood, *The Economics of the East of Suez Decision* (Aberdeen: Aberdeen University Press, 1973).
4. See also Matthew Jones, 'A Decision Delayed: Britain's withdrawal from Southeast Asia reconsidered', *English Historical Review*, CXVII/472 (2002), pp. 569–95.
5. The chapter therefore builds on an increasing interest among scholars in the role of embassies. See, for example: Michael Hopkins, Saul Kelly and John Young (eds), *The Washington Embassy: British ambassadors to the United States, 1939–77* (Basingstoke: Palgrave Macmillan, 2009); Jonathan Colman, 'Portrait of an Institution: the US Embassy in London, 1945–53', *Hague Journal of Diplomacy*, 4 (2009), pp. 339–60.

6. Nelson Lankford, *The Last American Aristocrat: the biography of David K.E. Bruce* (Boston: Little, Brown, 1995); Jonathan Colman, 'The London Ambassadorship of David K.E. Bruce during the Wilson–Johnson years, 1964–68', *Diplomacy and Statecraft*, 15/4 (2004), pp. 327–52; and 'Introduction' to Raj Roy and John W. Young (eds), *Ambassador to Sixties London: the diaries of David Bruce, 1961–69* (Dordrecht: Republic of Letters Publishing, 2009).
7. Association for Diplomatic Studies and Training, Arlington, Virginia, Foreign Affairs Oral History Collection (hereinafter FAOHC; available online at http: //www.adst.org/Oral_History.htm), Sheldon Krys interview.
8. Virginia Historical Society, Richmond, Virginia, David Bruce diary (hereinafter Diary), 16 January 1963.
9. Philip Kaiser, *Journeying Far and Wide* (New York: Scribner's, 1992), pp. 59–71.
10. Lankford, *American Aristocrat*, p. 312.
11. John W. Young, *The Labour Governments, 1964–70: Volume II, International Policy* (Manchester: Manchester University Press, 2003), 21–2; and see Jonathan Colman, *A Special Relationship? Harold Wilson, Lyndon Johnson and Anglo–American relations* (Manchester: Manchester University Press, 2004).
12. Italics in original. Quoted in Dockrill, *East of Suez*, 40.
13. Diary, 28 September 1963.
14. Diary, 21 July 1961.
15. Diary, 17 February 1962.
16. Diary, 29 March 1962.
17. See Dockrill, *East of Suez*, chapters 3, 4, 6 and 7; Young, *Labour Governments*, pp. 35–45.
18. Saki Dockrill, 'Forging the Anglo–American global defence partnership: Harold Wilson, Lyndon Johnson and the Washington summit, December 1964', *Journal of Strategic Studies*, 23/4 (December 2000), pp. 107–29.
19. Diary, 27 November 1964.
20. Dockrill, *East of Suez*, p. 116.
21. Diary, 9 February and 15 March 1965.
22. National Archives and Record Administration (NARA), College Park, Maryland, Record Group (RG) 59, POL7UK, box 2777, telegram, London to State, 6 February 1965.
23. Diary, 5 September 1965.
24. Diary, 17 October 1965.
25. Record of McNamara-Callaghan meeting, 30 June, and Ball memorandum, 6 August 1965, quoted in Dockrill, *East of Suez*, pp. 116–17.
26. Lyndon B. Johnson Library (LBJL), Austin, Texas, National Security File (NSF), Country File (CF), United Kingdom (UK), box 208, London to State Department, 10 September 1965.
27. Diary, 26 November 1965.
28. Cyrus L. Sulzberger, *An Age of Mediocrity* (New York: Macmillan, 1973), p. 265.
29. LBJL, Office Files of the President, box 13, Bundy to Johnson, 16 December 1965.
30. LBJL, Francis Bator papers, box 2, Notes of President's meeting with Wilson, 16 December 1965.

31. Dockrill, *East of Suez*, pp. 134–7, quote from 136; Pham, *Ending*, pp. 70–72.
32. Bruce Diary, 27 and 28 January 1966.
33. NARA, RG59, Lot 67D305, box 398, 'Summary of Joint State-Defense Scope Paper', 21 January 1966.
34. Dockrill, *East of Suez*, pp. 148–9 and pp. 155–6; Pham, *Ending*, pp. 74–7; John Subritzsky, *Confronting Sukarno: British, American, Australian and New Zealand diplomacy in the Malaysian-Indonesian confrontation* (Basingstoke: Macmillan, 2000), pp. 199–201.
35. On the 1966–7 review see: Dockrill, *East of Suez*, pp. 157–99; Young, *Labour Governments*, pp. 45–9; and, on the Washington meeting, Pham, *Ending*, pp. 154–8.
36. Diary, London to State (for Under-Secretary), 11 July 1966.
37. LBJL, Francis Bator papers, box 3, memorandum for the President, 27 July 1966; Colman, 'London Ambassadorship', pp. 336–7.
38. Diary, 22 July 1966.
39. Diary, 27 July 1966.
40. LBJL, Francis Bator papers, box 3, memorandum for the President, 29 July 1966; and see Pham, *Ending*, pp. 118–22.
41. The National Archives (TNA), Kew, PREM 13/808, Wilson to Johnson, 28 November 1967.
42. Bator memorandum, 29 July 1965, *Foreign Relations of the United States* (*FRUS*), 1964–68, Vol. XII, document 247, http://history.state.gov/historicaldocuments/frus1964–68v12/ch6 (accessed 23 June 2011).
43. Sterling Library, Yale University, Dean Acheson papers, draft memorandum to Robert Schaetzel, 10 September 1965. I am grateful to Prof. Donna Lee of Birmingham University for pointing out this source.
44. NARA, RG59, POL1UK-US, box 2786, Leddy to Rusk, 13 October 1966.
45. LBJL, NSF, CF, UK, box 210, London to State Department (signed Kaiser), 1 March 1967.
46. LBJL, NSF, CF, UK, box 211, Kohler memorandum for the Secretary, 14 April 1967.
47. Henry Brandon, *Special Relationships: a foreign correspondent's memoirs* (London: Macmillan, 1988), pp. 213–15; Pham, *Ending*, pp. 151–4.
48. LBJL, NSF, CF, UK, box 210, London to State, 14 and 18 April 1967; and see James Ellison, *The United States, Britain and the Transatlantic Crisis: rising to the Gaullist challenge, 1963–68* (Basingstoke: Palgrave, 2007), pp. 140–43.
49. Bruce Diary, 21 April 1967, with memorandum from Rusk to Brown.
50. TNA/PREM 13/1528, Palliser to Maclehose, 25 April 1967.
51. Diary, Benton to Bruce, 29 April 1967.
52. Diary, 1 May 1967.
53. Diary, Bruce to Rusk, 6 May 1967.
54. Diary, 10 May 1967; LBJL, NSF, CF, UK, box 211, London to State Department, 10 May 1967.
55. Diary, 12 May, with Rusk to Brown and copy of Bruce to Rusk, 12 May.
56. Dockrill, *East of Suez*, pp. 189–90.
57. Diary, Bruce to Rusk, 30 May 1967.
58. Diary, 2 June 1967; Pham, *Ending*, pp. 173–6.
59. Diary, Bruce to Leddy, 20 June 1967.

60. For example, LBJL, NSF, CF, UK, box 211, Rusk to Brown, 7 July 1967.
61. Dockrill, *East of Suez*, pp. 199–208; Pham, *Ending*, chapter 7; Young, *Labour Governments*, pp. 49–52.
62. Diary, 6 January 1968, with copies of telegrams.
63. Diary, 9 January 1968, with copy of telegrams.
64. Diary, 11 January 1968.
65. TNA/PREM 13/1999, New York to Foreign Office, 11 January (including Brown quote); LBJL, NSF, CF, UK, box 212, Rostow to Johnson, 11 January 1967 (including 'saddest days'); *FRUS, XII*, document 288, http://history.state.gov/historicaldocuments/frus1964–68v12/ch6 (accessed 23 June 2011).
66. Diary, 12 January 1968, with Johnson to Wilson telegram.
67. Diary, 14 January 1968.
68. Diary, Bruce to William Bundy, 15 January 1968.
69. Diary, Johnson to Wilson, 15 January 1968.
70. Diary, 16 January 1968; LBJL, NSF, CF, UK, box 211, London to State, 16 January 1968.
71. Diary, 17 January 1968.
72. Diary, 22 January 1968.
73. Diary, Bruce to Rusk, 23 January 1968.
74. Diary, 16 January 1968.
75. Diary, 8 February 1968.
76. For example: C. J. Bartlett, *The Special Relationship* (Basingstoke: Macmillan, 1992), pp. 109–18; David Dimbleby and David Reynolds, *An Ocean Apart* (London: BBC Books, 1988), p. 256; John Dumbrell, *A Special Relationship* (Basingstoke: Macmillan, 2001), p. 72.
77. Alan Dobson, *Anglo–American Relations in the Twentieth Century* (London: Routledge, 1995), p. 138.

9

'We Were always Realistic': The Heath Government, the European Community and the Cold War in the Mediterranean, June 1970–February 1974

Effie G. H. Pedaliu

The Mediterranean region and contemporary Mediterranean history fascinated Saki Dockrill. She discussed, often, with characteristic perspicacity, all aspects of American and British diplomacy and strategy in the region. For her, British concepts and attitudes to the Mediterranean were more nuanced and inclusive than American ones. She perceived these as having been moulded by emotion and strategic expediency in equal measure. It was this that made her all the more interested in how two American Republican administrations, in particular, dealt with the region. Both Eisenhower and Nixon had a 'whole Mediterranean' approach. This essay investigates the extent to which, during Edward Heath's premiership (18 June 1970–28 February 1974), Britain's preparations to join the European Community (EC) led to a 'Europeanisation' of its policies and approach towards the Mediterranean. It will examine also, how Britain sought to protect its interests in the Mediterranean during the years of détente with what had become, just, limited capabilities. In doing so, it will bring together some of the themes that were a constant source of interest to Saki, namely post-war British efforts to adopt a European role without compromising the 'special relationship' with the US and its world role.

The Mediterranean in British foreign policy

In 1945, the Mediterranean had been one of the uppermost priorities in British foreign policy because of London's need to safeguard its imperial lines of communication, to maintain its global role, to defend the metropolis and the Empire from the USSR and to push back the threat that communism posed to its national interests and social democratic ideology. British efforts to build a Mediterranean security pact in the late 1940s came to nothing because of American disinterest and because Italy, Greece and Turkey, despite flirting with the idea, preferred to join NATO rather than what could have been a second rate alliance. British economic decline and the repeated re-organisation of NATO's naval commands chipped away, slowly but surely, at British might in the Mediterranean.[1] Moreover, within twenty years, decolonisation in a rapidly evolving bipolar world, the fallout from the ill-fated Suez crisis and the retreat from 'East of Suez', about which Saki Dockrill wrote so eloquently,[2] reduced the all pervasive British presence in the sea, from the 'blue water empire'[3] of the past to just 'a small force of anti-submarine vessels'.[4] The Six Day war of 1967, compounded by Prime Minister Harold Wilson's defence cuts and US President Richard Nixon's adoption of détente in 1969, diminished further Britain's ability to take independent initiatives in the Mediterranean.[5]

Diminished national wealth also brought about a change in British views of the significance of the Mediterranean. By the time Edward Heath won the June 1970 general election, British interests in the Mediterranean had become very modest indeed. The new government asked the Overseas Policy and Defence Committee to define and prioritise the principal British foreign policy objectives.[6] As far as the Mediterranean was concerned, the tendency to perceive the sea as a strategic waterway was to remain because of the country's dependence on Middle Eastern oil but, from now, the focus shifted to trade with its riparian states rather than the sea itself.[7] Indeed, the Heath government continued with the policy review on Britain and the Mediterranean that the Wilson government had initiated at the beginning of 1970 and was to draw similar conclusions. British interests in the Mediterranean had now become primarily defined by the Cold War and trade.[8] The Cold War, however, ensured that Britain would continue to remain watchful and alert to political developments in the region. The Cabinet perceived that the 'Mediterranean [was] the Southern Front of Southern Europe and of NATO'.[9] Inevitably, this led to the conclusion that 'British political interests in the Mediterranean were coincidental with the strategic ones'.[10] The instability of the Southern Flank of NATO engendered deep concerns in the corridors of the Foreign and Commonwealth Office (FCO), the Ministry of Defence (MoD) and the Treasury. Graeco–Turkish relations simmered over Cyprus; the rise of the left in Italy and the unpopularity of the post-1967 Greek dictatorship with many of Britain's NATO allies were identified as issues of major worry. There was fear of an outbreak of war over Greek–Turkish differences in Cyprus and over imagined moves towards neutralism in both Greece and Italy, entailing the potential loss of NATO facilities which would adversely compromise the defence of the area.[11] The situation became bleaker from the moment Colonel Qaddaffi took over in Libya and the Maltese Prime Minister, Dom Mintoff, started cosying up to the Soviet Union and threatened to make Malta a NATO no-go area.[12]

In view of these problems, the cohesion and the strength of NATO's Southern Flank was deemed to be a paramount policy concern. The Ministry of Defence stated that Britain should aim to 'promote a political pattern that will permit the Southern Flank to be adequately defended by the alliance'.[13] By this stage, nearly all British military resources were committed to NATO. In the Mediterranean, the Royal Navy was actively involved in NATO's 'Naval On Call Force'. This consisted of a guided-missile destroyer, two frigates, occasionally backed the HMS Ark Royal, amphibious ships manned by Royal Marines Commandos, an infantry battalion, an armoured reconnaissance squadron and the Gibraltar garrison, including an infantry battalion.[14] The Cabinet was agreed that British interests in Southern Europe could be secured only through the preservation of peace and stability and that Britain's principal contribution to this lay in the fields of economic, political and military cooperation. This was particularly important as ministers were resigned to the idea that 'none of our [British] national interests can be preserved by military intervention on the national level'.[15] Success in cooperation here would also address another interrelated Cold War objective namely, the 'containment of Soviet influence' and 'the prevention of USSR from establishing military and non-military dominance in the area'.[16]

The desire to expand trade with the region, gave British decision-makers an added incentive to seek Mediterranean stability. At this time, British economic interests there were quite healthy. British trade and investment in Southern Europe, especially in France, Italy, Spain and Greece were quite substantial.[17] On the Southern littoral, the Maghreb formed a special area of concern since by 1969, 26 per cent of British oil came from Libya.[18] The fear here was that the USSR would exploit the Arab-Israeli conflict to expand its influence. Commercial relations, other than oil, with the non-European Mediterranean countries were quite small but the British government saw scope for improvement.[19] The competition for markets in the area had been hotting up. France and Italy had moved to secure their economic interests and security by embarking on their own Mediterranean initiatives. Similarly, Spain tried to use the Mediterranean as a means to end its political isolation, prop up its colonial interests and as a lever to negotiate better agreements with the US over American bases on Spanish territory.[20] For its part, the US was aggrieved by the nature of the EEC trade agreements with Mediterranean countries through the Yaoundé framework, which the Americans regarded as discriminatory.[21] The Soviet Union, in turn, was making inroads into the economic affairs of the region through increased aid to the Maghreb, Mashreq and Turkey, by signing trade agreements with Italy and also through active economic rapprochement with the Southern European dictatorships.[22] Thus, when Heath came to power, Mediterranean matters were becoming more complex just at the time that Britain had started to treat the region like any other part of the globe.

Mediterranean issues, thus, were not high on the foreign policy agenda of the new government, at least to begin with. Heath's priorities lay elsewhere. He was concerned not to be sidetracked from realising his major ideological ambition, namely, to bring Britain into the EC. His was a goal that was informed both by his deeply upheld political conviction that the Community was a natural place for post-colonial Britain and by his pragmatic take on international affairs. His views led him to believe that European integration would have a regenerative effect on Britain's world role, signalling 'a new era in British diplomacy' which would leave 'behind the years of retreat'.[23] As he put it, 'we were returned to office to change the course of history of this nation'.[24] To achieve all this he needed French backing. The end of Charles de Gaulle's control of French foreign policy in 1969 had increased the prospects for the EEC's first major enlargement. De Gaulle's successor, Georges Pompidou, had however, upgraded the importance of the Mediterranean in French foreign policy since it was one arena of the globe with which France could engage independently.[25] Heath was thus, determined to approach Mediterranean matters with caution so that Britain would not accidentally step on French toes and spark their displeasure.

Britain had to wade gently into Mediterranean affairs because of other reasons as well. The Mediterranean had been acquiring an increasing importance for the European Community during a time of heady development. The EC was trying to come to terms with its economic might whilst adapting to the new world of floating currencies ushered in by the Smithsonian Agreement in 1971. It was trying to redefine its relations with the Third World and also the Mediterranean. This was a time of rapid European institution and identity building. The EC states had to cope also, with new security threats emanating from the Middle East at a time when American attention was turned away to South East Asia, because of the Vietnam War, and European defence was compromised through the drawdown of American troops.[26] Matters were further exacerbated by superpower détente and the way it was practiced which created strains and stresses, especially in areas away from the Central Front such as the Mediterranean. Finding policies to negotiate successfully its way around these changes and strains had been difficult for Britain, but were exacerbated by its status as a former superpower that still had residual influence in the region. This was a critical problem since Britain's diminished circumstances were often not fully appreciated by local politicians.[27] By exploiting the inability and unwillingness of local politicians to comprehend fully British weakness, London was able to capitalise on its residual influence but at the same time, it could be drawn into issues that could antagonise those with whom it wished to have good relations, namely, the US and the EC. If British foreign policy was to be effective it needed to adjust to new realities by keeping a lower profile in the Mediterranean.

Even, as the new British government downgraded its Mediterranean focus further than its immediate predecessor had done, a series of regional developments and the by-products of détente conspired to make Mediterranean issues a headache for the Prime Minister. By the 1970s, changes in the region precipitated by decolonisation and modernisation fused with pressures arising from superpower détente to foment regional instability. Heath's attention was never able to veer away from the region for too long throughout his term in office. Indeed, the Mediterranean presented him with the first international crisis of his premiership in September 1970 and bookended it with a regional war in 1973 that prepared, in part, the path to his downfall. It also fomented tensions in Anglo–American relations and brought him closer to evolving EEC thinking on the region.

Superpower détente created its own dynamic in the Mediterranean.[28] Saki Dockrill was a pioneer in the study of the 'pre-history' of détente as an aspect of American policy towards the USSR under the coldest of Cold warriors President Eisenhower.[29] However, détente as a Cold War strategy in the 1970s would be applied differently than it had been in the 1950s. It was no longer just an item on the agenda of superpower relations which could be discarded at any time. It had now been elevated into the framework within which East–West relations would be exercised.[30] As a concept, it remained deliberately vague and ill-defined, so that the two superpowers could exercise full flexibility in their tactics and likewise, it was not to be constrained by doctrinal or pre-conceived expectations. The superpower détente process was to be a carefully orchestrated exercise in superpower relations, vigilantly controlled, so that they could focus fully on improving relations in Central Europe and not be sidetracked by events the peripheries of their spheres of influence. Cards were played so closely to the chest by the US administration that even whole swathes of the American bureaucracy, let alone America's trusted allies, were excluded from the diplomatic process.[31] One such peripheral area was the Mediterranean, which, during the 1960s and 1970s, was experiencing the effects resulting from the intersection of three destabilising forces: East–West rivalry, the intensifying North–South divide and an emerging and growing South–South divide.

In America, the assumption of power by a Republican President in 1969, ushered in an administration that held a 'whole Mediterranean' view which, like Eisenhower's, rested on keeping the status quo in the Mediterranean intact at all costs.[32] For Nixon and his National Security Advisor, Henry Kissinger, all change, in this part of the world, needed to be restrained and discouraged. In this world view, the Southern European dictatorships came to be seen as promoting stability in the region. Similarly, potential changes in Italian domestic politics were frowned upon and covertly inhibited.[33] American policies had the effect of making the Northern Mediterranean shore appear to be passive and masked its accruing tensions but, from Lisbon to Ankara there was disquiet and even resentment of superpower détente. It was perceived to be encouraging American inattention to the affairs of the basin and allowing the Soviets to build up their naval strength there.[34]

The September 1970 crises

The US focused on détente and tried to keep the lid on peripheral pressures, but the Mediterranean was evolving into an area where accidents could happen and with dangerous implications for world peace. The Southern Mediterranean shore was suffering local low intensity warfare from which a new security threat was beginning to emerge. Radical Palestinian groups had expanded their operations to areas outside the Middle East and adopted violence against international travel as a means of carrying their fight to Israel. Through a series of hijackings and taking of hostages they turned airports into battlegrounds and planes into potential coffins in order to publicise their case. Their aim was to shock world public opinion into turning against

Israel. George Habash, the leader of the Popular Front for the Liberation of Palestine (PFLP) and terrorist tactician, explained this penchant for highjacking thus: 'When we hijack a plane it has more effect than if we kill a hundred Israelis in battle'.[35] Initially, hijacks affected Northern Mediterranean countries with airports in Rome, Paris and Athens being particularly vulnerable.[36]

The hijackings of 6 September 1970 made such Palestinian actions a problem to both Northern and Southern European countries and not just the US and Israel. The Heath government had been in office for barely three months when four planes were hijacked. Two were forced to land at Dawson's Field in Jordan, one was blown up in Cairo after the evacuation of its passengers and the fourth hijack failed. The following day yet another hijack occurred and this plane too, landed in Dawson's Field. All the hijackings were perpetrated by the PFLP. The primary aim of the hijackers was to trade hostages for imprisoned terrorists in Israel, Germany and Switzerland. The plane involved in the failed air-piracy attempt had landed at Heathrow and the surviving highjacker Leila Khaled, was 'provisionally arrested'. London was propelled, suddenly, into what Heath described in Cabinet as a 'difficult and complex decision'.[37] What Britain, a co-signatory of the Tokyo Convention of 1963, was forced to decide was whether to negotiate the freeing of Khaled in exchange for the lives of the hostages, of whom 65 were British. Even as the crisis unfolded, the US State Department called the ambassadors of the UK, Switzerland and Germany to tell them that it was important that no unilateral action was taken and that 'any response be concerted here in Washington'.[38] The governments involved, in turn, decided that negotiations had to be carried out under the auspices of the International Committee of the Red Cross (ICRC).[39] The British Cabinet was both uneasy and split 'between those who wanted to hold firm and those who wanted to find a way out of the crisis',[40] but all were in agreement that a united front was of paramount importance. As negotiations were being initiated by the ICRC, the British like the Swiss, let the hijackers know that they were willing to negotiate.[41]

The negotiation process became complicated and protracted because of the deteriorating internal situation in Jordan and Israel's 'no deal' approach to hostage swapping especially since the PFLP was not prepared initially, to make specific demands. The prolongation of the negotiations created an awkward situation for the British government.[42] As the hostages became bargaining chips in the contest between the hijackers and King Hussein – after he declared martial law – relations amongst governments involved in the 'Berne group' deteriorated. The British, the Germans and the Swiss, mindful of their domestic public opinion, were eager to achieve a quick settlement and they became frustrated by the Americans' understanding attitude towards Israeli procrastination. Indeed, the British became fearful that the cohesion of the 'Berne Group' could collapse and took the lead in pressing the Israelis in Berne and also trying to persuade the US to pressure Israel into adopting a more conciliatory attitude to the PFLP's demands. London warned Washington that it, Bonn and Berne 'might be unable to maintain solidarity with the Governments of the United States and Israel in the attempt to promote a non-discriminatory settlement'.[43]

These events took their toll on Anglo–American relations at a critical time when both administrations were still sizing each other up. On 13 September 1970, Denis Greenhill, the FCO Permanent Under-Secretary, in trying to convey the urgency for a quick resolution ended up in a heated conversation with Joseph Sisco, the American Assistant Secretary of State for Near Eastern and South Asian affairs. He told Sisco bluntly that the best contribution the US could make to end the hostage crisis 'would be to persuade the Israelis to give up Palestinian prisoners in order to complete the exchange'.[44] Sisco did not pull any punches either when he warned that British government 'would want to weigh carefully the outcry in the [US]' against the Britain taking unilateral action. An exasperated Greenhill replied, 'there would also be an outcry in the UK. If we don't agree to bargain, our people get killed'.[45] His words mirrored the views of the British Cabinet.[46] At high political levels misunderstandings continued unabated with the US feeling that the UK was behaving as if the US 'was in collusion' with Israel. At lower levels however, the FCO, heeding the advice of John Freeman, the British Ambassador in Washington, who had warned strongly that such action would have 'potentially serious consequences for Anglo–United States relations', worked closely with the State Department to keep a united front and still secure the release of hostages.[47] Eventually, the US was able to convince all members of the Berne group 'to agree to consider the PFLP proposals at such time as the PFLP provides its total demands, including a specific list of the *fedayeen* it wants'.[48] Israel, despite profound concerns, made its contribution.[49] The swap took place and the few hostages remaining in captivity were released on 30 September.

As the hostage crisis was drawing to a close, new tensions arose when direct fighting erupted in Jordan between the Jordanian Armed Forces loyal to King Hussein and the Palestine Liberation Organization. Hussein's bid to reclaim authority over his Kingdom during that 'Black September' exposed the different policies of Britain and the US in the region and also how inimical British policy was to the priorities of superpower détente. King Hussein, fearing a Syrian Army intervention on the side of the Palestinians, pleaded with Britain and the US to ask Israel to attack the Syrian armed forces by air if they crossed the Jordanian border. Although the Hashemite Kingdom of Jordan had been, largely, their creation, the British decided that they should not be the ones to pass the message on to the Israelis, nor were they prepared to coordinate with the US to take military action in support of Hussein. The Cabinet decided that 'in no circumstances could we ourselves intervene in Jordan by military means; and the damaging consequences for Western interests in the Middle East as a whole which might result from United States intervention entitled us to represent forcefully to the United States Government that they, too, should refrain from intervention of their own'.[50] As the US began to fortify Israel and Jordan into bastions of Western interest by taking steps to ensure that there was no political change, Britain had decided, in contrast, that in the Mediterranean, stability did 'not mean necessarily the preservation of the status quo'.[51] London was sceptical to the idea that the presence of Western forces in the region could necessarily 'contribute to stability'.[52] Britain saw stability in the region as the need to prevent international conflicts and should they occur, be kept localised in order to prevent British economic relations with various countries 'from being interrupted by changes in their political complexions'.[53] Such views were quite different to US conceptions that had led the Americans to contemplate military intervention in support of Hussein.

Within a month of the Jordanian crisis being capped, the nautical dangers arising from an overcrowded Mediterranean sea surfaced again. Soviet naval presence there had grown and the USSR had acquired base facilities in the region as a result of the Six Day War. Fears increased over accidental collisions between Western and Soviet ships and its repercussions for East–West relations. The Mediterranean was a favourite area for naval and aerial manoeuvres for the NATO countries as well as the Soviet Navy. Shadowing NATO ships on exercises was a common practice of the Soviets and the danger for accidents was both high and real. On 9 November 1970, HMS Ark Royal took part in the military night flying exercise 'Line Jug'. Just west of Crete, a Soviet Kotlin destroyer collided with it. There were two Soviet casualties. The Ark Royal escaped with no loss of life and some superficial damage. On this occasion the incident was downplayed and the only action taken by the British government was to ask the British Ambassador in Moscow to make an official complaint to the Soviet government, but the dangers remained.[54]

The European dimension

The high levels of Mediterranean volatility, the presence of the *Eskadra* and air piracy in a period of increased air-travel and tourism became a major concern for European public opinion and politicians. It created a deep sense of insecurity in many EC members and the European Commission and led to a growing engagement with the region.[55] Britain was to be affected by the new agenda. The EC's drive to pacify the Mediterranean was to be spearheaded by Italy, France and Germany. Italy's impetus originated from its need for security and its desire to upgrade its political and commercial relevance in regional affairs. Its initiatives combined Europeanism and Atlanticism. Giulio Anderotti and Aldo Moro, the initiators of this process, who were, according to Elena Calandri, more 'cold warriers' than 'ardent' Europeanists,[56] sought to open up a broad discussion on the Mediterranean to improve regional security, to diminish the influence of radical Arab states on the Maghreb and to secure access to oil.[57] They were able to secure German support, since German trade with the Mediterranean was now substantial, but Italian plans were diametrically opposed to how the French wanted to proceed. Georges Pompidou had embarked on a series of Mediterranean initiatives designed to increase French prestige and independence of action. His favoured way of dealing with the Mediterranean was through bilateralism and he was not particularly keen on Italian plans because of their Atlanticist dimension. Pompidou preferred not to involve the Community in the process up until his realisation that its membership of the EC increased France's diplomatic weight in the Maghreb and could help it overcome disadvantages from to its colonialist past. Therefore, he adopted a multifaceted approach by courting the Maghreb and the Middle East Arab states through increased weapons sales in order to make France the interlocutor of Arab interests internationally. He supported Spanish efforts to join the EC in an attempt to balance out the Northern enlargement of the Community and tried to involve the Italians in his schemes whilst flirting with the Greek junta.[58] Thus, as Italy pushed for an overall Mediterranean approach, France set about on a tactic of dealing with 'Mediterranean problems' in a piecemeal manner.[59]

Up to this stage, the Community had used a 'hotchpotch' approach in its relations with Mediterranean countries consisting of trade agreements within the Yaoundé Convention framework and association agreements such as the Athens and Ankara treaties.[60] The upheavals in the Mediterranean necessitated the French and Italian positions be reconciled and that the EC move to elaborate a coherent Mediterranean policy. A series of plans were initiated within the Community, but also through the European Political Cooperation (EPC) process, the brainchild of the Davignon report. The EPC's remit included East–West relations, the Middle East, Asia, Africa, America and the United Nations.[61] In May 1971, the Political Committee of the EPC set up the Mediterranean Working Group (MWG) under pressure from Italy and Germany. Very soon, however, the European debate on the Mediterranean became embroiled in disagreements between those member states wanting to tackle it through the EPC–MWG and those who preferred a Commission-led initiative.[62] As Guia Migani has put it, Mediterranean policy became 'a battle between bilateralism and common action'.[63]

Heath's preference was the EPC. The new European Mediterranean activism coincided with what Hill and Lord have described as the 'later Heath', a man who had been growing more pessimistic about British diplomatic ability to bolster Britain's place in the world unilaterally and who was becoming increasingly convinced that the best way to promote British interests was through 'collective diplomacy within the EC'.[64] He admitted as much in Parliament, on 9 February 1972, when he said 'I believed until recently that we would carry fairly well outside'.[65] Heath considered the Commission to be the bastion of the old Community of the Six whereas he felt that the EPC's intergovernmental nature represented better the new era of the, soon to be, Community of the Nine, which would enable Britain to defend and better promote its interests since this structure existed outside the treaties of Rome.[66] This was also in line with Conservative thinking which went thus: 'It is only through a careful process of growing together, and not through the establishment of theoretical blueprints, that we shall advance'.[67] Indeed, Britain was to become a very active member of the EPC–MWG process and was involved from the initial stages of the EPC's Mediterranean debate, even before joining the Community officially. It had been treated as a *de facto* member and requested to report on Yugoslavia.[68] Another factor in Heath's support for the EPC process was the awkward relationship between Britain and France. Pompidou was still blowing 'hot and cold' about British entry. His constant jibes about 'Britain's tendency to remain too closely attached to US policies'[69] and his rejection of the Italian initiatives because of their Atlanticist orientation,[70] gave a clear indication of his views. Heath saw EPC as another means to woo over a still sceptical Pompidou. A Mediterranean solution within the EPC framework offered Heath a way of reminding Pompidou that

Britain was a natural ally against the supra-nationalist tendencies of the Commission.[71]

By mid-1972, the EPC Mediterranean initiative was beginning to run out of steam despite the support from Britain, Holland, Denmark and Ireland and gradually the Commission took the upper hand. In September 1972, the Commission recommended that a common vision had to be elaborated towards the Mediterranean.[72] The outcome was the Global Mediterranean Policy (GMP) that included EC-Mashreq and EC-Maghreb relations[73] and provided a framework for trade and cooperation between the EEC and the Mediterranean basin.[74] Although the GMP originated from security fears, in the end it would become an instrument for negotiation to integrate the democratised Southern European countries and to negotiate trade issues with the non-European Mediterranean states.[75] Political relations with the Southern Mediterranean countries, especially after the Yom Kippur war in 1973, were consigned to the Euro–Arab Dialogue process.[76]

As the EC was deliberating on to how to approach its relations with the Mediterranean, the countries of the Maghreb began high levels of diplomatic activity in order to ensure that the conclusions of the Helsinki process would be applied to the Mediterranean too. Tunisia and Algeria were at the forefront of the Southern littoral countries that felt that their region had been excluded from superpower détente and that the Mediterranean Sea was being turned into a theatre of East–West conflict and a border.[77] They were also facing severe economic problems too, whilst Morocco had experienced a failed coup. For years these countries had played the US against the USSR in their efforts to develop, but now they were becoming fearful that the Mediterranean Sea was turning into a veritable battlefield. The increasing Soviet activity and the home-porting arrangements for the US Sixth Fleet in Athens confirmed to them that the drift towards an inevitable Mediterranean clash between the superpowers needed to be arrested.[78] 'A détente in Europe might lead to a disengagement in the Mediterranean', Habib Bourguiba, the President of Tunisia, said to the German Foreign Minister Scheel, during his visit to Tunis in March.[79] President Boumedienne of Algeria suggested to Pompidou that the time was ripe to create a 'Mediterranean Lake of Peace' which would be based on 'a genuine cooperation' of all the riparian Mediterranean countries.[80] Bourguiba too, made similar comments during his visit to Paris in June 1972. President Makarios of Cyprus, in the Eastern Mediterranean, had expressed similar fears.[81] All demanded that their countries be invited to Helsinki on the basis that Mediterranean security and European security were interlinked. They were to find support from Malta and Italy but the superpowers and the French and the British combined to prevent all non-European riparian Mediterranean states from taking part in the Helsinki conference.[82] As far as the Heath government was concerned, Britain ought to adopt a 'firmly negative' approach.[83] In a meeting with the Algerian Ambassador, Sir Thomas Brimelow, Deputy Under-Secretary of State, FCO, explained the British position with regards to the geographic remit of the conference, namely, that the geographic scope of the CSCE needed to be kept tight so that effective debate could take place, and that any attempt to adopt a wider scope would make the conference almost meaningless because many more countries would wish to participate. He also assured him that 'all participants at the conference were well aware of the importance of the Mediterranean' and that many would raise the matter in their speeches.[84] Britain, here, was following its realist approach that happily happened to be 'Europeanist' too. Both the Commission and the EPC–MWG had come to the conclusion that their approach to the Mediterranean should be primarily economic in essence.

As Britain attempted to get closer to the EEC, its policies and priorities were being influenced by the Community, and the idea behind accepting this was that British interests would be better served. Heath's approach to the Mediterranean was a pragmatic one and geared towards winning more trade for Britain.[85] If this was to be achieved by following a Community approach it was not a problem since this was the very *raison d'être* for joining it. As he told his Cabinet: 'We are joining the Community in the belief that participation in a 'growing unity in Western Europe is the best way open to us to maintain our security and promote our prosperity' ... 'to develop the degree of common decision-taking within the Community necessary for the achievement of our other objectives'.[86] His pragmatic approach became clearly evident in these 'lean years' for British arms sales to the region through the courting of the Greek dictators and the adoption of a major arms export drive towards Spain and Portugal. The EEC also became a powerful card for Heath and his Foreign Secretary, Sir Alec Douglas-Home, to pressure unwilling Cabinet colleagues to subscribe to projects they wished to promote. The Suez-Mediterranean pipeline (SUMED) was one such. The SUMED project had begun as a reaction in 1968, by Egypt's President Nasser, to ameliorate the negative economic impacts of the Six Day War and the closure of the Suez Canal on the Egyptian economy.[87] The FCO, in the late 60s had advised Harold Wilson that the project was, for Britain, both unattractive financially and risky in security terms. The Wilson government, therefore, turned down a loan to Egypt to develop the pipeline.[88] Heath's first year in government had coincided with Nasser's death and Anwar Sadat's rise to power. It also coincided with another spurt of activity by the Egyptian government to bring to reality its SUMED dream. The government came under increased pressure from Egypt for Britain to be part of the construction process. Heath and Douglas-Home wished to improve relations with Egypt's new regime and they also believed that Britain's extensive interests in the Middle East meant they 'could not afford to ignore Egypt's position as the leading Arab State'.[89] Qaddaffi's control over Libyan oil reserves also played a part in their decision to bring the matter to the Cabinet again. Douglas-Home and Heath failed to convince their Cabinet colleagues in the economic ministries that Britain had 'little to lose and much to gain' from involvement in the project.[90] So, in January 1971, the matter was passed to the Defence and Overseas Policy Committee. The principal argument from those supporting the scheme was that Britain ought to be part of a consortium comprising France, Italy and Germany as this would be a clear declaration of 'Europeanism'.[91] As a result, over time, any Cabinet resistance ended and the decision was taken that a £12m export credit cover be extended to British firms involved in the construction of the SUMED pipeline.[92]

As far as the Heath government was concerned its Mediterranean priorities lay in the stability of NATO's Southern Flank, oil and energy security, trade, in particular trade with oil producing countries and investment in the oil industry.[93] The first two were paramount and another Arab–Israel war in the region could affect both adversely. By 1973, as the clouds of war thickened over the South Eastern Mediterranean shore, his nightmare scenario that the Arabs would use oil as a weapon against the West in a war with Israel became a reality. His foresight offered him little solace when the OPEC declared its oil boycott.[94] The impact of the Yom Kippur War was to coincide with British industrial strife and a miners' strike. All would have a direct effect on his premiership as 'the three day week' became a necessity to conserve energy supplies. Heath saw the British economy nose-diving into recession and Anglo–American relations severely strained. In an international environment suffering major Mediterranean instability, the close association of Britain with the US was both a plus and a minus. The advantage was that British military decline did not impact adversely on the military and political balance in the Mediterranean because the US could cover it and thus, British interests in the region did not need suffer.[95] Throughout Heath's time in office, despite hiccups in the relationship and tensions arising from personal vanities and the practices of the Nixon White House over foreign policy matters, the special relationship remained strong. Authors who have suggested otherwise seem to have been seduced by the *zeitgeist* of the time and the political bickering between allies.[96] This was a period that brought to the fore differences between the US and Europe in the way the Europeans sought to redefine the transatlantic relationship, as the furore over the 'Year of Europe' disclosed.[97] However, the Heath government had no wish to sever the 'special relationship' since Britain's entry in the Community was not an 'either or' choice.[98] The Community was seen as an engine to drive forward Britain's economic prosperity and also its continuation as a relevant power in international affairs.

Notes

1. Elena Calandri, *Il Mediterraneo e la difesa dell' Occidente: ereditá imperiali e logiche di guerra fredda,* (Firenze: Manent, 1997); idem., 'Unsuccessful Attempts to Stabilize the Mediterranean: the Western powers and the Mediterranean Pact, 1948–1958', in Varsori, A. (ed.), *Europe 1945–1990s: The End of an Era?* (Basingstoke: Macmillan, 1995), pp. 275–9; Effie G.H. Pedaliu, *Britain, Italy and the Origins of the Cold War* (London: Palgrave Macmillan, 2003); Alessandro Brogi, *L'Italia e l'egemonia americana nel Mediterraneo* (Firenze: La Nuova Italia, 1996); Dionyssios Chourchoulis, 'High Hopes, Bold Aims, Limited Results: Britain and Establishment of the NATO Mediterranean Command, 1950–1953', *Diplomacy & Statecraft*, 20/3, 2009, pp. 434–45.
2. Saki R. Dockrill, *Britain's Retreat From East of Suez: The Choice between Europe and the World?* (Basingstoke: Palgrave Macmillan, 2002).
3. Robert Holland, *Blue-Water Empire: The British in the Mediterranean since 1800* (London: Allen Lane, 2012).
4. Michael L. Dockrill, *British Defence since 1945* (Oxford,: Blackwell), 1988), p. 105.
5. Dockrill, *Britain's Retreat, passim.*
6. Daniel E. Furby, *The Revival and Success of Britain's Second Application for Membership of the European Community*, 1968–71, Unpublished PhD Thesis, Queen Mary, University of London, p. 166, https://qmro.qmul.ac.uk/jspui/bitstream/123456789/706/1/FURBYRevivalAndSuccess2010.pdf
7. TNA/FCO49/301/RS11/2, Memorandum MoD, 15 September 1970.
8. Ibid.
9. TNA/CAB129/161/10, CP(72)10, 25 January 1972.
10. Ibid.
11. TNA/FCO49/301/RS11/2, Memorandum MoD, 15 September 1970).
12. TNA/CAB128/49/38, CM(71)38,15 July 1971.
13. TNA/CAB129/167/3, CP(73)3, 16 January 1973; Konstantina Maragkou, 'Favouritism in NATO's South-Eastern Flank: the Case of the Greek Colonels, 1967–74', *Cold War History* (August 2009), pp. 347–366; Effie G.H. Pedaliu, 'A Discordant Note: NATO and the Greek Junta, 1967–74', *Diplomacy and Statecraft,* 22/1, 2011, pp. 101–120.
14. TNA/CAB129/167/3, CP(73)3, 16 January 1973.

15. TNA/FCO49/301/RS11/2, Memorandum MoD, 15 September 1970.
16. Ibid.
17. Ibid., Annex A: *The Pattern of British Trade in the Mediterranean area 1969*, undated; ibid., Annex C: *Measurement of Mediterranean Countries Importance to the UK* (source priorities for British Interests Overseas, undated).
18. Ibid.
19. TNA/FCO9/2133, WS 45 memo British interests in Eastern Mediterranean, undated; TNA/FCO49/301/RS11/2, Annex A: *The Pattern of British Trade in the Mediterranean area 1969*, undated; FCO49/300/RS11/1, minute, 19 June 1970.
20. Effie Pedaliu, '"A Sea of Confusion": The Mediterranean and Détente, 1969–1974', *Diplomatic History*, 33/4, 2009, pp. 735–41.
21. Foreign Relations of the United States (hereafter FRUS), 1969–1976, Volume III, *Foreign Economic Policy; International Monetary Policy*, 1969–1972, Docs: 47 and 105.
22. FRUS, 1968–76, Volume I, *The Foundations of Foreign Policy, 1969–72*, (hereafter FRUS, 1968–76, I), Doc. 71; Steele, *The Limits of Soviet Power: The Kremlin's Foreign Policy* (London, Penguin, 1985), p. 205; Marta Dassú, 'The Italian View' in R. Davy, *European Détente: A Re-Appraisal* (London: Sage, 1992), p. 117.
23. John Campbell, *Edward Heath: A Biography* (London: Jonathan Cape, 1993), p. 310.
24. Sir Alec Cairncross, *The Heath Government and the British Economy*, in Stuart Ball and Anthony Seldon, (eds), *The Heath Government 1970–74*, (London: Longman, 1996), p. 107.
25. http://www.persee.fr/web/revues/home/prescript/article/polit_0032-342X_1978_num_43_3_1623, Houda Ben Hamouda, France, the European Community and the Maghreb, 1963–1976: From Inertia to Key Player, in E. Calandri, D. Caviglia and A. Varsori (eds), *Détente in Cold War Europe: Politics and Diplomacy in the Mediterranean and the Middle East*, (London, I.B. Tauris, 2013), pp. 195–205; Daniel Colard, 'La politique méditerranéenne et proche-orientale de G. Pompidou', in *Politique étrangère*, 43/3, 1978, pp. 283–306; Serge Berstein and Jean Pierre Rioux, *La France de l'expansion: L'apogee Pompidou, 1969–1974* (Paris: Ed du Seuil, 1995); Thierno Diallo, *La politique e'trangere de Georges Pompidou* (Paris: Librairie générale de droit et de jurisprudence, 1992).
26. Gfeller, Auriéle E., 'Imagining European Identity: French Elites and the American in the Pompidou-Nixon Era', *Contemporary European History*, 19/2 (2010), pp. 133–149; Pedaliu, 'A Sea of Confusion', pp. 735–41.
27. Holland, *Blue-Water Empire*, 2012, pp. 328–344; Effie G.H. Pedaliu, 'Human Rights and Foreign Policy: Wilson and the Greek Dictators, 1967–1970', *Diplomacy & Statecraft*, 18/1, 2007, pp. 185–214.
28. Pedaliu, 'A Sea of Confusion', pp. 735–41.
29. Saki Dockrill, *Eisenhower's New Look National Security Policy, 1953–61*, (New York: Macmillan Press, 1996), pp. 116–139; Günter Bischof and Saki Dockrill (eds), *Cold War Respite: The Geneva Summit of 1955* (Baton Rouge, Louisiana State University Press, 2000).
30. FRUS, 1968–76, Volume I, *The Foundations of Foreign Policy, 1969–72*, (hereafter FRUS, 1968–78, I), 1969–72, Docs 4, 41, 71; John Gaddis, *Strategies of*

Containment: A Critical Appraisal of American National Security Policy During the Cold War (Oxford, Oxford University Press, 2005), p. 277; Jeremy Suri, *Power and Protest: Global Revolution and the Rise of Détente* (Cambridge, MA: Harvard University Press, 2003); Raymond Garthoff, *Détente and Confrontation: American-Soviet Relations from Nixon to Reagan*, 2nd edn, (Washington, DC., Brookings Institution, 1994).

31. Geraint Hughes, 'Britain, the Transatlantic Alliance, and the Arab-Israeli War of 1973', *Journal of Cold War Studies*, Volume 10, Number 2, 2008, p. 12; FRUS, 1969–76, I, Docs 61, 71 and 72.
32. Pedaliu, 'A Sea of Confusion', pp. 735–41.
33. James E. Miller, *The United States and the Making of Modern Greece: History and Power, 1950–1974* (Chapel Hill: University of North Carolina Press, 2009); Alexandros Nafpliotis, *Britain and the Greek Colonels: Accommodating the Junta in the Cold War*, (London: I.B. Tauris, 2012); Effie G.H. Pedaliu, 'Human Rights and Foreign Policy: Wilson and the Greek Dictators, 1967–1970', *Diplomacy and Statecraft*, 18/1, 2007, p. 205; Pedaliu, 'A Discordant Note', pp. 101–120.
34. FRUS, 1969–1976, Volume XXXIV *National Security Policy*, 1969–1972, docs 192 and 183; Pedaliu, 'A Sea of Confusion', pp. 735–41.
35. *The Times*, 16 September 1970 (interview with *Der Stern*).
36. Fromkin, David, 'The Strategy of Terrorism', *Foreign Affairs*, 53/4, 1975, p. 683; Edward Mickolus, *Transnational Terrorism: A Chronology of Events, 1968–1979*, (Westport, Conn.: Greenwood Press, 1980).
37. TNA/CAB128/47, CM(70)13, 9 September 1970.
38. FRUS, 1969–1976, Volume XXIV, *Middle East Region and Arabian Peninsula, 1969–1972; Jordan, September 1970*, (hereafter FRUS, 1969–1976, XXIV), Document 205.
39. Ibid.; TNA/CAB128/47 13 9/9/1970; FRUS, 1969–1976, Volume: XXIV, *Middle East Region and Arabian Peninsula, 1969–1972*, (hereafter FRUS, 1969–1976, XXIV) doc. 206.
40. Ibid.; TNA/CAB128/47, CM(70)18, 16 September 1970.
41. Ibid; FRUS, 1969–1976, XXIV, doc. 199
42. Ibid., docs 230 and 231.
43. TNA/CAB128/47, CM(70)19, 17 September 1970; FRUS, 1969–1976, XXIV, doc. 202.
44. FRUS, 19691976, XXIV, doc. 236.
45. Ibid., doc. 255.
46. TNA/CAB128/47 CM(70)18, 16 September 1970.
47. TNA/CAB128/47, CM(70)19, 17 September 1970.
48. FRUS, 1969–1976, XXIV, doc. 250.
49. TNA/CAB128/47, CM(70)20, 21 September 1970.
50. TNA/CAB128/47, CM20(70), 21 September 1970; FRUS, 1969–1976, XXIV, docs. 282, 284 and 287.
51. TNA/FCO49/301/RS11/2, memorandum MoD, 15 September 1970.
52. Ibid.
53. Ibid.
54. Hansard, HoC Debates, vol.: 806, colmns.: 388–90, 11 November 1970; TNA /CAB128/47/37, CM(70)37, 13 November 1970.
55. David Fromkin, The Strategy of Terrorism, *Foreign Affairs*, 53:4, 1975, p. 683; Edward Mickolus, *Transnational Terrorism: A Chronology of Events, 1968 1979*, (Westport, Conn.: Greenwood Press, 1980).

56. Elena Calandri, The United States, the EEC and the Mediterranean: Rivalry or Complementarity?, in Calandri, Caviglia and Varsori (eds), *Détente in Cold War Europe*, pp. 46–7.
57. Daniele Caviglia and Massimiliano Cricco, *La diplomazia italiana e gli equilibri mediterranei. La politica mediorientale dell'Italia dalla guerra dei Sei Giorni al conflitto dello Yom Kippur, 1967–1973* (Soveria Mannelli: Rubbettino, 2006); Elena Calandri, 'Il Mediterraneo nella politica estera italiana', in Agostino Giovagnoli and Silvo Pons (eds), *L'Italia repubblicana nella crisi degli anni settanta* (Soveria Mannelli: Rubbettino, 2003), pp. 351–82; Massimo De Leonardis (ed.), *Il Mediterraneo nella politica estera italiana del secondo dopoguerra* (Bologna: Mulino, 2002).
58. Colard, 'La politique méditerranéenne', pp. 283–306; Migani, Re-Discovering the Mediterranean, p. 52; Pedaliu, A Sea of Confusion, p. 739.
59. Calandri, 'The United States, the EEC and the Mediterranean', pp. 44–7; Guia Migani, 'Re-Discovering the Mediterranean: First Tests of Coordination among the Nine', in Calandri, Caviglia and Varsori (eds), *Détente in Cold War Europe*, p. 53.
60. Elena Calandri, 'L'eterna incompiuta: La politica mediterranea fra sviluppo e sicurezza', in Elena Calandri, (ed.), *Il primato sfuggente. L'Europa e l' intervento per lo sviluppo 1957–2000* (Milano: Franco Angeli, 2009), pp. 89–117.
61. http:/aei.pitt.edu/4541/1/EPC_Eur_File_13_83.pdf, accessed on 10 August 2012.
62. Georges-Henri Soutou, 'L'attitude de Georges Pompidou face à l'Allemagne', in Association Georges Pompidou, *Georges Pompidou et l'Europe: Colloque, 25 et 26 Novembre 1993* (Brussels: Editions Complexe, 1995), pp. 267–313; Marc Trachtenberg (ed.), *Between Empire and Alliance: America and Europe during the Cold War* (Lanham, MD: Rowman and Littlefield, 2003); Georges-Henri Soutou, 'President Pompidou, Ostpolitik, and the Strategy of Détente', in Helga Haftendorn, Georges-Henri Soutou, Stephen F. Szabo and Samuel F. Wells Jr. (eds), *The Strategic Triangle: France, Germany and the United States in the Shaping of the New Europe* (Washington: John Hopkins University Press, 2006), pp. 229–260.
63. TNA/FCO30/1258, report, undated; Migani, Re-Discovering the Mediterranean, p. 53.
64. Christopher Hill and Christopher Lord, The Foreign Policy of the Heath Government, *The Heath Government*, in Stuart Ball and Anthony Seldon (eds), *The Heath Government 1970–74* (London: Longman, 1996), p. 284.
65. Ibid.
66. TNA/CAB128/51/16, CM(73)15, 8 March 1973.
67. Quoted in John W. Young, 'The Heath Government and British Entry into the European Community', in Ball and Seldon (eds), *The Heath Government*, p. 284.
68. TNA/FCO 30/1258, report, undated; Daniel Möckli, *European Foreign Policy during the Cold War: Heath, Brandt, Pompidou and the Dream of Political Unity*, (London: I.B. Tauris, 2008), pp. 95–248, *passim*.
69. TNA/PREM15/370, tel. no.: 1197, Paris to FO, 23 Nov. 1970; Furby, *The Revival and Success of Britain's Second Application*, p. 178; Young, 'The Heath Government', p. 284.

70. Migani, 'Re-Discovering the Mediterranean', pp. 49–60.
71. Young, 'The Heath Government', p. 265; Möckli, *European Foreign Policy*, p. 47.
72. http://www.cvce.eu/obj/statement_from_the_paris_summit_19_to_21_october_1972-en-b1dd3d57–5f31–4796–85c3-cfd2210d6901.html Statement from the Paris Summit (19 to 21 October 1972), accessed 1 August 2012.
73. John Calabrese, 'Beyond Barcelona: The politics of the Euro-Mediterranean Partnership', *European Security*, 6/4, 1997, pp. 86–110; Roy Ginsberg, *Foreign Policy Actions of the European Community: The Politics of Scale* (Boulder, CO: L. Rienner, 1989).
74. Federica Bicchi, *European Foreign Policy Making toward the Mediterranean* (Basingstoke: Palgrave Macmillan, 2007).
75. Eirini Karamouzi, *Greece's Path to EEC Membership, 1947–1979 : The View from Brussels*, Unpublished PhD Thesis, London School of Economics and Political Science University of London, 2011, http://etheses.lse.ac.uk/217/1/Karamouzi_Greece%E2%80%99s_Path_to_EEC_membership.pdf
76. Calandri, 'The United States, the EEC and the Mediterranean', pp. 46–7; Robert Bideleux, *The Southern Enlargement of the EC* (London, Routledge, 1996); Glenda Rosenthal, *The Mediterranean Basin, its Political Economy and Changing International Relations* (London, Butterworths Scientific, 1982); David Allen, Political Cooperation and the Euro-Arab Dialogue, in David Allen, Reinhardt Rummel, and Wolfgang Wessels, (eds), *European Political Cooperation* (London: Butterworths, 1982), pp. 79–82; Haifaa A Jawad, *Euro-Arab Relations: A Study in Collective Diplomacy* (Reading: Ithaka, 1992), pp. 21–80, *passim*; Saleh Al-Mani and Salah Al-Shaikhly (ed.), *The Euro-Arab Dialogue, A Study in Associative Diplomacy* (London: Frances Pinter Publishers, 1983).
77. Nicolas Badalassi, 'Sea and Détente in Helsinki: The Mediterranean Stake of the CSCE, 1972–1975', in Calandri, Caviglia and Varsori (eds), *Détente in Cold War Europe*, p. 61.
78. NARA, Central Files 1970–73, Box: 1677, telegram, 11 April 1970; telegram, 23 April 1970; telegram, 30–31 April 1970; NARA, Central Files 1970–73, Box: 2036, telegram, 27 May 1970; TNA/FCO39/1029, letter, A.R.K. Mackenzie, British Ambassador, Tunis to Alex Douglas-Home, 16 June 1972.
79. TNA/FCO39/1029, MWG meeting report by A. Brooke-Turner, 20 June 1972.
80. *Le Monde*, 6 January 1970.
81. TNA/FCO39/1029, letter, Rex Goring Morris, Tunis to AJM Craig, NENAD, 6 July 1972.
82. TNA/FCO66/629/DS11/516/1/2, minute, 1 May 1974; TNA/FCO 39/1029, minute by P.W. Marsden, FCO Research Department, 12/6/1972.
83. TNA/FCO39/1029, letter, Crispin C.C. Tickell, FCO, to A.RK. Mackenzie, British Ambassador, Tunis, 26 June 1972.
84. TNA/FCO30/1260, letter, FCO to Algiers, 7 December 1972; TNA/FCO 39/1031, memorandum, Tickell, 4 December 1972.
85. TNA/FCO39/1032, minute J.P. Goolden, Planning Staff FCO, undated.
86. TNA/CAB129/161/15, CP(72)15, 8 February 1972.
87. *The Guardian*, 7 October 1971; *Economist*, 28 October 1967; Eliyahu Kanovsky, 'The Economic Impact of the Six-Day War', *Middle East Journal*, 22/2, 1968, pp. 131–143.

88. TNA/FCO93/306, Walker to Holding, 25 June 1968; TNA/PREM 13/2073, record of meeting with the Prime Minister, 24 September 1968; TNA/FCO 39/753, minute, 20 February 1970.
89. Elie Podeh, 'Making a Short Story Long: The Construction of the Suez-Mediterranean Oil Pipeline in Egypt, 1967–1977', *The Business History Review*, 78/1, 2004, p. 75.
90. TNA/FCO39/1030, memorandum, Douglas-Home, 31 December 1970.
91. TNA/PREM15/534, 25 January 1971; ibid., DOPC(71)4, 2 February 1971.
92. Podeh, 'Making a Short Story', pp. 75–77.
93. TNA/FCO93/2, minute, A.D. Parsons, 24 January 1973.
94. Hughes, 'Britain, the Transatlantic Alliance', pp. 4, 37, 39.
95. FCO39/1032, 'The Community's Policy Towards Mediterranean Countries', 11 October 1972.
96. Henry Kissinger, *White House Years* (New York: Weidenfeld and Nicholson, 1979), p. 933; John Dickie, *'Special' No More: Anglo–American Relations: Rhetoric and Reality* (Weidenfeld and Nicholson, 1994), p. 147; C.J. Bartlett, *The Special Relationship: A Political History of Anglo–American relations since 1945* (Longman, 1992), 133; David Reynolds, *Britannia Overruled: British Policy and World Power in the Twentieth Century* (Longman, 1991), p. 244; Robin Renwick, *Fighting With Allies: America and Britain in Peace and War* (Basingstoke: Macmillan, 1996), p. 212.
97. Keith Hamilton, 'Britain, France and America's Year of Europe, 1973', *Diplomacy and Statecraft*, 17/4 (2006), pp. 871–895.
98. John Young, *Britain and European Unity, 1945–1999*, 2nd edition (Macmillan, 2000), p. 193; Hughes, 'Britain, the Transatlantic Alliance', pp. 4, 37, 39; Niklas Rossbach, *Heath, Nixon and the Rebirth of the Special Relationship*, (Palgrave Macmillan, 2009), pp. 202–222; Alex Spelling, 'Edward Heath and Anglo–American Relations 1970–1974: A Reappraisal', *Diplomacy & Statecraft*, 20/4, (2009), pp. 638–658; Andrew Scott, *Allies Apart: Heath, Nixon and the Anglo–American Relationship* (Basingstoke: Palgrave Macmillan, 2011).

10

'At The Top Table': British Elites' Perceptions of the UK's International Position, 1950–91

Michael D. Kandiah and Gillian Staerck

Since the end of the Second World War, Britain's global status has been a subject of intense debate. When the former US Secretary of State, Dean Acheson, famously stated in 1962 that 'Great Britain has lost an Empire and has not yet found a role',[1] he was suggesting the country should scale back its expectations of a world position, not rely upon a relationship with the US to project power and, importantly, reconcile itself to being just another major European state. Echoes of such views can be found in the pronouncements of French President Charles de Gaulle when he vetoed UK entry to the European Economic Community, in 1963 and again in 1967. The General believed that Britain was too close to Washington, not sufficiently European in outlook and too interested in maintaining a global presence. Over the decades such views have been repeated by others right down to the present day and, in all likelihood, will continue for some time to come. But, what did the British elite – politicians, policy-makers, civil servants and diplomats – think of this debate? This chapter will examine the question by utilising group oral testimonies, called 'witness seminars', of those who were at the heart of the UK policy-making elite as collected by the Institute of Contemporary British History (ICBH). The chapter will focus on three distinct but closely interrelated themes which consistently and identifiably run through the testimonies in these seminars: the internal debates about the UK's global position; Anglo–American relations; and relations with Europe. It is especially appropriate to rely on this source, because Saki Dockrill was considered a stalwart of the programme, attending most of those witness seminars relating to foreign and defence policy-making. She attended most, but not all, of the witness seminars that will be referred to in this chapter. Her final attendance at a witness seminar was in the summer of 2009.

The source: ICBH witness seminars

Before going any further, it is important to say a few more words about the prime source, the collection of witness seminars organised by ICBH. As already indicated, they are a type of group oral histories or group interviews. Since 1986, the year that the ICBH was established by Peter Hennessy and Anthony Seldon, over 100 witness seminars have been organised and several dozen transcripts have been published in journals or are available on the ICBH's website. Topics cover the spectrum of British policy-making and institutions, but a solid core of them broadly relate to British foreign and defence policy-making. Both authors of this chapter have contributed to the creation and maintenance of this resource. Those contributing their testimonies include senior civil servants and diplomats, ministers including several Foreign Secretaries and Defence Secretaries, and even Prime Ministers, in total consisting of over a thousand individuals from across the various branches of British public life.[2]

ICBH witness seminars are organised around a particular issue, institution or event. Individuals who were involved with, connected to, or knowledgeable about, the subject of the witness seminar are invited to attend and contribute their testimony with others, in a discussion which is facilitated by a Chair. Prior to the witness seminar, an academic-based brief with a chronology is prepared and circulated to all the participants, and a list of areas of discussion is drawn up. The discussion is semi-structured and the Chair uses his or her judgement when cutting short a discussion or developing it. The discussion usually consists of two sessions of no more than an hour and a half each. An audience, consisting of academics and other interested individuals (such as other colleagues and journalists), is also invited, and, if there is time, the audience is allowed by the Chair to ask questions or make other comments to contribute to the discussion. All participants are instructed beforehand that their utterances will be recorded, transcribed and they will be identified in both the transcript and the recordings. Nothing is 'off the record'. Once transcribed and lightly edited for the purposes of verbal smoothing, participants are asked to go over and correct the manuscript for sense and accuracy. The agreed transcript is then made available by the ICBH.[3] It is the agreed transcripts of various witness seminars that have been used and quoted in this chapter.

As with any oral history, narratives are constructed by the interviewees. These narratives are based on experience, both individual and collective, and a desire to communicate an interpretation of experience. Witness seminars, being as they are group interviews, have the potential to reveal layers of narratives: that of the individual; the collective group and institutional narratives that the individuals belong to; and, additionally, national narratives.[4] These narratives may be interconnected but they can also be discordant – participants can agree or disagree with each other as they respond to what others have said. This been described as 'a kind of "chaining" or "cascading" effect; talk links to, or tumbles out of, the topics and expressions preceding it'.[5] Thus, these witness seminars can provide dense information relating to the experiences of the individual and the group – for the purpose of this chapter, the UK's policy-making elite.

The members of the political and policy-making elite who have participated in ICBH witness seminars are a self-selecting group. This is for no other reason than these individuals have had to make time available to attend and contribute to a witness seminar. It can be inferred, therefore, that they have a stake in providing their testimonies – their particular narratives and interpretation of events – and that they know their memories will thus be recorded, preserved and disseminated, because these are the explicit aims of the Programme. This is not to say that the oral testimonies thus collected are unusually biased or self-interested. But the participants are aware and self-aware, and this can be a useful dynamic at a group interview. Interventions from participants can provide a necessary, alternative viewpoint. For instance, during a 2006 witness seminar series devoted to surveying foreign policy-making during the Thatcher years, Lord Powell of Bayswater, who had been Margaret Thatcher's principal foreign policy adviser, observed, 'I thought that the … session had the characteristics of an orgy of Foreign Office self-congratulation' and he proceeded to a contrary view that helped to give added texture to the testimonies gathered.[6]

The distinguished oral historian, Alessandro Portelli, has convincingly argued that those collecting and analysing oral testimonies should learn to value the primacy of the narrative, whether or not that narrative is strictly or objectively accurate. According to Portelli, we need to go beyond the observations of those who are sceptical of the value of oral history: that memory and recall is inherently faulty and that oral testimony is therefore fundamentally untrustworthy and consequently not useful. Portelli has argued that those who give us their oral testimonies tell us not only what they recall they did in the past but also, inevitably, tell us what they would have liked to have done and they reflect their current views.[7] Much of Portelli's work has sought to uncover and analyse both the untruths and essential truths in oral accounts and his work suggests that it is rewarding to understand what is revealed by the broad narratives that are recounted by individuals and groups.[8] The approach that this chapter will adopt is to understand and analyse the witness seminar oral histories and it takes the view that much can be revealed about the British ruling elite's individual, group and national narratives.

The individuals participating in the various ICBH witness seminars were (and in some cases, still are) professional politicians and policy-makers who, during the course of their careers and afterwards, have been used to recalling, recounting and analysing the significant experiences of their working lives. If they were diplomats or civil servants, they would write reports based not only on research and analysis of particular events but also upon their own experiences and judgements. Politicians who were ministers would have had to provide, as a matter course, accounts of events and analysis of situations to colleagues in Cabinet or Parliament and, of course, deal with the press. Members of Parliament who were backbenchers routinely participated in parliamentary committees and are used to giving and dealing with oral testimonies. Those who were junior observers at the time were very often involved in keeping accurate records of events. Some of the witness seminar participants have written their own memoirs or autobiographies. This is not to make a special claim for the veracity or accuracy of the testimony of individuals who participated in witness seminars, but it can be said that they are more used to recalling and analysing their experiences and having those experiences queried and put on record. Additionally, because the subjects they talked about are of national and perhaps even international significance, and because the chronology is provided beforehand, errors about events, the sequence of events, and dates tend to be minor. Additionally, many of the diplomats have also provided their life stories to the Diplomatic Oral History Programme, based at the Churchill Archive Centre, Cambridge. So they may be said to speak from positions of knowledge and authority, which suggests that their testimonies are reasonably robust for the purposes of this chapter.

At the top table in world affairs

It is perhaps significant that in none of the witness seminars did any single participant articulate precisely why Britain *should* have a significant world role. Instead, they reflected that it did. The UK's world role, they agreed, had started to diminish after the end of World War II, but it had not been extinguished – not yet, at any rate. Indeed, by broad consensus they believed that, overall, Britain had contributed more than other powers to the international order through, for instance, her contribution to NATO and other international bodies. Nevertheless, they also believed that whatever power and prestige that the UK had, and has, internationally was uncertain – it was something that might easily slip away. Making sure that it did not slip away entirely was something that they, and Britain, had had to work very hard to prevent.

Consequently, according to most participants, having a significant military capability and the ability to wage war has been vitally important to the UK. At a 1997 witness seminar, which examined the workings of the British Embassy in Washington, Sir Bernard Burrows, who worked at the Embassy in the late 1940s and early 1950s, was asked why he thought the Ambassador at the time, Oliver Franks, and the UK government had been keen for Britain to participate in the Korean War, the first major international conflict after the end of World War II. Burrows stated: 'The obvious answer…is that it thought to help our claim to "a place at the top table", which seemed to be of almost overriding value at that time'. He wondered, nevertheless, in 'hindsight, could we rightly afford the diversion of resources to this major military operation at that time, when there were so many other calls on British resources?' He said that Britain's view of the Korean conflict was, in fact, fundamentally 'neutral'. But, participation in the War was necessary: because of wider Cold War considerations, particularly because of British interests in the Far East; because of British policy in the Middle East with regards to growing Arab nationalism; and because the UK saw it as a gesture to facilitate better Anglo-American relations, at a time when the Americans were relatively new to the world stage. For these reasons, participation in the Korean War was deemed vital.[9]

Held twenty years after the conclusion of the 1982 Anglo-Argentine Falklands War, a witness seminar was organised in order to record the testimony of the members of the British government and senior members of the armed forces who were involved at the policy-making level. The sovereignty of the Falkland Islands had been a long-term matter of dispute between the UK and Argentina, with the former taking the view that as long as those resident in the South Atlantic islands wished to remain British, it would be British; and the latter believing that the Malvinas, as the Argentinians called the islands off their coasts, had been forcibly taken from them by the British, not long after their state was established in the early nineteenth century. For the participants of the witness seminar, the situation whereby the British continued to have possession of the Falklands was a result of an Imperial past and, most importantly, the continuing willing consent of the inhabitants. The Defence Secretary at the time, Sir John Nott, recalled that most politicians did not actually know where the Falkland Islands were until shortly before the invasion. But, nevertheless, for him and for the others, it was considered British territory, therefore it was worth fighting for. Additionally, Nott pointed out that the early 1980s was a period of renewed high Cold War tensions, so the UK could not be seen to be weak. According to Nott, 'The Warsaw Pact was a direct threat to the independence and freedom of the United Kingdom and was growing stronger, not weaker. That was the context of the Falklands'.[10] Reflecting on the period before the Argentine invasion of the South Atlantic islands in April 1983, Cecil Parkinson, who at the time was a member of the War Cabinet, said that: 'I remember during the Heath government [1970–74] a huge effort was made to persuade the Falkland Islanders to think more kindly about the Argentineans'.

Additionally, he recalled when a Foreign Office Minister had put forward a plan to the House of Commons that would allow the Argentinians to leaseback the islands, the proposal, he noted, 'went down like the proverbial lead-filled balloon.' When he had visited Argentina the year or so before the invasion, with a view to promote Anglo–Argentine trade, he said: 'I remember getting off the plane in Argentina and the very first question I was asked was "What is your attitude to the Malvinas", I said, "We call them the Falklands and they are British"'.[11] Sir Nicholas Henderson, who at the time of the Falklands crisis was the British Ambassador in Washington, identified the key stumbling block to negotiations that the US President Reagan and Secretary of State, George Shultz, were keen to promote: 'We were not prepared to talk about sovereignty. It was put up to ministers – this was the alternative, either reinforce or negotiate about sovereignty– and they said we can do neither'.[12] In short, despite the fact that they knew the UK's sovereignty was disputed, right across the British policy-making elite the Falkland Islands were considered to be basically British, and so they were – and this guided their actions. Prime Minister Margaret Thatcher may have been the most obvious and vocal defender of Britain's determination to keep hold of the Islands but these views, in different degrees, were shared by other ministers and the diplomats followed this lead.

The military humiliation that haunted all policy-makers during the Falklands war was the *débâcle* of the 1956 Suez operation. Nott recalled that, 'I vividly remembered Suez'. And he added, 'I know that…I and Terry Lewin, the Chief of the Defence Staff, never stopped thinking about Suez and what a frightful cock-up that had been'.[13] For him and for the others, although it was not articulated but it can be inferred, the successful outcome of the Falklands War had helped extirpate the memory of Suez and, they hoped, had helped rehabilitate the UK on the international stage. Britain's claims to her position at the top table were vindicated.

The Suez Crisis was very much in the minds of the participants of a witness seminar held in 1988, on the subject of the 1957 Sandys Defence White Paper,[14] which among other things was about the future of British military commitments and containing defence expenditure while maintaining a world role. However, none of the participants thought that Suez marked a watershed. Sir Richard Powell, who spent most of his career in the Ministry of Defence and was Deputy Secretary from 1950 to 1956, stated: 'Suez was certainly the proximate cause of the White Paper, in the sense that it led to a change of Prime Minister and Minister of Defence.' Instead, Powell argued that the Sandys Report was the result of longer-term debates within the foreign and defence policy-making elites. In particular, Powell suggested why post-war British governments had developed, then and subsequently, had been generally keen to maintain the nuclear deterrent. Firstly, it was believed that nuclear weapons would be cheaper than maintaining and supporting conventional forces. Secondly, the nuclear deterrent would be an expression of British might. According to Powell, 'the Attlee government [of 1945–51] felt that, as we were a world power, this was something we must have. That is why they decided to make their own bomb, being debarred of course by the McMahon Act [1946], which cut off co-operation with the United States. If we wanted it, we had no alternative but to go on our own. It was thought to be a necessary adjunct to a position of being a world power.' Powell went on to say, 'Later, it was also thought that it would give us greater influence with the United States if we had it than if we did not have it. We would be more on a level with them.' He concluded: 'I think the third consideration was that, however close we were to the US and however they were tied to us by alliances, one could not rule out circumstances in which they might go isolationist. These were the three basic reasons why we must have an independent deterrent. Those arguments', Powell observed, 'have gone on ever since'.[15]

Therefore, for British elites, if the UK was to have a credible international position, it was vital that the country have, and be seen to have, a strong military force and as cutting edge weaponry as it could afford. This had to be done, if Britain wished to be the globally significant country that they believed it was.

Anglo–American relations

For British elites, the maintenance of good Anglo–American relations was an imperative – it allowed Britain 'power by proxy'[16] – and this is a *leitmotif* that runs through all the ICBH witness seminars relating to foreign affairs and defence. However, as has already been seen, another recurrent theme was the elite's ambivalence towards the US. Reference has already been made to the 1997 witness seminar on the role of the Washington Embassy. This was organised to explore the nature of relations between the two countries with participants who had worked as diplomats at the Embassy spanning a period of forty years, from the Korean War to the 1991 Gulf War. The Chair was Lord Wright of Richmond, who had been Permanent Under-Secretary and Head of Diplomatic Service between 1986 and 1991, and who had served in Washington between 1960 and 1965 as Private Secretary to the Ambassador and later First Secretary. Wright stated that, in his opinion, 'the wartime alliance, and still the intelligence and defence relationship, has actually given the British Embassy in Washington a status...which no other Embassy in Washington has ever had or is ever likely to have'.[17] Concurring with this opinion was Sir Antony Acland, who had been Washington Ambassador between 1986 and 1991. Acland observed:

> If [the Americans] haven't made up their minds: if they are uncertain, if they are groping, if they are fumbling for a policy, then I do think still that there is an ease of communication and consultation with the British which probably doesn't apply with any other country and that there we can have a big input. They still respect our intelligence input. They still respect the fact that, like them, we have representation in most parts of the world and knowledge about most parts of the world. If they really want to do something and have made up their minds, they are going to do it. I don't think we are going to be able to ride them off. If they are fumbling, if they are groping for a solution, and because they don't want to walk alone they want someone with them, we will have influence. I think they will still probably look to us as the country of influence most likely to join them in a policy.[18]

Also present at the witness seminar was Mariot Leslie, UK Permanent Representative to NATO since 2010. During the mid-1980s, when she was at the British Embassy in Bonn, she had caught sight of a report that had been generated as a result of an exchange of lower level German and British diplomats in Washington. The German report, she said, had expressed astonishment 'at the degree of contact with the Hill the British Embassy had.' Furthermore, the German diplomats who had participated in the swap reported that they 'admired our ability to keep the door open, which the British Embassy had repeatedly done, because they found it very difficult to do sometimes. Also, our contacts right across the American administration, and not just in the State Department, were much more extended than they had imagined or thought possible'.[19] The general ease of interaction between the UK and the US could somehow produce advantages, according to Acland and Leslie.

However, Edmund Dell, who had been Paymaster General in Harold Wilson's Labour Government, 1974–76, was of the opinion that 'this cosying up to the Washington administration through the British Embassy and otherwise has repeatedly been contrary to British interests, particularly in the economic field.' To illustrate this, Dell gave the example of the negotiations he had led during his tenure in office that produced the Bermuda II Civil Aviation Agreement, 1977. This agreement, which according to Dell was the outcome of tough bargaining, had been to in the UK's best interests with regards to the very lucrative trans-Atlantic air travel business. But, throughout the negotiations, the Foreign Office and the Washington Ambassador, Sir Peter Ramsbotham, had repeatedly advised him to take a more conciliatory approach in his dealings with the Americans. Dell concluded that 'this feeling exists that we have, in order to maintain our relationship with the United States in certain areas, in order perhaps to get some return for bearing with them on all sorts of issues, repeatedly sacrificed British interests'.[20] Responding to Dell's charge, was Mark Pellew. He had been a Counsellor in the Washington Embassy between 1983 and 1989, and he believed this was an incorrect interpretation. Pellew recalled Ambassador Sir Oliver Wright telling him that 'it was a measure of the strength of the relationship' that there were 'at least half-a-dozen good economic rows going on with the Americans at any one time.' Furthermore, Pellew said, 'I do not recall a single occasion when we pulled our punches because it was felt it would damage the relationship'.[21]

In another witness seminar in 2006, which considered the broad areas of foreign policy-making during and since the Thatcher years, a similar disagreement emerged during the discussion. Sir Malcolm Rifkind, Defence Secretary, 1992–95, and then Foreign Secretary, 1995–7, noted that in his experience he had found that 'the Americans are grown up and that we can actually be pro-American and strongly disagree with them from time to time'. He gave an example: 'At the height of the Bosnian conflict [in the early 1990s], we were on the same side as most of the European countries. We were in deep disagreement with the United States about whether a more aggressive attitude should be taken, about bombing from the air and so on.' However, he suggested that this did not interrupt good relations more broadly: 'The fact is that they are grown up. They knew perfectly well that Bosnia, however much we disagreed about it, was one element of a much wider relationship'.[22] According to Rifkind, he and most other policy-makers and diplomats understood that the UK had earned the right to fight her own corner *vis-à-vis* the US, and that this was respected by the Americans. However, Rifkind was critical of the approach taken by Tony Blair's government when committing the UK to the Second Iraq War in 2003:

> If I have a problem with Tony Blair's policy, it is not that he has been pro-American. Every British Prime Minister wants to do that. It has been that he has given the impression of being unconditional. That has not been the attitude of all previous Prime Ministers, Labour or Conservative.[23]

Blair's determination to keep in with the Americans at what appeared to be any cost – by massaging intelligence evidence, for example – was, in Rifkind's view, contrary to previous practice and would not be to the UK's ultimate advantage. His comments met with broad agreement by other witness seminar participants, not all of whom were Conservatives.

The apogee of Anglo–American relations during the Cold War period is generally considered to be in the 1980s, during the Thatcher–Reagan years. A witness seminar was organised in 2009 focusing on the 1983 Grenada Crisis, which saw a very public rift between the two leaders when the US mounted military action against the Caribbean Commonwealth country.[24] One of the participants was Sir Bernard Ingham, who was the Prime Minister's Press Secretary. In his view, 'Margaret Thatcher found her mission in life in 1981 when President Reagan came to office'. He said that, while 'She saw it as her job to support the leader of the free world as best she could', nevertheless, 'She did not believe that a person was a friend unless that friend gave their honest, candid advice.' Thatcher, unlike Reagan and the rest of his administration, did not believe that the

Grenadian regime, run by the Marxist New Jewel Movement, posed a threat to the security of other countries in the Caribbean or more broadly. Consequently, she was surprised when US troops invaded Grenada and ousted the left-wing government. Thatcher was also furious, Ingham recalled, because Grenada was part of the Commonwealth, gaining independence as recently as 1974, and the Queen was still the new country's Head of State: Thatcher felt, therefore, that the UK should have been consulted about an action against a country that was within the British sphere. Ingham also recalled another important objection that she had: 'How would we stop the Soviets walking into wherever they want?'[25]

Lord Bramall, who was Chief of Defence Staff between 1982 and 1985, indicated that he had actually previously intimated to Prime Minister Thatcher that an American invasion was a possibility. He recalled she dismissed this prediction, saying, 'What on earth would make them do a stupid thing like that?' So Bramall told her: 'They have just lost 241 men in the Lebanon.... [T]here are a couple of Cuban officers there [in Grenada], some Black Power element, something that they could believe or make themselves believe was destabilising in the West Indies and I think that President Reagan will want an easy, quick victory, which he can put against this ghastly tragedy in the Lebanon to restore morale.' Bramall was present when, subsequently, Thatcher made a series of telephone calls to Reagan, in which she freely expressed her strongest opposition to US actions. According to Bramall, 'The interesting thing was that...it made no difference to the wonderful relationship between Margaret Thatcher and President Reagan, although they disagreed fundamentally on that point'.[26]

That same year, 1983, the Strategic Defense Initiative (SDI) was announced by President Reagan. The aim of SDI was to develop a strategic ballistic defence system that would eliminate the need for nuclear weapons: this would require the development of new technologies. For UK policy-makers, if SDI were workable – and they were not sure that it actually was – it would nevertheless fundamentally undermine British defence policy that had been put in place since the end of World War II – that of keeping the US closed tied to the UK and Europe. Michael Heseltine, who was Defence Secretary between 1983 and 1986, recalled that: 'There was deep concern ... [because] President Reagan was going to negotiate with the Soviet Union a serious diminution in the numbers of nuclear weapons systems available to either side.' He pointed out that the UK had invested 'huge sums of defence money' on the deterrent; therefore, British policy-makers were confronted with 'in the hypothetical (and I personally think much to be deplored and avoided) situation of a decoupling of the United States from the NATO Alliance and from Europe'.[27] Lord Powell, who was the Prime Minister's Foreign Policy Adviser, recalled that 'Margaret Thatcher said of Ronald Reagan and SDI, "This is Ronald Reagan, so I must support him; Ronnie believes in the same things as me, on lower taxes, on the evil empire of communism and so on, if he wants the SDI he is going to get it and I should support him".' However, he said that she then added:

> But the man is mad, he wants to get rid of nuclear weapons, this is intolerable, we can't allow this to happen, nuclear weapons are vital to Britain's defence, I have an agreement to purchase *Trident* and I would look very silly indeed if I was left without a nuclear weapon. So we must stop that side of it: we must have SDI *and* we must have nuclear weapons and the two go hand in hand, and indeed I can construct an argument which says that deterrence is actually enhanced by the SDI as long as you keep the nuclear weapons as well, possibly in slightly smaller numbers.[28]

Therefore, when the US asked allies if they were interested in participating in research and development which would bring the SDI programme to fruition, the Prime Minister and other British policy-makers had already concluded that they had to do so. Sir Michael Quinlan, Permanent Under-Secretary of State at the Ministry of Defence, 1988–92, explained that once Reagan had made his intentions public, 'The question was never, "Is this a good idea?". It was, "What are we going to do"?'[29] Dr Frank Panton, formerly Assistant Scientific Advisor (Nuclear), explained what followed: 'What was done was, in effect, to construct an arrangement similar to the arrangement under the atomic agreement, the 1958 agreement, where specific areas were determined as areas in which a pretty free exchange of views and work between the American side and the British side would be established'.[30]

Maintaining good Anglo–American relations was, therefore, held to be a cornerstone of British external policy-making by British elites. Not good relations at all costs: British interests, they believed, had to be primary. But achieving this goal, as they found in their experience, was not always easy.

Europe

Finding the right policy toward Europe has been notoriously difficult for the British political and policy-making elite. The post-World War

II movement for greater European unity has posed challenges for the British them *vis-à-vis* the country's international role, particularly since the 1957 Treaty of Rome was signed by West Germany, France, Italy and the Benelux countries. At a 1998 witness seminar on Britain and Brussels, Sir Roy Denman reflected on what British reactions had been towards the newly-formed EEC. Denman, then a junior civil servant at the Board of Trade, was sent to the Bonn Embassy. When he was there, he recalled, 'A message arrived from London, almost like a message from the Pope, saying that rumours had appeared in the press that Britain might join this new-fangled European Community.' It was Denman's job to talk to West German press 'how we couldn't join the EC, because of our relationship with the Commonwealth, our special relationship with the US and our links with Switzerland and Scandinavia.' However, he was surprised when 'The Germans pointed out that the Commonwealth was disappearing as a political force, and the US would go where power was, which would be with a big continental bloc.' When Denman reported back to the Ambassador, Sir Christopher Steel, 'he rose to his feet like a great Edwardian stage actor and said, "Her Majesty's Government could never possibly join this continental rag, tag and bobtail, but it was damned impertinent of these fellows to go it on their own". Up to 1960 that was the Foreign Office attitude'.[31] Even after the UK joined in 1973, Denman felt things were not much better: 'the picture in Whitehall generally ... has been a depressing case of English insularity'.[32] Unsurprisingly Denman went on to join the European Commission and became a senior figure there.

In 1990, a witness seminar was organised to examine the 1967 decision to withdraw from defence bases 'East of Suez', that is in Southeast Asia and the Persian Gulf. For the participants, the broad economic imperatives that had driven Harold Wilson's Labour government to take this decision had also led to the UK's second application to join the EEC. According to J.K. Wright, a senior government economist in the 1950s and 1960s, 'The destination of UK exports and trade was changing. In 1965 we still exported more to the Commonwealth than to Europe, but within the next ten years that had changed, and it was becoming quite clear that the Commonwealth market was falling away from us.' He noted that politicians and policy-makers had begun to conclude that 'the future of Britain lay in closer co-operation with Europe and that the Commonwealth, if anything, was neutral in this and as often as not would turn out to be to our disadvantage'.[33]

UK elites were also led to believe by the Americans that the US wanted Britain to have a closer relationship with Europe. At the 2006 witness seminar on foreign policy-making during the Thatcher years, participants reflected on this. One of them was Lord Kerr of Kinlochard, who had been Permanent Under-Secretary of State at the Foreign Office, 1997–2002, and previously Ambassador to Washington, 1995–97. He observed: 'It is a complete myth that the United States would prefer a wider English channel. It talks to us not only because we speak well and we are interesting people, but in the hope that we may affect the policy of the European Union'. It was clear to him that 'the thing that matters most about being seen to be influential in Europe is that it makes the United States listen to you more'.[34] Kerr also noted that, 'We are seen by the Europeans as reasonably important, partly because we cut ice in Washington'.[35] Thus, whichever way one looked at it, it was important for Britain to try and get its European policy right. However, almost every British government has found it impossible to do so. Why? According to another participant at the witness seminar, Sir Malcolm Rifkind, 'It is an interesting question why every British Prime Minister has either directly or indirectly wanted to be at the heart of Europe, but all have failed to do so.' He remembered that:

> 'Before she became Prime Minister, Margaret Thatcher was not particularly anti-Europe in most of her speeches or comments. That began during her Prime Ministership'. John Major actually said that he wanted to be at the heart of Europe.... Both John Major and Tony Blair had no emotional hostility towards a European project; nevertheless they have ended up being pretty well as awkward as their predecessor.[36]

Another participant at the witness seminar, Lord Howell of Guildford, who claimed to be 'very pro-Europe',[37] attempted to answer this question by giving his point of view from his long experience as a Conservative backbench parliamentarian. He noted that, 'A good deal of fun tends to be made by those outside party politics of the way various people were said to be pro-Europeans and then became sceptics, while others who were sceptics became pro. Look at how the Conservative Party started as a party of Europe, then somehow had the reputation of being the party of the Eurosceptics. Look at how the Labour Party... ended up being the party that wanted to be at the heart of Europe.' However, he said the paradox was that 'I felt that I was watching the scenery change round us'. That is to say, the changing European and international scene had altered the way that politicians like him viewed British relations towards Europe:

> The Europe of the markets – that wonderful place across the Channel that would talk about markets and market forces...somehow evaporated and became a Europe of social partners and corporatist language and intentions, always with the market elements too, while it was Britain that became the island of market forces. So there was an extraordinary turnaround. It seems that that turning is still going on.[38]

Howell said that he came to see that 'the modern Commonwealth...contains six of the fastest growing high-tech and potentially rich and dynamic nations on earth and constitutes a network that stretches across continents and faiths and encompasses and can address some of the really horrific issues of the twenty-first century.' Therefore, he believed that 'going through our European partners, is too small a channel – too narrow a gate – for us to fulfil our wider ambitions and make the wider contribution that we can make as a nation. That is how I see matters from the parliamentary side'.[39] Of course, his views were not in line with the views of most other participants, but accurately capture the dilemmas of some with regards to Britain's European policy.

The significance of the defence aspects of Britain's European policy were articulated in a witness seminar held in 2001 on the Nott Defence Review of 1981. For the then Defence Secretary John Nott, 'money, money' was at the heart of his problems. He had to cut defence expenditure while allowing the UK to maintain its NATO commitments. This would meet the security needs of Britain and its European partners, and ensure that an American presence in Europe was maintained: 'We were paying 10 per cent towards the defence of the United Kingdom, that was our contribution to NATO. The Americans were contributing 50 per cent of the cost of NATO. It was absolutely fundamental that we kept those American troops on the Central Front.' As a result, he said, his 1981 Defence Review determined that what needed to be done was to reduce the size of the Royal Navy. He found that he 'didn't have any option but to go the Continental route....it really wasn't that I was unsympathetic to the naval case, I just didn't have the choice'.[40] For the security of the British Isles, first line of defence was, ultimately, Western Europe.

Maintaining European stability was also an important feature of British policy in the closing years of the Cold War. To examine this, a witness seminar was held in 2000, which focused on Anglo–German relations at the time of German unification. At that time, the British

Ambassador to Germany was Sir Christopher Mallaby. He observed that UK policy-makers feared instability in Russia might cause instability in the East Central European area: 'We did not think that liberalisation in the Soviet Union was necessarily irreversible and there was a fear that rapid movement towards German unification could endanger Russian Premier Gorbachev's position. He could find himself in a position where he could not defend domestically in Moscow some of the things that were going on in Central Europe'.[41] However, above all, what was making things worse for British policy-makers was the hostility of Prime Minister Thatcher even to consider the prospect of German unification, following the fall of the iconic Berlin Wall in November 1989.

The British Ambassador to Moscow, Sir Rodric Braithwaite recalled that a month before the Berlin Wall fell, he and a number of the other participants at the witness seminar attended a Heads of Mission Conference to discuss the future of NATO and European security. At that time, events were moving at a breakneck pace and they were hoping for political leadership from the top. However, Braithwaite remembered, 'one of the interesting things about that conference was that we were told right at the beginning that the Prime Minister did not wish us to consider the consequences of a possible reunification of Germany'. Nevertheless, he went on to say, 'We were worried that, if Germany were reunited and the Russians withdrew, it would be possible that NATO would go.' At this point, he said he thought that Thatcher's grip on the realities of foreign policy had slipped: 'That was really, I think, the first clear indication that I had that Mrs Thatcher wasn't in touch with reality. There were serious concerns both in Bonn and in Paris, but also in Washington, that she was taking herself out of the discussion by the views that she was taking'.[42]

Similarly concerned was Sir Michael Alexander, then UK Ambassador and Permanent Representative on the North Atlantic Council. He recalled:

> I myself wasn't in the least worried about the threat of the Germans dominating Europe. But I was extremely worried about – I remember talking about it with [Foreign Secretary] Geoffrey Howe at that time – the prospect that 15 years out (i.e., about now [at the time of the witness seminar in 2000), Germany and Berlin would matter even more to the UK than Russia and Moscow. That made it pretty foolish to run the risk of alienating the German Government in their history

> since the end of the Second World War, i.e. unification. For us to alienate them by trying to stop it struck me as mad – and I said so.[43]

Leadership from politicians was what the diplomats said they were looking for, but it was something that they did not find. Sir Michael Burton, who was Minister in Berlin during the entire period commented that, 'It was therefore disappointing when the Foreign Secretary [Douglas Hurd] came to Berlin … that he brought the message, "Unification is not on the agenda". That was not how we were seeing it on the ground.' Burton noted, 'Although no-one at that stage could put a time-table on re-unification, it was my view that, as far as the long decades of the Allied presence in Berlin were concerned, we were into the end-game'.[44] Unfortunately, the political inertia in London caused by the Prime Minister meant that the British were not to play a significant role during this key moment in time in Europe.

For British elites, therefore, European policy was an area that caused the deepest of disputes. It can be seen from their testimonies that this was because relations with Europe called into question and challenged what they believed was Britain's wider, and proper, international role.

Conclusion

It might be said that, notwithstanding Acheson's belief that the British had not found their proper place in the post-war world, the country's elites believed that, diminished though British power may be, it *had* a position and they wanted to do what they could to maintain that position, not to let it slip away. Hanging on to, and harnessing, US power was one of their principal strategies but, as has been seen, other aspects of foreign and defence policy-making were also orientated to that end. Following this through was what they saw was in the UK's best interests. That the findings arising from the ICBH Witness Seminars are not radically dissimilar from the analysis found in document-based research is not surprising, but it is significant. It is not surprising, because the members of the elite who provided the testimony in the seminars were the same people who formulated British foreign and defence policy-making and wrote the documents on which archival researchers depend. It is significant, because it is possible to infer that these narratives are fundamental to the workings of the policy-makers, politicians and diplomats, and suggest a remarkable unanimity of views, despite certain areas of divergence and dispute on the details.

Notes

1. See Douglas Brinkley, 'Dean Acheson and the "Special Relationship": The West Point Speech of December 1962', *Historical Journal* Vol. 33 No. 3 (1990), p. 599.
2. For a full list of witness seminars, see the ICBH website: http://www.kcl.ac.uk/innovation/groups/ich/index.aspx.
3. If not published, the transcript is available from ICBH, King's College, London.
4. Herbert Ruben and Irene Ruben, *Qualitative Interviewing: the Art of Hearing Data* (Thousand Oaks, CA: SAGE, 1995).
5. Thomas R. Lindlof and Bryan C. Taylor, *Qualitative Communication Research Methods* (2nd Edition, Thousand Oaks, CA: SAGE 2002), p. 182.
6. Lord Powell of Bayswater, in Michael Kandiah and A. Riley (eds), 'Making Foreign Policy in the Thatcher Years and Beyond', 6 February 2006, unpublished manuscript, p. 67.
7. See in particular his *The Death of Luigi Trastulli and Other Stories: Form and Meaning in Oral History* (Albany: State University of New York Press, 1991); *The Battle of Valle Giulia: Oral History and the Art of Dialogue* (Madison: University of Wisconsin Press, 1997); and *The Order Has Been Carried Out: History, Memory and Meaning of a Nazi Massacre in Rome* (Basingstoke: Palgrave Macmillan, 2003).
8. Betsy Brinson, 'Crossing Cultures: An Interview with Alessandro Portelli', *Oral History Review*, 28/1 (Winter/Spring 2001), p. 88.
9. Sir Bernard Burrows in Gillian Staerck and Michael Kandiah (eds), *The Role of HM Embassy in Washington,* 18 June 1997 (London: ICBH, 2002), pp. 19–20.
10. Sir John Nott, in Andrew Dorman, Michael Kandiah and Gillian Staerck (eds), *The Falklands War,* 5 June 2002 (London: ICBH, 2005), p. 18.
11. Lord Parkinson, in ibid., p. 19.
12. Sir Nicholas Henderson, ibid., p. 25. Sir Crispin Tickell, in another witness seminar, recalled that at the time of the Falklands Crisis: 'I was then Ambassador to Mexico and the Latin Americans made clear to me their deep embarrassment. On the one hand, they disliked colonialism and, on the other, they did not like the Argentine Government at all. The Mexican President proposed to me that Margaret Thatcher and General Galtieri should meet on the beach at Cancun bilaterally without observers and note-takers. He said that there was only one problem: who will throw the other into the sea first? I think that we know!' in Kandiah and Riley (eds), 'Making Foreign Policy', pp. 55–6.
13. Nott, in Dorman, Kandiah and Staerck (eds), *Falklands War*, pp. 32–3.
14. The *1957 White Paper on Defence* (Cmnd. 124, London: HMSO, 1957), known as the Sandys Report after Defence Secretary, Duncan Sandys.
15. Sir Richard Powell in Michael Kandiah and Gillian Staerck (eds), *The Move to the Sandys White Paper*, July 1988 (London: ICBH, 2002), pp. 21–2.
16. See James Ellison and Kevin Ruane, 'Managing the Americans: Anthony Eden, Harold Macmillan and the Pursuit of "Power by Proxy" in the 1950s', *Contemporary British History*, 18/3 (2004), pp. 147–67.
17. Sir Antony Acland, in Staerck and Kandiah (eds), *Washington*, p. 21.
18. Ibid., p. 34.

19. Mariot Leslie, ibid., p. 43.
20. Edmund Dell, ibid., p. 47.
21. Mark Pellew, ibid., p. 48
22. Sir Malcolm Rifkind, in Kandiah and Riley (eds), 'Making Foreign Policy', p. 113.
23. Ibid.
24. See Gary Williams, *US-Grenada Relations: Revolution and Intervention in the Backyard* (Basingstoke: Palgrave Macmillan, 2007).
25. Sir Bernard Ingham in M. Kandiah (ed.), 'Britain and the Grenada Crisis, 1983: Cold War in the Caribbean', 29 May 2009, unpublished manuscript, p. 13.
26. Lord Bramall, ibid., pp. 50–51.
27. Lord Heseltine, in Michael Kandiah and Gillian Staerck (eds), *The British Response to SDI*, 9 July 2003 (London, 2005), p. 31.
28. Lord Powell of Bayswater, ibid., pp. 32–3.
29. Sir Michael Quinlan, ibid., p. 72.
30. Dr. Frank Panton, ibid., p. 36
31. Sir Roy Denman, in R. Broad, Michael Kandiah and Gillian Staerck (eds), *Britain and Europe*, 5 May 1998 (London: ICBH, 2002), p. 47.
32. Ibid., pp. 47–8.
33. J.K. Wright, in Peter Catterall, Michael Kandiah and Gillian Staerck (eds), *The Decision to withdraw from East of Suez*, held 16 Nov. 1990 (London: ICBH, 2002), p. 29.
34. Kerr, in Kandiah and Riley (eds), 'Making Foreign Policy', p. 113.
35. Ibid.
36. Rifkind, ibid., p. 111.
37. Lord Howell of Guildford, ibid., p. 121.
38. Howell, ibid., p. 117
39. Ibid., p. 120.
40. Sir John Nott in Michael Kandiah and Gillian Staerck (eds), *The Nott Review*, 20 June 2001 (London: ICBH, 2002), p. 47.
41. Sir Christopher Mallaby, in Michael Kandiah and Gillian Staerck (eds) *Anglo–German Relations and German Unification*', 18 October 2000, (London: ICBH, 2003), p. 26.
42. Sir Rodric Braithwaite, ibid., pp. 27–28.
43. Sir Michael Alexander, ibid., p. 30.
44. Sir Michael Burton, ibid., p. 45.

11

The British Embassy in Washington and Anglo–American Relations during the Blair Governments, 1997–2007

Michael F. Hopkins

Tony Blair served as British Prime Minister for ten years, the first Labour Party leader to win three successive general elections. By the time he came to power in 1997, Britain was, at best, a second tier power in the world economically, and a significant military force only when compared with other European nations, for America, Russia and China easily surpassed British strength. Nevertheless, Britain was a permanent member of the UN Security Council, it possessed nuclear weapons and Blair was determined to play a role on the world stage. In foreign policy, he was in the forefront of a new interventionist approach and he encouraged the United States to be less hesitant about intervening in regional problems for humanitarian reasons. At the core of his foreign policy was the country's relationship with the United States, as had been the case for British premiers since the Second World War (with the possible exception of Edward Heath, in 1970–1974). Given the centrality of the Anglo–American relationship to British foreign policy and American dominance of that partnership, Washington was where the power resided. The British Embassy in Washington had the proximity to the levers of American power and the expertise to be a vital ingredient in advising Blair and his government and in pursuing policy. It merits detailed analysis. Yet, the mission has rarely been the focus of scholarly scrutiny.[1] Indeed, it has scarcely even been mentioned in studies of Tony Blair and his governments' foreign policy.[2] This chapter helps to fill this gap in the literature.

Of course, the records for such recent events remain classified and they will do so for some time, even under the new twenty-year rule on the release of documents, which is now being introduced by the

British government. Yet, it is possible to find a range of sources: publicly available government materials from speeches to press conferences to White papers to interviews; the memoirs and diaries of politicians and officials, including one ambassador (Sir Christopher Meyer); and various oral history interviews conducted by the British Diplomatic Oral History Project, now based at Churchill College, Cambridge. I also interviewed ambassadors to Washington and other officials who served in this period. In addition, there are the studies by well-informed journalists, whose accounts frequently depend on the testimony of key individuals. These materials provide a window into the activities and influence of senior figures in London from Tony Blair to successive foreign secretaries to permanent under secretaries at the Foreign Office. They also shed light on the activities of ambassadors. However, they give little indication of the roles of more junior individuals, whose contributions will only become clear when their minutes and memoranda and other records are opened to the public. So, this analysis of the role of the British Embassy in Washington is dominated by the activities of the ambassadors, although the contributions of other officials make intermittent appearances.

This study is an examination of diplomatic practice rather than a scrutiny of the details of policy. It explores the key individuals and the systems and procedures in which they operated. First, it considers Tony Blair and his successive foreign secretaries in London and how he ran his government; and pays particular attention to the mechanisms for making foreign policy. Then it addresses its central concern: how the British Embassy in Washington functioned in this process. The analysis is divided into three parts: the situation in 1997 when Blair came to power; the course of developments from 1997 to the war in Iraq in 2003; and the years from the war to the departure of Blair in summer 2007. These divisions coincide with the three ambassadorships to Washington during Tony Blair's term as Prime Minister: Sir John Kerr, 1995–1997; Sir Christopher Meyer, 1997–2003; and Sir David Manning, 2003–2007.

Tony Blair and British foreign policy

Anthony Charles Lynton Blair was born in Edinburgh in May 1953 and educated at Fettes and St John's College, Oxford where he read jurisprudence. On graduation he trained as a barrister under the guidance of Derry Irvine, whom he later appointed as Lord Chancellor. He entered Parliament in 1983, became Shadow Home Secretary in 1992 and, after the death of John Smith, was elected Labour leader in 1994. He then won the 1997 general election, becoming Prime Minister at the age of 44; and won again in 2001 and 2005, before retiring in 2007. The premiership was the only Cabinet office Blair held, a unique feat among twentieth century British premiers. The ease with which he assumed the post and executed his duties indicated his self-belief. Blair brought an intelligent, bright, lively, and socially comfortable personality to his work. He had an intuitive feel for, rather than an intellectual appreciation of, politics. As his memoirs make clear, he also displayed toughness, a readiness to stand up for what he regarded as important matters, and, perhaps above all, a sense of conviction. Blair brought religious belief to his political drive. Indeed, his recent conversion makes him the only British Prime Minister to be a Catholic, albeit only after leaving office. His Christian faith led him to pursue improvement at home and abroad, but he was not dogmatic; rather he always appreciated the need to be pragmatic. He also had a strong sense of his ability to persuade. He won selection for his parliamentary constituency after initially being rejected.[3]

As soon as he became Prime Minister, Blair challenged the traditional practices of Cabinet government. The first decision of his new government, in May 1997, which gave operational control of the setting of interest rates to the monetary policy committee of the Bank of England, was made before the first Cabinet meeting. An official maintained that 'This is not a collective government. We have to accept that the old model of Cabinet government is dead as a doornail.' Paragraph 88 of the *Ministerial Code*, as amended by Blair's government, read:

> In order to ensure the effective presentation of government policy, all major interviews and media appearances, both print and broadcast, should be agreed with the No 10 Press Office before any communications are entered into. The policy content of all major speeches, press releases and new policy initiatives should be cleared in good time with the No 10 Press Office; the timing and form of announcements should be cleared with the No 10 Press Office.

Commenting on the change, Peter Riddell of *The Times* observed: 'Goodbye Cabinet government. Welcome to the Blair presidency'.[4]

The post of British Foreign Secretary was held by Robin Cook (May 1997-June 2001), Jack Straw (June 2001-May 2006) and Margaret Beckett (May 2006-June 2007). None enjoyed especially close relations with Blair, who turned, instead, to his team of advisers at 10 Downing

Street. Many of these were personal appointments: Jonathan Powell, who served as Blair's chief of staff for the whole of his term as Prime Minister; Alastair Campbell, his press secretary from 1997 to July 2000, and director of communications and strategy from July 2000 to August 2003; and the Policy Unit, under the leadership of David Miliband, which was renamed as the Policy Directorate in 2001. But the Foreign and Commonwealth Office had a voice in No 10 through the Prime Minister's Private Secretaries for foreign affairs, John Holmes (1997–1999) and John Sawers (1999–2001). Indeed, John Holmes made so favourable an impression that he was appointed Principal Private Secretary to the Prime Minister.

By spring 2001 Blair wanted to strengthen his team at No 10. He told the Cabinet Secretary, Sir Richard Wilson, that he did not understand why, when each Cabinet minister had a Permanent Secretary, there could not be one at No 10. After a series of discussions, it was agreed that there would be two posts at Permanent Secretary level: Stephen Wall would be in charge of European Union (EU) matters and David Manning would oversee policy for all other areas of the world.[5] For Sir John Kerr this was a good solution to changing circumstances. 'Prime Ministers are always going to interfere in foreign affairs ... Any Prime Minister is going to have his own view on quite a number of dossiers. It is not going to be possible to wait in all cases for the Foreign Office's advice.' So, 'what really matters for the Foreign Office is who whispers in his ears, who is there encouraging good ideas, and discouraging bad ideas.' The arrangements made in 2001 did create 'an embryo National Security Council in No 10', but those appointed did not lose their links with the Foreign Office and wanted to 'maintain reasonably good links with base camp because they would quite like another job when this one ends.' Indeed, Manning and his replacement, Nigel Sheinwald, went on to be successive ambassadors to Washington.[6]

Robin Cook arrived in office preoccupied with his private life and his first year contained a number of mishaps, but his undoubted talents impressed both Kerr and Meyer. Meyer called him 'a man more to be admired than liked.' 'People in the Foreign Office told me later that Cook was idle about reading his briefs. If that was so, he managed to conceal it through a natural intelligence and a lucid style of exposition'.[7] Kerr noted that he had 'an absolutely coruscating intelligence', but he felt that 'prior homework is not of the essence'. He would turn his mind to a subject and 'filter advice, suck up the relevant facts, memorise them incredibly fast and polish his oratorical style.' He never acted as though he was in charge: he 'felt someone else should be running the ship, leaving him unencumbered to pick and choose the issues he would handle.' He managed these issues brilliantly, but 'he didn't want to know about other dossiers'.[8] Cook's private secretary, Sherard Cowper-Cowles, was more understanding. He describes his time working for Cook as amongst the most difficult of his career, but, in many ways, the most rewarding and enjoyable. Cook had a 'wry sense of humour' and was 'free of cant and pomposity'. He was not lazy; he was profoundly disorganised. He felt he should concentrate on what interested him and those topics where he believed he could make an impact. Although he did not have good relations with FO officials or with his junior ministers, he did have excellent relations with the foreign ministers of other countries. In particular, he and the US Secretary of State, Madeleine Albright 'got on exceptionally well one on one'.[9] At first, Blair and Cook worked well together. Both spoke about ethics in foreign affairs and about Britain's leadership in this area. In a speech to the Royal Institute of International Affairs, at Chatham House, on 28 January 2000, Cook maintained that 'the global interest is becoming the national interest'.[10] Cowper-Cowles, however, is right to describe their relationship as 'warily respectful rather than close'. Cook was unimpressed with Blair's lack of a thorough grasp of the issues at European meetings and by his 'reluctance to tell his interlocutors what they didn't want to hear'.[11]

After the election victory in May 2001 Blair replaced Cook with Jack Straw, who was chosen *faute de mieux* and because he was, as one figure in No 10 Downing Street said, 'fundamentally loyal. They'd have their arguments in private, but then Jack would stick to the script and decisions in public, something Robin hadn't done'.[12] Kerr observed: 'The sigh of relief when Jack Straw arrived, clubbable and polite, a man who held meetings and allowed into his room the people who drafted the papers, and wanted to know who they were, and shook their hands, and then, if he disagreed with them, explained why'.[13] All agreed that the new Foreign Secretary was a much more agreeable person to work for. Cowper-Cowles noted how Straw, with 'typical tact and generosity', made space available in the Foreign Office for Cook's farewell party.[14] Meyer observed: 'It took Jack Straw, someone more to be liked than admired, a long time to find his feet'.[15] Straw became, in Meyer's judgement, a solid performer, but no more than that, after a year or so. Straw and Blair established a functional relationship, but neither Prime Minister nor the No 10 staff seemed to have much regard for the Foreign Secretary. One official said that they had sent a boy to do a man's job.[16] Nonetheless, Straw built up good relations with Secretary of State Colin Powell and National Security Adviser Condoleezza Rice, who succeeded Powell in

2005. She observed in her memoirs, 'We'd become close friends as well as close colleagues'.[17]

Doubts about Straw led to plans to replace him before the 2005 election, but Blair's preferred candidate, Charles Clarke, had to take over at the Home Office, after it was revealed that the incumbent, David Blunkett, had fast-tracked a visa application for the nanny of his mistress. So, Straw stayed until 2006 by which time Clarke's performance as Home Secretary had failed to impress the Prime Minister. To general surprise, Blair appointed the competent, but uninspiring Margaret Beckett, who had demonstrated a deft touch in various international issues at the Department for Environment, Food and Rural Affairs. Her undoubted loyalty and the prospect of appointing the first woman as Foreign Secretary were probably important contributing factors.[18] Although in office only for the last year of Blair's premiership, Beckett drew some harsh judgements on her performance.[19]

In campaigning for office and in his first months as Prime Minister, Blair adopted a non-ideological, pragmatic outlook on foreign affairs. In his only speech on foreign policy in the 1997 general election campaign, he declared 'I am a British patriot and I am proud to be a British patriot. I love my country. I will always put the interests of my country first. The Britain in my vision is not Britain turning its back on the world – narrow, shy, uncertain. It is a Britain confident of its place in the world, sure of itself, able to negotiate with the world and provide leadership in the world.' He talked about 'the destiny of Britain to lead other nations'.[20] But he then began to develop a foreign policy vision. He gave a speech to the Economic Club of Chicago on 24 April 1999 entitled the 'Doctrine of the International Community', which argued that intervention was legitimate in certain circumstances. For Blair, foreign policy should pay attention to values. 'It is by furthering our values that we further our interests in the modern era of globalisation and interdependence'; 'Idealism becomes realpolitik'.[21] These values should be pursued by the combined use of soft and hard power. This outlook was articulated in the deliberately simultaneous appearance of the Foreign Office's first ever strategy White Paper and a Defence White Paper, in 2003.[22]

The Washington embassy in 1997

The structure of Britain's Washington embassy and the range of its activities in May 1997 remained surprisingly similar to those established during the Second World War and adapted to peacetime use after 1945. Its main departments were the Chancery, the engine room of the mission, which handled foreign policy and US domestic issues; the Economic section, which tackled Treasury matters; Trade Policy, which also embraced aviation and science; the Press; Defence; Intelligence; Internal Management; and the British Council. There was also a branch devoted to matters of protocol. The Ambassador, Minister and Counsellor were the three senior figures who sought out contact with figures of similar status in the American hierarchy. The two main areas of activity, overseen by ministers, were political strategic issues and various economic matters ranging from trade and commerce to labour questions. In 1997 there were five ministers: the senior one was David Logan, who was succeeded by Michael Arthur, Stephen Wright and Anthony Brenton; the senior economic minister was Huw Evans, who had been seconded from the Treasury; and there was a minister with oversight of defence material and another two with responsibilities for Hong Kong.[23] Connected to the embassy, but separate from the diplomats, was the British Defence Staff, successor to the wartime British Joint Staff/Services Mission, and a substantial presence. There were approximately 600 staff at the embassy, more than half of them working for the Ministry of Defence.[24] The Defence Staff and the diplomats pursued largely separate lives. Kerr recalled that, shortly after arriving as ambassador, he met a naval captain and asked him what he did, only to receive the reply that he was not allowed to tell him.[25] Around the country there was a network of consulates. Other important players on American soil were those who served as the Permanent UK Representative to the UN in New York: John Weston, 1995–1998; Jeremy Greenstock, 1998–2003; and Sir Emyr Jones Parry, 2003–2007.

This machinery and these individuals aimed to accomplish two main tasks. First, was the representation of the British case on a range of issues and, where possible, to secure American acceptance of that position. Secondly, there was reporting to London of an accurate picture of the American outlook and attitudes on key areas; and more especially on how the United States approached various matters, so that the British could develop ways of pursuing their goals that would appeal to the Americans. Meyer has admirably summed up the embassy's role:

> We are expected to report on, and to influence, American policy on: trade, aid, agriculture, the economy, defence, the environment, energy, science, education, law and order, welfare, health, narcotics, and transport. We also have staff who promote US investment into the UK and help UK investors in the US; look after distressed British subjects; issue passports and visas; analyse and report on, US politics;

> represent Scotland and Northern Ireland; maintain close relations with the US armed forces; and liaise equally closely with all branches of US intelligence and the FBI. All of this is in addition to staff who pursue the traditional Foreign Office agenda: relations with the US and third countries; the UN; weapons of mass destruction; Iraq and the Middle East; international crises of one kind or another; terrorism; war and peace, and so on.[26]

Kerr has emphasised the importance of retaining the range of expertise in the embassy: 'On the day Cambodia is on the front page, the Embassy in Washington needs to be delivering down the Hill in Foggy Bottom a stream of analysis of the situation in Cambodia as good as, or I would hope better than, the stuff that is coming up from the State Department and the CIA, and someone delivering it who understands it, and has personal credibility'.[27]

Sir John Kerr, 1997

John Kerr was born in Grantown-on-Spey in the Scottish Highlands on 22 February 1942 and educated at Glasgow Academy, before studying modern history at Pembroke College, Oxford. He graduated in 1963 and intended becoming a don but changed his mind about his career. He joined the Foreign Office in 1966, after finishing top in the Civil service examinations. He served in a number of posts over the next years, becoming private secretary to the Permanent Under-Secretary from 1974 to 1979. He was then seconded to the Treasury between 1979 and 1984, acting as Principal Private Secretary to Sir Geoffrey Howe, when the latter was Chancellor of the Exchequer. In 1984, Kerr moved to the Washington embassy and served as Head of Chancery until 1987. He returned to London as an Assistant Under-Secretary from 1987 to 1990, before being appointed Britain's Permanent Representative to the European Union, a post he held until 1995. Kerr brought his range of experience, and his economic expertise, which was unusual among Foreign Office officials of his generation, and his considerable skills as an analyst and operator to bear as ambassador, and to good effect. Jack Straw later described him as 'brilliantly wily',[28] while Norman Lamont, Chancellor of the Exchequer in 1990–1993, wrote in his memoirs: 'John was a very political civil servant, albeit an able one. He once summed himself up to me thus: "There are two sorts of civil servants. Those who do what they are told and those who try to save Ministers from their folly. I am the second."'[29]

Kerr had arrived as Ambassador in September 1995, a few weeks after the departure of his predecessor, Sir Robin Renwick (1991–1995). He had had few preparations in London, but he visited Northern Ireland before leaving for Washington in order to get a feel for what he expected to be an important issue. He wisely calculated that it would be better to meet and make contacts in Washington and then return to London, which he did in October, and report on what their opposite numbers were thinking. It was not possible for him to return to London as frequently as he had done in his previous post as Permanent Representative to the EU, when he would visit London each Friday. He made two or three scheduled visits each year, but he also accompanied senior American figures on their trips to Britain. So, he travelled with the outgoing US Defense Secretary, William Perry in January 1997. More significantly, he came over with President Bill Clinton when he went to Belfast in December 1995.[30] The Prime Minister, John Major, ignored opposition from the Tory Right and Unionist parties and welcomed Clinton's interest. Kerr played an important role as go-between, discussing the idea, and the risks, with both leaders. Because his visit went so well, Clinton wanted to remain involved in the Peace Process, and, as Kerr notes, 'admired the way Blair later handled it, and was loud in his praise for the Good Friday Agreement...which in turn cemented the relationship between Blair and Clinton'.[31]

Kerr enjoyed excellent contacts with politicians in London – he had sat alongside virtually all the main members of John Major's Conservative Cabinet of 1990–1997. Therefore, he could telephone one of them and speak about an issue. For example, he rang up Michael Ancram, the Minister of State for Northern Ireland, and arranged for David Trimble, leader of the Ulster Unionists, to visit the United States. To Kerr such contacts with politicians were vital, to avoid being cut off from London and the Prime Minister in particular. John Major would ring him up to bounce ideas around. He would often test Kerr on whether President Clinton would support a particular idea. Tony Blair was less inclined to do this.

Sensing the shift in the political mood in Britain and the strong likelihood of a Labour Party victory in the general election, Kerr obtained the approval of the Foreign Secretary, Douglas Hurd, and the Permanent Under-Secretary, Sir John Coles, to make contact with the key members of Labour's shadow Cabinet, including Tony Blair and Robin Cook, when they visited the United States in 1996–97. As a result, when Labour achieved a sweeping victory in the May 1997 general election, Kerr could build on the ties he had begun to establish. He knew the new Chancellor, Gordon Brown, best, Foreign Secretary Cook a little and Blair the least. But he got to know Blair and Cook much better when he returned to London as Permanent Under-Secretary (1997–2002). He was less critical of the so-called 'sofa diplomacy', not least because he enjoyed good relations with Jonathan Powell and Alastair Campbell, while the Cabinet secretary, Robin Butler, was a friend.

Blair and President Clinton had first met in April 1996 and got on well, partly because they were ideologically close to one another, but also because each man admired the other's political skills.[32] Once he was Prime Minister, Blair also benefited from a shrewd and experienced ambassador. Relations soon flourished. Kerr later recalled, 'I found Ronald Reagan a much easier President to understand and predict... Bill Clinton was extremely difficult to predict. ... His was a very brilliant White House team; and they sat up all arguing... I didn't think Clinton had very many fixed points in his compass... he was always capable of being sidetracked or seduced by an attractive argument, by a new thought.' Thus, Kerr observed that, when he wanted to approach the President 'I used to leave that moment as late as possible because I always had in mind how the President let down Robin Renwick, my predecessor as Ambassador.' [He had promised he would not give a visa to IRA leader Gerry Adams, then did so, saying a new factor had come up.][33] Relations were friendly between Kerr and Clinton's two Secretaries of State, Warren Christopher (1993–1997) and Madeleine Albright (1997–2001). Although he had regular contact with Thomas Pickering and Richard Holbrooke in the State Department, he saw less of that department's officials than he did of those from the National Security Council (NSC). He also devoted more time to working with Congress than with the administration.[34] In the early months of his ambassadorship, the Clinton administration was pushing to secure Congressional backing for the Dayton Agreement to bring peace to Bosnia and enlisted him to help in the lobbying. This taught Kerr an important lesson about the standing of the British ambassador: 'you are part of the system. Of course one has to be careful that one is used in the right cause, and now and again one is going to say no, because UK policy will be different from the Administration's policy. But one is seen, at least in part, as an Insider. Which makes it easy to get to know the real Insiders, and develop a knowledge of what's really going on Inside'.[35]

Although Kerr served as ambassador until September 1997, his departure was already planned before Blair took office. The Foreign Secretary, Malcolm Rifkind, had offered him the post of Permanent Under-Secretary. The ever-astute Kerr asked whether he had spoken to

Blair and Cook, since they were looking likely to win the impending general election. Rifkind said he had spoken to them and that they were happy about the appointment.[36] There then arose the question of who would be his successor. According to Meyer, Kerr first suggested the idea to him in late 1996 or early 1997. Meanwhile, he was appointed in March 1997 as Ambassador to Bonn, but Jonathan Powell broached the idea with him (during Blair's visit to Germany) in June.[37] Kerr says the final decision was taken in June when he accompanied Blair on the airplane to a G7 summit in Denver. Robin Cook told him that the Prime Minister had turned down the Foreign Office's choice of new Ambassador in Washington. Cook asked what they should do. Kerr said that it was the Foreign Secretary's right to recommend someone. Cook asked him to suggest someone. Kerr spoke to Jonathan Powell, who confirmed Cook's story of the rejection of the Foreign Office choice. Kerr thought the matter over and asked about Christopher Meyer; Powell said he thought that Meyer would not be turned down. So, he told Cook.[38] Then, Sir John Coles offered him the post.

Sir Christopher Meyer, 1997–2003

The new ambassador was another highly intelligent man from the Foreign Office, but he had a different personality. Both were clubbable but Kerr was more a political operator, while Meyer was completely at ease in socialising. Christopher John Romer Meyer was born on 22 February 1944 and was educated at Lancing and Peterhouse, Cambridge, where he gained a first in history in 1965. He passed the Foreign Office entrance examination but deferred for a year, so that he could study at the Johns Hopkins School of Advanced Studies in Bologna. He entered the Foreign Office in 1966, the same year as Kerr. He held various posts in London and in Madrid, Moscow and Brussels. He was Head of Chancery in Moscow from 1982 to 1984, before returning to lead the Foreign and Commonwealth Office's News Department for four years. He studied at Harvard for a year before becoming Minister (Commercial) at the Washington embassy in 1989 and in 1992 assumed the post of deputy head of mission. He then served as Press Secretary to Prime Minister Major from 1994 to 1997. Meyer's arrival in Washington coincided with complications in his personal life: he was in the midst of divorcing his first wife, while his second wife-to-be, Catherine, was also recently divorced. They remarried on 30 October and travelled to the United States the next day.[39]

Meyer therefore arrived as ambassador with the invaluable assets of a considerable experience of the mission and the United States and with a clear talent for handling the media. He modelled his approach to running the embassy on the example set by Sir Robin Renwick (1991–1995), rather than Sir Antony Acland (1986–1991), who had delegated a great deal: Meyer later described the approaches as Renwick acting as executive chairman, while Acland acted as non-executive chairman.[40] Meyer soon established effective relations with the President and with Albright, but his closest relations were with Thomas Pickering, the Under-Secretary for Political Affairs at the State Department, whom he described as 'State's driving force' and 'among the best' American diplomats.[41]

In February 1998, Blair made his first trip as Prime Minister to Washington. Meyer and his staff at the Embassy played an important part in ensuring the visit went well: organising events, inviting the 'right' people, accurately briefing Blair and his retinue. It came at the height of the trouble over Clinton's sexual liaison with a White House intern, Monica Lewinsky. Blair acquired massive credit with the President for standing by him on this issue. He utilised it to gain Clinton's support for his efforts to make progress on Northern Ireland. In April 1998, Blair helped to forge the Good Friday Agreement which promised a devolved Northern Ireland Assembly in Belfast. In return, the IRA and Protestant paramilitary organisations agreed to lay down their arms. This was a major breakthrough but it would take until May 2007 before effective power-sharing was achieved.

In 1999, Blair made a memorable speech in Chicago on the need to intervene into sovereign territories in certain circumstances. This was delivered in the midst of a further crisis in Europe. The disintegration of Yugoslavia in 1990–91 had led to the creation of the independent states of Croatia and Slovenia and a war between Serbia (the dominant part of the former Yugoslavia) and Bosnia-Herzegovina, which sought independence from Serbia. The United States had brokered the Dayton Agreement of 1995 on Bosnia. But now another territory, Kosovo, sought to break away and the Serbs were responding brutally. Blair urged tough action. NATO agreed to launch an air campaign against Serbia, but its leader Slobodan Milosevic did not yield. Blair argued strongly for the use of ground forces. During the drafting of the speech Meyer had told him that the Americans were set against using troops, but this did not deter the Prime Minister. Indeed, after a sharp exchange with Clinton, whom he visited in Washington en route to Chicago, Blair toughened his language. Then, Milosevic backed down and withdrew his forces from Kosovo because the Russians told him they would not help if there was all-out war. Peter Riddell believes 'Blair was very, very lucky.' But the episode was revealing about the intensity of Blair's commitment to the issue.[42]

As Clinton's second term came to an end in 2000, Blair and most of his advisers expected the Vice President, Al Gore, to become the new President. However, the Republican candidate, George W. Bush, was elected by a narrow margin. Meyer considered Bush an untutored conviction politician, but he advised London that he had a real chance of winning. Following the victory, Meyer was very adept in cultivating contacts with senior figures in the new administration. He already knew many of them from his previous time in Washington. At that time, Vice President Dick Cheney had been the Defense Secretary, while the new Secretary of State, Colin Powell, had been Chairman of the Joint Chiefs of Staff and the new National Security Adviser, Condoleezza Rice, had been a Russian expert at the NSC. The prospects for a good relationship between Bush and Blair were not good, they had never met and seemed far apart politically. Clinton advised the Prime Minister to get as close to the new administration as possible, to 'hug them close'.[43] He followed this advice and Jonathan Powell crudely advised Meyer to 'get up the arse of the White House'.[44] Meyer set about planning Blair's first meeting with the new President. He returned to London to brief the Prime Minister, offering him brief character sketches of Bush and Cheney. Matthew Rycroft and other embassy officials liaised with members of Bush's staff and arranged an impressive schedule of meetings. Besides talks with Bush, there would be conversations with Cheney, Powell, Rice and a number of other figures. As the February 2001 discussions began Blair was nervous but Bush adeptly put him at ease. They were soon chatting in a relaxed and easy fashion and probing the issues in a constructive way.[45]

Within six months their bonds were deepened by the response to the dramatic attacks of 9/11, when hijacked airplanes were flown into the World Trade Center in New York and the Pentagon in Washington DC. Blair expressed Britain's solidarity with the Americans and soon joined with them in the campaign to punish the perpetrators. The two men brought a similar outlook, what William Shawcross calls 'passionately held certainties', arising out of their Christian faith.[46] In December, British forces joined the Americans in an assault on Afghanistan, to overthrow the Taliban regime which was harbouring al-Qaida, the terrorist group behind the 9/11 attacks and earlier strikes against American targets. Soon there was talk of acting against another long-standing problem,

Saddam Hussein's Iraq. The key figures in pushing this agenda were Cheney and the Secretary of Defense, Donald Rumsfeld. Both demonstrated their expertise in winning Washington's turf wars. They pressed for, and secured, policies rooted in the wielding of American power. British readiness to join in action against Iraq emerged from frequent communications between Blair and Bush, between the White House and 10 Downing Street. Both the Secretary of State and the British Embassy played lesser roles.[47]

In the course of 2002, the momentum for military action against Iraq intensified and Blair endorsed the American case, though he persuaded the administration to obtain a UN resolution declaring Iraq to be in 'material breach' of its commitment, made at the end of the Gulf War of 1990–1991, to destroy its weapons of mass destruction (WMD). In March 2003, the Americans launched an attack on Iraq in a coalition with the British and a number of smaller allies. Anthony Seldon believes that Blair supported the Americans in a war against Iraq because he disliked Saddam, wanted to tackle the problem of WMD, thought this was another instance of legitimate humanitarian intervention, and that it was in the British national interest to be on the side of the Americans.[48] Meyer did not accept the popular critique of Blair as an 'American poodle'. Rather, like Bush, Blair was a 'true believer'. However, his high moral ground and unconditional support for an ally in the service of an idea had a disadvantage: it put him in the hands of an ally.[49]

By the time the Iraq war began, Meyer had retired from the diplomatic service. In fact, his term of four years had been due to end in 2001 but he was persuaded to stay for another eighteen months. This would mean departure in March 2003, but as the time approached London did not want him to leave in the middle of a war and so asked him to remain in post until August. Meyer, however, needed minor heart surgery and insisted on leaving at the end of February. Blair did not want to release the ambassador-designate, David Manning, from his duties in London in the middle of hostilities. In consequence, Meyer's deputy, Anthony Brenton, took charge of the Embassy until the arrival of the new ambassador in September.

Sir David Manning, 2003–2007

The change of ambassador in 2003 did not take place with its customary smoothness. Indeed, it was associated with some bitterness. A flavour of this is evident in Jack Straw's memoirs where he noted that Manning replaced Meyer 'to great relief on both sides of the Atlantic'.[50] The reasons for Straw's view are not clear. After all, he hosted a valedictory dinner at the Embassy.[51] Perhaps he was irritated by both Meyer's refusal to stay after March 2003 and his urging of a tougher stance in talks with the Americans.

Born on 5 December 1949, Manning was educated at Ardingly College, Oriel College, Oxford and the Paul H. Nitze School of Advanced International Studies of the Johns Hopkins University. He entered the Foreign and Commonwealth Office in 1972 and accumulated an impressive range of posts at home and abroad. He served in Warsaw (1977–1980), New Delhi (1980–1982), Paris (1988–1990) and Moscow (1990–1993); was head of the Eastern Department (1993–1994) and the Planning Staff (1994–1995); and became ambassador to Israel (1995–1998). He briefly served as ambassador to the UK Delegation to NATO at Brussels in 2001 before assuming his duties as foreign policy adviser at No 10. In running the Embassy, he gave direction to his staff but also wanted to allow them space to operate: he trusted able specialists with more detailed knowledge than he to execute their tasks, but he let them know that he was available if needed. He recognised it was important that the Ambassador should provide a consolidated view.

Appointment as Ambassador to Britain's most important ally was just reward for such a talented man, but it undoubtedly benefited from his work at No 10. He therefore arrived in Washington with the securest of foundations in London. Manning was trusted by Blair, who described him as 'calm, matter-of-fact, and a brilliant adviser, someone of deep integrity, great loyalty and not insignificant courage'.[52] The Downing Street staff held him in the highest regard; he knew Powell very well. Manning also enjoyed excellent relations with Jack Straw. During his time as foreign policy adviser he had built up contacts with a wide range of politicians and officials, so that, when he was Ambassador he could telephone them and handle issues directly with them. In Washington, he enjoyed similarly good relations with Secretary of State Powell and National Security Adviser Rice. She described Manning as 'exceptionally capable and trustworthy… elegant and urbane – and funny.' Their friendship was built on their shared 'fascination and frustration with Russia and Russians'; 'We became very close, and I'm grateful to have found pals like David and Catherine Manning, a friendship that has outlasted our government service'.[53] As her memoirs make clear, they were already in regular communication when she was National Security Adviser and he was Blair's foreign policy adviser. After he became Ambassador in September 2003, they maintained their contacts, although she now dealt on a regular basis with his successor at No 10, Nigel Sheinwald.

When she became Secretary of State in January 2005, they met more frequently.

Manning also appreciated the importance of economics. He met Federal Reserve chairman, Alan Greenspan, every three to four months, but saw his successor, Ben Bernanke, less frequently. He made sure that he was accompanied by staff from the embassy's economic section who, thanks to their expertise, were able to pick up on points that he did not notice. He took a prominent role in a number of trade issues, including securing a fair share of work for Britain in the Joint Strike Fighter. He found, like earlier Ambassadors to Washington, that a great deal of time was devoted to the broad area of lobbying on a range of political issues and on matters of trade. This involved him in frequent visits to Congress to persuade senators and congressmen to support British schemes. In such a large, democratic society as the United States, it was also necessary to travel extensively, partly to present Britain's position on various questions, but also to gauge opinion across the country. Manning aimed to visit the major consulates each year, to go to New York every six to eight weeks, and tried to spend five working days in the Bay Area of California annually. He persuaded Blair to make the first prime ministerial visit to California in July 2006.[54] Manning undertook a major initiative in the management of the embassy, which occupied 10–15 per cent of his time for about a year. It came partly as a result of budgetary pressures, but also because of the need to be more efficient. A management committee of all the counsellors was established, so that the building became the responsibility of everyone and not just one section of the embassy's staff. Open plan offices were constructed. A change management counsellor, Peter Hayes, oversaw the process. Many posts previously held by British citizens were now taken by locally-employed Americans. The changes involved some painful adjustments, but the new practices came to be accepted over time.

Both Afghanistan and Iraq continued to be important issues as the two countries continued as allies in war. Given his detailed involvement at No 10, no one was better placed than Manning to handle these topics which, if anything, became more challenging. Initial success in Iraq in 2003, when Saddam's regime was toppled, gave way to an insurgency and major difficulties for British forces in southern Iraq. The Baker-Hamilton Iraq Study Group Report of December 2006 argued against a sustained increase of American troops and recommended an accelerated handover to Iraqi forces. Bush, however, wanted a 'surge' in US forces, which he implemented in January 2007, despite Blair's opposition. The surge, together with various arrangements with local leaders, helped to stabilise Iraq by the end of Bush's presidency. In Afghanistan, too, there was an upsurge of violence after 2004 and a recovery of the Taliban. Nonetheless, the important point for the Embassy was that Britain and the United States remained largely in harmony on these issues and on the broader question of fighting Bush's 'war on terror'. The question of Iran and its possible development of nuclear weapons, which could be used to threaten Israel and the West, became pressing towards the end of the ambassadorship and Manning took a leading role in discussing the matter with American officials. Lebanon also became a major problem. After repeated attacks by Hezbollah from within the country, Israel invaded Lebanon in April 2006. Blair instinctively backed the Americans in their sympathy for Israel. Manning, however, explained robustly to the prime minister that this was an issue on which the two countries might legitimately differ; and that condoning Israeli action would hinder the Middle East peace process.[55]

If the Middle East dominated the immediate issues, Manning recognised longer-term trends, in particular how American attention was increasingly turning to Asia. There was recognition of China's growing economic power, with predictions that its economy could overtake the US in size within a generation, and a desire to build better relations with India, which also experienced rapid economic growth. Such shifts in global power would continue to test the Anglo–American relationship in future.

Conclusion

Under the Blair premiership, the British enjoyed remarkably good relations with both Clinton and Bush, despite the fact that London remained a secondary player in world affairs. Ambassadors and senior officials had easy access to key administration figures. Americans continued to welcome the opportunity to test their ideas on a dependable ally. Thanks in large part to the work of John Kerr and the embassy staff, better contacts were developed with Congress, a development that was continued under Meyer and Manning. The longer-established defence and intelligence network continued largely unaffected by changes of government and unnoticed by the public. Of course, Britain's standing in Washington was helped by Blair's personal ability to work closely with US Presidents and by his readiness to play a more interventionist role abroad. However, much turns in Washington on personal relations. Kerr, Meyer and Manning, and the missions they oversaw, were highly effective throughout Blair's governments. All three envoys were admired for their talents and stature in London. They offered accurate and timely reporting; they submitted shrewd judgements on multifarious features of American life and politics; they undertook the groundwork to ensure Blair's visits were successful; and they often gave unpalatable advice. Manning possessed better ties with Blair's No 10 than either Kerr or Meyer, and he had happy relations with Jack Straw, who was Foreign Secretary for most of his term. He also had excellent relations with Condoleezza Rice. In terms of mutual respect and trust, their relationship bears comparison with that between Oliver Franks and Dean Acheson during the Truman administration. However, it yielded less, because Rice did not have the dominant voice in foreign affairs in the Bush presidency that Acheson had enjoyed when Truman was President. There were face-to-face meetings between the Prime Minister and the President in these years but, as Meyer points out, such direct contacts are 'like a flash of lightning across the landscape. That is important; but it is not enough without the constant illumination that a good embassy should provide'.[56] Furthermore, as Kerr observes, no other embassy in Washington had 'the same across-the-board access and influence as the British'.[57]

Notes

I am grateful to Dr Richard Smith of the Foreign and Commonwealth Office for help on points of FCO practice and facilitating contacts with former officials.

1. One of the few studies is Michael F. Hopkins, Saul Kelly and John W. Young (eds), *The Washington Embassy: British Ambassadors to the United States, 1939–77* (Basingstoke: Palgrave Macmillan, 2009).
2. See, for example, Paul David Williams, *British Foreign Policy under New Labour, 1997–2005* (Basingstoke: Palgrave Macmillan, 2005) which has a chapter, 'Closest Ally', pp. 35–55, on Anglo-American relations but does not mention the embassy or any ambassador.
3. Tony Blair, *A Journey* (London: Hutchinson, 2010). See also, Anthony Seldon, *Blair* (London: Simon & Schuster, 2004); idem., *Blair Unbound* (London: Simon & Schuster, 2007); Christopher Meyer, *DC Confidential* (London: Weidenfeld & Nicolson, 2005).
4. Peter Hennessy, *Prime Minister* (London: Penguin, 2000), pp. 480, 483–484; *Ministerial Code: A Code of Conduct and Guidance on Procedures for Ministers* (London: Cabinet Office, July 1997), p. 30.
5. Seldon, *Blair Unbound*, pp. 35–36.
6. Churchill College, Cambridge, British Diplomatic Oral History Project (hereinafter BDOHP), Lord Kerr interview by Malcolm McBain, 6 January 2004, pp. 63–64.
7. Meyer, *DC Confidential*, p. 33.
8. BDOHP, Kerr interview, pp. 46–47.

9. Sherard Cowper-Cowles, *Ever the Diplomat: Confessions of a Foreign Office mandarin* (London: HarperPress, 2012), pp. 200–201, pp. 204, 211, 217 and 218.
10. Robin Cook, 'Foreign Policy and the National Interest', at www.fco.gov.uk/news/speechtext.asp?3259; Christopher Hill, 'Foreign Policy', in Anthony Seldon (ed.), *The Blair Effect: the Blair Government, 1997–2001* (London: Little, Brown, 2001), pp. 333, 349. See also Robin Cook, *The Point of Departure* (London: Simon & Schuster, 2003).
11. Cowper-Cowles, *Ever the Diplomat*, pp. 227–228.
12. Quoted in Seldon, *Blair Unbound*, pp. 34–35.
13. BDOHP, Kerr interview, p. 47.
14. Cowper-Cowles, *Ever the Diplomat*, p. 230.
15. Meyer, *DC Confidential*, p. 78.
16. Author's interview with Sir Christopher Meyer, London, 2 May 2012.
17. Condoleezza Rice, *No Higher Honour: a memoir of my years in Washington* (London: Simon & Schuster, 2011), p. 453.
18. Seldon, *Blair Unbound*, pp. 446–449.
19. Simon Heffer, 'Not Up to the Job', *The Spectator*, 12 August 2006.
20. Speech at Bridgewater Hall, Manchester 21 April 1997; quoted in John Kampfner, *Blair's Wars* (London: The Free Press, 2004), p. 3.
21. Tony Blair, 'Doctrine of the International Community', speech to the Economic Club of Chicago, 24 April 1999; http://www.pm.gov.uk/output/Page1297.asp; Tony Blair, 'Terrorism must be tackled head-on', speech to the Foreign Policy Centre, 21 March 2006, http://www.number-10.gov.uk/output/Page9224.asp; Tony Blair, 'Our Nation's Future', lecture, 12 January 2007, quoted in Michael Clarke, 'Foreign Policy', in Anthony Seldon, (ed.), *Blair's Britain, 1997–2007* (Cambridge: Cambridge University Press, 2007), p. 598; Tony Blair, 'A Battle for Global Values', *Foreign Affairs*, 86:1 (January–February 2007), p. 90. See also Caroline Kennedy-Pipe and Rhiannon Vickers, 'Blowback' for Britain?: Blair, Bush, and the war in Iraq', *Review of International Studies*, 33 (April 2007), pp. 210, 217.
22. Cm 6052, *United Kingdom International Priorities: A Strategy for the Foreign and Commonwealth Office* (London: The Stationery Office, 2003); Cm 6040-I, *Defence White Paper: Delivering Security in a Changing World* (London: The Stationery Office, 2003); statement by Defence Secretary, 11 December 2003, cited in Clarke, 'Foreign Policy', p. 599.
23. For a sense of the operations in the Chancery, see Cowper-Cowles, *Ever the Diplomat*, pp. 104–131.
24. BDOHP, Kerr interview, p. 23.
25. Author's interview with Lord Kerr, London, 11 April 2012.
26. Meyer, *DC Confidential*, p. 64.
27. BDOHP, Kerr interview, p. 42.
28. Jack Straw, *Last Man Standing* (London: Macmillan, 2012), p. 327.
29. Norman Lamont, *In Office* (London: HarperCollins, 1999), p. 117. John Kerr confirmed this: author's interview with Kerr, 11 April 2012.
30. Author's interview with Kerr, 11 April 2012.
31. Correspondence with Lord Kerr, 10 February 2013.
32. Bill Clinton, *My Life* (London: Hutchinson, 2004), pp. 686 and 756. See also, Peter Riddell, *Hug Them Close* (London: Politico's, 2003), p. 70.

33. BDOHP, Kerr interview, p. 37.
34. Ibid., p. 38.
35. Ibid., p. 41.
36. Ibid., p. 43.
37. Meyer, *DC Confidential*, p. 46.
38. Author's interview with Kerr, 11 April 2012.
39. Meyer, *DC Confidential*, pp. 50–53.
40. Author's interview with Meyer, 4 May 2012.
41. Meyer, *DC Confidential*, p. 84.
42. Meyer, *DC Confidential*, pp. 98–103; Riddell, *Hug Them Close*, pp. 103–114; correspondence with Lord Kerr, 10 February 2013.
43. Quoted in Andrew Rawnsley, *The End of the Party* (London: Penguin, 2010), p. 28.
44. Meyer, *DC Confidential*, p. 1.
45. Ibid., pp. 167–170, 175.
46. William Shawcross, *Allies: The United States, Britain, Europe and the War in Iraq* (London: Atlantic Books, 2003), p. 46.
47. Meyer, *DC Confidential*, pp. 178, 210–214; Christopher D. O'Sullivan, *Colin Powell* (Lanham, Maryland: Rowman & Littlefield, 2009), pp. 130–135.
48. Seldon, *Blair Unbound*, pp. 84–86.
49. Meyer, *DC Confidential*, p. 284.
50. Straw, *Last Man Standing*, p. 405.
51. Tina Brown in *The Times*, 30 January 2003, p. 3.
52. Blair, *A Journey*, p. 459.
53. Rice, *No Higher Honour*, p. 39.
54. Seldon, *Blair Unbound*, pp. 474–475.
55. Andrew Rawnsley, *The End of The Party* (London: Penguin, 2010), pp. 384–385.
56. Meyer, *DC Confidential*, p. 64.
57. BDOHP, Kerr interview, p. 42.

12
Beyond the Horizon

Peter Hennessy

Institutions often reflect a particular human anxiety or aspiration and are driven by a desire for certainty. Some reflect the desire to institutionalise social justice (such as, in Britain's case, the Department of Work and Pensions); altruism (the National Health Service), national protection (the Ministry of Defence) or public safety (Home Office and Ministry of Justice). The last century has seen a succession of government-led attempts in the UK to reduce *uncertainty* through improved forward planning. The intelligence and security services are a classic example, by trying to anticipate events, good and bad, and to increase the chances of good happening and to reduce the prospects of the harmful. Today, such 'horizon-scanning' is a trans-Whitehall activity on a substantial scale. The pursuit of top-of-the-range horizon-scanning has been a kind of Holy Grail for Whitehall and the horizon-scanner's craft has been central to the British state's preparations for the worst. This chapter will look at the institutions that 'horizon-scanning' spawned in Britain after 1945, and in particular, during the 1970s and the early 2000s, as well as the contributions of individual horizon-scanners. It will do so in the light of Fernand Braudel's belief that:

> When it comes to the present day, with all its different potential dénouements, deciding which are the really major problems essentially means imagining the last line of the play – discerning, among all the possible outcomes, those which are most likely to occur. The task is difficult, hazardous and indispensable ... forecasting the near future – the 'futurible', to use a frightful word beloved of certain economists. The 'futurible' is what now can legitimately be described in the future tense – that thin wisp of tomorrow which can be guessed at and very nearly grasped.[1]

Origins of horizon-scanning

The very first horizon-scanning institution in British government was the Committee of Imperial Defence (CID), created in 1902. Then came the Chiefs of Staff Committee (COS), which came into formal existence in 1923.[2] However, it was the pressure of total war that gave impetus to government-based horizon-scanning. The next innovation was spawned from within the COS and led to the establishment of the Joint Intelligence Committee (JIC), in June 1936, to co-ordinate inter-services intelligence.[3] Initially, the JIC was not a serious shaper of the British horizon-scanners' craft, because neither the Foreign Office nor the individual service intelligence departments wished it to have such a capacity in the first years of its life, leaving it 'a peripheral body' until just before the outbreak of the Second World War.[4] War however, is a great tester and refiner of institutions as well as people. When Winston Churchill became Prime Minister, he issued a new directive for JIC to 'take the initiative in preparing at any hour of the day or night, as a matter of urgency, papers on any development in the international situation whenever this appears desirable to any member in the light of information that might be received'.[5] In May 1941, the JIC's Joint Intelligence Staff was created and rapidly developed into a considerable Whitehall player. It can be seen as the lineal begetter of today's Assessments Staff, which works to the JIC in the Cabinet Office.[6]

The Second World War was remarkable, too, as a test-bed for *post-war* institution-building and the special kind of horizon-scanning required for that. The most enduringly example concentrated on welfare rather than warfare. Indeed, it was wartime conditions that enabled Sir William Beveridge to declare that: 'A revolutionary moment in the world's history is a time for revolutions, not for patching.' Beveridge was not engaged in preparing for the worst and avoiding the worst – a return to the 1930s. 'Preparing for the best' would be a better way of describing his purpose when he seized upon a commission from the wartime Coalition Government to tidy up existing social insurance provision and turned his inquiry into a comprehensive plan for a post-war transformation, designed to conquer what he called the 'five giants on the road of reconstruction.' These were, 'Want, Disease, Ignorance, Squalor and Idleness'.[7] Horizon-scanning infused Beveridge's craft, because he rightly sensed that unless these 'giants' were hammered simultaneously, the tough shell created by interlocking deprivations would not crack. For example, without full employment reducing dole payments *and* raising tax revenue, post-war governments would not be in a financial position to fund a comprehensive welfare system (including a free health service) or provide secondary education for all.[8]

Post-1945 insecurities

The precarious position of the UK's economy, with almost a third of the country's wealth gone during the war, saw changes to old innovations and some new ones introduced during the years of the Attlee governments 1945–51.[9] On the industrial side, some ministers, most notably Sir Stafford Cripps, President of the Board of Trade, and Aneurin Bevan, the Minister of Health, objected to the revival of the old Supply and Transport Organisation after the war. Among other things, they wanted the trade unions consulted about any successor system, which struck the Cabinet Secretary, Sir Norman Brook, as impractical.[10] In April 1947, amidst a rash of unofficial industrial action in the docks, a new Emergencies Committee of the Cabinet was created. Later in the year an Emergencies Organisation to service it and engage in forward planning was created in the Home Office.[11] The EC/EO structure was to remain in place until replaced by the Civil Contingencies Committee and the Civil Contingencies Unit in the Cabinet Office in the 1970s.

Economic and industrial planning generally was one of the big ideas of the post-war Labour governments and in the spring of 1947 a Central Economic Planning Staff, led by the businessman and wartime temporary civil servant, Sir Edwin Plowden, was created for the purpose. It was largely ineffectual, confining itself to an annual *Economic Survey* of the year just past and general aspirations for the future with ministers adding vocal exhortation.[12] But it did horizon-scan and after the Conservatives returned to power in the 1950s, it was the body which oversaw the compilation of the Trend Report, the first comprehensive plan for civil nuclear power in the UK, which was published in 1955.[13] This involved a high degree of horizon-scanning and what turned out to be hugely optimistic forecasts about the cost of nuclear-generated electricity, compared to that produced by coal-burning power stations.[14]

Indeed, the greatest leap in the imaginative capacities of Whitehall's post-war horizon-scanners was required on the part of those charged with contemplating a different kind of nuclear revolution, 'the bomb'. Its dreadful potential stretched the craft in several directions further than anything previously encountered. It was, in its way, to adapt a 1945 phrase of Ronald Knox's, 'a baptism of uranium'.[15] Attlee, in an August 1945 memorandum on 'The Atomic Bomb', for the Cabinet Committee on Atomic Energy, told his ministers in effect, that the world passed through a valve when the bombs were dropped on Hiroshima and Nagasaki: 'Scientists agree that we cannot stop the march of discovery,' he wrote.[16] Ever since, the 'bomb' has been a constant horizon-scanning imperative for Whitehall.

Cold War horizons may have been compelling for four decades, but the configurations of the scanners changed from time to time. Among the more significant refinements were the shifting of the JIC, post-Suez in 1957, from the orbit of the Chiefs of Staff Committee to the Cabinet Office, where it has remained ever since.[17] As Percy Cradock put it, the purpose was to have the JIC's 'requirements set in part by the Cabinet or individual ministers rather than just by the Minister of Defence and the Chiefs'.[18] In 1968, its supporting administration was beefed-up by the creation of an Assessments Staff in the Cabinet Office (still its underpinning today).[19] The creation, in 1964, by the Foreign Office of its own Planning Staff (revived in 2008 as the FCO's Strategy Unit) was a valuable addition to Whitehall's overall horizon-scanning capacity and for several decades, was a crucial rung on the career ladder of many of the Office's highest flyers.[20]

Post-war Whitehall also undertook the occasional one-off scan of significance, such as the first ever cost-benefit analysis of the British Empire in 1957. Prime Minister Harold Macmillan commissioned it because the Colonial Office complained they had no methodology for completing it easily or swiftly.[21] In fact, *Future Constitutional Development in the Colonies*[22] fed into yet another post-Suez review overseen by the Cabinet Secretary, Sir Norman Brook, entitled *The Position of the United Kingdom in World Affairs*, circulated to ministers in 1958.[23] A further piece of horizon-scanning of the Macmillan period was the *Future Policy Study* which he commissioned in great secrecy (only the Foreign Secretary, Selwyn Lloyd, knew about it amongst his ministerial colleagues) in June 1959. The *Future Policy Study*'s horizon-scan was a decade forward, predicting where Britain would be by 1970 on present policies – increasingly dwarfed by the superpowers, falling behind the European Economic Community 'Six' (as they then were) in economic and trade terms, and, possibly, struggling to maintain both a comprehensive welfare state and substantial defence spending. The only thing Macmillan's scanners got seriously wrong was Northern Ireland; in their treatment of Ireland they did not foresee a recrudescence of 'the Troubles'.[24] The final paper, once again a Norman Brook production, was so gloomy that Macmillan pulled it from the intended full Cabinet discussion in February 1960 and took it to a special Cabinet committee instead.[25]

Edward Heath, as part of his new style of government after winning the 1970 general election, sought to institutionalise an approach to horizon-scanning with his creation of the Central Policy Review Staff (CPRS), led by the former head of research at Shell, Lord Rothschild. From its inception in 1971, reflecting Victor Rothschild's background, it kept a close eye on energy problems, especially the supply of oil. More widely, it sought to meet the ministers' need, most vocally expressed by Willie Whitelaw, to avoid being taken by surprise so often. Whitelaw said he 'did not want to read about V and G [Vehicle and General, an insurance firm that collapsed in 1972] in the newspapers in his bath'.[26] Rothschild set up an Early Warning System (EWS) and attempted to persuade Whitehall departments to share their anxieties about the future. The EWS was a brave stab at horizon-scanning, but it was hobbled by two things: the Treasury were highly reluctant to pool information on sensitive economic matters, the exchange rate of Sterling in particular; and Heath's reluctance, given the top secret nature of much of the material, to circulate the EWS reports to all his ministerial colleagues.[27] As the pace of leaks grew from the mid-1970s, fear of disclosure became a considerable problem for the more candid 'what if?' exercises.

In the Heath years, anxieties about the security of energy supplies were made still more fraught by the miners' strike of 1972, the first national one since 1926. Rothschild submitted his first CPRS paper on 'Oil Economics and Supplies' to Heath, in September 1971, before the strike began.[28] A refined version of the paper was circulated by the Prime Minister to ministers in April 1972, arguing that the country should increasingly rely less on coal, more upon a mix of natural gas and nuclear-powered or oil-fired stations.[29] In May 1973, the CPRS prepared a report for the Cabinet Committee on Economic Strategy on the possible rise in oil prices due to growing scarcity over the next decade, possibly to, what was then, an eye-watering $9 a barrel.[30] Two months later, seven months before the outbreak of the Yom Kippur war, a Task Force on Oil Supplies chaired by Lord Carrington, the Defence Secretary, warned the Economic Strategy Committee that a war in the Middle East would have a serious impact on the price of oil, although such a war was not thought to be imminent.[31]

On 6 October 1973, Egyptian troops crossed the Suez Canal into the Sinai and the fourth Arab–Israeli war began. On 16 October, the Organisation of Petroleum Exporting Countries (OPEC) raised the price of oil from $2.90 a barrel to $5.11. In mid-December 1973, they raised it again to $11.65.[32] The price had quadrupled in less than four months. The Carrington contingency and Rothschild's worst-case-by-1985 possibility had met and struck a British economy already reeling from rising commodity prices abroad and growing industrial strife at home. Very shortly, the country was plunged into another miners' strike. The new Civil Contingencies Unit created after the miners' strike of 1972, with its new horizon-scanning system for monitoring the 16 key industries where strikes could hit the essentials of life, was put to the test.[33] In fact, as Heath moved towards his 'who rules?' general election campaign in February 1974, British industry did not collapse, but for those inside the contingency planning world, in the words of one of them, 'it was pretty close at the end'.[34]

During the critical weeks of early 1974, the Foreign Office Planning Staff's horizon-scanners struggled to assess new, post-OPEC, realities. Its blunt title was 'A Policy for the Lean Years'. It confronted head-on the geopolitical transformation engineered by the OPEC price rises. As far as Britain was concerned, it was poorly placed to cope in these stretching circumstances:

> We are vulnerable because of our relatively high dependence on essential imports,..., our heavy dependence on imported oil during the next few years, our domestic difficulties, and our need to borrow. Our borrowing will have to be on an unprecedented scale if we are to maintain the level of the country's economic capacity. Our ability to borrow on such a scale will depend on the estimates that others make of our credit-worthiness. This will depend on the belief of others in our ability to survive our transitional difficulties...; on their assessment of our readiness and ability to honour our international obligations, political and financial; and on their assessment of our intention and our ability to repay our debts.[35]

This remarkable paper, mixing candour and prescience, the twin gold standards of the horizon-scanner's craft, went to a group of permanent secretaries, chaired by the Cabinet Secretary, Sir John Hunt, on the very morning of the February 1974 general election, including the forceful Sir Douglas Allen, Permanent Secretary to the Treasury. The key point made in the discussion sounded very like Allen, a veteran of every sterling crisis since 1947:[36] 'the emphasis should be on policies which inspire confidence in the markets rather than ones which, though they might find favour with other Governments...'.[37] Given the failure of the incoming Labour government to either control public spending or curb inflation (which peaked at 26.9 per cent in August 1975), the prediction that the money markets alone would provide was confounded in a very public way in the autumn of 1976, by which time Jim Callaghan had replaced Harold Wilson as Prime Minister. On 29 September 1976, the Chancellor of the Exchequer, Denis Healey, announced that the UK was applying to the International Monetary Fund (IMF) for a £3.9 billion loan.[38]

Even after an extraordinarily prolonged and dextrous exercise in collective Cabinet government, there remained the possibility in November–December 1976 that Callaghan and Healey would not be able to carry their colleagues with them on the terms the IMF demanded for the loan.[39] The Treasury, Cabinet Office and the Ministry of Defence were all intimately involved. Hunt, the Cabinet Secretary, warned Callaghan that 'if sterling begins to slide, we should have to let it go. There would be no obvious floor and we should probably be forced back to the IMF'.[40] The Treasury also warned Healey that, if Britain was forced into creating a 'siege economy', by surrounding itself with import controls and tight controls on foreign exchange, it 'would be a virtually irreversible step away from Europe and away from the system into which we have progressively integrated ourselves since the war'.[41] The UK's foreign and defence policies would also be shredded, seriously injuring relations with the US and NATO. Possibilities included severe cuts to the British Army on the Rhine, withdrawal from Cyprus (where signals intelligence installations were housed, crucial to the US–UK's capacities for eavesdropping on the southern Soviet Union and the Middle East), serious reductions in Royal Naval capacities in the Eastern Atlantic and the possible abandonment of the Polaris strategic nuclear force.[42] Callaghan finally eased his Cabinet into line on 2 December 1976.[43] The abyss was avoided.

Thus far, this survey of horizon-scanning illustrates a number of things. Firstly, on a practical historical level, the indispensability of primary archival material for mining the story, given the inherent sensitivity of so much of the horizon-scanners' product. Secondly, the mix of careful foresight and rather desperate reaction to the unforeseen – the contingency planners version of muddling through. Thirdly, a serious gap on the economic side compared to the politico-military. For a time in the late 1960s and early 1970s, the JIC was split into two: 'A' dealt with its traditional concerns and 'B' with economics. The dual approach never really worked. As a 1970s Cabinet Office insider put it, 'the Treasury has never been keen for anyone else in Whitehall to produce alternative economic forecasts, not that JIC (B) tried to; it concentrated mainly on economic aspects of the Cold War'.[44] Some of these problems persisted into the twenty-first century.

Post-Cold War developments

Mervyn King, the previous Governor of the Bank of England, talked of the 'Panic of 2008', 'because of the almost complete collapse of confidence in financial institutions and the flight of funding that ensued' after the collapse of Lehman Brothers in September of that year.[45] It was the Queen, to whom all the horizon-scanners on the Crown Services payroll constitutionally answer, who asked the question on everyone's mind at the time. Opening a new building at the London School of Economics, on 5 November 2008, she enquired of Professor Luis Garicano, a management economist, 'if these things were so large, how come everyone missed them?'[46] The Queen might have wondered whether somewhere deep in her Crown Services there was an intelligence capacity for this. Indeed, the Cabinet Office's *National Risk Register*, published as the 'Panic of 2008' struck, in its diagram of 'high consequence risks facing the United Kingdom' was completely silent on the financial chaos descending ever more destructively on the UK and the world.[47] Across its range of a dozen anxieties and horrors, nowhere were the four horsemen of the financial apocalypse to be seen. Sir Richard Mottram, former Co-ordinator of Security and Intelligence in the Cabinet Office, spoke publicly about how unwelcome a paper on derivatives would have been during his chairmanship of the Joint Intelligence Committee between 2005 and 2007.

It would have been genuinely difficult to forecast the especially malign concentration of events in 2007–08 before they began to happen. For even a fully-functioning and brilliantly staffed UK financial and economic intelligence committee to have picked all of these pieces up and integrated them into an assessment would have been a tall order. There were several fuses lit over the previous generation that went 'bang' in 2007–08. For example, a significant one was ignited in 1973–75 amid the ruins of the Bretton Woods system, when the economics departments of the University of Chicago and the Massachusetts Institute of Technology began to work on money-making financial techniques made possible by speculating against fluctuating currency rates. Deregulation in the 1980s and globalisation in the 1990s, following the collapse of the Soviet bloc, also put matches to huge fuses.

Having said this however, one group of Whitehall horizon-scanners, at the Foresight Horizon Scanning Centre, did come very close, in December 2006, as we shall see, as did Christopher Ondaatje in 2008. The former financier and British-based philanthropist in his *The Power of Paper: a history, a financial adventure and a warning* wrote:

> paper, not tax revenues or earned income, is fuelling record levels of US consumer debt, an overvalued stock market, a housing bubble and, not least, an aggressive foreign policy....The mindset among US investors and leaders is clearly that housing prices have only one way to go up. The housing bubble continues but, like all bubbles, the larger it grows, the worse will be the fallout when it finally bursts. The end of the housing bubble will remove a prop to the US economy that stimulated consumer spending.... [T]he impact on the US economy will be far greater than the bursting of the technology stock bubble in 2000...Many of its fundamental problems, such as its bubbles and its under-funding of pensions, are shared by other advanced economies. Even more important, the financial markets are now global, with capital increasingly free to move across national boundaries in defiance of national taxes and financial regulations....[48]

Ondaatje's was a truly remarkable piece of economic and financial horizon-scanning on the housing-related aspects of the crisis, as liberal capitalism moved towards its biggest systemic shock since the 1930s.

The threat of terrorism has sharpened the horizon-scanning capabilities of the Joint Terrorism Analysis Centre and the Cabinet Office secretariats and groups that feed into the annual National Security Strategy. So widespread an activity has horizon-scanning become in Whitehall, that in April 2007, the Chief Scientific Adviser, Sir John Beddington, created the Future Security and Intelligence Outlook Network (FUSION), embracing more than twenty departments and agencies. FUSION is serviced by the Horizon Scanning Centre, which is part of the Foresight programme inside the Government Office for Science.[49] In recent times, probably the most consistent of publicly-available, Whitehall-created horizon-scanning products, is the series created by what is now called the Ministry of Defence's Development, Concepts and Doctrine Centre (DCDC), based at Shrivenham near Swindon. Since it was first commissioned, as the Joint Doctrine and Concepts Centre, in May 2001, 'to assist the Ministry of Defence to gain a strategic understanding of the future threats, risks, challenges and opportunities that might be faced by UK Armed Forces',[50] it has produced four editions of *Global Strategic Trends*, three of which have been published.[51] The centre's origins lie in the work done for the 1998 Strategic Defence Review.[52] As its Permanent Secretary from 1998 to 2005, Sir Kevin Tebbit, put it, the Ministry of Defence thought 'the process should be captured and carried on. We decided to do it very seriously and to survey the marketplace of those who were doing futures and to use that as a compass to help us with how to do it. We've built it in every two years. Simon Webb [Policy Director, Ministry of Defence, 2001–04] was particularly active in all that'.[53]

The 'Shrivenham scans', as they might be called, are propelled by three themes. These are: 'trends' (discernible patterns of change, such as the fact that the average age of the UK population is increasing); 'drivers' (factors that directly influence or cause the change, as when better healthcare allows greater life expectancy); and 'shocks' (high impact, low probability events, such as a global collapse of the financial system).[54] The Shrivenham scans are primarily intended to examine risks that impinge upon defence and security policy – and the overwhelming proportion of their paragraphs are devoted to 'trends' and 'drivers', rather than 'shocks'.[55] The scanners, using early 2003 mentalities looked forward to the period 2003–30 and broke down 'possible shocks' into seven types: physical (for example, the Gulf Stream could be switched off, dramatically cooling the UK); social (such as a Christian revival in the West, prompting a reverse in secularisation); scientific and technological (computers gaining a widespread autonomous decision-making capability, perhaps, or a biomedical breakthrough that slows human ageing); economic (like a sustained economic downturn, causing transnational companies to withdraw their interests back to their home base, hurting open economies dependent on foreign direct investment); legal (for example, the UK reasserting national supremacy over European courts); political (such as a crisis of democratic legitimacy in the West, a US withdrawal from international organisations like the UN and NATO, or the collapse of the Euro); and military (such as the re-emergence of a conventional military threat to Europe, perhaps from a resurgent Russia or the Middle East). Much of this overlapped with the work of the intelligence agencies and the JIC's Assessments Staff.[56]

In its 'The Economic Dimension' section, the 2003 scan elaborated a little on this a brief whiff of September 2008. It detected, albeit as a 'low probability', that a shock in one part of the world economy could be transmitted to others as a by-product of globalisation:

> the relative risk of *economic shocks* having major detrimental impacts on states is likely to increase. This is one of the potential prices of globalisation... The impacts of such crises are likely to be increasingly severe in terms of national prosperity and potentially more likely to precipitate knock-on consequences for other closely dependent states.[57]

The cartography of anxiety (and hope) changed in terms of low probability/high impact events amongst the Shrivenham scanners between 2003 and 2007. In the January 2007 edition of *Strategic Trends* their list of 'possible shocks' made 'no claim to be comprehensive', but sought 'to demonstrate how the world might develop in ways that are radically and intuitively different from outcomes derived from linear analysis'.[58] The ingredients were fewer in number, all harmful and all but unmitigated by the odd benign possibility (as in 2003). The range of possibilities was more infused, too, with climate and medical/disease-related anxieties and what used to be called 'Acts of God' natural disasters, such as mega volcanic or seismic events, as well as the dangers of abrupt climate change and a globalised economic collapse.

The DCDC's early 2010 version, which cast its forward look to 2040, made plain that the bulk of their product was devoted to trends that are already viable or events likely to happen, whilst recognising that others may be beyond our experience to anticipate, conceive or understand. It is not a comprehensive list. Acknowledgement that shocks *will* happen is important. It is recognition that the future cannot be predicted in detail or with certainty. However, shocks will inevitably influence defence and security in some way, providing a strong argument for versatile and adaptable Defence institutions, equipment and personnel to deal with the unexpected challenges they will present.[59] This time, the Shrivenham scan was a tad shorn in its 'Strategic Shocks' section, brigading them together under five headings which they deemed 'credible': the collapse of a Pivotal State; a cure for Ageing; development of New Energy Sources; a collapse of Global Communications; and External Influences.[60]

A cluster of scanners on the Whitehall payroll, who operate in a similar fashion to the Shrivenham team, are those at the Foresight Horizon Scanning Centre which works to the Chief Scientist, in the Office of Science and Innovation (now part of the Department of Business). In global terms, they gaze out to 2020 in their *Scenarios for the Future International Environment*;[61] in domestic terms, they reach for 2030 in their *UK Futures: Society and Economy*.[62] These foresighters, in their *Financial Faultlines* paper which they distributed in December 2006, almost two years ahead of the 2008 financial crisis, stated that they thought a serious financial crisis might happen inside two years.[63] This remarkable, two-page piece of concentrated prescience was available to those ministers and officials who wished to read it 22 months *before* the collapse of Lehman Brothers. They wrote: 'Regulators have found it hard to keep up with the multitude of new instruments and risks involved during global capital market growth. The accepted view that risk-taking and financial fragility have been dispersed and reduced by new financial institutions and hedge fund growth has yet to be tested by adverse events such as an unexpected policy shift adversely affecting risk pricing'.[64]

Different in style and reach from both DCDC and the Foresight Horizon Scanning Centre productions was the document *Realising Britain's Potential*, commissioned by premier Gordon Brown from his Downing Street Strategy Unit on 'Key strategic challenges facing Britain' published in February 2008.[65] There was a great deal of accumulated horizon-scanning in its scope which reflected, understandably, the interests, political language and approach of its patron. The headings included: Global Britain; Economic Prosperity; Life Chances; The Population Picture; Families and Communities; Safe Britain; Personalised Public Services; The Climate Challenge; Democratic Renewal. But their conclusions did not match the Foresight Horizon Scanners in foreseeing, the economic storm ahead, although, in the 'Implications' section of their 'Global Britain' chapter included a whiff of unease when it stated that, 'Globalisation ... may create new risks of economic instability and pose new challenges in counter-terrorism and conflict prevention/resolution'.[66]

Ongoing weaknesses

Each generation of horizon-scanners is shaped by a particular cluster of anxieties, especially with regard to competitor states: Russia and Germany in the early twentieth century; Russia in the Twenties; Germany again in the Thirties; the Soviet Union and the Bomb during the Cold War; energy (oil in particular) in the Seventies; jihad-inspired terrorism after 9/11; and financial collapse from September 2008, with the cumulative impact of carbon emissions now providing the constant percussion reaching into several other worrying possibilities. The horizon-scanner's craft should blend smartness and a sense of history (enlivened by a sense of the wreckage of predictions past plus an acknowledgement of 'thin wisps' missed in the past). A certain promiscuity of approach is valuable, too, because of the necessary humility this brings. There should be no 'no-go areas'. Horizon-scanning teams should mix insiders and outsiders. The future should not be subject to the Official Secrets Act. It should also look for what might be called benign/malign conjunctions.

When one scans the Whitehall scanners in late 2009/early 2010, the craft was, in terms of range and people, more heavily resourced than ever before. It was more a part of the central intelligence machinery than in the past. The Cabinet Office's Strategic Horizons Unit, for example, fed into the second National Security Strategy directly with its still classified 'Vulnerabilities and Challenges of a Networked World' paper of March 2009. The JIC Assessments Staff now ran a fortnightly Current Intelligence Group on Futures, chaired by the head of the Strategic Horizons Unit, Dr Lynette Nusbacher, which drew together the work of the wider Whitehall horizon-scanning community.[67]

There remained, however, a gap in the Whitehall horizon-scanning machinery which was discussed at a British Academy Forum on 15 December 2009, the second of a pair summoned to answer the Queen's question about the financial crisis. Tim Besley, Kuwait Professor of Economics and Political Science at LSE signed a letter, on 22 July 2009, about the causes and nature of the crisis that had prompted her question.[68] A second letter, signed by Besley and Peter Hennessy on 8 February 2010, examined how the Queen's crown servants, scattered across a host of departments, institutions and agencies, might so organise themselves that she would never have to ask such a question again. None of the senior crown servants present at the 15 December 2009 forum 'volunteered either individually or institutionally' to pull all the scattered horizon-scanning financial and economic material together on a regular basis. This could take for example, the shape of a monthly economic and financial horizon-scanning summary from, say, the Cabinet Office, comparable to the JIC's 'Red Book', which the Queen had received each week from 1952 until 2008, when it was abandoned.[69]

Scans of the horizon today must contain one critical, overarching ingredient: climate change, powerfully influenced by carbon emissions. As George Soros noted, a future economic shock comparable to that of 2007–08 would, if triggered by a climate change-related event, produce an immense problem for those seeking to put it right. Professor Nicholas Stern of the London School of Economics, an economist, also produced an analysis and a remedial prescription for the economics of climate change almost exactly two years before the Lehman collapse.[70] Prepared whilst he was Chief Economic Adviser to the Treasury, the Stern review on *The Economics of Climate Change* scanned the horizon to the period 2030 to 2060 and reckoned that, by then, there would have been a doubling of pre-industrial revolution levels of carbon dioxide in the atmosphere, with a 20 per cent probability that the related temperature increase could be over 5°C. All current Whitehall horizon-scanning that seeks global reach now builds in climate change as both a pacemaker and an omnipresent conditioner of forecasting. For example, the best of the regular productions, The Global Strategic Trends Programme, run by the Ministry of Defence's Developments, Concepts and Doctrine Centre in London and at the Defence Academy in Shrivenham, treats climate change as one of its three 'Ring Road Issues' (the other two being globalisation and global inequality).[71]

Horizon-scanners *par excellence*

Martin Rees, the Astronomer Royal, delivering the Lord Speaker's Mile End Group Lecture on 'The World in 2050' in June 2009, pointed out that the 'past record of scientific forecasters is dismal. Lord Rutherford averred that nuclear energy was moonshine; Thomas Watson, founder of IBM, thought there might be a world market for five computers; and one of my predecessors as Astronomer Royal said space travel was utter bilge.' Yet, Lord Rees insisted, we owe it to the generations to come to try:

> one thing seems clear: The UK's standing depends on sustaining our competitive edge as discoverers and innovators – on ensuring that some of the key ideas of the 21st century germinate and – even more – are exploited here in the UK.[72]

Braudel's 'thin wisps' of tomorrow problem has absorbed the energies of some of the best primed clusters of grey cells in crown service since the establishment of the very first horizon-scanning institutions in British government. Before concluding this chapter however, it is important to identify those individual horizon-scanners who picked up possibilities ahead of events that turned out to be of considerable significance when they materialised. The first was the physicist, Frederick Soddy who coined the word 'isotope'. In 1908, during the course of six public lectures at Glasgow University he held up a mysterious mineral for inspection. 'This bottle', he said, 'contains about one pound of uranium oxide, and therefore about fourteen ounces of uranium. Its value is about £1. Is it not wonderful to reflect that in this little bottle there lies asleep and waiting to be evolved the energy of about nine hundred tons of coal?'[73]

Another prescient scanner was the economist John Maynard Keynes. In a famous lecture delivered in Madrid, in June 1930, as the Great Depression deepened, Keynes looked ahead to 2030 and the 'Economic Possibilities for Our Grandchildren'.[74] Keynes was determined to counter what he called the 'bad attack of economic pessimism'.[75] Out of Keynes' optimism came the insightful forecast: '... assuming no important wars and no important increase in population ... I would predict that the standard of life in progressive countries one hundred years hence [in 2030] will be between four and eight times as high as it is today [in 1930]'.[76] There *was* an 'important war' between 1939 and 1945; and the UK population increased from about 44 million to 60 million over the 80 years since 1930, but Keynes' prediction *has* proved remarkably accurate.

Tam Dalyell, Labour MP for West Lothian and then Linlithgow, from 1962 to 2005, was on the trail of A.Q. Khan, the father of the Pakistani nuclear bomb, 20 years before Khan began to figure in the discussions of the JIC. Dalyell's was one of the most remarkable examples of the value of the lone, persistent backbencher in twentieth-century British politics. Speaking during an Adjournment Debate in the House of Commons, at 5:12 a.m. on 18 December 1979, Dalyell raised the alarm on Khan.[77] Nearly 25 years later, the 2004 Butler Report, *Review of Intelligence on Weapons of Mass Destruction*, with full access to UK intelligence files, sought to find out 'what was known' and when, about Khan's activities. It concluded that, 'By early 2000,...it became clear that Khan was at the centre of an international proliferation network....By September 2000, it was pointing out that the network was expanding to mass-produce components for large-scale centrifuge cascades'.[78]

In 1988, Donald McLaren, a young diplomat, back from a spell in the Moscow Embassy, covering Soviet bloc matters for the Foreign Office's Planning Staff in the late 1980s, circulated a think-piece entitled 'East/West Relations and the Future of Europe'.[79] MacLaren wanted Britain to embrace the idea of a unified Germany (a tricky prospect with Margaret Thatcher in No 10) and 'harness the most powerful forces in Europe – the ambitions and aspirations of the Germans and the Russians – and turn them to our, and Europe's account, before we find ourselves steam-rollered'. MacLaren reckoned there were two hurdles to be cleared when his paper circulated in the Foreign Office, sixteen months before the Berlin Wall was breached: the Germans themselves and the Russians. It is these sections of his piece, though they had not the slightest influence on the conduct of UK policy, that are still the stuff of legend in the Foreign Office over 20 years on. 'There are' wrote MacLaren,

> two important hurdles for the Germans to overcome on the way. One is...that no current or immediate prospective member of that leadership would acquiesce willingly in the subsuming of the GDR...into an all embracing German entity...Tomorrow East Germans will

> not be moulded by the previous generation's propaganda. To them Germany will be as good a name, and a better home, than DDR. The wall will be pushed down from both sides.

But would the Soviets let it 'be pushed down'? In reply, McLaren asked his own question:

> how much is the GDR now contributing to socialism as a unifying ideological concept at a time when that concept is undergoing its greatest crisis? How much is she contributing to the process of perestroika, vital to Soviet economic, social and political survival?... Not at all. Then who will rid me of this troublesome daughter since her absence will cause me little grief, and will leave behind a more cohesive family living in even greater security than now?[80]

Given the level of knowledge available in the summer of 1988, that piece of horizon-scanning is a piece of incredible foresight.

In contrast, in his 2008 Ditchley Foundation Lecture, 'The Next Half Century: A Scientist's Hopes and Fears', Martin Rees has given us some examples from the 1950s, whose life-shaping possibilities were not appreciated at the time:

> It was in 1958 that Jack Kilby of Texas Instruments and Robert Noyce of Fairchild Semiconductors built the first integrated circuit – the precursor of today's ubiquitous silicon chips, each containing literally billions of microscopic circuit elements. This was perhaps the most transformative single invention of the past century. A second technology with huge potential began in Cambridge in the 1950s, when Watson and Crick discovered the bedrock mechanism of heredity – the famous double helix. This discovery launched the science of molecular biology, opening exciting prospects in genomics and synthetic biology.

Conclusion

There are other, wider problems with the horizon-scanning craft. There is a danger, after a fairly deep immersion into a century or more of the horizon-scanners' craft, of either becoming faintly obsessed with the 'thin wisps of tomorrow' and/or growing fatalistic about what can be done about a considerable number of the grimmer contingencies. John Maynard Keynes, wrote in September 1931 that: 'It is so difficult to predict what is ahead... some of the things which I vaguely apprehend are, like the end of the world, uninsurable risks, and it's useless to worry about them.' Ministers can get like that when confronted, on top of all their instant preoccupations, with less than cheerful material on what might await. Prediction fatigue has afflicted pretty well every set of political customers in Whitehall, partly because the pictures painted are so rarely jolly. History can help a bit, since History helps us avoid the danger of what Bryan Magee has called being 'provincial in time'.[81] As Professor Sir Michael Howard put it in the autumn of 2007: 'In 1989 [after the fall of the Berlin Wall] I felt we were on an even keel again. As a historian, I should have known better... We have not yet seen the end of History. There is a good deal of life in the old girl yet which is very good news for historians'.[82] A sense of Braudel's fast, medium and slow pulses of history[83] also helps those listening for the hissing of multiple fuses. Unless a reasonable proportion of the best British intellects are deployed in horizon-scanning, those 'thin wisps of tomorrow' that *are* discernible will be lost on us and the Queen's Question will be applicable across a wider range of subjects than needs be.

Notes

1. Fernand Braudel, *A History of Civilisations*, (Harmondsworth: Penguin edn, 1995), pp. xxxvii–xxxviii.
2. Keith Jeffery and Peter Hennessy, *States of Emergency: British governments and strikebreaking since 1919* (London: Routledge, 1983), pp. 10–39, 102–29, 32–3.
3. F.H. Hinsley, *British Intelligence in the Second World War: its influence on strategy and operations, Volume I* (London, 1979), p. 36.
4. Ibid., p. 37.
5. Percy Cradock, *Know Your Enemy: how the Joint Intelligence Committee saw the world*, (London: John Murray, 2002), p. 12.
6. Noel Annan, *Changing Enemies*, (London: Harper Collins, 1995); Cradock, *Know Your Enemy*, pp. 12–14.
7. *Social Insurance and Allied Services, Report by Sir William Beveridge*, Cmd. 6404, (London: Her Majesty's Stationery Office, 1942), p. 6.
8. Angus Calder, *The People's War: Britain 1939–1945* (London: Granada, 1971), p. 609.
9. Alec Cairncross, *Years of Recovery: British Economic Policy 1945–51* (London: Methuen, 1985), pp. 7–8.
10. The National Archives (TNA), Kew, PREM 8/673, 7 March 1946; Jeffery and Hennessy, *States*, p. 181.
11. Jeffery and Hennessy, *States*, pp. 184–5.

12. Keir Thorpe, '"The Missing Pillar": Economic Planning and the Machinery of Government during the Labour Administrations of 1945–51', (PhD thesis, Queen Mary, University of London, 1999); TNA/T229/208, 'central Economic Planning Staff Work, 1947–52', 25 April 1951.
13. *A Programme of Nuclear Power*, Cmd. 9389, (London: Her Majesty's Stationery Office, February 1955).
14. Roger Williams, *The Nuclear Power Decisions: British policies, 1953–78*, (London: Croom Helm, 1980), pp. 60–79.
15. Ronald Knox, *God and the Atom*, (London: Sheed and Ward, 1945), p. 9.
16. TNA/CAB130/3, GEN75/1, 'The Atomic Bomb', 28 August 1945.
17. TNA/CAB158/30, JIC(57)101, 'Terms of Reference for the Joint Intelligence Committee', P.H. Dean, 1 October 1957.
18. Cradock, *Know Your Enemy*, p. 262.
19. Ibid., pp. 265–6.
20. Geoffrey Moorhouse, *The Diplomats: The Foreign Office Today*, (London: Cape, 1977), p. 121.
21. TNA/CAB134/1555, 15 February 1957.
22. Ibid., CPC(57)30 (Revise) 'Future Constitutional Development in the Colonies. 6 September 1957; Peter Hennessy, *Having It So Good: Britain in the Fifties* (Harmondsworth: Penguin, 2007), pp. 472–81.
23. TNA/PREM 11/2321, 'The Position of the United Kingdom in World Affairs', undated memorandum.
24. TNA/CAB129/100, FP(60)1, 'Future Policy Study 1960–70', 24 February 1960.
25. TNA/CAB134/1929, FP(60)1st Meeting, 23 March 1960.
26. TNA/PREM15/927, 'Review of Government Strategy by CPRS, Part 3', 18 July 1972.
27. Jon Davis, *Prime Ministers and Whitehall 1960–1974*, (London: Continuum, 2007), pp. 121–4.
28. TNA/CAB184/57, 'International Oil Questions', 21 September 1971. I am grateful to my research student, Rosaleen Hughes, for steering me through the thickets of energy policy and the CPRS.
29. TNA/CAB184/58, 27 April 1972.
30. TNA/CAB134/3607, ES(73)18, 'An Energy Policy for Britain', 9 May 1973.
31. TNA/CAB134/3609, ES(73)35, 'First Report from the Task Force on Oil Supplies', July 1973.
32. Leonardo Maugeri, *The Age of Oil: the mythology, history and future of the world's most controversial resource* (New York: Praeger, 2006), pp. 112–14.
33. Jeffery and Hennessy, *States*, p. 238; TNA/CAB130/590, GEN108(72)1st, 16 June 1972; TNA/CAB134/3653, IRP(73)4, 'Civil Emergencies: Action to Increase Preparedness', 8 January 1973.
34. Jeffery and Hennessy, *States*, p. 240.
35. TNA/FCO49/503, Note of a meeting of the US/EEC group of Permanent Secretaries in Sir John Hunt's room, Cabinet Office, 28 February 1974, at 11 a.m.
36. Peter Hennessy, *Whitehall* (London: Pimlico, 2001), pp. 102–3, 273–4, 490–92.
37. TNA/FCO49/503, 'Note of a Meeting of the United States/EEC Group of Permanent Secretaries', 28 February 1974.

38. Edmund Dell, *The Chancellors: A History of the Chancellors of the Exchequer, 1945–90*, (London: HarperCollins, 1996), pp. 426–7.
39. Hennessy, *The Prime Minister: the office and its holders since 1945* (Harmondsworth: Penguin, 2001), pp. 385–89.
40. TNA/PREM 16/804, 'What happens if we do not get the IMF loan?', 1 December 1976.
41. TNA/PREM 16/805, 'Plans contingent on a failure of the application for an IMF standby, Annex A', 5 December 1976.
42. Ibid., Annex 5.
43. Hennessy, *Prime Minister*, p. 386.
44. Cradock, *Know Your Enemy*, pp. 266–67 and private information. I am grateful to my research colleague, Peter Davies (formerly of the Defence Intelligence Staff) for his thoughts on JIC (B).
45. King, 'Finance: A Return from Risk', speech to the Worshipful Company of International Bankers, Mansion House, 17 March 2009.
46. *Daily Telegraph*, 6 November 2008; *Financial Times*, 14 November 2008.
47. *National Risk Register* (London: Cabinet Office, 2008), p. 5. I owe my appreciation of this omission to Sir David Omand, former Co-ordinator of Security and Intelligence in the Cabinet Office.
48. Ibid.
49. Dr. Harry Woodruff to the author, 4 June 2008.
50. *Strategic Trends* (London: Joint Doctrine and Concepts Centre, Ministry of Defence, March 2003), 'Methodology, Key Findings and Shocks', p. 1.
51. Ibid; *The DCDC Global Strategic Trends Programme 2007–2036: Strategic Trends*, (London: DCDC, MOD, January 2007), *DCDC Strategic Trends Programme: Global Strategic Trends – Edition 4*, (London: DCDC, MOD, January 2010).
52. *The Strategic Defence Review*, Cm 3999, (London: The Stationery Office, 1998).
53. Author's conversation with Sir Kevin Tebbit, 13 September 2009.
54. *Strategic Trends*, [2003], 'Methodology, Key Findings and Shocks', p. 6.
55. Ibid., p. 26.
56. Ibid., pp. 7, 27–9.
57. Ibid., 'The Economic Dimension', p. 5.
58. *The DCDC Global Strategic Trends Programme 2007–2036*, p. 77.
59. *The DCDC Strategic Trends Programme: Global Strategic Trends out to 2040*, p. 81.
60. Ibid., pp. 95–6.
61. *Scenarios for the Future International Environment, 2010–20* (London: Office of Science and Innovation, 2010).
62. UK Futures: society and economy 2030 (London: Office of Science and Innovation, 2010).
63. *Financial Faultlines: could global financial fragility be exposed by a sudden interest rate shock?* (London: Government Office for Science/The Sigma Scan, December 2006), p. 1.
64. Ibid., pp. 1–2.
65. *Realising Britain's Potential: Future Strategic Challenges for Britain*, (Strategic Unit, February 2008), Prime Minister's 'Foreword', p. 4.
66. Ibid., p. 20.
67. Private information.

68. *British Academy Review*, Issue 14, November 2009.
69. *British Academy Review*, Issue 15, March 2010.
70. Sir Nicholas Stern, *The Economics of Climate Change*, (London: HM Treasury, 30 October 2006).
71. *The DCD Global Strategic Trends Programme 2007–2036*, (Third Edition, London: Ministry of Defence, 2007), p. xiii.
72. Lord Rees of Ludlow, 'The World in 2050', The Lord Speaker's Mile End Group Lecture 2009, House of Lords, 18 June 2009.
73. Frederick Soddy, *The Interpretation of Radium, being the substance of six free popular experimental lectures delivered at the University of Glasgow, 1908*, (London: John Murray, 1909), p. 223. I am very grateful to Dr. Robert Bud of the Science Museum for bringing this to my attention.
74. John M. Keynes, *Essays in Persuasion*, (London: Macmillan, 1931).
75. *The Collected Writings of John Maynard Keynes, IX, Essays in Persuasion*, (London: Royal Economic Society/Macmillan, 1972), p. 321.
76. Ibid., pp. 325–26.
77. House of Commons, *Official Report*, 18 December 1979, col. 554 p. 55.
78. *Review of Intelligence on Weapons of Mass Destruction: Report of a Committee of Privy Councillors*, HC898, (London: The Stationery Office, 14 July 2004), pp. 17–18.
79. Private information.
80. Private information.
81. Bryan Magee, *Confessions of a Philosopher* (London: Weidenfeld and Nicolson, 1997), p. 25.
82. Sir Michael speaking at the International Institute of Strategic Studies, 3 October 2007.
83. Braudel, *History of Civilisations*, pp. xxxvi–xxxvii.

Index

9/11, 210, 229

Acheson, Dean, 65, 69, 71, 72, 147, 179, 215
Acland, Sir Antony, 186, 209
Adams, Gerry, 207
Aden, 48
Adenauer, Konrad, 148
Adoula, Cyrille, 126–32
Afghanistan, 210, 213–14
Africa, 119–35
Afro-Asian bloc, 90, 97, 109
Akihito of Japan, HIH Prince, 111
Albright, Madeleine, 202, 207, 209
Alexander, Sir Michael, 194
Alexandra of Kent, HRH Princess, 111
Algeria, 94, 170
Aliyah Beth Haganah, 44–5, 50, 56
Allen, Sir Douglas (Lord Croham), 223
Al Qaida, 210
American League for a Free Palestine (ALFP), 47
Ampiah, Kweku, 112
Andaman and Nicobar Islands, 90
Ancram, Michael, Earl of, 206
Anderson, Sir John, 22
Anderotti, Giulio, 168
Anglo-American Committee of Inquiry (AAC), 45
Anglo-American relations, 53, 62–72, 109, 119–55, 186–92, 198–215, 224
Anglo-Soviet alliance, 5
Anti-European, 192
Arab nationalism, 183
Argentina, 183, 184
Ark Royal, HMS, 161, 167
Arthur, Michael, 204
Assessments Staff, 219, 221
Athenagoras, Archbishop, 17
atomic bomb, 73, 74, 76, 220
Attlee, Clement (Earl Attlee), 25, 44, 62, 65, 67, 68, 69, 71, 82, 185, 220
Australia, 66, 84, 85, 95, 107–8, 142, 144, 145

Baker-Hamilton Iraq Study Group Report, 2006, 213
balance of payments, British, 140, 142, 147–8
Balkan countries, 8
Ball, George, 126, 128, 143, 144
Bank of England, 200
Basutoland, 90
Bator, Francis, 146, 155
Baudouin, King of the Belgians, 121
Beckett, Margaret, 200, 203
Bechuanaland, 90
Bedell Smith, Walter, 76
Beddington, Sir John, 226
Beisner, Robert, 66
Belgium, 83, 85, 87, 90, 93, 96, 119, 120, 121, 122, 124, 128, 133, 134, 191
Bell, George, 13
Benelux countries, 191
Benjamine, Metropolitan, 12
Bentinck, Victor, *see* Cavendish-Bentinck, Victor (9th Duke of Portland)
Benton, William, 148
Bergin-Belsen, 44
Berlin, 27, 29, 110, 111, 141, 142, 195
Berlin Wall, Fall of, 194, 232, 234
Bermuda summit of 1953, 73, 74
Bermuda II Civil Aviation Agreement 1977, 187
Bernanke, Ben, 213
Berne group, 165, 166
Besley, Tim, 230
Bevan, Aneurin, 220
Beveridge, Sir William (Lord Beveridge), 219
Bevin, Ernest, 12, 25, 33, 50, 52, 64–5, 67, 68

Bidault, Georges, 43
Bierut, Bolslaw, 23, 25, 32, 36
Black Power, 189
Black September, 166
Blair, Tony, 188, 192, 198–215
Blunkett, David, 203
Board of Trade, 112, 191
Bosnia, 188, 207
Bosnia-Herzegovina, 209
Boumedienne, Houari, 170
Bourdillon, Harry, 93
Bourguiba, Habib, 170
Braithwaithe, Sir Rodric, 194
Brammall, Lord, 189–90
Brandon, Henry, 148
Braudel, Fernand, 218, 231, 234
Brenton, Anthony, 204, 211
Bretton Woods system, 225
Brimelow, Sir Thomas (Lord Brimelow), 171
British Army of the Rhine (BAOR), 139, 141, 142, 147, 224
British Defence Staff, 204
British Diplomatic Oral History Archive, Cambridge, 182, 199
Brook, Sir Norman (Lord Normanbrook), 66, 220, 221
Brown, George (Lord George-Brown), 143, 145, 147, 148, 149, 150, 151, 152, 153, 154, 155
Brown, Gordon, 207, 229
Bruce, David, 127, 130, 131, 132, 133, 139–55
Bruce, Evangeline, 140
Bulgaria, 55
Bundy, McGeorge, 144
Burton, Sir Michael, 195
Burrows, Sir Bernard, 183
Bush, George W, 210, 213, 214
Butler, Sir Robin (Lord Butler of Brockwell), 207
Butler Report, *Review of Intelligence on Weapons of Mass Destruction* (2004), 232
Byrnes, James, 33, 47

Cabinet, British
  Cabinet Committee on Atomic Energy, 220–1
  Decisions and government, 49, 52, 66, 73, 86, 93, 94, 106, 148, 150, 160, 161, 165, 167, 171–2, 200, 224
  Defence and Overseas Policy Committee, 56, 69, 75, 160, 173
  War Cabinet (Falklands), 184
Cabinet Office, 219, 230
Cadogan, Sir Alexander, 25, 82, 84, 88
Calandri, Elena, 168
Callaghan, James (Lord Callaghan of Cardiff), 143, 150, 224
Cambodia, 205
Campbell, Alastair, 201, 207
Canada, 66, 92, 95
Carrington, Lord, 222
Cavendish-Bentinck, Victor (9th Duke of Portland), 23–4, 25, 26–7, 33, 34, 35, 36
Central African Federation (CAF), 91, 94, 121
Central Economic Planning Staff, 220
Central Europe, 164, 194
Central Front, 193
Central Intelligence Agency (CIA), 103, 133
Central Policy Review Staff (CPRS), 222
Central Standing Commission on Religious Questions, 4
Ceylon, *see* Sri Lanka
Cheney, Dick, 210
Chiefs of Staff, British, 64, 65, 66, 69, 70, 71, 73, 75, 146, 150, 184, 189–90, 221
Chiefs of Staff Committee, 219
Chief Scientist, 228
Chieftain, HMS, 50
Childers, HMS, 50
China, Nationalist, *see* Taiwan
China, People's Republic (PRC), 62–77, 101, 103–4, 109, 148, 198, 214
Christianity, 2, 34, 36, 200, 210a
Christopher, Warren, 207
Church of England Council on Foreign Relations (CFR), 3, 7, 8, 13

churches
  Catholic, 4, 9, 13, 16, 34, 36, 47, 200
  Church of England, 2–15
  Evangelical, 4
  Orthodox, 2, 4, 7, 8, 9
  Serb Orthodox, 13
  Uniate, 6
Churchill, Sir Winston, 10, 22, 24, 26, 63, 70, 71, 72, 73, 75, 86, 93, 104, 219
Churchill Archive Centre, Cambridge, 182
Civil Contingencies Committee, 220
Civil Contingencies Unit, Cabinet Office, 220, 223
Clarke, Charles, 203
Clinton, Bill, 206, 207, 209, 210, 214
Clutton, Geroge, 13–14
Cohen, Ben, 84
Cold War, 1–2, 9, 13, 15, 18, 55, 62, 66, 72, 75, 82, 88, 89, 100–2, 105–7, 112, 113, 114, 119, 120, 122, 123, 124, 125, 128, 131, 133, 134–5, 159, 160, 161, 163, 168, 183, 184, 188, 193, 221, 224, 229
Coles, Sir John, 206, 208
Colombo Plan, 107, 110
Colonial Office, 42–58, 81–97, 122
Comité Spécial du Katanga (CSK), 129
Committee of Imperial Defence (CID), 219
Commonwealth, 65, 66, 67, 81–95, 102, 104, 111, 112, 141, 188, 189, 191, 193
Commonwealth Relations Office (CRO), 89–90, 95, 97
Communists, Japanese (JCP), 102–5
Compagnie du Katanga (CK), 129
confrontation, Malaysian-Indonesian, 141, 144
Congo, 119–35
Congress, US, 3, 65, 71, 75, 207, 213, 214
Conservative Party, British, 63, 70, 71, 77, 122, 126, 127, 130, 131, 139, 141, 142, 143, 169, 188, 192, 206, 220
consular services, 12, 14, 26, 154, 204, 213
Cook, Robin, 200, 201, 202, 206, 208
Cowper-Coles, Sherard, 202
Cradock, Sir Percy, 221
Creech-Jones, Sir Arthur, 83
Crick, Francis, 233
Cripps, Sir Stafford, 220
Croatia, 209
Cuba, 85, 189
Cunningham, Alan, 48
Cyprus, 48, 51, 52, 55, 84, 92–6, 160–1, 224
Czechoslovakia, 9, 16, 28, 46

Daily Herald, 30, 48, 52
Dalton, Hugh (Lord Dalton), 66
Dalyell, Tam, 232
Damaskinos, Archbishop, 10
Dawson's Field, Jordan, 165
Dayton Accords, 207, 209
Defence Committee, British, 56, 69, 75, 160, 173
defence expenditure, 141, 142, 143, 145, 154
Defence White Papers
  1957 (Sandys Defence Review), 141, 185, 221
  1962, 142
  1966, 142, 145
  1967, 145, 151, 154
  1981 (Nott Review), 193
  1998, 226
  2003, 203
De Gaulle, Charles, 140, 162, 179
Dell, Edmund, 187
Dening, Sir Esler, 102, 103, 106, 107
Denman, Sir Roy, 191
Denmark, 170
Denver Summit 1997, 208
Department for Environment, Food and Rural Affairs (DEFRA), 203
Department of Business, 228
Department of Work and Pensions, 218
Détente, 160, 163
Development, Concepts and Doctrine Centre (DCDC), 226–9
Devlin, Larry, 124

Dictators, South Europe, 164
Dien Bien Phu, 75
Dixon, Sir Pierson, 63, 64, 77, 94
Dobson, Alan, 154
Dockrill, Michael, ix–xi
Dockrill, Saki, ix–xv, xvi, xix, xx, 1, 100, 115, 139, 143, 144, 149, 159, 160, 163, 179
Double helix, 233
Douglas, J.A., 8, 9
Douglas-Home, Sir Alec (Lord Home of the Hirshel; disclaimed: 14th Earl of Home), 101, 110, 112, 113, 126, 128, 131, 132, 141, 171, 172
Duff Cooper, Alfred (1st Viscount Norwich), 51
Dulles, John Foster, 72, 75, 76, 93, 94
Dumbarton Oaks Conference, 84
Dundee, the 11th Earl of, 130, 131–2

Early Warning System (EWS), 222
East of Suez position, 93, 139, 142, 143, 144, 145, 146, 147, 148, 149, 150, 152, 160, 191–2
Economic Club of Chicago, 203
Economic Strategy Committee, 222
economy (British), 140, 141, 142, 145, 146, 147, 155, 161, 220, 221, 224, 229
Eden, Sir Anthony (Earl of Avon), 22, 23, 70–7, 86, 87, 91, 92, 93, 106
Egypt, 70, 87, 96, 171, 172, 222
Eisenhower, Dwight, 1, 72, 73, 74, 75, 93, 94, 109, 122, 159, 163
Elizabeth II, HM, 225, 230, 234
Embassy (British)
  Berlin (GDR), 195
  Bonn, 187, 191, 208
  Moscow, 10–11, 167, 194, 208, 212
  New Delhi, 212
  Paris, 53, 212
  Poland, 23
  structure of Washington Embassy, 203–5
  Tokyo, 104
  Warsaw, 212
  Washington, 46, 51, 69, 183–4, 186–7, 198–215
Embassy (US) in London, 139–55
Emergencies Committee, 220
Emergencies Organisation, 220
Empire, British, 11, 52, 84, 105, 134, 160, 179, 221
Empire, French, 63, 75, 85–6, 87, 95–7, 119, 120, 135
Eskadra, 168
Euro-Arab Dialogue process, 170
European Commission, 191
European Community, 145, 146, 159–78, 162–3
European Economic Community, 139, 162, 168, 191, 221
  1967 Application to join, 191
European Political Cooperation (EPC)
  EC-Maghreb, 170
  EC-Mashreq, 170
  Global Mediterranean Policy (GMP), 170
  Mediterranean Working Group (EPC-MWG), 169–70, 171
European Recovery Programme, *see* Marshall Plan
European Union, 201
Evans, Huw, 204
Exodus 1947 (AKA *President Warfield*), 42, 50–4

F-111 aircraft, 139, 142, 144, 150, 151, 152, 153
Falkland Islands (Islas Malvinas), 183–4
Falklands War, 1982, 183–4
Federation of British Industries, 111
Financial crisis, 2008, 229
Financial Faultlines, 2006, 228
Fitzmaurice, Gerald, 89
Foreign and Commonwealth Office, 159–78, 187
Foreign Office, 1–19, 22–37, 42–58, 62–77, 81–97, 119–35, 191, 201, 205, 219
Foreign Office White Paper 2003, 203
Foresight Horizon Scanning Centre, 225, 228, 229
France, 8, 83, 85, 87, 90, 93, 94, 96, 119, 128, 133, 135, 140, 161, 162, 168, 172, 191

Franks, Sir Oliver (Lord Franks), 66, 69, 183, 215
Fredericks, Wayne, 131
Freeman, John, 166
Fujiyama Aiichiro, 108, 110
Future Constitutional Development in the Colonies, 221
Future Policy Study, 1959, 221
Future Security and Intelligence Outlook Network (FUSION), 226

G7 Summit, *see* Denver Summit 1997
Gaddafi, Muammar, *see* Qaddaffi (Gaddafi), Muammar
Gainer, Sir Donald, 36
Gaitskell, Hugh, 66, 67
Garbett, Cyril (Archbishop of York), 8, 10, 15, 16
Garicano, Luis, 225
General Agreement on Tariffs and Trade (GATT), 106, 113
Geneva conference on Indochina, 1954, 75
genomics, 233
German unification, 193–5, 232
Germany, Democratic Republic, 194
Germany, Federal Republic, 100, 112, 114, 140, 143, 146, 147, 165, 166, 168, 172, 191, 193–4, 229
Germany, Nazi, 5, 8
Gibraltar garrison, 161
Gizenga, Antoine, 125, 126, 127, 128
Global Strategic Trends (Shrivenham Scans), 226–8
Good Friday Agreement, 209
Gorbachev, Mikhail, 194
Gore, Al, 210
Government Office for Science, 226
Greece, 10, 95, 160, 161, 168, 171
Greek Patriachate, 10, 11, 17
Greenhill, Denis (Lord Greenhill of Harrow), 166
Greenspan, Alan, 213
Greenstock, Sir Jeremy, 204
Greenwood, Sean, 18
Gregory, Metropolitan, 12
Grenada, 189
Grenada Crisis, 1983, 188–9
Griffiths, Jim, 66, 67
Grocholski, Count, 35
Gruber, Ruth, 50
Gulf War, 1990–1991, 186, 211
Gullion, Edmund, 128, 130
Gurion, Ben, 45

Habash, George, 165
Halifax, 1st Earl of, 12, 16
Hammarskjöld, Dag, 120, 124, 126, 130
Hankey, Robin, 22, 23, 26, 36
Harlech, Lord, *see* Ormsby Gore
Harpham, William, 108
Hatoyama Ichiro, 106
Hayashi, Lieutenant-General, 107
Hayto, Ikeda, 112
Hazell, Ronald, 32
Heads of Mission Conference 1989, 194
Healey, Denis (Lord Healey), 144, 147, 149, 151, 153, 154, 224
Heath, Sir Edward, 110, 159–78, 162, 184, 198, 222
Helsinki Conference (CSCE), 170, 171
Henderson, Sir Nicholas, 184
Hennessy, Peter (Lord Hennessy of Nympsfield), 180, 230
Heyes, Peter, 213
Hezbollah, 214
hijackings (1970), 165
Hiroshima, 221
Hitler, Adolf, 4, 8, 44
Holbrooke, Richard, 207
Holliday, G.L.G., 26
Holmes, John, 201
Home, Lord, *see* Douglas-Home
Home Office and Ministry of Justice, 218, 220
Hong Kong, 68
Hopkinson, Henry, 91
Horizon Scanning Centre, 226
House of Commons, 33, 34, 105, 128, 184, 232
Howard, Sir Michael, 234
Howe, Sir Geoffrey (Lord Howe of Aberavon), 194, 205
Howell, David (Lord Howell of Guildford), 192–3
Hudson, Lord, 91, 92
Humanite, 51

Hungary, 15, 96
Hunt, Sir John (Lord Hunt of Tanworth), 223, 224
Hurd, Douglas (Lord Hurd of Westwell), 195, 206
Hurley, Bishop Joseph, 13, 14, 16
Hussein, King of Jordan, 165, 166, 167

IBM, 231
Ikeda Hayato, 112
India, 66, 85, 89, 90, 91, 95, 214
Indochina, *see* Vietnam
Indonesia, 141
Information Research Department (IRD), 103, 104
Ingham, Sir Bernard, 188
Institute of Contemporary British History (ICBH), 179
International Committee of the Red Cross (ICRC), 165
International Refugee Organisation (IRO), 55
International Monetary Fund (IMF), 224
Inverchapel, Lord (Sir Archibald Kerr), 47
Inboden, William, 1–2
Iran, 214
Iraq, 86, 211, 213
Iraq War, 2003-, 188, 211, 213
Ireland, Republic of, 170
Irish Republican Army (IRA), 209
Israel, 165, 166, 214
Italy, 100, 114, 160, 161, 162, 168, 172, 191

Japan, 100–15, 140
Jebb, Gladwyn (Lord Gladwyn), 84, 88, 89, 130
Jenkins, Roy (Lord Jenkins of Hillhead), 150, 152, 153
Jewish Agency, 47, 53, 55
Johnson, Lyndon B, 140, 143, 144, 146, 148, 149, 152, 153, 154
Joint Intelligence Committee (JIC), 219, 221, 224, 225, 230, 232
Joint Chiefs of Staff, US, 64, 210
Joint Strike Fighter, 213
Joint Terrorism Analysis Centre, 226
Jowitt, 1st Earl (Sir William Jowitt), 48

Kaiser, Philip, 140, 143, 147
Karpov, Georgii
Kasavubu, Joseph, 122, 123, 124
Katanga, 120–34
Katyn massacre, 23
Kennan, George, 11–12
Kennedy, John F, 119, 120, 123, 125, 126, 127, 128, 132, 134, 140, 141
Kerr, Sir John (Lord Kerr of Kinlochard), 192, 199, 201, 202, 204, 205–8, 215
Keynes, John Maynard (Lord Keynes), 231–2, 234
Khaled, Leila, 165
Khan, A.Q., 232
Khrushchev, Nikita, 123
Kielce pogrom (1946), 46
Kilby, Jack, 233
King, Mervyn (Lord King), 225
Kipping, Sir Norman, 111
Kirkpatrick, Sir Ivone, 34
Kishi Nobusuke, 108, 110
Kishi Plan, 109
Kissinger, Henry, 164
Kitona Agreement, 127–30
Knox, Ronald, 220
Kol Israel (The Voice of Israel), 50
Korea, North, 62, 63
Korea, South, 62, 63, 73
Korean War, 62–77, 183, 186
Kosovo, 209–10
Kurile Islands, 104

Labour Party, British, 25, 44, 69, 105, 147, 148, 192, 198, 206
Lambert, Charles, 30
Lamont, Norman (Lord Lamont of Lerwick), 205
Lane, Arthur Bliss, 26–7, 35
Lansdowne, the 8th Marquess of, 110–11
Latin America, 125
League of Militant Godless, 4
League of Nations, 88
Lebanon, 189, 214
Leddy, John, 147, 155
Lehman Brothers collapse, 225, 229
Leopold, King of the Belgians, 121, 129

Leslie, Dame Mariot, 187
Lewin, Terry (Lord Lewin), 185
Libya, 161
Lie, Trygve, 49
Lewinsky, Monica, 209
Liberal Democratic Party, Japanese, 108
Lloyd, Selwyn (Lord Selwyn-Lloyd), 73, 86, 87, 91, 92, 108–9, 221
Logan, David, 204
London Conference 1947, 49
Lumumba, Patrice, 119–20, 122, 123, 125, 131
Luxemburg, 191

Magee, Bryan, 234
Maghreb, 161, 162, 168, 170
MacArthur, Douglas, 62–3, 68–9, 71, 72, 76
Macdonald, Malcolm, 102–3
MacGillivray, 50
Macmillan, Sir Harold (1st Earl of Stockton), 106, 110–12, 125, 128, 132, 140, 141, 142, 221
Major, Sir John, 192, 206
Makarios, President of Cyprus, 170
Malawi, 121
Malaysia, 113, 145, 150
Mallaby, Sir Christopher, 194
Malta, 161
Manning, Sir David, 199, 201, 211–14
Mao-Khrushchev manifesto of October 1954, 103
Marshall Plan, 15, 16
Marx, Karl, 6
Marynowska, Miss, 35
Mashreq, 162
Mason, Paul, 86
Mayhew, Christopher (Lord Mayhew), 148
McLaren, Donald, 232–3
McMahon Act 1946, 185
McNamara, Robert, 143, 144, 145, 146, 149, 155
Mediterranean policy (British), 142, 159–78
Menon, Mrs., 91, 92
Menzies, Sir Robert, 107
Mermaid, HMS, 50
Meyer, Sir Christopher, 199, 201, 202, 204, 208–11, 214
MI5, 49, 56
Middle East, 142, 160, 183, 214, 224
Middle East war
  of 1967 (Six Day War), 150, 160
  of 1973 (Yom Kippur War), 167, 170, 171, 172, 222
Migani, Guia, 169
Mikolajczyk, Stanislaw, 23, 28, 32, 35
Miliband, David, 201
Milosevic, Slobodan, 209–10
Ministerial Committee on Illegal Immigration, 49, 52, 54–5
Ministry of Defence, 160, 204, 218, 226
Ministry of Information, 5, 7
Mintov, Dom, 161
Mobutu, Joseph, 124
Montgomery of Alamein, 1st Viscount, 47
Morgan, Kenneth O (Lord Morgan), 43
Moro, Aldo, 168
Morocco, 85, 87
Morrison, Herbert (Lord Morrison), 66, 68
Moscow Patriachate, 10, 11, 12
Mottram, Sir Richard, 225
Multilateral Force (MLF), 143
Munich Agreement 1938, 152
Muslim, 4

Nagasaki, 221
Napoleon, 8
Nasser, Gamal Abdel, President of Egypt, 171
National Health Service, 218
National Risk Register, 225
National Security Council (NSC), 207, 210
Neisse River, 25
Netherlands, 83, 170, 191
New Jewel Movement (Grenada), 189
New Look, 74–5
New York Times, 17, 36
New Zealand, 66, 84, 85, 93, 95, 145
NKVD, 23
Nicholson, Sir Godfrey, 109
Nixon, Richard, 159, 160, 164, 172

North Atlantic Council, 194
North Atlantic Treaty Organisation (NATO), 65, 87, 92, 100, 112, 120, 122, 128, 139, 141, 143, 154, 160, 161, 167, 183, 187, 190, 193, 194, 212, 224
Northern Ireland, 'The Troubles', 206, 209, 221
North-South divide, 164
Norway, 92
Nott, Sir John, 184–5, 193
Noyce, Robert, 233
Number 10 (Downing Street), 202, 211, 215
Number 10 (Downing Street) Press Office, 200
Nuclear deterrent (British), 142, 146, 185, 189–90, 220
Nuclear policy, 141
Nuclear tests, British, 107
Nusbacher, Lynnette, 230

O'Brien, Conor Cruise, 130
Oder-Neisse Line, 28, 33, 37
Office of Science and Innovation, 228
Ōhira Masayoshi, 113
oil economics and supplies, 222
Ondaatje, Sir Christopher, 225–6
Ōno Katsumi, 108–9
Organisation for Economic Cooperation and Development (OECD), 112
Organisation of Petroleum Exporting Countries (OPEC), 222
Ormsby Gore, David (Lord Harlech), 127, 130, 132, 133, 140
Osborne, Sir D'Arcy, 13
Overseas Policy and Defence Committee, 160

Pacelli, Cardinal, 6
Pakistan, 85, 90, 95, 232
Palestine, 42–58
Palestine Committee, *see* Ministerial Committee on Illegal Immigration
Palestine groups, 164
Palestine Liberation Organisation, 166
Palestine Patrol, 57
Palestine Post, 53
Palmer, Lord, 26
pan-Slavism, 8–9, 11
Panton, Frank, 190
Parkinson, Cecil (Lord Parkinson), 184
Parry, Sir Emry Jones, 204
Parsons, J. Graham, 17
Parsons, Richard, 13, 14
Peck, Sir Edward, 112
Pellew, Mark, 187
Perowne, J.V., 13
Perry, William, 206
Persia, *see* Iran
Persian Gulf, 139, 144, 146, 150, 151, 191–2
Philippines, 85
Pickering, Thomas, 207, 209
Pius XII, Pope, 15, 16
Planning Staff (FO), 221
Plowden, Sir Edwin (Lord Plowden), 220
PM, 51
Poland, 22–37
Polaris missile, 142, 224
Policy Unit, 201
Polish Western frontier, 15, 24–36
Political Advisers (at No. 10 Downing Street), 200–1, 212
Pompidou, Georges, 162, 168, 170
Popular Front for the Liberation of Palestine (PFLP), 165, 166
Port de Bouc, 51, 52, 53, 55
Portelli, Alessandro, 181–2
Portugal, 83, 85, 87, 96, 164, 171
Position of the United Kingdom in World Affairs (1958), 221
Potsdam Conference. 1945, 22, 28
Powell, Charles (Lord Powell of Bayswater), 181, 190
Powell, Colin, 202, 210, 212
Powell, Enoch, 143
Powell, Jonathan, 201, 207, 208, 210
Powell, Sir Richard, 185
President Warfield, see *Exodus 1947*
Protestant paramilitary organisations, Northern Ireland, 209

Qaddafi, Muammar, 161, 172
Quai d'Orsay, 51

Quinlan, Sir Michael, 190

Radford, Arthur, 74, 75, 76
Ramsbotham, Sir Peter, 187
Reagan, Ronald, 184, 188–90, 207
Realising Britain's Potential, 229
Red Army, 22, 25, 26
Red Cross, *see* International Committee of the Red Cross
Rees, Sir Martin (Lord Rees of Ludlow), 231, 233
Renwick, Sir Robin (Lord Renwick of Clifton), 206, 209
Rice, Condoleezza, 202–3, 210, 212, 215
Richards, Brigadier, 20
Riches, Derek, 129
Riddell, Peter, 200, 210
Ridgway, Matthew, 69
Ridsdale, Julian, 110–11
Rifkind, Sir Malcolm, 188, 192, 208
Roosevelt, Eleanor, 89
Roosevelt, Franklin D, 18
Rothschild, Robert, 132
Rothschild, Victor (3rd Lord Rothschild), 222
Royal Institute of International Affairs (Chatham House), 202
Royal Navy, 46, 48, 51, 161, 193, 224
Rumsfeld, Donald, 211
Rusk, Dean, 128, 132, 145, 146, 148, 149, 151, 152, 155
Russia (Russian Federation), 198, 210, 229
Rutherford, Lord, 231
Rycroft, Matthew, 210

Sadat, Anwar, 172
Saddam, Hussein, 211
Sandstrom, Emil, 50
San Francisco Conference 1945, 84
San Francisco peace conference 1951, 101
Sargent, Orme, 15
Satterthwaite, Joseph, 123
Sawers, John, 201
Scandinavia, 191
Scenarios for the Future International Environment, 228
Schwede-Coburg, Franz, 28
Scott, Ian, 121, 122
Second World War, 1, 2, 100, 140, 141, 179, 183, 189, 195, 198, 203, 219
Selborne, the 3rd Earl of, 122
Seldon, Anthony, 180, 211
Selkirk, the 10th Earl of, 107
Serbia, 209
Shawcross, William, 210
Sheel, Walter, 170
Sheen, Monsignor Fulton J, 12
Sheinwald, Nigel, 201, 213
Shultz, George, 184
Silkin, Lewis, 35
Simic, Vladimir, 50
Simonstown base, 90
Singapore, 142, 143, 144, 150
Sino-Soviet bloc, 105, 225
Sino-Soviet split, 112
Sisco, Joseph, 166
Six Day War, 1967, *see* Middle East War of 1967
Sixth Fleet (US), 170
Smith, John, 200
Slovenia, 209
Sobor (Council of Bishops), 5
Socialists, Japanese, 102
Socièté Gènèrale Belgique, 123, 128
Soddy, Frederick, 231
Soros, George, 230
South Africa, 66, 84, 85, 87, 89, 95, 96
Southeast Asia Treaty Organisation (SEATO), 112, 145, 147, 148
South-South divide, 164
South West Africa (later Nambia), 89
Soviet bloc, *see* Warsaw Pact
Soviet Navy, 167
Soviet Union, *see* Union of Soviet Socialist Republics
Spaak, Paul-Henri, 128, 132
Spain, 161, 162, 171
Spalding, Elizabeth Edward, 1, 2
Spiers, Ron, 151, 153
Sri Lanka (formerly Ceylon), 85, 95
Stalin, Josef, 3–6, 9, 12, 23, 25, 73
State Department, US, 89, 93, 103, 127, 129, 132, 133, 165, 187
Steel, Sir Christopher, 191

Sterling Bloc, 105–6
Sterling crises, 142, 143, 146, 150, 223
Sterling devaluation, 1967, 150
Sterling payments agreement with Japan, 105
Stern, Nicholas, 230
Stern Review on *The Economics of Climate Change*, 230
Stettin, 27–34
Stevenson, Adlai, 126
Stewart, Michael, 144
Strachey, John, 66
Strang, William (Lord Strang), 64, 71
Strategic Defense Initiative (SDI), 189–90
Strategic Horizon's Unit, 230
Strategy Unit (FCO), 221
Straw, Jack, 200, 202, 205, 211, 212, 215
Suez Canal, 95, 222
Suez crisis 1956, 96, 107, 160, 184–5, 221
Suez-Mediterranean pipeline (SUMED), 171, 172
Sunday Times, 148
superpower relations and strategy (also East-West rivalry), 162–4, 166–7, 232
Swaziland, 90
Swinton, the Earl of, 106–7
Switzerland, 8, 165, 166, 191
Syria, 51, 167

Tablet (Roman Catholic newspaper), 9
Taiwan, 101
Taliban, 210, 214
Tanganyika Concessions, 128, 130–1, 132
Taylor, Myron, 15, 16
Tebbit, Sir Kevin, 226
Thatcher, Margaret (Baroness Thatcher of Kesteven), 181, 187–9, 192, 194, 232
Third World, 101, 109, 112, 162
Times newspaper, 30, 34, 53, 200
Tito, Josip, 16
Tobias, Channing, 88
Tokyo Convention of 1963, 165
Trade, Anglo-European, 191
trade promotion, by ambassadors, 213
Treasury, British, 141, 142, 160, 223, 224
Treaty of Rome 1957, 191
Trend, Sir Burke (Lord Trend)
Trend Report 1955 (civil nuclear power), 220
Trimble, David (Lord Trimble), 206
Truman, Harry S, 1, 15, 16, 17, 18, 24, 44–5, 62, 63, 65, 68
Truman Doctrine, 15, 16
Tshombe, Moishe, 121–34
TSR-2 aircraft, 141, 142
Tunisia, 170
Turkey, 95, 160, 162, 164

U Thant, 127, 129
UK Futures: Society and Economy, 228
Ukraine, 6
Union Menière du Haut Katanga (UMHK), 120, 122, 126, 128, 131
Union of Soviet Socialist Republics (USSR), 2–15, 18, 47, 71, 74, 76, 82, 84, 87, 88, 93, 100, 120, 122, 123, 127, 141, 161, 162, 167, 170, 189, 194, 224, 229
United Arab Republic, 109
United Nations (UN), 81–97, 107, 112, 131
  Charter, 82, 83, 84
  Fourth Committee of the General Assembly, 82, 83, 84, 85, 86, 88, 92, 108, 119
  General Assembly, 55, 56, 82, 83, 84, 94
  Political Committee, 65
  Relief and Rehabilitation Agency, 47
  Secretary-General, 49
  Security Council, 82, 88, 121, 127, 198
  Trusteeship Council, 83
  United Nations Command (UNC), in Korea, 62–77
  UNSCOP, 50, 54
United States of America (USA)
  anti-colonialism, 81–97

United States of America (USA) – *continued*
  Japan, policy towards, 100–2
  religion, 15
  Senate, 88
Urquhart, Sir Brian, 130
US–UK Mutual Defence Agreement 1958, 190

Versailles Conference (1919), 88
Viet-minh, 75, 77
Vietnam, 63, 75
Vietnam War, 63, 140, 148, 149, 163

Waddams, Herbert, 5, 14
Wall, Sir Stephen, 201
Walters, Joseph, 31, 32, 34
War on Terror, 214
Warner, Christopher, 13, 15
Warsaw Pact, 141, 184
Washington summits
  1967, 145
  1968, 154
Watson, James, 233
Watson, Thomas, 231
weapons of mass destruction (WMD), 211
Webb, Simon, 227
Weston, Sir John, 204
Waterhouse, Charles, 122
White House, 211
Whitelaw, William (1st Viscount Whitelaw), 222
Wigny, Pierre, 122, 123, 124
Williams, Mennen, 126
Wilson, Sir Harold (Lord Wilson of Riveaux), 139, 140–55, 160, 171, 187, 191, 224
Wilson, Sir Richard (Lord Wilson of Dinton), 201
Wilson, Woodrow, 18
Winch, Michael, 26, 29
witness seminars (ICBH), 179–82, 186, 195
World War III, 65, 66, 71, 76
Wright, J.K., 191
Wright, Sir Oliver, 187
Wright, Sir Patrick (Lord Wright of Richmond), 186
Wright, Stephen, 204
Wyatt, Woodrow (Lord Wyatt of Weeford), 148

Yalu River, 72, 73
Yaoundé Convention, 162, 168
Year of Europe, 1973, 173
Yom Kippur War, *see* Middle East War of 1973
Yoshida Shigeru, 101, 103, 105, 109
Younger, Sir Kenneth, 65, 66, 67, 70
Yugoslavia, 209

Zambia, 121
Zionism and Zionist propaganda, 42–58
Zimbabwe, 121

CPSIA information can be obtained
at www.ICGtesting.com
Printed in the USA
LVHW020448231118
597987LV00008B/230/P

9 780230 360396